ABBOTT'S AMERICAN WATCHMAKER

*An Encyclopedia for the
Horologist, Jeweler,
Gold and Silversmith*

HENRY G. ABBOTT

Skyhorse Publishing

Skyhorse Publishing books may be purchased in bulk at special discounts for sales promotion, corporate gifts, fund-raising, or educational purposes. Special editions can also be created to specifications. For details, contact the Special Sales Department, Skyhorse Publishing, 307 West 36th Street, 11th Floor, New York, NY 10018 or info@skyhorsepublishing.com.

Skyhorse® and Skyhorse Publishing® are registered trademarks of Skyhorse Publishing, Inc.®, a Delaware corporation.

Visit our website at www.skyhorsepublishing.com.

10 9 8 7 6 5 4 3 2 1

Library of Congress Cataloging-in-Publication Data

Abbott, Henry G., 1858-1905.
[American watchmaker and jeweler]
Abbott's American watchmaker : an encyclopedia for the horologist, jeweler, gold and silversmith / Henry G. Abbott.
p. cm.
Originally published: 1894.
ISBN 978-1-61608-532-2
1. Clock and watch making--Dictionaries. I. Title.
TS540.7.A23 2012
681.1'103--dc23
2011038749

Printed in the United States of America

PREFACE.

F OR some years there has been a demand among the watchmaking and jewelry fraternity in this country, for a book that would furnish them some information in regard to tools of American manufacture, drawings and descriptions of the various escapements, definitions of various words and phrases used in the trade, etc. There are upon the market several very valuable books, compiled by English, French and German authors, but these works are silent in regard to tools and methods distinctively American. Most of these works devote considerable space to the use of the bow lathe, the turns and other devices long since abandoned by the American watchmaker.

The ambitious workman is always in search of knowledge, in search of new ideas, new tools and new methods. Patient study, constant practice and ambition are requisite to become proficient in any art. The demand for skilled workmen is constantly increasing, and a person wishing to thoroughly master any art, must be to a certain extent capable of self-instruction. To be a proficient in any art a man must not be deft of touch alone, but the head must also play its part. In America the watchmaker is somewhat differently situated from his European brothers. In the country towns he is often called upon not only to clean and repair watches and clocks, but is often asked to put in order or repair music boxes, fishing reels, musical instruments, sewing machines, electric motors, statuettes, pipes, and a variety of other articles too numerous to mention. It would be next to impossible for the ordinary workman to remember all the various instructions, hints, pointers, formulas and recipes which he has read or heard about, and the author believes such persons will welcome this volume and that it will prove valuable for reference in cases of emergency. This, the fourth edition, has been revised and enlarged so that it is more complete than former editions. In this work the compiler makes no claims of originality. The best authorities have been drawn upon for the information here given.

THE AMERICAN

WATCHMAKER AND JEWELER

AN ENCYCLOPEDIA FOR THE

HOROLOGIST, JEWELER, GOLD AND SILVERSMITH

ABBEY. To him or his assistant, Graham, is attributed the invention of the cylinder escapement.

ACCELERATION. This term in horology is applied to the steady gaining in the rate of a time-keeper, particularly to be observed in new movements. It is positively known to occur in marine chronometers, watches as a rule not being subjected to tests sufficiently accurate to detect it in them. There is but little doubt that the hairspring is the cause of acceleration. Old movements after being re-sprung sometimes accelerate, particularly if the overcoil is manipulated too much when timing. Britten declares that there is little doubt that the tendency of springs is to increase slightly in strength for some time after they are subjected to continuous action, just as bells are found to alter a little in tone after use. Sometimes the very best chronometers, after going for a year or two, will accelerate by about three or four seconds per day. M. Jacob attributes this acceleration to the fact that chronometers are exposed to heat oftener and for longer periods than to cold, and since the balance is thus more frequently contracted it follows that after a time the segments will not return exactly to their initial positions. There will therefore be necessarily a slight acceleration of the rate.

Dent believed that it was due to the combination of oxygen of the air with the steel hairspring, so that after a time its rigidity is increased.

M. Villarceau attributed it to the influence of the escapement and that it arises from the fact that the impact communicating the impulse occurs before the balance has arrived at its neutral position.

M. H. Robert attributes it to the fact that the resistance opposed by oil at the pivots of the escape wheel differs from that at the pivots of the balance.

Flat springs do not accelerate as much as those having overcoils. Palladium springs accelerate very much less than hardened steel springs.

ACIDS AND SALTS. Acids and salts of various kinds are employed by the watchmaker and jeweler, but he should never keep them in proximity to his tools or work, or he may have cause to regret it some day. It is advisable to keep them in glass stoppered bottles.

Acetic Acid of commerce varies considerably in concentration and is usually of a very light yellow color. It is very acid in taste and has a pungent odor by which it is easily distinguished.

Alum is sometimes used for removing the stains left by soldering, in lieu of acids, and is also used in removing broken screws from brass plates by immersing the plates in a strong solution of alum and water, the best results being obtained from a boiling solution, which rapidly converts the steel into rust, while it does not attack the brass plate.

Ammonia, or spirits of hartshorn, of commerce is sold usually in the form of a colorless liquid known as aqua ammonia, which is obtained from the ammonical liquor which results from the distillation of coal for the manufacture of gas. Its properties are somewhat similar to those of soda, potash and other alkalies. It will restore the blue color of litmus paper which has been reddened by acid, and counteracts the strongest acids.

Ammonia Phosphate of commerce is a salt produced by the exact saturation of phosphoric acid with ammonia. It is very useful in baths for producing thick platinum deposits.

Ammonium Sulphide of commerce is a liquid produced by saturating ammonia with sulphuretted hydrogen gas. In combination with metals it rapidly forms sulphides and is used on silver for producing the black coating sometimes called oxidation, and is employed for bronzing metals.

Aqua Regia is a combination of 1 part nitric acid and 2 parts hydrochloric acid, and its strength greatly depends upon the degrees of strength of the two ingredients that form it, which vary in commerce considerably. It is the strongest solvent of metals, and the only one that dissolves gold and platinum.

Boric Acid is employed for decomposing the subsalts deposited in cyanide electro-baths, and for increasing the whiteness of silver alloys.

Borax of commerce is usually met with in the form of colorless crystals. When heated by means of the blow-pipe these crystals expand and finally run into a kind of glass which dissolves nearly all the metallic oxides, and on this account it is used as a flux in hard soldering. It is also used in assaying with blow-pipe, for destroying the sub-salts of silver formed in electro-plating baths, and for restoring the shade of defective gilding baths.

Chromic Acid is generally made by a combination of bichromate of potash and sulphuric acid. It is used to excite galvanic batteries and as an etching agent.

Hydrochloric Acid of commerce, is a mixture of the acid proper and water. The acid proper is gaseous, and is therefore combined with water. It is a by-product in the manufacture of soda.

Hydrofluoric Acid will dissolve nearly all the metals except sil ver, platinum and lead. It is a dangerous acid to handle unless you are thoroughly acquainted with its nature. It is used for etching on copper, enamel and glass.

Magnesia Calcine is calcined carbonate of magnesia, and is sold in commerce in the form of a white powder.

Nitric Acid, or aqua fortis, may be purchased of various colors and degrees of strength, and it dissolves most of the metals. As it is frequently used in a dilute state, it is well to remember that WATER SHOULD NEVER BE POURED INTO THE ACID, but rather POUR THE ACID IN A SMALL STREAM INTO THE WATER, stirring meantime with a glass rod. As this and other acids heat rapidly, it is well to place the vessel, while mixing, in another vessel filled with water.

Oxalic Acid of commerce is sold in the form of white crystals, and is very poisonous.

Potassium Cyanide of commerce is a colorless salt having an odor somewhat similar to prussic acid. It is highly poisonous. Solutions of potassium cyanide will dissolve metallic silver. It is used in electro-plating, and the plating is more or less effective, depending on the power of the solution of the salts to dissolve the cyanides of gold and silver.

Potassium Bicarbonate of commerce is a colorless crystal. This salt is soluble in tepid water.

Potassium Bitartrate, or tartar, is a salt produced from the crystals found on the sides of wine casks. When purified it is known as cream of tartar. It is acid, and is slightly soluble in water.

Potassium Hydroxide, or caustic potash of commerce, is sold in the form of small sticks, which must be kept in air-tight bottles.

Potassium Nitrate, or saltpetre, is used as a flux, and as it readily yields a portion of its oxygen to other bodies, it is used extensively for oxydizing metals.

Potassium Sulphide is a salt which in commerce is sold in brown masses, and is sometimes called liver of sulphur.

Prussic Acid, or hydrocyanic acid, should be used with the greatest care, as it is one of the most deadly substances used in the art. It may be distinguished by its smell, which resembles that of peach pits, apple seeds or bitter almonds, and, in fact, these substances owe their peculiar odor to the presence, in small quantities, of this acid. It is used for decomposing the alkaline carbonates formed in baths with cyanide of potassium, and for maintaining the strength of the hypophosphite of gold in immersion baths.

Sal-Ammoniac, or Chloride of Ammonium, is used as a flux in soldering tin and other metals in the form of a paste obtained by combining with sweet oil. It is also used in battery solutions in electroplating.

Sodium Bicarbonate corresponds in properties very closely with potassium bicarbonate.

Sodium Hydroxide of commerce is solid, in thick white masses, and is readily converted into carbonate of soda by the absorption of carbonic acid from the air.

Sodium Pyrophosphate of commerce is sold in the form of a white salt which is soluble in water.

Sodium Phosphate of commerce is usually sold in the form of crystals. It is used in hot electro-gilding baths.

Sulphuric Acid or oil of vitriol is a colorless, odorless fluid. Like nitric acid, it should be carefully mixed when diluting with water, and the same water-bath used.

Tartaric Acid of commerce is usually sold in the form of crystals and also in the form of a powder. Solutions of this acid should only be prepared for immediate use, as it readily decomposes.

ADAMS, J. C. Born in Preble, N. Y., October 7, 1834. As a watch factory organizer he has probably had more experience than any

living man. He served a five years' apprenticeship to John H. Atkins, an old Liverpool watchmaker, then located in Elgin, Ill. After serving his apprenticeship he worked for two years as watchmaker for I. E. Spalding, Janesville, Wis. He was afterwards engaged in business in Elgin, the firm being known as G. B. & J. C. Adams. The partnership was dissolved at the end of two years, and he accepted a position in the watch department of Hoard & Hoes, Chicago. In 1861 he had the management

J. C. Adams. of the watch department of W. H. & C. Miller, the largest jewelry store in Chicago. In 1862 he was appointed time-keeper for the various roads centering in Chicago. In 1864, together with

Charles S. Moseley and P. S. Bartlett, he organized the Elgin Watch Company. In 1869, together with Paul Cornell, he organized the Cornell Watch Company of Grand Crossing, Ill. One of the movements made by this company bore his name. In 1869, together with Springfield capitalists, he organized the Illinois Watch Company. In 1874 he organized the Adams & Perry Manufacturing Company. In 1883 and 1884 he was in the employ of the Independent Watch Company of Fredonia, N. Y. In 1885 he organized the Peoria Watch Company of Peoria, Ill., and remained with that company until April 14, 1888. He is the inventor and patentee of the Adams System of Time Records, now used by nearly every western railroad.

ADENDUM CIRCLE. The distance or space between the pitch line of a gear and the circle touching the ends of the teeth.

ADHESION. Adhesion is the mutual attraction which two bodies have for one another, as attraction between the liquid and the substance of the vessel containing it. See also *Oil* and *Capillarity*. Saunier says that the working parts in contact with each other should separate by sliding action and not by a sudden drawing asunder in a direction perpendicular to their touching surfaces, as such an action would involve the inconvenience of variable resistances, depending on the greater or less adhesion or cohesion of these surfaces. The amount of adhesion between clean surfaces is difficult to determine and it is impossible to give its exact proportion. In the case of oiled surfaces the resistance due to adhesion is proportional to the extent of the surfaces in contact.

ADJUSTING ROD. A device for testing the pull of the mainspring.

ADJUSTMENT. The manipulation of the balance, its spring and staff, for the purpose of improving the time-keeping qualities of a watch. Three adjustments are usually employed for this purpose, viz.: positions, isochronism and compensation.

Adjustment to Positions. The manipulation of the hairspring and balance so that the movement keeps time in the different positions. In ordinary watches two positions are taken, viz.; pendant up or vertical and dial up or horizontal. In the finer grade of work adjustments are made in the quarters, that is, with 3 up and 9 up. This adjustment is a delicate and often a difficult operation and it is only by constant study and application that the watchmaker can hope for success. Several excellent essays on this subject are in print, among which may be mentioned Modern Horology in Theory and Practice and the Watchmaker's Hand Book by Claudius Saunier, the Watch and Clockmaker's Hand Book by F. J. Britten, and Adjustments to Positions, Isochronism and Compensation, published by G. K. Hazlitt & Co., Chicago. Isochronal adjustments are thoroughly reviewed in an excellent little work by Moritz Immisch entitled Prize Essay on the Balance Spring. The object of timing or adjusting to positions is to ascertain how far a change of position modifies the compensation and isochronism and to verify the poising of the balance. Saunier says the balance can not possibly be accurately poised in all positions if the pivots and pivot holes are not perfectly round, and the poising will be modified with a change of temperature if the two arms do not act identically; as will be the case when the metals are not homogeneous, when one or both arms have been strained owing to want of skill on the part of the workman, or careless work, etc. After accurately timing in a vertical position with XII. up, make it go for twelve hours with VI. up and the same number of hours with III. and IX. up. Observe with care both the rates and the amplitude of the arcs and note them down. Assuming the pivots and pivot holes to be perfectly round and in good condition and that the poising of the balance has been previously tested with care by the ordinary means, if the variations in the four positions are slight the poising may be regarded as satisfactory. As a general, but not invariable rule, a loss in one position on the rate observed in the inverse position may be taken to indicate that the weight of the upper part of the balance is excessive when it does not vibrate through an arc of 360° or the lower part if the arcs of motion exceed this amount. Independently of the balance this loss may be occasioned by excessive friction of the pivots due to a too great pressure owing to the caliper being faulty, or to a distortion of the hairspring causing its center of gravity to lie out of the axis of the balance. If these influences become at all considerable their correction will be beyond the power of the isochronal hairspring, and indeed it will be impossible to counteract them. Changes in the rate on changing from the vertical to the horizontal position may also arise from the following causes: 1. The action of the escape wheel, which is different according as it tends to raise the balance staff or to force it laterally. 2. A hairspring that starts to one side and so displaces its center of gravity, a balance that is not well poised, pivots or pivot holes that are not perfectly round, faults which although of but little importance in the vertical position of the balance staff become serious when it is horizontal. 3. The more marked portion of the friction of the pivots may take place against substances of different degrees of hardness in the two cases, the end stones being frequently harder than the jewels. Saunier further says that satisfactory results will be obtained in most cases by employing the following methods, either separately or two or more together, according to the results of experiments or the rates, the experience and the judgment of the workman:

1. Flatten slightly the ends of the balance pivots so as to increase their radii of friction; when the watch is lying flat the friction will thus become greater.

2. Let the thickness of the jewel holes be no more than is absolutely necessary. It is sometimes thought sufficient to chamfer the
jewel hole so as to reduce the surface on which friction occurs; but this
does not quite meet the case since an appreciable column of oil is maintained against the pivot.

3. Reduce the diameters of the pivots, of course changing the jewel
holes. The resistance due to friction, when the watch is vertical, increases
rapidly with any increase in the diameters of pivots.

4. Let the hairspring be accurately centered, or it must usually be so
placed that the lateral pull tends to lift the balance when the watch is
hanging vertical. In this and the next succeeding case it would sometimes be advantageous to be able to change the point at which it is fixed,
but this is seldom possible.

5. Replace the hair-spring by one that is longer or shorter but of
the same strength; this is with a view to increase or diminish the
lateral pressure in accordance with the explanation given in the last
paragraph.

6. Set the escapement so that the strongest impulse corresponds with
the greatest resistance of the balance.

7. Replace the balance. A balance that is much too heavy renders
the timing for positions impossible.

8. Lastly, when these methods are inapplicable or insufficient there
only remains the very common practice of throwing the balance out of
poise.

Adjustment to Isochronism. The manipulation of the hairspring so that the long and short arcs of the balance are performed in the
same time. The theory of isochronism advanced by Dr. Robert Hooke
and more commonly known as Hooke's law, " as the tension so is the
force," is an axiom in mechanics with which everybody is, or should be
familiar. This law has like nearly all others its exceptions, and it
is only partially true as applied to hair-springs of watches; "otherwise,"
says Glasgow, "every spring would be isochronous." Pierre Le Roy
says that there is in every spring, of a sufficient extent, a certain length
where all the vibrations, long or short, great or small, are isochronous,
and that this length being secured, if you shorten the spring the great
vibrations will be quicker than the small ones; if, on the contrary, it is
lengthened, the small arcs will be performed in less time than the great
ones. Glasgow says that a hair-spring of whatever form to be isochronous must satisfy the following conditions: Its center of gravity must
always be on the axis of the balance, and it must expand and contract in
the vibrations concentrically with that axis. When these conditions are
secured in a properly made spring it will possess the quality of isochronism, that is, its force will increase in proportion to the tension, and it
will not exert any lateral pressure on the pivots.

Britten says, it should be remembered that if the vibrations of a balance are to be isochronous the impulse must be delivered in the middle of its vibration, and that therefore no spring will be satisfactory if the escapement is defective in this particular.

The recognized authorities conflict considerably in their various theories in regard to adjustment to isochronism and particularly in regard to the length of spring. Immisch says that mere length has nothing to do with isochronism. Glasgow contends that length has everything to do with it, and that a spring too short, whatever its form, would make the short arcs of the balance vibration be performed in a less time than the long arcs, and a spring too long would have just the contrary effect. Charles Frodsham advanced the theory that every length of spring has its isochronous point. Britten declares the length is all important; that a good length of spring for one variety of escapement is entirely unfitted for another variety. Saunier says that the discussion of the question whether short springs are preferable to long ones is a mere waste of time and can result in no good. In horology everything must be relative. Whatever be the escapement under consideration, it requires neither a long nor a short hairspring, but one that is suited to its nature and mode of action, that is to say, the length must bear a definite relation to the extent of the arcs of vibration, etc.

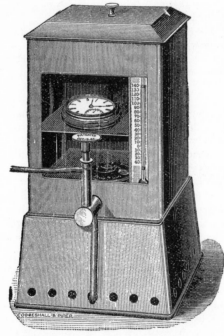

Fig. 2.

Owing to the conflict of opinion it is advisable that the student read the various arguments set forth in the works referred to above and form his own conclusions.

ADJUSTMENT HEATER. The Simpson heater, shown in Fig. 2, will be found invaluable when adjusting movements to temperature. The variation of temperature in this heater is one and one-half degrees in twenty-four hours. It is designed to be heated by gas, the cost of heating being but about three cents in twenty-four hours. A small lamp can be used if the watchmaker has no gas at command.

ALARM. The mechanism attached to a timepiece by which at any desired time a hammer strikes rapidly on a bell for several seconds. Generally a weight or spring actuates an escape wheel, to the pallet staff of which a hammer is fixed to act on a bell. The alarm is usually set off ,by a wire attached to the hour wheel lifting a detent that stops the escape wheel.

ALCOHOL OR BENZINE CUP. The watchmaker should keep the alcohol and benzine on his bench in a glass cup having a tight fitting cover to prevent evaporation and contamination with dust. It also adds to the appearance of his bench and is a great improvement over an old saucer and bottle. The cup shown in Fig. 3 has a ground glass cover or stopper that fits tightly into the neck of the cup.

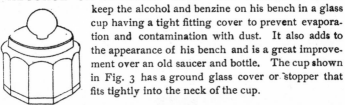

Fig. 3.

ALCOHOL LAMP. The Clark patent simplicity lamp shown in Fig. 4 is a favorite one with American watchmakers. It has nine facets on the font that it may readily be adjusted to any required position. The wicks of alcohol lamps should not be too tight, and the interior and exterior of the font should be kept free from dirt. The Clark lamp should not be filled more than one-third full. The wick should be removed when it gets so short that it fails to reach well down into the alcohol.

Fig. 4.

ALL OR NOTHING PIECE. That part of a repeating watch that keeps the quarter rack off the snail until the slide in the band of the case is pushed around. The lifting piece of the hour hammer is kept free from the twelve-toothed ratchet, while the quarter rack is locked, so that the hours cannot be struck until the quarter rack has fallen. It is sometimes called the hooking spring. It was invented by Julien Le Roy.

ALLOY. A compound of two or more metals. It is usual to melt the less fusible metal first and add the more fusible.

Alloys for Compensation Balances. Breguet used for his compensation balances the following alloy: Silver, two parts, by weight; copper, two parts; zinc, one part. First melt the silver and throw in the zinc, reduced to small pieces, stirring the metals and leaving it on the fire for as short a time as possible to prevent the volatilization of the latter metal; then pour it out and let it get cold. Melt the copper and add the cold alloy, stirring the three together until intimately mixed. Pour out, cut into pieces, and smelt anew, to obtain a perfect incorporation. Be careful, however, to leave the alloy as short a time as possible over the fire, because the zinc dissipates easily. This alloy is hard, elastic, very ductile, and quickly smelts in the furnace. It does not stand much hammering.

Alloy for Composition Files. These files, which are frequently used by watchmakers and other metal workers, for grinding and polishing, and the color of which resembles silver, are composed of 8 parts copper, 2 parts tin, 1 part zinc, 1 part lead. They are cast in forms and treated upon the grindstone; the metal is very hard, and therefore worked with difficulty with the file.

Aluminium Alloys. Aluminium is alloyed with many metals, but the most important are those with copper. Lange & Sons have obtained a patent in the United States for an alloy consisting of ninety-five parts of aluminium and five of copper, which is malleable and is used for clock springs. An alloy of ten parts of aluminium and ninety of copper is hard but nevertheless ductile. It takes a high polish and somewhat resembles gold.

Aluminium Bronze. This alloy contains from 6 to 10 per cent. of aluminium, and is prepared by fusing chemically-pure copper with aluminium. The standard bronze in use consists of ninety parts of copper to ten of aluminium. It gives sharp castings, is easier to work than steel, can be engraved, rolled into sheets or drawn into wire and when exposed to the air suffers less change than cast iron, steel, silver or brass. It can be soldered only with an aluminium alloy.

Aluminium Silver. Aluminium and silver are easily alloyed and these alloys are more easily worked than silver although harder. An alloy of ninety seven parts aluminium and three of silver is not affected by ammonium hydrosulphide and has a beautiful color. An alloy of ninety-five parts of aluminium and five of silver is white, elastic and hard. It is used for making blades of desert and fruit knives.

Aluminium Gold. One part of aluminium to 99 of gold gives a metal the color of green gold, very hard but not ductile. An alloy of 5 parts of aluminium to 95 parts of gold gives an alloy that is nearly as brittle as glass. An alloy of 10 parts of aluminium to 90 parts of gold is white, crystalline and brittle. An imitation of gold, used as a substitute for the precious metal in cheap jewelry, is made by fusing together 5 to 7½ parts of aluminium, 90 to 100 parts of copper and 2½ of gold. The color of this alloy resembles gold so closely as to almost defy detection.

COMPOSITION OF SOME VALUABLE ALLOYS.

	Palladium	Aluminium	Gold	Silver	Bismuth	Tin	Zinc	Lead	Copper	Antimony	Iron	Platinum	Nickel	Black Cobaltic Oxide	Manganese	Cadmium
Alloy for Tea Pots						88.55	9.94		0.88	9.53						
Alloy for Knives and Forks						10							100			
Alloy for Opera Glasses						20							100			
Alloy Resembling Silver									55				25		25	
Alloy Resembling Silver									57				6.5		20	
Alloy for Gongs and Bells				5		25			100							
Alloy, Non-Magnetic	45 to 75			20 to 25					15 to 30							
Bell Metal, American						11	20		54.50							
Bell Metal, Japanese						3	1		39							
Bronze, Japanese						4.86	1.86	9.9	54.50							
Bronze, Manganese						4	20		82.72		0.55				25.50	
Bronze for Medals						3	18	2	50							
Bronze for Ornaments									83							
Bronze, Paris									99.60							
Clock Bells, German				1.44		1.70	5.33		73							
Clock Bells, Swiss						24.3	2.7	1.37	74.5							
Clock Bells, French						25		5	72			1				
Clock Wheels, Black Forest						26.56	36.88		60.66		5	20				
For Spoons						1.36	25		50							
Nurnburg Gold									90							
Oreide		7.5	2.5			0.48			86							
Prince's Metal						1	30		68.21		.74					
Pinchback							13.52		90		0.24					
Soft Solder					7	18		6								
White Metal							72		750				140	20		1

Alloys of Gold used by Jewelers.

COLOR.	GOLD.	SILVER.	COPPER.	CADMIUM.	STEEL.
Blue	250				250
Blue	500				250
Gray	800				200
Gray	857	86			57
Gray	725	275			
Green	750	125		125	
Green	750	166		84	
Green	746	114	97	43	
Red	666	67	268		
Red	750	104	146		
Red, Pale	600	200	200		
Red, Very	583	42	375		
Yellow	583	250	167		
Yellow	666	194	139		
Yellow	750	146	104		
Yellow, Dark	583	125	292		
Yellow, Pale	666	333			

The alloys of gold should not be overheated and ought to be poured immediately after the proper fusion has taken place. The mixture should be well stirred from time to time after it has commenced to melt, using a cherry red iron rod, or a stick of very dry poplar or other slow burning wood. This serves two purposes; it makes the metal homogeneous in its composition and it enables the operator to judge by the feeling when the mass is thoroughly melted. As long as the metal feels curdy or cloggy, it is unfit to pour; when the stirred mass feels thin and watery it should be thoroughly agitated, fresh charcoal added, and allowed to stand for a minute, then poured.

In melting silver alloys, great care and strict attention to the points given below are necessary in order to secure homogeneous alloys of the proportions required. Especially is this the case when the alloys contain the more readily oxidizable metals, such as zinc and tin. The weighing of the metals, the arrangement of them in the crucible, the management during the time they are in the furnace, all are points requiring steady care and constant attention to produce accurate results.

When the alloy consists only of copper and silver they should both be put in the crucible before putting it in the furnace. Put the copper at the bottom and the silver over it, as copper has the highest melting point and the heat is greatest at the bottom; then, too, the silver being the heaviest, will descend through the copper when melting, thus producing a more perfect mixing than when the copper is placed on the top.

Alloys Resembling Silver. The following alloys have a close resemblance to silver: Minargent is composed of 100 parts copper; 70 nickel; 1 aluminium and 5 of tungstate of iron. Trabak metal is composed of tin 87.5, nickel 5.5, antimony 5 and bismuth 2. Warne metal is composed of tin 10, bismuth 7, nickel 7 and cobalt 3.

Aluminium Zinc. Alloys of aluminium and zinc are very hard and take a beautiful polish. An alloy of 97 parts of aluminium and 3 of zinc gives a result that is as white as the pure metal, harder than aluminium and very ductile.

Artificial Gold. A metallic alloy, at present very extensively used in France as a substitute for gold is composed of: Pure copper, 100 parts; zinc, or preferably tin, 17 parts; magnesia, 6 parts; sal-ammoniac, 3 to 6 parts; quicklime, ⅛ part; tartar of commerce, 9 parts, are mixed as follows: The copper is first melted, and the magnesia, sal-ammoniac, lime and tartar are then added separately and by degrees, in the form of powder; the whole is now briskly stirred for about one-half hour, so as to mix thoroughly, and then the zinc is added in small grains by throwing it on the surface and stirring until it is entirely fused; the crucible is then covered and fusion is maintained for about 35 minutes. The surface is then skimmed and the alloy ready for coating. It has a fine grain, is malleable, and takes a splendid polish. It does not corrode readily, and is an excellent substitute for gold for many purposes. When tarnished, its brilliancy can be restored by a little acidulated water. If tin be employed instead of zinc, the alloy will be more brilliant.

Bell Metal. An alloy of copper and tin, in proportions varying from 66 to 80 per cent. of copper and the balance of tin.

Brass. An alloy consisting of about 65 parts of copper to 35 parts of zinc. This proportion is varied according to the uses to which the alloy is to be put. See *Bronzing*, *Plating* and *Coloring Metals*.

Brittania. This alloy as prepared by Koller consists of 85.72 parts of tin, 10.34 of antimony, 0.78 of copper and 2.91 of zinc.

Chrysorine. This alloy is sometimes used for watch cases and parts of the movement. In color it closely resembles 18 to 20 carat gold. It does not tarnish when exposed to the air and has a beautiful luster. It consists of 100 parts of copper and 50 of zinc.

Fictitious Silver. No. 1: Silver, 1 oz.; nickel, 1 oz., 11 dwts.; copper, 2 oz. 9 dwts.; No. 2, silver 3 oz.; nickel, 1 oz. 11 dwts.; copper, 2 oz 9 dwts.; spelter 10 dwts.

Malleable Brass. A malleable brass is obtained by alloying 33 parts of copper and 25 parts zinc; the copper is first thrown into the pot, which is covered slightly and fused. As soon as the copper is smelted, the zinc, to be free from sulphur, is added, and cast into ingots.

Aluminium. Aluminium, or aluminum, is an extremely light, ductile and malleable metal, which is rapidly coming into favor for many purposes since the great improvements in its manufacture and the consequent reduction in cost. It can now be purchased in quantities at ninety cents per pound, which makes it nearly as cheap as copper, when the great difference in weight of a cubic foot of the two metals is considered. It is silvery in appearance, melts at 1,300 degrees F., has a specific gravity of 2.56 to 2.60, which is one-fourth the weight of silver, does not oxidize readily and resists most acids and alkalies, but is very easily attacked by others, especially when heated, or when present during chemical reactions on other metals. It is three times as ductile as silver, and has 50 per cent. more tenacity or strength. Much nonsense has been written about this metal, such as that it is stronger than steel; will not rust; is not attacked by acids, etc., all of which are untrue. It is readily attacked by many chlorides, such as common salt (chloride of sodium), etc., and by some of the organic acids, in which respect it resembles silver. In regard to the hardening, tempering, etc., of the pure metal, comparatively little is known at present; but it is probable that as its use becomes more common it will be greatly improved in these respects, as has been done with iron. At all events, it will have an extended trial in the fine arts and mechanics, and it will probably displace platinum and nickel in the various alloys to some extent, on account of the great difference in weight. One great difficulty remaining to be overcome is that of soldering. At present it can be soldered only by using an alloy of which aluminium forms a part.

Aluminium forms alloys with many metals; those with copper, silver and tin are largely employed for many purposes, and their use is rapidly extending. The most important are those of copper, with which aluminium easily unites. See *Alloys*.

AMALGAM. A compound of mercury with another metal; as an amalgam of tin.

AMPLITUDE. The full extent or breadth. As applied to pendulums, the amplitude of a simple oscillation or vibration; properly the distance from the middle to the extremity of an oscillation, but the term is usually applied to the distance from one extremity of the swing to the other.

ANCHOR ESCAPEMENT. The recoil escapements used in most house clocks. A variety of the lever escapement made with a very wide impulse pin, is also known as an anchor escapement. Authorities differ as to the inventor of the anchor escapement. Britten gives the credit of the invention to Dr. Hooke, whom he claims invented it in 1675, while Saunier says that the first anchor escapement appears to have been invented in 1680, by Clement, a London clockmaker.

Glasgow says: This escapement was the first step in the direction of securing isochronism in the vibrations of the pendulum, as it involved a longer pendulum, shorter arcs, a heavier pendulum bob and less motive power. Consequently this combination resulted in the pendulum being

less controlled by the escapement, and therefore less influenced by variations in the impulse, although the escapement can not be considered
detached in the sense that a dead-beat one is.

In Clement's escapement, the entrance pallet was convex, and the
exit pallet concave, and they were afterwards made flat, but in both cases
they were found to cut away very fast, owing to the friction when the

Fig. 5.

recoil takes place; to prevent this, they were subsequently made both
convex, as shown in the Fig. 6, which lessens the angle, and consequently the friction, at the recoils.

There are still people, says Britten, who believe the recoil to be a
better escapement than the dead-beat, mainly because the former
requires a greater variation of the driving power to affect the extent of
the vibration of the pendulum than the latter does. But the matter is

beyond argument; the recoil can be cheaply made, and is a useful escapement, but is unquestionably inferior to the dead-beat for time-keeping.

There is no rest or locking for the pallets, but directly the pendulum in its vibration allows a tooth, after giving impulse, to escape from the impulse face of one pallet, the course of the wheel is checked by the

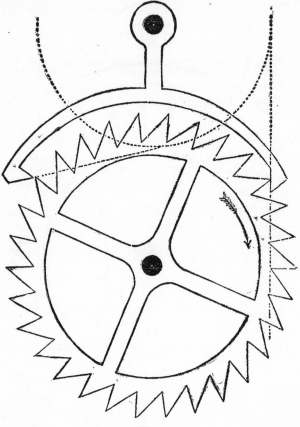

Fig. 6.

impulse face of the other pallet receiving a tooth. The effect of this may be seen on looking at the drawing (Fig. 6), where the pendulum, traveling to the right, has allowed a tooth to fall on the left-hand pallet. The pendulum, however, still continues its swing to the right, and in consequence the pallet pushes the wheel back, thus causing the recoil which gives the name to the escapement. It is only after the pendulum

comes to rest and begins its excursion the other way that it gets any
assistance from the wheel, and the difference between the forward motion
of the wheel and its recoil forms the impulse.

Setting out the Escapement. Draw a circle representing the escape
wheel, which we assume to have thirty teeth, of which the anchor
embraces eight. Mark off the position of four teeth on each side
of the center one, and draw radial lines which will represent the backs
of the teeth.

Space between one tooth and the next $= \frac{360}{30} = 12°$; and 8 spaces $= 96°$.
Then $\frac{96}{2} =$ equal 48° to be set off on each side of the center.

The distance of the pallet staff center from the center of escape
wheel $=$ radius of wheel $\times$ 1.4. From the pallet staff center describe a
circle whose radius $=$ seven-tenths of the radius of escape wheel, that is,
one-half the distance between the escape wheel and pallet staff centers.
Tangents to this circle just touching the tips of the teeth already marked,
as shown by dotted lines in the drawing, would then form the faces of
the pallets if they were left flat. When a tooth has dropped off the right-
hand pallet, which is the position of the escapement in the drawing, the
amount of impulse is shown by the intersection of the other pallet in
the wheel. The impulse, measured from the pallet staff center, is usually from 3 to 4°.

The pallet faces are generally curved full in the middle, as shown in
Fig. 5. The object of curving the pallets is to lessen the "pitting" which
the wheel teeth make on the pallets. There will, however, be very
little "pitting" if the wheels are made small and light, and there is not
excessive drop to the escapement.

The advantage of making the backs of the escape wheel teeth radial
and the foresides curved, as shown in Fig. 5, is that if the pendulum gets
excessive vibration the pallets butt against the roots of the teeth and
the points are uninjured.

There is another form of the recoil escapement often used in long-
cased clocks, in which the anchor embraces ten teeth of the escape
wheel, and the foresides of the teeth are radial. It is shown in Fig. 6.
In other respects the construction is substantially the same as the one
just described.

ANGULAR GEARING. Toothed wheels of irregular outline,
used in transmitting variable motion, as shown
in Fig. 7.

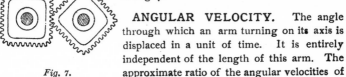

ANGULAR VELOCITY. The angle
through which an arm turning on its axis is
displaced in a unit of time. It is entirely
independent of the length of this arm. The
approximate ratio of the angular velocities of

Fig. 7.

the balance with the cylinder and (pocket) chronometer escapements in the same unit of time (one-fifth second when there are 18,000 vibrations per hour), is about 270°: 360°. The velocity, properly so called, is the space transversed in a unit of time by the point under consideration (which in this case is taken on the circumference of gyration). For a given angular movement we obtain the aproximate ratio of the velocities by multiplying each radius by the number of vibrations in a unit of time.—*Saunier*.

ANNEALING. The process of heating metals and then manipulating them in order to increase their ductility. Gold, silver, copper and brass are annealed by heating them to redness and then plunging them in water, while steel is annealed by heating and then allowing it to cool slowly.

ANNULAR GEAR. A gear wheel in which the teeth are on the inside of an annulus or ring, while its pinion works within its pitch circle, turning in the same direction.

ANODE. The positive pole of an electric current, that pole at which the current enters; opposed to cathode, the point at which it departs.

ARBOR. An axle or spindle on which a wheel turns.

ARC. Any given part of the circumference of a circle, or other curve.

ARCOGRAPH. An instrument sometimes used by watchmakers for drawing a circular arc without the use of a central point.

ARNOLD, JOHN. Born in Cornwall, England, in 1744, and died at Eltham, England, in 1799. He was the inventor of the helical form of balance spring and a chronometer escapement. The English Government awarded him £1,320 for the superiority of his chronometers in 1799, and his son, who followed up the successes of his father, was awarded £1,680 in 1805.

John Arnold.

ASSAY. To subject an ore, alloy or metallic compound to chemical examination in order to determine the amount of a particular metal contained in it.

AUXILIARY. See *Balance*.

BALANCE. The wheel in a watch, clock or chronometer which is kept in vibration by means of the escapement and which regulates the motion of the train. The size and weight of a balance are important factors in the time-keeping qualities of a watch, although the dimensions of a balance are not criteria of the time in which the balance will vibrate. The balance is to a pocket time-piece what the pendulum is to a clock; although there are two essential points of difference. The time of vibration of a pendulum is unaffected by its mass, because every increase in that direction carries with it a proportional influence of gravity; but if we add to the mass of the balance we add nothing to the strength of the hairspring, but add to its load and therefore the vibrations become slower. Again, a pendulum of a given length, as long as it is kept at the same distance from the earth's center, will vibrate in the same time because the gravity is always the same; but the irregularity in the force of the hairspring produces a like result in the vibration of the balance. Britten says there are three factors upon which the time of the vibration of the balance depends:

1. The weight, or rather the mass, of the balance.*

2. The distance of its center of gyration from the center of motion, or to speak roughly, the diameter of the balance. From these two factors the moment of inertia may be deducted.

3. The strength of the hair-spring, or more strictly its power to resist change of form.

Balances are of two kinds, known as plain or uncut, and cut or compensation. The plain balance is only used in this country on the very cheapest variety of movements. The compensation balance is used on the better grades of watches. The plain balance is usually made of brass or steel, while the compensation balance is made of steel and brass combined. Some English makers use gold for plain balances, it being denser than steel and not liable to rust or become magnetized. The process of compensation balance making as carried on in our American factories is as follows: A steel disc, one-eighth of an inch thick and five-eighths of an inch in diameter, is first punched from a sheet of metal. It is then centered and partially drilled through, the indentation serving as a guide in the operation to follow. A capsule of pure copper three-fourths of an inch in diameter is then made, and in the center of this capsule the steel disc is lightly secured. A ring of brass one-sixteenth of an inch in thickness is then made and placed between the copper capsule and the blank, and the whole is fused together. It is then faced upon both sides. It is then placed in a lathe and cut away in the center until a ring is formed of steel, which is lined or framed with brass. It then goes into the press, where two crescents are cut from it, leaving only the inner lining of the ring and the cross-bar of steel. The burr is then removed and the balance is ready to be drilled and tapped for the balance screws. This method of making balances is known as the "capsule method."

---

*The mass of a body is the amount of matter contained in that body, and is the same irrespective of the distance of the body from the center of the earth. But its weight, which is mass X gravity, varies in different latitudes.

The Expansion and Contraction of Balances. The American Waltham Watch Co. use a simple little contrivance shown at Fig. 9 for indicating the expansion and contraction of balances. It is composed of a steel disc, on one side of which a scale is etched and opposite the scale a hole is drilled and tapped to receive the screw that holds the balance. One of the screws of the balance to be tested is removed and the indicating needle is screwed in its place. The steel disc is held by means of a pair of sliding tongs over an alcohol lamp, or can be heated in any other

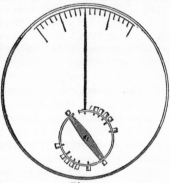

way, and the expansion will be indicated by the movement of the needle on the scale. Fig. 10 illustrates the expansion and contraction of balances. With an increase of temperature the rim is bent inward, thus reducing the size of the balance. This is owing to the fact that brass expands more than steel, and in endeavoring to expand it bends the rim inward. The action is, of course, reversed by lowering the temperature below normal. Some adjusters spin a balance close to the flame of a

Fig. 9.

lamp before using, in order to subject it to a higher temperature than it is likely to meet in use. The balance is then placed upon a cold iron plate and afterward tested for poise. The balance is then trued, if found necessary, and the operation is repeated until it is found to be in poise after heating. Britten says that it has been demonstrated that the loss in heat from the weakening of the hair-spring is uniformly in proportion to the increase of temperature. The compensation balance, however, fails to meet the temperature error exactly, the rims expand a little too much

Fig. 10.

Original Position of Rim.   Position Under Extreme Cold.   Position Under Extreme Heat.

with decrease of temperature, and with increase of temperature the contraction of the rims is insufficient, consequently a watch or chronometer can be correctly adjusted for temperature at two points only. Watches are usually adjusted at about 50° and 85°. In this range there would be what is called a middle temperature error of about two seconds in twenty-four hours with a steel hair-spring. The amount of the middle temperature error cannot be absolutely predicated, for in low temperatures, when the balance is larger in diameter, the arc of vibration is less than in high temperatures when the balance is smaller, and consequently its time of vibration is affected by the isochronism or otherwise of

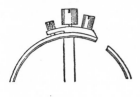

the hair-spring. Advantage is sometimes taken of this circumstance to lessen the middle temperature error by leaving the piece fast in the short arcs. To avoid middle temperature error in marine chronometers various forms of compensation balances have been devised, and numberless additions and auxiliaries have been attached to the ordinary form of balance for the

Fig. 11.

same purpose. Poole's auxiliary, shown in Fig. 11, and Molyneaux's, shown in Fig. 12, may be taken to represent the two principles on which most auxiliaries are constructed. Poole's consists of a piece of brass attached to the fixed ends of the rim and carry-

ing a regulating screw, the point of which checks the outward movement of the rim in low temperature. Molyneaux's is attached to each end of the arm by a spring, the free ends of the rim acting on it in high temperatures only. Fig. 11 illustrates this auxiliary when the temperature has been raised,

Fig. 12.

its free ends, to which the adjusting screws are attached, having approached nearer the center of the balance, carrying with them the free ends of the auxiliary, so that the small projection no longer comes in contact with the short end of the balance rim, as it would in a temperature of 55°. This auxiliary is made of steel.

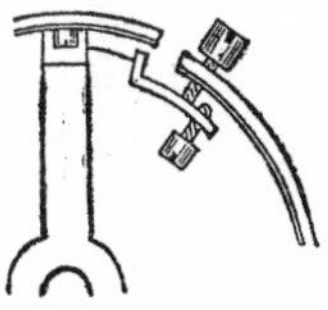

Sizes and Weights of Balances. The size and weight of the balance are two very important elements in the timing of a watch and especially in adjusting to positions. The rules governing the sizes and weights of balances, says Mr. Chas. Reiss, are of a complex nature, and though positive, are difficult of application on account of the impracticability of determining the value of the elements on which we have to base our calculations. These elements are the main-spring or motive power, the hairspring representing the force of gravity on the pendulum, momentum and friction. The relation of the motive power, or the main-spring, to the subject under discussion lies first in the necessary proportion between it and the amount of tension of the spring to be overcome, according to the extent and number of vibrations aimed at; and, second, to that of friction affecting the motion of the balance and incidental to it. In an 18,000 train the main-spring has to overcome resistance of the hairspring for 432,000 vibrations daily. The hairspring, having its force established by the relative force of the motive power, circumscribes the proportions of the mass called balance and is a co-agent for overcoming friction.

Momentum overcomes some of the elastic force of the spring and friction. It is the force of a body in motion and is equal to the weight of the body multiplied by its velocity. Velocity in a balance is represented by its circumference, a *given point* in which travels a *given distance* in a *given time*. Weight is that contained in its rim. A balance is said to have more or less momentum, in proportion as it retains force imparted to it by impulsion. If a watch has a balance with which it has been brought to time, and this is changed to one-half the size, it requires to be four times as heavy, because its weight is then only half the distance from the center, and any given point in its circumference has only half the distance to travel. On the other hand, a balance twice the size, would have one-fourth the weight. In the first case the balance would have twice as much momentum as the original one, because if we multiply the weight by the velocity we have a product twice as great. In the latter case a like operation would give a product half as great as in the original balance.

It follows that the smaller and heavier a balance the more momentum, and, vice versa, the less momentum it has, always on condition that the hairspring controls both equally. Friction, affecting the vibration of the balance, is that of the pivots on which it moves and that of the escapement. It is in proportion to the force with which two surfaces are pressed together and their area. In a balance, weight is synonymous with pressure. Area is represented by the size of its pivots and the thickness of the pivot holes. The first, pivot friction, is continuous and incidental and is overcome by combined forces, the motive power, the elasticity of the hair-spring, and the momentum of the balance. The latter, or escapement friction, is intermitting and is overcome by contending forces, the hair-spring and the momentum of the balance on one side and the motive power on the other.

Having in our power, as shown above, to obtain the desired momentum of the balance by differing relative pressure and diameter, we can regulate pivot friction within certain limits and distribute the labor of overcoming it, among the co-operative forces, in such a manner that the proportions of such distributions shall not be disturbed during their (forces) increase or decrease. Incidental pivot friction is that caused by the unlocking on the impulse. The first causes retardation, the latter acceleration in the motion of the balance, regardless of isochronism. It is easy to comprehend that a heavy balance would, by its greater momentum, unlock the escapement with less retardation than a light one; but, on the other hand, the acceleration by the impulse would be less also; and with a varying motive power a disturbing element would be introduced by a change in the relative proportions of these forces, the momentum of the balance decreasing or increasing faster than the motive power, constituting as it does relatively a more variable force. In argument the reverse of this might be advanced in regard to a balance which is too light. Without, however, entering further into the subject it is plain how the rate of a watch under such conditions might be affected after being apparently adjusted in stationary positions, by being used on a locomotive or under conditions where external disturbances should lessen the extent of vibration, and making the contact between the balance and the escapement of less duration.

The almost universal abandonment of watches with uniform motive power and the introduction of stem-winders with going barrels, invest the subject with special interest; and, as stated in the beginning, applying rules for defining these desirable proportions being impracticable, the only solution of the problem which remains to us is the study, by observation of certain symptoms which do exist, to determine that which by other means cannot be done. During the progress of horology, similar difficulties had to be met in every kind of watch which happened to be in use. The old Verge watch had its balance proportioned thus: that it could lie inside in the main-spring barrel, and the watch, when set going without a balance spring, would indicate, by the hand on the dial, a progress of twenty-seven and one-half minutes during one hour running. It was said that under these circumstances it would be least affected by inequalities of the motive power, and the verge would not be cut by the escape wheel. The balance in the Cylinder watch was to be sized according to the proportion of the train, each successive wheel to be one-half smaller than the preceding one, and the balance to be twice the size of the escape wheel, the weight to be determined by the equal running of the watch during all the changes of an unequal motive power. The cutting of the steel pallets in Duplex watches or chronometers is caused more by too heavy balances than by any other defect in their parts. It might be well to note the following which is very important and too often neglected. That is the arrangement of the mainspring in the barrel so as to avoid coil friction The smallest advantage of the old Fusee watch was not the facility of obtaining five turns of the fusee to three or three and one-half of the mainspring, but being enabled thereby to arrange the latter around a small arbor in such a manner that the coils never touched, insuring a smooth motive power and lessening the chances of breakage beyond estimation.

Poising the Balance. In merely poising a balance for a cheap movement there is no great difficulty, that is, putting it in equipoise sufficient for the reasonably good performance of the movement; but to well and thoroughly poise for a high grade of movement embraces means and methods not necessary in the first mentioned. In a cheap balance a high degree of accuracy is not expected, and so the manipulations are, in the poising, simple, provided all the parts are in condition to admit of poising. The following will be about all the conditions and means used generally: In the outset the balance should be in poise without its staff, and this is approximated before the staff is in by putting into the staff socket in the arm a piece of true wire, sufficiently tight to allow of the balance being held onto it with friction, so that the balance can be trued in the flat by the fingers or with tweezers and remain while poising on the parallel bars.

Fig. 13 illustrates a form of tweezers made especially for balance truing. To here explain the parallel bars and give a few points regarding the essential features will be well, and help to make clear some

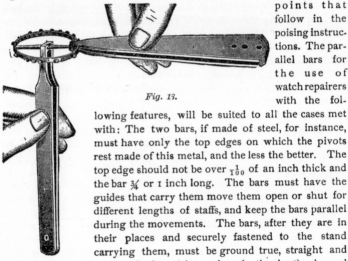

points that follow in the poising instructions. The parallel bars for the use of watch repairers with the following features, will be suited to all the cases met with: The two bars, if made of steel, for instance, must have only the top edges on which the pivots rest made of this metal, and the less the better. The top edge should not be over $\frac{1}{100}$ of an inch thick and the bar $\frac{3}{4}$ or 1 inch long. The bars must have the guides that carry them move them open or shut for different lengths of staffs, and keep the bars parallel during the movements. The bars, after they are in their places and securely fastened to the stand carrying them, must be ground true, straight and parallel, on a flat piece of glass (plate glass is the best), charged with emery of about 140, with oil sufficient to make a paste. The glass can be held and used as a file or the bars can be held down on the glass and moved about with a circular stroke, but if the stand is large and heavy this operation will not be readily performed with good results. The main reason for using the glass referred to, is that it is a ready way of getting a grinding bed comparatively true without labor or preparation. A flat metal surface, marble or stoneware, would answer well, but would not be so readily had. After the emery has ground the surface true, clean off all the emery and use fine oil stone powder or pumice stone; clean, and follow the pumice stone with any polishing powder, or follow the pumice stone with a large and true burnishing file, keeping the surface wet slightly. In making the parallel edges, the object is to give them a perfectly straight surface on the edge and highly polished. These parallels are probably best made of bell metal, as there is then no danger of their being affected or accumulating

Fig. 13.

magnetism. In the construction of a poising tool, to avoid the use of iron or steel in its make-up, will be found the most satisfactory, as then magnetism will not be a disturbing element that it might otherwise be. The whole tool should be heavy and low and stand on the bench firmly, and, if a fine one, have two level vials set in its base to level up the parallels with, before using. With a level bench and a tool made so that the feet are parallel to the top edge of the parallels, there will be little trouble in the balance rolling by gravity while poising. There are a great variety of poising tools, and any that have the parallel bars true and straight and parallel to one another, readily adjusted for distance, and have a firm and heavy stand, will be easily and satisfactorily handled.

Holes for the staff pivots are not good for poising, although jeweled, as the pivots must turn in them with a slipping action, whereas they roll without slip or friction on the parallels. The extreme top edge of the parallels, if of hard substance, can be made as thin as the $\frac{1}{200}$ of an inch and be all the better, as will be explained. The plain, straight portion of a conical pivot of a fine staff is frequently not over the $\frac{1}{100}$ of an inch long, and this is the part of the pivot that is to be exactly concentric with the center of gravity of the balance after poising is accomplished and is that part of the pivot that rests on the jewel. Now, from this it will be seen that the thickness of the parallels can not be great, not over the $\frac{1}{200}$ of an inch, as the conical part of the pivot must not touch the

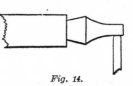

Fig. 14.

parallel, and the end of the pivot should be outside of the parallel. Fig. 14 will show the situation and give the best idea. After the balance has been trued on the wire, then test on the straight edge, and if the balance rolls freely and gravitates, then lighten it on the down or heavy side. Or in the event that the balance is rather light it may be advisable to weight it on the top or light side.

It will take a little practice to poise in this first operation, and there are several points to look at. First, if the balance is a heavy one, then in poising take away weight; second, if a plain (not comp.), remove little bits from the under side of the rim with a graver or drill; if very light, add weight by drilling in the rim and driving in several pins and then filing away till poised. The pins must be put into the rim at such points as are indicated by the circumstances. Soft solder, if used on the under side of a plain balance, is very easily handled, but the risk from the soldering fluid is great and requires great care in cleaning, but when all is well done, it serves a good purpose. As the wire on which the balance is hung is large in diameter, the poising will not be very delicate, but can be made good enough for the end served. In poising a compensating balance, the balance must be hung on a wire with each end pointed, turned to points, so that the wire can be held in the calipers and the balance made true in the round.* Set the gauge of the calipers so that the rim at the end of one arm shall exactly coincide with it, and then turn the balance slowly under the gauge and see if the rim turns truly under it. If not true, bend in or out with the fingers and try by gauge till the balance will turn true in the round, then put onto the parallels and poise as in case of the plain balance, but alter the weight with the screws. The screws that are at the bottom can be put into a split chuck and a little turned away from the under side of the head, or a washer† can be put under the head of the top screw, and this method pursued till a reasonably fine poising is obtained. In these operations all the points relating should be well considered, and not make moves without method and good reasons. Care is required all through poising in all its branches.

These washers are very convenient to use in cases where a balance requires a little more weight, and where it is not advisable to change the hairspring or regulator when regulating to time, and in such cases must be put under the heads of the screws at the ends of the arms. All things being equal, in poising a weighted balance, it is better to add a little weight than to take away any, by turning the heads of screws as described, and then the balance is not in any way injured, and if it was all correct when found, although indications led to other conclusions, by removing a washer or two the balance would be left as originally, and much trouble saved in trying to remedy a mistake. Never make any changes in a fine compensated balance, as, in all probability, it was correct when made and some injudicious handling is to blame for any defect. After a balance has been trued in the calipers as described, so that the rim is truly concentric with the hole in the arm, it should, if it has not been injured, be virtually in poise, but if it is not, add washers to the screws on the light side, and by them try to poise it rather than by lessening the weight. Many times, taking a screw from the heavy side and putting it in place of one on the light, and the light in place of the heavy, will tend to an equilibrium, and so far as it does, is so much gain In removing the screws in a compensating balance, care must be used when they are replaced, to see that they are left just tight enough to stay in place, and at the same time not bind the head hard down on the rim. Screws badly handled in this respect may derange the compensation, also the poising. All the screws of a balance, except those at the ends of the arms, and occasionally a pair of the quarters, should be down, heads close to the rim. The others can be turned in and out at pleasure to poise, or for timing, as required. With a balance with a screw at each end of the arm, it is best not to move them in or out in poising, but proceed as described and leave these screws to be moved in timing afterward,

*See *Gauges.*
†See *Balance Screw Washers.*

if required, as it helps to make that operation easy.   When a balance has four screws they may be moved to do all the poising and afterward any pair opposite, or the whole, may be moved in timing and not disturb the poising.   A compensating balance with four screws as described is much the easiest balance to handle, for by these screws the finer adjustments in poising and timing can be easily performed with greater certainty than by the old methods as described.

The balance staff is a very important element in poising and its pivots should be perfect, that is, perfect cylinders, and all that part that touches the hole jewel should be of equal diameter.   By referring to cut of staff, it will be seen that the end after leaving the cone is straight, of equal diameter throughout its whole length, and this is the shape of all staff pivots at that point riding in the jewel holes, no matter what curve or shape may be given to the balance of the pivot.   When there is a different diameter in the top and bottom pivots they are each true cylinders and their cylindrical diameters are parallel to each other and to the axis of the staff. When pivots are bent, or out of parallel with the axis of the staff, they are then not in condition to make poising possible, as a bent pivot will make a balance gravitate and act as though out of poise in itself, and with a bent pivot, poising can only be approximately attained.   Perfectly cylindrical and parallel pivots to a staff are, in poising, a very essential feature, and without which poising cannot be attained.

When a balance has been poised as indicated and a staff made and fitted with perfectly cylindrical and parallel pivots, proceed as follows, and there will be little to do to complete the operation: First put the balance on the staff with a hollow punch and only press it on sufficiently to hold for preliminary tests; then place on the parallels of the poiser and examine; should the balance appear in poise, it must not be taken for granted that it is so, but try a very slight jar given the poising tool, like rubbing over the frame an old file, which will impart to it a very slight vibration, and if the balance is actually out, it will roll and then remain with the heavy side down.   If a jar, such as a series if taps with a hammer, be given, the balance will rotate and stop for an instant and then rotate again, and finally jar off the bars and the operation will not prove anything.   The jar is such that the balance raises up bodily, when made with a file, and then falls down exactly on the same place on the parallels, rather the pivots come to rest always at the same point; and it will be seen by this means that if any point of the rim is in reality heavier from gravity, that it will by the momentum imparted, fall, overcoming the pivot friction, and finally seek a point in a direct line under the staff.

Repeated movements of a balance while on the parallels are necessary, together with great cleanliness of pivots and parallels, to thoroughly ascertain the true poised condition of the balance.   When it is ascertained that a balance is out of poise or has a heavy side, punch out the staff and put the balance again on it only turned just one-half way around, and repeat as above. In this way a staff can be put into a balance to the best advantage and such little items all tend to save time and make easy the whole handling. When the best position is found for the staff, stake it, and true in the flat, and test again on the bars, and if necessary make further changes as above to affect a poise. When a balance is in poise and a staff perfectly true as has been described, and well staked on, it will in the most cases be found poised and nothing further to do. After putting on the roller it is advisable to test again for position, but it is generally unnecessary, as this will not disturb the poising only in exceptional cases. By staking on the roller too tight the staff may be bent and may destroy the poise.

Care is necessary in handling a balance for any purpose, not to bend the rim, soil or corrode the metal and finish, and in making slight alterations in the curve of the rim, not to bend it at the holes and so destroy its true circle and injure the strength of the metal and change its adjustment.

Any one, after poising a balance and testing the movement carefully in different positions, will in many cases be aware of quite a change of rate in the changes of position, and this, at the first thought, would seem to rather reflect on the accuracy of the poising; but it will be found to occur at times with the most carefully poised balance, and that the operation of poising by the parallels does not comprehend the whole, nor the very nicer requirements. In any case the most careful mechanical poising must be attended to first, before any operations of a more delicate nature are attempted. In short, the parallels are to be used in the most delicate methods, but precede the others. When a movement is placed in its case and hung up, after poising on the parallels, its rate should be carefully noted for a given time, then it should be just reversed and set up with the pendent down, when it will be found, as a rule, that after a trial of same duration as the first, that the rate will not be the same. Now, when this occurs in a fine movement, it will be advisable to investigate all the parts which in any way relate to this action. Both hole jewels must be examined, for finish, thickness and truth of the bore; the roller jewel and the lever-fork examined; guard pin and its action with the table; the hairspring and all its relations and connections; the balance must be removed and then the lever, and the lever placed on the parallels by its staff pivots, as in the balance, and tested for poising. The lever should, when placed on the parallels, lay horizontal, like the beam of pan scales, and not swing or hang either end down; the weight should be removed from the heavy end, in such an event, until the lever will lie as indicated. Levers can be, and are made, that will stand in any position, like a poised balance, but it will, in most cases, be difficult to poise a lever for any position other than horizontal. Next, the escape wheel must be poised so that it will perform as a poised balance, when on the parallels; lever and escape jewels examined, as in those of the balance staff.

After all has been so far attended to, and the parts in place again, the balance must stand, when the mainspring is entirely run down, with its arms either perpendicular or horizontal; with a movement, whose balance is near the center, the arms can stand pointing to 6 and 12, or 3 and 9, as the most convenient. In requiring balance arms to stand in some fixed relation to prominent points of the movement, the manipulations are greatly facilitated, though any position the arms may chance to have will not interfere with the result, but a more expert hand will be required to get along with ease and certainty.

When all the foregoing operations are attended to, hang up the watch and take its rate for 12 hours, with main spring fully wound up; then reverse its position, with main spring wound up, and test for another 12 hours. On examination, if there should be any considerable variation in the rates in the two positions, say 10 to 15 seconds, then proceed by changing the screws as follows: in a case where the watch loses when hanging, it indicates that a screw of the balance nearest to 12 or 6, when the movement is entirely run down, must be moved a very little in or out. In this case, it is fair to suppose that the balance is too heavy on the side nearest 6—that this side gravitates, and, to an extent, acts like a pendulum. Assuming this to be the case, turn the lower screw in and the upper one out, where there are four timing screws, and, where not, washers may be added to the top screws, and the two trials repeated. After trial, if the result is improved, then the lower screw may be made a little lighter, but not at the first trial. In the first trials the balance should not be altered in weight, as indications in these manipulations are changed or modified by conditions not yet mentioned.

We will assume that the balance has four screws, and when one is turned in and the other out, as indicated, and the end attained, then the watch is to be placed with the 3 or 9 up, and two trials made, as in the first, and the same method used, if indications are similar.

When the handling of the balance has been correctly done, the poising will be found to equalize the rates of the different positions, and the total performance improved. There are, of course, many chances for mistakes, but, with caution, they will do no harm, for if the balance is not changed other than a change in distribution of its weights, the act of restoring will be merely setting all the screws back to the position they were when poised by the parallels, and then proceed again on a new method, reversing the first; and then gradually it will be made clear to the most inexperienced, remembering that what held good in one case may not in another; and that various cases are only compassed by trial; and that the indications in the one may be just reversed in the other.

Instead of changing the lower screw as previously suggested, another trial may be made with 12 down, and the rate taken for the same period as for 6 down, and the two compared. Now if the watch maintains its former record it is pretty good evidence that the two rates will be its rates for these two positions, and then the alterations may be made. Now, while hanging in this case the watch lost, 6 down, and relatively gained with 12 up, and a very natural conclusion would be, if losing with 6 down, that the lower side of the balance would be the heaviest. Such is not the case, but the indications are that the upper side is the heaviest, and that the screw there should be turned in, and that the lower one may or may not be changed. Change the top screw first, in this case, and then make another trial and compare with the first. In all average cases, after changing the screw, the two rates should be found to be closer than in the first trial, and this will give a pretty good index of how to proceed. The philosophy of the action is the same as that of the action of the musical measuring instrument used to beat music measures, called a metronome. It has a short pendulum with the rod prolonged above the shaft that it swings on, and on the upper end of this rod is a small weight that slides up and down and so regulates the beats. The position of this weight, being above the center of motion, has a very great control of the vibrations and controls them for a wide range. For instance, the whole pendulum of one of these instruments is not over 2 or 2½ inches long, but with the little counter weight it can be made to beat seconds and slower measures, which could not be accomplished with anything short of a 39 inch pendulum and over. Then move the screw as already indicated, keeping in mind the compared pendulum action and its philosophy.

Gravitating on the principle of the simple pendulum is not the whole problem in moving the screws of the balance, but they embrace the philosophy of the instrument described, and this must be kept in mind in the handling. In experiments it will be found that a screw moved at at the top of a balance, will make twice as much changing in the rate as the same movement of a screw at the bottom. Hang up a watch and turn out the lower screw one-half a turn, and the rate will be, for instance, ten seconds slow in six hours. Now put up just reversed, and for the next six hours the watch will be found twenty seconds slow or more. Now, if we proceed in this case on the simple pendulum philosophy, we should make a mistake in moving the screws.

In practice it is not necessary to make only tests for 3 and 9, assuming we have an open face watch. First regulate on full spring for 6 or eight hours hanging, and when well regulated place the watch 3 up and then 9 for the same period on full spring, and if any material change in rate is found in the two last, then move the screw as already indicated, keeping in mind the compound action and its philosophy.

The handling of the screws in poising on the parallels and in the running watch are for some indications just reversed, and this is due to the action of lever and hairspring on the balance, with gravity in one case and to gravity alone in the other. In experimenting with the running watch always wind fully up for each trial, and periods of six to eight hours will be found the most convenient. The upper coils of a main-spring are much the most equal in power, and consequently give best results; that is, the fourth, fifth and sixth turns of a spring are much nearer each other in strength than are the second, third and fourth. If a balance is perfectly poised mechanically, and the whole train in perfect mechanical poise and condition, then the running watch should not give any very considerable difference in rate in four positions, but as this is not the case generally there will be a change of rate in the positions and the balance can be then manipulated to correct the error, although it in itself may not be at fault. The reason for not testing a watch for the whole range of four positions, is that in the pocket, a watch is not sup-posed to get into a position with the stem down, three and nine are apt to be up and down, and so with twelve are the three positions used. The isochronal condition of the hairspring is apt to make trouble in these experiments, and this is another reason for using full spring invariably. The extent of motion of the balance is another element in the mat-ter, and any movement when in perfect poise for a balance motion of ¾ of a revolution, each side of the center or dead point (1½ revolution) would not be found in as accurate poise for ¾ of a revolution. A bal-ance making one and a half revolutions, to a certain extent, is self-cor-recting, as will be seen, and is to be preferred to any other movement, for if any point of the rim is out of poise then the fault is brought just opposite in each excursion, and so does not relatively gravitate. Owing to the fusee, an English lever with a balance making one and one-half revolutions, is the highest form of movement for accurate adjustments of any kind and so is the easiest to realize perfect poising. The Ameri-can watch is so uniformly well and evenly made by machinery that poising is in it quite easy, and much more so than in foreign makes. A Waltham movement that I tested, just as it left the factory, only changed its rate about three seconds for the four positions. This could not be realized in any medium grade of foreign watch, and I presume this is not a single case, but probably rather a type. The American movement is made mechanically so near perfection that the watchmaker will find poising a balance comparatively easy, and that what he finds to hold good in one case will be pretty sure in another, due to this mechanical perfec-tion. J. L. F.

BALANCE ARC. That part of the vibration of a balance in which it is connected with the train, used only in reference to detached escapements.

BALANCE BRIDGE OR COCK. The standard that holds the top pivot of the balance in an upright position. In some of the old En-glish and French full plate watches the balance cock was spread out to cover the entire balance, as shown in Fig. 15, and was sometimes artistically wrought and set with precious stones.

BALANCE PROTECTOR.   No matter how careful a person may be, accidents will happen, and the least accident to a compensation balance gives the workman considerable trouble.   The Arrick patent balance protector, Fig. 16, is intended for guarding balances from contact

Fig. 15.   Fig. 16.

with turning tools, polishers and the hand rest, while work is being done upon the pivots.   The staff is passed through the hole in the protector, and held in a wire chuck, and the protector is secured to the arms of

Fig. 17.

the balance by two screws.   The Bullock protector, shown in Fig. 17, is designed to protect the balance and other wheels from heat while drawing the temper from staff or pinion for the purpose of pivoting.

BALANCE SCREW WASHERS.   All watch adjusters and expert repairers time their watches by the balance screws, without unpinning the hairspring, and have their regulator in the center.   After the curve of the hairspring is once correct, it should never be let out or taken up.   The portion of the spring where it is pinned is naturally stiffer and often abruptly bent to make the first coil conform to the stud and regulator.   In unpinning the spring this curve is necessarily altered and the spring thrown out of the center, the heat and cold adjustment is altered and the isochronal adjustment often entirely destroyed.

When a watch has timing or quarter screws and they move in or out friction tight, you can very soon bring your watch to time without molesting the spring and have the regulator in the center, and also poise by these screws. Very often some of these timing screws are so tight that there is danger of twisting them off. You will also find that two-thirds of the watches of the best makes do not have timing screws. In this case time by a pair of screws opposite the balance arms. If it runs too slow lighten an opposite pair of screws (just mentioned) in a split chuck or file in the slot with slotting file. If it runs too fast put a pair of washers under the screws near the balance arms, or four at right angles or more under other screws. Whatever may be required in pois-ing put the required amount on the light side of the balance rim. Do not tamper with an adjusted hair-spring or any other. If you are anxious to do your work quickly and accurately, compare your seconds hand with that of the regulator. See *Poising the Balance.*

BALANCE SPRING. See *Hair Spring.*

BALANCE STAFF. The axis or staff to which the balance is attached. In some makes of watches the balance staff and collet are one piece, while in others the collet is made of brass and is fitted tightly to the staff.

Making a New Staff. It is a very common thing for American workman, especially those who reside in the large cities, to depend upon the stock of the material dealer for their staffs. The country watch-maker must, however, rely upon his mechanical ability, and even in the large cities the workman will have to make his own staffs when repair-ing many foreign watches. The following instructions relate more particularly to staffs for American watches, though they may be applied to foreign watches as well. Before proceeding further I would call the attention of the trade to a most valuable series of essays on the balance staff, published in the columns of *The American Jeweler*, and would advise those interested to read them carefully*

The material used should be the best, say Stubb's steel wire, a little larger in diameter than the largest part of the staff and a trifle longer than the old one. A wire that fits the No. 45 hole in the pinion guage will be about right in the majority of cases. Put this in the split chuck of your lathe, if you use an American lathe, and rough it out to the form shown at *B* in Fig. 18. If you use a Swiss or wax-chuck lathe, the form of chuck shown at *A*, Fig. 18, will be found very useful.† It is made from a piece of brass rod, threaded to fit the lathe spindle and bored out to receive

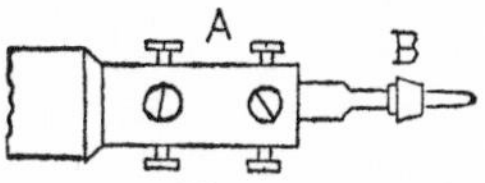

Fig. 18.

---

* Making and Replacing the Balance Staff, a series of seventeen essays published in *The American Jeweler* for December, 1888, and January to September, 1889, inclusive. The Illustrations are from these essays.

† From the essay by "Pasadena," *American Jeweler* March, 1889.

the work, which is held by set screws, three or four at each end of the chuck.   By the aid of these screws the work may be held very firmly and yet can easily be brought to center.

After bringing the work to the general form of the staff, in the rough, remove from the lathe, smear with soap and harden by heating to a cherry red and plunge endwise into oil. Re-chuck in the lathe, and while revolving, whiten by applying a No. ooo emery buff, so that you may observe the color while drawing the temper. Now place the roughed-out blank in the bluing pan, and draw to a deep blue in color.

The heights may be taken from the old staff, providing it was not faulty and is at hand, but all things considered it is better to make your measurements and construct the new staff independent of the old one.

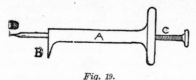

A simple tool, and one which any watchmaker can make, is shown in Fig. 19. It will be found very convenient in taking the measurements of heights of a staff.‡ It consists of a hollow

Fig. 19.

sleeve *A*, terminating in a foot *B*. Through this is screwed the rod *C*, terminating in a pivot *D*, which is small enough to enter the smallest jewel. To ascertain the right height for the roller, place it upon the foot *B*, indicated in Fig. 20, and set the pivot of the tool in the foot jewel,

and adjust the screw until the roller is in the proper relation to the lever fork as shown in the illustration.   In Fig. 20 the potence and plate of the watch are shown in section at *A*. The roller is indicated at *c* and the lever fork at *d*. After the adjusting of the roller is completed, remove the tool and apply it to the rough staff as indicated in Fig. 21, at *A*, and the point at which the seat for the roller should be cut will be shown.   In order to ascertain the height of the balance, apply the

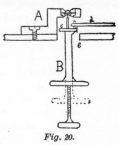

Fig. 20.

gauge as before and bring the point *e*, so as to give sufficient clearance below the plate as indicated by the dotted lines at *B*, Fig. 20.   Then apply the gauge to the work as indicated at *B*, Fig. 21, and turn the

A   B

Fig. 21.

balance seat at the point indicated.   The diameter of the seat for the roller, balance and hairspring collet, can be taken from the old staff,

‡ Other measuring instruments for this purpose will be found under *Gauges.*

or gauge the holes with a taper arbor or a round broach, and then take the size from the broach with calipers.

The diameter of the lower pivot should be taken from the jewel, and the ordinary pivot gauge, when used in connection with a round pivot broach, is all that is necessary even for the finest work. At A, in Fig. 22, is shown the gauge, each division of which corresponds to about $\frac{1}{2500}$ of an inch. Slip the jewel on the broach as far as it will go without forcing, as shown at B, Fig. 22, and then take the size of the broach,

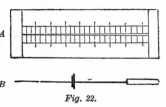

Fig. 22.

close up to the jewel, by means of the slit in the gauge. This will not give you the exact size of the jewel hole, but will be just enough smaller to allow of the proper freedom of the pivot.

The best shape for the pivots is shown in Fig. 23, known as conical

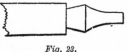

Fig. 23.

pivots; the straight portion of the pivot which enters the jewel hole being truly cylindrical and about $\frac{1}{100}$ of an inch long. Many very good workmen employ but one graver for performing the entire work, but it is better to have at least three, similar in shape to those shown in Fig. 23; A for turning the staff down in the rough, B for under-cutting, and C for turning the conical shoulders of the pivots. A graver like that shown at D will be found excellent for beginners and others who find it difficult to hold the

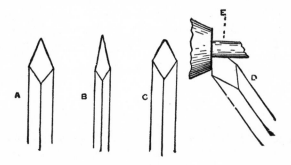

Fig. 24.

shoulder square and at right angles to the staff E, without leaving a groove in one or the other. The all important thing is to keep the gravers sharp. Upon the least sign of their not cutting, stop the work and sharpen them.

Next in importance is the position in which the graver is applied to the work. It must, under all circumstances, *cut* and not *scrape*. If held as shown at *A*, Fig. 25, it will cut a clean shaving, while if applied as at *B*, it will only scrape. If held as shown at *C*, the force of the cut will be in the direction of the hand, as indicated by the arrow. If the point

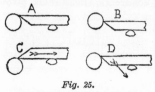

should catch from any cause, the hand would yield and no harm would be done, while if held as at *D*, the force of the cut would be downward upon the rest, as indicated by the arrow, and the rest being unyielding catching would be dangerous.

Fig. 25.

The roughing out should be done with the point of the graver held as at *C*, Fig. 25, and then finished with the edge held diagonally as at *A*, Fig. 26. It is difficult to show the exact position in the cuts, but the idea is to have the shavings come away in a spiral may be as fine as a hair, but in perfect coils.

To turn the pivot, hold the graver nearly in line with the axis of the lathe, as shown at *B*, Fig 26, and catching a chip at the extreme end with the back edge of the graver, push forward and at the same time rolling the graver towards you, which will give the pivot the conical form. Very small pivots can be turned in this way with perfect

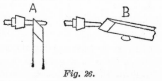

Fig. 26.

safety, and very smoothly. Of course, this method of turning will not give sharp corners; such places as the seat of the roller, balance, etc., must be carefully done with the point of the graver.

The pivot and seat of the roller should be left slightly larger than required, to allow for the grinding and polishing, the amount of which will depend upon how smoothly the turning is done. The grinding is done

with a slip of bell-metal or soft iron or steel of the shape shown at *A*, Fig. 27. *B* is a bell-metal polisher, and may also be made

Fig. 27.

of box wood. *A* should be used with oil-stone powder and oil, and *B* with crocus and diamantine for polishing.

When the staff is finished from the lower pivot to the seat of the balance, the upper part should be roughed out nearly to size, then cut off, reversed in the lathe and the top part finished. It is better to do this in a wax chuck even if you use a split chuck, for the lower part of the staff is tapered and it is ten chances to one that you could select a split chuck that would hold it true and firm In using a wax chuck the important point is to get a perfect center. It should be turned out with the graver at an angle of about 60°, care being taken not to leave a little "tit" in the center. Before setting the staff in the wax it is necessary to get its full length as follow: Screw the balance cock in place with both cap jewels removed, and if the cock has been bent up or down, or punched to raise or lower it, see that it is straightened and put right; then with a degree gauge or calipers take the distance between the outer surfaces of the hole jewels, and shorten the staff with a file to that length.

A very handy tool can be made by adding a stop-screw to the common

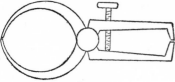

double calipers as shown in Fig. 28. The improvement is that they can be opened to remove from the work and closed again exactly the same.

When fixing the staff in the chuck, care should be taken not

Fig. 28.

to burn the wax. Use a small lamp and heat the chuck until the wax will just become fluid. The staff should be set in the wax about to the seat of the balance, the finished pivot resting in the center of the chuck, and the outer end trued up by the finger and the point of a peg while the wax is still soft.

Fig. 29 shows it with the staff finished, but, of course, it is not, when put in the wax. The dotted lines show about the right quantity and shape of the wax, which must be true and round, or in cooling it will draw the work out of center. If necessary, when cool, the wax can be turned true with the graver, again heated and centered. The turning and finishing is to be done as previously described. The seat

Fig. 29.

for the balance should be slightly undercut and fitted to drive on tightly without riveting. Take the size of the top pivot from its jewel the same as the lower. The ends of the pivots should be finished as flat as possible, and the corners slightly rounded. When done, remove from the wax and boil in alcohol to clean, and it is ready to receive the balance, which should first be poised as described on page 27.

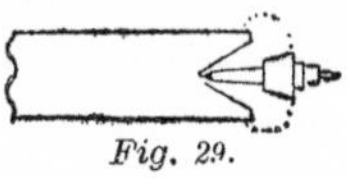

BANKING. In a lever watch, the striking of the outside of the lever by the impulse pin owing to excessive vibration of the balance. In a horizontal or verge, the striking of the pin in the balance against the fixed banking stud or pin.

BANKING ERROR. When by a sudden circular motion of the watch in the plane of the balance (a very frequent occurence when wearing the watch, or winding it up in a careless way), the vibration increases to more than two full turns, the impulse-pin strikes against the outside of the fork, which cannot yield, because it is leaning against the banking-pin or edge. By the violence of this percussion there is some danger of injury, not only to the ruby-pin, but also to the balance-pivots, which are often bent or broken by the reaction. But more than that, all such cases are accompanied by a considerable acceleration of the rate of the watch, producing under unfavorable circumstances great differences in its time-keeping.

BANKING PINS. The two pins that limit the motion of the lever in the lever escapement, are known as banking pins. The pins used for limiting the motion of the balance in verge and horizontal escapements are also known as banking pins. The two pins in the balance arm which limit the motion of the balance spring in pocket chronometers are also known as banking pins.

BANKING SCREW. An adjustable screw in the chronometer escapement, the head of which regulates the amount of locking by forming a stop for the pipe of the detent.

BARLEYS. The little projections formed by the operation of engine-turning.

BARLOW, EDWARD. A clergyman who invented the rack striking work for clocks in 1676. With this mechanism clocks could be made to repeat the hour at will, and its popularity on this account led to the introduction of repeating watches a few years later. Barlow and Quare both applied for a patent for repeating watches, and the English government decided in favor of the latter in 1687.

BAR MOVEMENT. A watch movement in which the top plate is omitted and the upper pivots of the movement are carried in bars. A bar movement is sometimes called a " skeleton " movement.

BAROMETRIC ERROR. The alteration in the timekeeping of a clock due to changes in the density of the atmosphere through which the pendulum has to move. Chronometers and watches are doubtless affected from the same cause to a lesser extent. Experiments by Mr. Ellis showed that if a magnet were fixed vertically to a pendulum, just above the pole of another magnet attached to the clock case, the rate of the clock could easily be altered by causing the magnets to recede from or approach each other. When the adjacent poles of the two magnets were similar, the repulsion retarded the clock, and the attractive power of dissimilar poles caused it to gain. Taking advantage of this fact, he devised a barometric compensation for the standard sideral clock at the Greenwich Observatory, where it answers admirably. Two bar magnets, each about six inches long, are attached to the pendulum bob, one behind and one in front. The latter is marked *a* in the engraving. A lever resting at A on knife edges carries a horse-shoe magnet *b*, whose poles are exactly under the bar magnets and about 3.75 inches below them. At the other extremity of the lever is a rod (*d*) carrying a float *e*, which rests on the mercury in the short leg of a barometer, as shown. The area of the cistern part of the short leg is four times the area of the upper part of the barometer tube, so that a variation of one inch in the barometric pressure would affect the height of the mercury in the cistern but .25 of an inch. As the clock gained with a falling barometer, the bar magnet over the south pole of the horse-shoe magnet was placed with its north pole downwards, and the bar magnet over the north pole of the horse-shoe magnet with its south pole downwards, so that there should be attraction between the bar magnets and the horse-shoe magnet. The bracket supporting the knife edges can be shifted, to increase or diminish the action of the magnet, and the lever is balanced by placing the weights in the pan *f*.

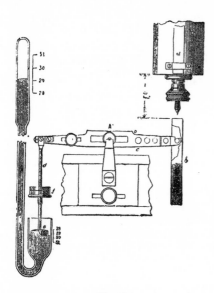

Fig. 30.

BARREL. The circular brass or steel box that encloses the mainspring of a watch or clock.

BARREL ARBOR. The barrel axis, around which the mainspring coils. M. Roze calls attention to the importance of the proper diameter of barrel arbors, and points out that if the arbor is too large part of the elastic reaction of the spring will be wasted, and if too small there will be a rupture or straining of the spring and therefore a loss of elastic reaction. It is, then, he says, the thickness of spring that determines the diameter of the arbor or conversely, and from this it follows that the diameter is not an arbitrary quantity, since it depends on the duration of flexible and thickness of spring. See *Mainsprings.*

BARREL CONTRACTOR. An instrument for contracting distorted mainspring barrels. It consists of a die with a series of tapered holes and punches to correspond. The barrel being forced into a hole slightly smaller than its circumference necessarily contracts.

BARREL HOOK. A hook in the barrel to which the mainspring is attached. The mainspring is sometimes attached by means of a hook on the spring which fit in a hole in the barrel.

BARREL RATCHET. A wheel which is placed on the barrel arbor and kept from turning backward, when the mainspring is wound, by a click or dog.

BARTLETT, P. S. The first ladies watch made in America was turned out by the American Waltham Watch Co., in 1861 and named the P. S. Bartlett. Previous to this however, in 1859 the company placed an 18 size movement on the market which was named the P. S. Bartlett, but its manufacture was discontinued in 1859. Mr. P. S. Bartlett, after whom these movements were named, was born in Amesbury, Mass., September 3, 1834. His first connection with watchmaking was in 1854, when he went to work for the Boston Watch Co., just after its removal to Waltham Mass., where he occupied the position of foreman of the plate and screw department. In 1864 he visited Chicago, and together with Messrs. Moseley, Adams and Blake, organized the National Watch Co., of Chicago, afterwards known as the Elgin National Watch Co. He subsequently signed a contract with the company for five years, as foreman of the plate and screw departments. He was for seven years assistant superintendent and general traveling agent for the company, during which time he introduced Elgin watches into Europe, selling them in Moscow, St. Petersburg and other large cities. He is now in the wholesale and retail watch and jewelry busines in Elgin.

BASCULE ESCAPEMENT. A form of chronometer escapement in which the detent is mounted on a pivoted axis. It is also known as the pivoted detent escapement to distinguish it from the spring detent.

BEAT. The striking of the escape wheel upon the pallet or locking device. When an escapement is in adjustment, so that the striking of the escape wheel upon the pallets is even and equal it is said to be in beat and when it is not in adjustment it is said to be out of beat. The latter, says Saunier, may be due to any of the foliowing causes: 1. One or even both of the pins that secure the hairspring in the collet and stud are loose. 2. The spring is strained between the two curb pins. 3. The Hairspring stud not having been placed immediately over the dot on the balance when putting the escapement together.

BEAT BLOCK. A device for obviating the necessity of marking the balance to see that it is in beat.

Before taking off the hair spring lay it on the block, turn the balance so the roller pin hits on the side the arrow points, then turn the table so that the line comes under the stud. In replacing the balance put the stud over the line and it will then beat the same as before. By using this tool you also avoid getting the balance out of true.

BEAT PINS. Small screws or pins to adjust the position of the crutch in relation to the pen-

Fig. 31.

dulum. The pins at the end of the gravity arms that give impulse to the pendulum in a gravity escapement.

BELL METAL. See *Alloys*.

BENCH. An excellent arrangement for a watchmaker's bench is shown in Fig. 32. This bench was designed by G. W. Laughlin and is complete in every detail. Benches can be purchased ready made

Fig. 32.

from almost any tool and material house in the country but many pre- fer to make their own or to have them made in order to vary the details to suit their peculiarities. The bench shown in Fig. 33 is one of the latest designs on the market, the points claimed for it being that it is raised sufficiently from the ground to allow sweeping under it, its small

weight and its low price. The frame is made of iron and is similar to those used for sewing machines. The foot-wheel is fastened to the iron frame on the left, instead of being supported by uprights from the floor. It is neat in appearance, substantial, and reasonable in price. From the sketch (Fig. 32) any first-class cabinet maker should be able to make a good bench. This bench is made of black walnut, veneered with French walnut and bird's eye maple. The top is twenty-one inches wide by forty-one long, and is thirty-three inches high. The drawers on the right hand side are ten inches wide. In the center are two drawers and the left hand side is entirely boxed in. The lathe wheel can be varied to suit the ideas of the watchmaker, a space of five inches being left for its reception. For the various styles see *Lathe Wheels.*

Fig. 33.

Well seasoned black walnut, cherry or red cedar are the best woods for a bench. The little pin attached to the right hand side of the bench is a pegwood cutter, an enlarged view of which is shown in Fig. 34.

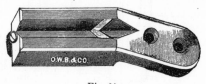

O.W.B.&CO.

Fig. 34.

BENZINE. A light oil of petroleum used for cleaning movements. For directions for use see *Watch Cleaning.*

BERTHOUD, FERDINAND. A Swiss horologist who was born in 1729 and died in 1807. At the age of nineteen he visited Paris, never afterward leaving it. Saunier says that "his technical training was matured and perfected by contact with the great masters of that day, of whom he subsequently became a rival. He was possessed of a very extensive knowledge and real talent, coupled with indefatigable energy; these are sufficient to explain and justify his great reputation. He published ten quarto volumes on horology. Berthoud did much valuable work, and his name will therefore long remain one of the glories of the horological art."

BERTHOUD, LOUIS. A French chronometer maker and nephew of Ferdinand Berthoud. He died in 1813.

BEVEL GEARS. Gears in which the two wheels working together stand at an angle to each other.

BEZEL. The grooved metal ring of a watch or clock that holds the crystal or glass in position.

BEZEL CHUCK. See *Chuck.*

BINDING WIRE. Fine malleable iron wire used for binding articles while soldering, etc.

BITE. To adhere to; to hold fast; as a set screw *bites* a shaft. The eating of metal by means of acid.

BLOWER. The form of bellows shown in Fig. 35 is known as the Fletcher Foot-Blower, and is applicable wherever an air-blast is required, either for the blow-pipe or for operating melting furnaces. It is simple compact, portable and powerful; giving a steady blast of air at a pressure of from one to nearly two pounds to the inch. Two patterns of this blower are made, one with the air reservoir on the top of the bellows, and the other like the one shown in the illustration. The latter form is preferable, as it obviates the risk of injury to the rubber reservoir or its net, by dropping tools or corrosive liquids upon them.

Fig. 35.

BLOW-PIPE. A tapering metal tube, used to direct the flame from a lamp or gas jet upon an article for soldering, annealing and similar purposes.

Fig. 36 shows the automatic hand blow-pipe, which is used in connection with the foot-blower. One of the rubber tubes shown is connected to the blower and the other to the gas supply. It is self-adjusting, for

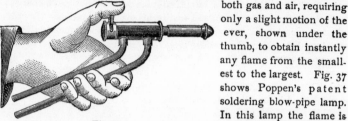

both gas and air, requiring only a slight motion of the ever, shown under the thumb, to obtain instantly any flame from the smallest to the largest. Fig. 37 shows Poppen's patent soldering blow-pipe lamp. In this lamp the flame is made by igniting the fumes

Fig. 36.

of the gasoline contained in the can and forced through the pipe, as shown in the illustration. Flame can be made any size. Unscrew top A, fill can one quarter with gasoline (this fluid gives best results), handle same as an ordinary blow-pipe. Blowing through pipe B causes the fluid

Fig. 37.

in C to bubble, which separates the fumes from the fluid and at the same time forces them through pipe D to outlet E, then light wick at pipe G. For a small flame insert pin F in outlet E, which is also inserted to preserve the strength of fluid while the blow-pipe is not in use.

BLUESTONE. A soft blue stone, sometimes used for reducing brass and gold before polishing. It must not be confounded with blue vitriol, sometimes called bluestone.

BLUING. The changing of the color of steel by heat.

BLUING PAN. A pan used for bluing screws and other small articles. It is sometimes very desirable to match the color of screw heads in a watch. By making the following described simple little tool you can very readily color your screws straw, purple, or blue, as the case may require, to match the other screws in the watch. Select a very large mainspring barrel, drill a hole in the side of the barrel the size of an ordinary pendulum rod for an American clock, cut a thread in this hole and also on the piece of wire and screw it firmly into the main-spring barrel, cutting off about four or five inches long, to which attach a neat piece of wood to serve as a handle. Now take out the head and fill the barrel full of fine marble dust or brass or iron filings and replace the head in the barrel, after which drill any number and size of holes in

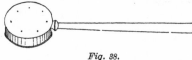

the barrel you wish, to accommodate all sizes of watch screws, and the tool is ready for use. Bluing pans, similar to the one shown in Fig. 38,

Fig. 38.

can be purchased from material dealers, and are similar to the one described. After fitting the screw to the proper place in the watch, harden and temper in the usual manner. Polish out all the scratches or other marks, and selecting a hole in the tool to fit the screw loosely, press it down level with the face of the barrel and hold the tool over a small alcohol lamp flame until the color desired appears. Heat up slowly and the effect will be much better than if it is done

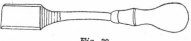

Fig. 39.

rapidly. First blue the screws without any special regard as to uniformity of color. Should they prove to be imperfect, take a piece of clean pith and whiten the surface with rouge, without letting it be too dry. Pieces when thus prepared, if cleaned and blued with care will assume a very uniform tint.

Soft screws are sometimes very difficult to blue evenly, but this difficulty may be overcome by finishing them with a slightly soapy burnisher. Bluing shovels, like that shown in Fig. 39, can be purchased from material dealers.

Pieces that are not flat will rarely assume an even color when placed in a flat pan. To overcome this dificulty, sprinkle the bottom of the pan with fine brass filings or marble dust and press the article into it. The bluing pan or shovel should be thoroughly warmed before the articles are placed in it, in order that any moisture present may be dispersed.

BOB. The metal weight at the bottom of the pendulum.

BOILING-OUT PAN. A copper or brass pan, which is also

known under the name of pickle pan. It is used for boiling steel pieces in alcohol to remove shellac, and for boiling out

Fig. 40.

jewelry after soldering. For the latter purpose use sulphuric acid one part, and water fifteen to twenty parts.

The pan, which is shown at Fig. 40, will also be found useful for tempering small steel articles by boiling them in oil.

BORT. A collective name for diamonds of inferior quality, especially such as have a radiating crystalization, so that they will not take a polish. These are crushed to form diamond powder, or diamond dust, which is used for cutting and polishing diamonds and other precious stones; also the steel work of watches, and other instruments of precision.

BOTTOMING FILE. A file constructed like those shown in

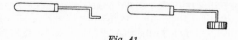

Fig. 41.

Fig. 41, so that it may be used for filing sinks, or other depressions, where an ordinary file cannot be brought into use.

BOUCHON. A hard brass tubing sometimes inserted in watch and clock plates to form pivot holes, and known in America as bushing wire. See *Bushing.*

BOW. A device now obsolete, which consisted of a strip of whalebone, to both ends of which a cord or gut was attached, and which was used to rotate a drill or mandril, before the introduction of watchmakers lathes.

The ring of a watch case, by which it is attached to the chain. See also *Pendant Bow*

Bow Tightener. See *Pendant Bow Tightener.*

BOW COMPASSES. A pair of compasses furnished with a bow

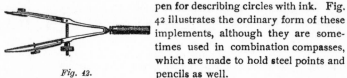

Fig. 42.

pen for describing circles with ink. Fig. 42 illustrates the ordinary form of these implements, although they are sometimes used in combination compasses, which are made to hold steel points and pencils as well.

BOW PEN. A metallic ruling pen, similar to the one attached to the bow compasses.

BOXWOOD. The fine, hard-grained timber of the box, much used by wood engravers, and in the manufacture of musical and mathematical instruments, etc. The wood is very free from gritty matter, and on that account its saw-dust is much used in cleaning jewelry, drying small polished articles, etc.

BRASS. An alloy, consisting of about 65 parts of copper to 35 parts of zinc. This proportion is varied, according to the uses to which the alloy is to be put.

Brass Polishes. 1. Rottenstone 4 oz., oxalic acid, powdered, 1 oz.; sweet oil, 1½ oz.; turpentine to make a paste; apply with soft leather. 2. Equal parts of sulphur and chalk, made into a paste with vinegar. Allow to dry on the article and clean with a chamois brush. 3. Dip the brass in a mixture of 1 oz. alum, 1 pint lye, and polish with tripoli on a chamois. This gives a brilliant luster.

Magic Polish for Brass. Add to sulphuric acid half its bulk of bichromate of potash; dilute with an equal weight of water, and apply well to the brass; rinse it well immediately with water, wipe dry, and polish with pulverized rotten stone.

Polishing Paste for Brass. Dissolve 15 parts of oxalic acid in 120 parts of boiling water, and add 500 parts of pumice powder, 7 of oil of turpentine, 60 of soft soap, and 65 of fat oil. The polishing agent is usually mixed with oil, alcohol or water, to prevent scattering, and is then applied to the polishing tool in the shape of cloth and leather buffs, polishing files, etc. Either the work or the tool should revolve with great velocity, in order to secure good results. Many articles are brought to a high degree of polish, by the use of the burnisher, after subjecting them to the action of the ordinary polishing agents.

Etching Fluids for Brass. 1. Dissolve 6 parts chlorate of potash, 100 parts water, add 160 parts water to 16 of fuming nitric acid; mix the two solutions. 2. One part sulphuric acid, 8 parts water. 3. One part nitric acid, 8 parts water. 4. Nitric or sulphuric acid 1 part saturated solution of bichromate of potash 2 parts, water 5 parts.

Gold Yellow for Brass. A gold like appearance may be given to brass by the use of a fluid prepared by boiling for about 15 minutes, 4 parts caustic soda, 4 parts milk sugar, and 100 parts water, after which 4 parts of a concentrated solution of sulphate of copper is added with constant stirring. The mixture is then cooled to 79 degrees C., and the previously well cleaned articles are for a short time laid into it. When left in it for some time they will first assume a blueish and then a rainbow color.

Lacquers for Brass. 1. Dragon's blood 40 grains; seed lac 6 ounces; amber and copal, triturated in a mortar, 2 ounces; oriental saffron, 36 grains; alcohol 40 ounces; extract of red sanders ½ dram; coarsely powdered glass 4 ounces. 2. Gamboge, seed lac, annatto, dragon's blood, each 1 ounce; 3½ pints alcohol, ¼ ounce saffron.

Gold Lacquer for Brass. Twenty-four grains extract red sanders wood in water, 60 grains dragon's blood, 2 ounces amber, 6 ounces seed lac, 2 ounces gamboge, 36 grains oriental saffron, 36 ounces pure alcohol, 4 ounces powdered glass. The amber, gamboge, glass, drag-on's blood and lac should be thoroughly pounded together. Infuse the saffron and the sanders wood extract in the alcohol for 24 hours. Pour this over the other ingredients and strain.

Lacquer for Brass. Coat it with the following varnish; 1 part white shellac and 5 alcohol; 1 shellac, 1 mastic, 7 alcohol; or 2 sandarac, 8 shellac, 1 Venetian turpentine, 50 alcohol; or, 12 parts sandarac, 6 mas-tic, 2 elemi, 1 Venetian turpentine, 64 alcohol. Clean the article well, do not touch with your hands, and warm to about 75° C.

Blackening Brass. Dissolve copper wire in nitric acid, weakened by adding, say, three or four parts of water to one of acid. The article to be blackened is made hot and dipped into the solution; it is then taken out and heated over a Bunsen burner or spirit lamp. When the article is heated, the green color of the copper first appears, and as the heat is increased the article becomes of a fine dead black. If a polished surface is desired, finish with a coat of lacquer. This process is the very best for fine work, though articles soft-soldered cannot be safely subjected to it. For such, and rough work generally, the following, which is equally applicable for zinc and other metals, may be substituted: Mix lampblack on a stone with gold size; if a dull black is desired, make it to a very stiff paste; if a more polished surface, then use more gold size. Add turpentine to thin it, and apply with a camel's hair brush

BREGUET, ABRAHAM LOUIS. Born in Switzerland in 1747 and died in Paris in 1823. An eminent watchmaker of French par-entage, and the inventor of the form of hairspring of that name. He was endowed with great ingenuity and a taste for complicated and remarkable mechanisms.

BREGUET SPRING. See *Hair Spring*.

BRIDGE. The standard secured to the plate, by means of screws, and in which a pivot works.

BROCOT SUSPENSION. The method of suspending a pen-dulum which is in use on nearly all mantel clocks of modern make, by means of which they may be regulated from the front of the dial by means of a key.

BROACH. A tapering piece of steel used for enlarging holes and made with from two to eight cutting edges. Some broaches are made without cutting edges and are called polishing broaches. They are used for burnishing pivot holes. Care should be taken to see that the handles of your broaches are properly fitted so that they revolve truly. To test this, rest the points against the fingers of one hand and causing the handle to rotate by two fingers of the other hand and the broach itself should appear to remain true. Sealing wax answers the purpose as a handle for broaches very nicely, and the broach can be centered in it without much trouble. In the latter case hold the broach between two fingers with the handle downward, and rotate it while close to the flame of an alcohol lamp, so that the sealing wax forms a regular oblong handle. It is well to gently draw a piece of iron charged with rouge along the edges of pivot broaches in order to remove the thread of metal from them. Minute particles of this thread might otherwise remain in the holes, and occasion wear of the pivots.

To Broach a Hole Vertically. It is quite a serious thing for young watchmakers to broach a hole vertically, a hole in a plate, or that in a barrel, is seldom maintained at right angles to the surface, when they have occasion to employ a broach. They may be certain of success, however, by adopting the following method: Take a cork of a diameter rather less than that of the barrel or other object operated upon, and make a hole in the length of the cork through which the broach can be passed. When the cork has been turned quite true on its end and edge, the broach is passed through, and used to enlarge the hole; by pressing against the back of the cork, it is kept against the barrel, whereby the broach is maintained in a vertical position.

To Solder Broken Broaches. Steel broaches and other tools are soldered by cleaning well the parts broken, then dipping them into a solution of sulphate of copper, and soldering them with ordinary soft solder. The joint is a good one and will stand ordinary hard wear.

BRONZING. See *Electro-Plating, Bronzing and Staining.*

BUFF. A device for polishing or reducing metals. Emery buffs are round or square sticks on which emery paper or cloth is glued. They are used to reduce the surfaces of metal. Fig. 43 illustrates a ring buff used for polishing the inside of rings, preferably used on a polishing lathe.

Fig. 43.

BULLSEYE. A thick watch resembling a bull's eye in shape. A term usually applied to old fashioned English verge watches.

BURNISHER. A polished steel or agate tool used for glossing the the surface of metals. Fig. 44 is a jewel burnisher. The article to be burnished must be first freed from all scratches, for scratches would only be brought out more prominently by the use of the burnisher. The burnisher must be kept highly polished or you cannot expect to do good work with it. Saunier gives the following method of re-facing a burnisher: Prepare a dry smooth piece of wood, rather thick, and of a width equal to the length of the burnisher. On this board carefully glue a piece of emery paper of a fineness corresponding to the degree of cut

Fig. 44.

required, stretching it as even as possible, and turning the edges down towards the under side. Then lay the board on a firm smooth surface, resting a weight upon it, and allow it to dry. In using this lap, it is fixed or allowed to rest against the side of the bench; holding the burnisher with two hands at its extremities, the workman places himself at one end of the board, and draws the burnisher along it towards him, maintaining the surface quite flat and applying considerable pressure. On reaching the nearer end, raise it, and after again placing it on the furthest end, draw towards the body, and so on. By proceeding in this manner all risk of rounding the angle will be avoided.]

BUSH. A perforated piece of metal let into a plate to receive the wear of pivots. See *Bouchon.*

. **Bushing Pivot Holes.** The bush may be either a turned or tapped one. A bush is selected as small as the pivot will admit. Open the hole in the plate or cock and finish with a rat-tail file. Slightly taper the end of the bush with a fine file until it will fit the hole. With a knife score the bush just above the edge of the plate and press it firmly into the hole. Break off the bush at the point scored and drive it firmly into place by means of the bushing punch shown at Fig. 45, and you will find your bush is riveted firmly into the plate. Observe the endshake your pinion requires and make due allowance when finishing off your bushing. In bushing a plate, particularly where the bushing must be large, some watchmakers prefer to use a solid wire and drill the hole after fitting. If this method is followed be careful to see that you accurately center the work before drilling, and drill first with a small drill, subsequently passing through a larger one, or open up the hole by means of a small broach. It is always well to use bushing wire with a hole smaller than is ultimately required, and enlarging afterwards while the work is centered in the lathe. A tapped bushing is very firm, but

unless the threads are well made is apt to be out of center   The closing
hole punch shown in Fig. 45 often obviates the use of a bushing, if skill-
fully used.

To Bush a Wheel. A watch will frequently stop because a wheel
is improperly centered in itself, whereby one side will gear too deep, the
other too shallow, into the pinion driven by it.   Such a wheel likely is
of the proper size and has good teeth, but the difficulty is its proper centering, when fitted to its pinion.   The following will be found to be an
easy way of correction.   Take a piece of lead of about the thickness of a
silver half dollar, and clip and file it round so that it will fit into one of
the larger steps in a step chuck of an American lathe.   Screw it fast into
the lathe, and while revolving, center and drill a hole of about the size
of a winding arbor.   Then, with a graver, turn out a recess, the size and
a trifle more than the thickness of the wheel, so that it will fit in exact,
with its teeth touching the outside of the cut.   Drive the wheel from its
pinion, and broach out the center, so as to take a bush of sufficient
length, which should be firmly riveted in and filed smooth on the lower
side.   Turn a small groove around the outside of the cut in the lead,
crowd in the wheel, with a burnisher set as a gavel.   This fixes the
wheel perfectly true on the outside.   Now center and drill, leaving a
little to be turned with a fine polished graver, to fit the same pinion.
Rivet on, and your wheel is all right.

BUSHING OR CLOSING HOLE PUNCH.   This tool is very
simple in construction and will be found very useful in repairing both
watches and clocks.   Fig. 45, Goeggel's Bushing and Closing Hole

· *Fig. 45.*

Punch, consists of two counter-sunk steel punches, with a post in the
lower punch.   In using, fasten the lower punch in vise and place the
work over it.   They are made in various sizes for watches and clocks
and are quite inexpensive

BUSHING WIRE.   Hard brass tubing for bushing the pivot holes
of watches and clocks.   This wire is kept by most material houses in the
various sizes applicable to watch and clock work, and is put up in assorted sizes.   See *Bouchon* and *Bush.*

BUTTING.   The touching of the points of the teeth of two wheels
acting with one another.   It is caused by the wheels being planted incor-
rectly, or by pinions or wheels of improper size.   See *Depthing Tool*
and *Wheels and Pinions.*

CALIPERS. Compasses having two curved legs or fingers pivoted together and used either to measure the inside or outside diameter of bodies. Calipers are divided into two classes, known as inside and outside calipers. They are used by watchmakers for determining the diameter of staffs and pinions, for testing the truth of wheels, etc. Calipers are sometimes used in poising balances, the balance staff being centered between the points of the calipers. For this purpose a hole is drilled in the calipers and jewels are inserted. Thompson's jeweled calipers, shown in Fig. 46, have garnet jewels inserted in the points of the arms at one end, and hardened steel

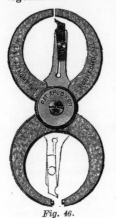

Fig. 46.

bearings in the other. The Euclid Double Calipers are very useful tools, as they give on the lower limbs an inside measure-

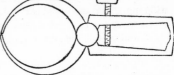

Fig. 47.

ment corresponding to the outside measurement of the upper limbs. By adding a stop screw to the common double calipers as shown in Fig. 47, a very handy tool can be made, as the tool can be opened and removed from the work and closed again exactly the same amount. See *Gauge.*

CALLET, F. A thorough mechanic and skilled calculator. He was born at Versailles, France, in 1744, and died in 1798.

CARBORUNDUM. A substitute for diamond powder, used in polishing. It is made in two grades. No. 1, which is an olive tinted powder, is used by lapidaries for polishing the facets of gems, as it is so much finer than diamond powder that a superior finish can be secured on the gem by its use. It is also much cheaper than diamond powder. No. 2 is a black powder, which resembles the other in hardness, but is impure and still cheaper. It has extensive use among metal workers as an abrasive. Both varieties are used by watchmakers in the various polishing operations, as substitutes for diamond powder, bort, diamantine, etc.

CAM. A moveable piece of irregular contour, so shaped as to give a variable motion to another piece pressing against it by sliding or rolling contact.

CANNON PINION. The pinion to which the minute hand is attached; so called on account of the pipe attachment resembling a cannon.

To Tighten a Cannon Pinion. The cannon pinion is sometimes too loose upon the center arbor. Grasp the arbor lightly with a pair of cutting nippers, and by a single turn of the nippers around the arbor, cut or raise a small thread thereon.

CAP. The part of the case that covers the movement. A thin metal cover used in some English, Swiss and German watches to cover the movement and attached by studs and a sliding bar or spring.

CAPILLARY ATTRACTION AND REPULSION. The cause which determines the ascent or descent of certain fluids when in contact with certain solid substances. See *Oil Sinks.*

CAPPED JEWEL. A jewel having an end stone as shown in Fig. 48. In all movements, except the cheapest grades, capped jewels are used for the balance pivots.

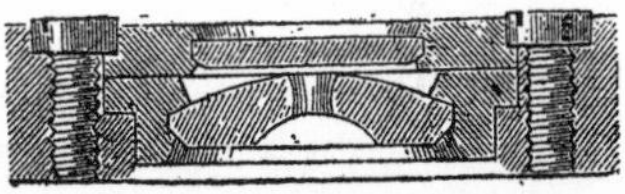

Fig. 48.

CARDINAL POINTS. The four intersections of the horizon with the meridian and the prime vertical circle, or North and South, East and West.

CARON, PETER AUGUSTUS. A celebrated French watchmaker, born January 25th, 1732, in the Rue St. Denis, Paris. When nineteen years of age he invented an escapement known in France as the double virgule, which may be said to be a combination of the cylinder and duplex. He disputed in 1753, with Lepaute, the honor of being the inventor, and was awarded the merit of the discovery by the Academy of Sciences, on February 24, 1754. At the age of twenty-five he obtained a situation at court, under Louis XV., and received permission, on giving up the watch business, to style himself Monsieur de Beaumar, and under this name he wrote and published two well known works, the " Barber of Seville" and " The Marriage of Figaro."

CARRIER. A piece fastened to work in a lathe and connecting it with the face plate. A dog.

CASE-HARDENING. A process of carbonizing the surface of wrought iron, thus converting it into steel. See *Steel.*

CASE SPRINGS. The springs in a watch case that cause it to fly open and that keep it in position when closed.

Adjustable Case Springs. The Harstrom Adjustable Case Spring shown in Fig. 49 is easily fitted and is said to be a very excellent spring. The holder should be fitted securely in a vice and with a three cornered

Fig. 49.

file cut down near the rear end on the back of the spring enough to rest a punch against; then with a tap of a hammer you can move it backwards. To move it forward, rest your punch against the end of the spring. Thus you can easily make it correspond with the screw hole in the case. Then, near to where it protrudes from the holder, bend the spring upward enough to make the front end level with the upper edge of holder, or move, if greater strength is required.

CASE SPRING VISE. The Boss case spring tool, shown in Fig. 50, is a very handy little tool. By turning the thumb screw you can bind the spring in the desired position and hold it there

Fig. 50.

Fig. 51.

until the screw is inserted in its proper place. It will be found much handier than the ordinary plyer-shaped tools designed for the same purpose. Another form of case spring vise is Hall's, which is shown in Fig. 51.

CASE STAKE. A stake made with a large head, generally of steel, and used for taking out dents from battered watch cases. The

Fig. 52.

stake shown in Fig. 52 is of the reversible pattern, and while using is held in the vise.

CEMENTS. Cement for use in the lathe can be purchased from material dealers generally, at so small a cost that it will scarcely pay the watchmaker to bother in preparing it, but circumstances often arise where a cement is desirable for other purposes, such as attaching metal letters to show windows, etc., and the following recipes will be found very reliable:

Acid-Proof Cement. A cement that resists acid is made by melting one part India rubber with two parts linseed oil; add sufficient white bolus for consistency. Neither muriatic nor nitric acid attack it; it softens a little in heat, and its surface does not dry easily; which is produced by adding one-fifth part litharge.

Alabaster Cement. Melt alum and dip the fractured faces into it; then put them together as quickly as possible. Remove the exuding mass with a knife.

Alabaster Cement. 1. Finely powdered plaster of Paris made into a paste with water. 2. Melt rosin, or equal parts of yellow rosin and beeswax, then stir in half as much finely powdered plaster of Paris. The first is used to join and to fit together pieces of Alabaster or marble, or to mend broken plaster figures. The second is to join alabaster, marble, and other similar substances that will bear heating.

Amber Cement. For cementing amber and meerschaum, make a thick cream of finely powdered quicklime and white of egg, apply with a camel's hair brush, dry slowly and scrape off surplus after thoroughly dry.

Acid Proof Cement. Form a paste of powdered glass and a concentrated solution of silicate of soda.

Cement for Thin Metal Sheets. Cut isinglass into small pieces and dissolve in a little water at a moderate heat; add a small quantity of nitric acid, the quantity being determined by experiment; with too much acid the cement dries too slowly, while with too little it does not adhere well.

Cement for Glass and Brass. Melt together 1 part of wax and 5 parts of resin, and after melting stir in 1 part of burned ochre and ¼ part plaster of Paris. This is a good cement for attaching letters to windows. Apply warm to heated surfaces where possible.

Cement for Glass and Metals. The following cement is used extensively for fastening brass and enamel letters to show windows: Mix together boiled linseed oil, 5 parts; copal varnish, 15 parts; glue, 5 parts; and oil of turpentine, 5 parts; add to this solution 10 parts of slaked lime and thoroughly incorporated.

Cement for Knife and Fork Handles. Melt 2 parts of pitch and stir in 1 part of sand or brick dust; fill the cavity in the handle with the mixture, and push in the previously heated tang.

Cement for Paper and Metals. Dissolve dextrine in water, adding 20 parts of glycerine and 10 parts of glucose. Coat the paper with this mixture, and, after rubbing the metal with a piece of onion, attach the paper.

Engravers' Cement. Resin, 1 part; brick dust, 1 part; mix with heat.

Fireproof Cement. A very tenacious and fireproof cement for metals is said to be made by mixing pulverized asbestos with waterglass, to be had in any drug store; it is said to be steam tight, and resist any temperature.

Glass and Metal Cement. Brass letters, and other articles of a like nature, may be securely fastened on glass windows with the following: Litharge, 2 parts; white lead, 1 part; boiled linseed oil, 3 parts; gum copal, 1 part. Mix just before using; this forms a quickly drying and secure cement.

Gold and Silver Colored Cement. For filling hollow gold and silver articles. Consists of 60 parts shellac, 10 parts Venetian turpentine, and 3 parts gold bronze or silver bronze, as the case may be. The shellac is melted first, the turpentine is then added, and finally, with constant stirring the gold or silver bronze.

Jewelers' Cement. Put in a bottle 2 ounces of isinglass and 1 ounce of the best gum Arabic, cover them with proof spirits, cork loosely and place the bottle in a vessel of water, and boil it until a thorough solution is effected; then strain for use.

Metal Cement. Take plaster of raris, and mix it to proper thickness by using water containing about one-fourth of gum Arabic. This cement is excellent for metal exposed to contact with alcohol, and for cementing metal to glass.

Strong Cement. Mix some finely powdered rice with cold water, so as to form a soft paste. Add boiling water, and finally boil the mixture in a pan for one or two minutes. A strong cement is thus obtained, of a white color, which can be used for many purposes.

Transparent Cement. A good transparent cement for fastening watch glasses, etc., in bezels or settings, is made by dissolving 7 parts of pure gum Arabic and 3 parts crystalized sugar in distilled 'water; the bottle containing the mixture should be placed in a utensil of hot water until the mixture assumes the consistency of syrup, and then left well corked for use.

Watchmakers' Cement or Wax. Eight ounces of gum shellac, heated and thoroughly incorporated with one-half ounce of ultramarine, makes the strongest and best wax for use on cement brasses and chucks.

CEMENT BRASSES. Attachments to a lathe to which work is fixed by means of cement. These brasses are made in various shapes and sizes by tool manufacturers, or the ingenious watchmaker can make them for himself during his leisure hours, Figs. 53 and 54. The watchmaker should have a supply of these brasses, varying in sizes from one inch to the smallest size necessary. Should you have a watch that has a broken cock or foot jewel, and among your supply you are unable to find one that fits both the pivot and the recess in the cock or potence, you will find these brasses very useful. If you find a jewel

Fig. 53.

that fits the pivot nicely, and the brass setting is too large, select a cement brass that is just a trifle smaller than the recess in the potance, cement the jewel to the end of the brass, with the flat side of the jewel to the brass, so that if the brass setting of the jewel is too thick it can be turned to exact thickness of the old setting at the same time that the diameter is turned. Bring to an exact center

Fig. 54.

by the hole in the jewel, by means of a pegwood, and as soon as the cement is hard, turn down with a sharp graver. With a full set of these brasses a watchmaker can utilize odds and ends, without waiting to send for new jewels. The above is only one of many uses to which these brasses may be brought.

CENTERS. Pins used in conjunction with a lathe for holding work while revolving. They are usually made of steel. They are of two forms, known as male and female centers.

Female Centers. These very useful adjuncts to a lathe are easily made by any watchmaker. He should have at least six pairs, the largest being one-fourth of an inch in diameter, which will accommodate as large a piece as you will wish to handle on your watch lathe, viz: winding arbors for clocks. These female centers are made from steel tapers, the same as male centers are made, but instead of turning the end to a sharp point they are countersunk, Fig. 55. First place the taper in a chuck and turn off the outside and end true; drill a small hole in the center of the taper, while the lathe is running, and deep enough so the countersink will not reach the bottom of the hole, or one-eighth of an inch deeper than the counter-sink. Harden the end only, and after tempering polish off the bluing. After you have made all the sizes you require, test all of them in your lathe to make sure they did not get out of true in tempering.

These female centers are very useful for holding or suspending any article in the lathe that is too large to be held in the split chucks. Pivots of clocks can be turned and polished very quickly and accurately in these centers.

Almost any kind of large work can be done on a medium sized watchmaker's lathe by fitting a face plate to the lathe, say one and three-

Fig. 55.

fourths inches in diameter, with four slots, and fitted to a chuck with a taper hole to receive both male and female centers. The taper hole being standard, the centers are interchangeable, and with two styles of dogs, almost any kind of large clock work can readily be handled.

These centers prove very useful for many odd jobs. As an example: It is a very common occurrence to hear an American clock beat irregularly, caused by the 'scape being out of round. Select a pair of female centers that will admit the ends of the pivots of the 'scape wheel snugly; place one center in the taper chuck and the other in the tail stock spindle, and suspend the 'scape pinion in these centers; fasten on a dog, run the lathe at a high speed and hold a fine, sharp file so it will touch the teeth of the 'scape wheel slightly, and in a moment the wheel will be perfectly round, after which sharpen up the teeth that are too thick.

Male Centers. Conically pointed pins; the opposite of female centers.

CENTERING ATTACHMENT. The Potter patent self-centering lathe attachment, shown in Fig. 56, will be found useful in rapidly bringing work to an accurate center, when pivoting, staffing, etc.

The attachment, which may be fitted to any make of American lathe, consists primarily of the side bed pieces R and D, the upright plate A, and the reversible anti-friction sliding jaws $o\,o\,o$. The upright plate A is attached to the slide D in such a way that it may be readily raised or lowered or adjusted in any other direction at pleasure; and may be set with either side facing the lathe head. Of the reversible sliding jaws $o\,o\,o$, which are made of Phosphor Bronze Anti-Friction Metal, not requiring the use of oil, four sets of three in a set, are furnished with each attachment. These are of different form, as shown at $X\ V\ O\ U$, to adapt them to the various kinds of watch work, and are operated in radial grooves in the upright plate A, by means of the rotating lever L, which moves the three jaws in and out, to and from the center, or opens and closes them in perfect unison. One set of jaws may be withdrawn and another set substituted therefor in a few moments. With each change of the jaws, however, the plate A requires readjustment; but this, too, may be done in a few moments, as follows: Having previously provided yourself with a bit of straight wire or small steel rod, turned to run perfectly true in your lathe, and having fastened this in the chuck in your lathe, loosen the nuts *C C* so as to give freedom of movement to the plate *A*; then bring the attachment to proper position on the lathe

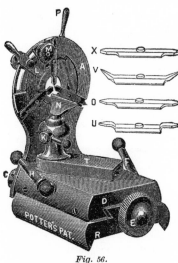

Fig. 56.

bed and fasten it there; after which move the sliding jaws inward until they bind lightly on the bit of straight wire held in your chuck, and in this position again tighten the nuts *C C*. Once adjusted to accurate center in this way no further adjustment, whatever the size of work to be operated upon, is required, until another change of jaws.

In use, the end of the work to be operated upon is placed in an accurate split chuck in the lathe and the chuck tightened on it just sufficiently to hold it in place and to rotate it, the other end being supported in the centered bearing formed by the jaws *o o o*. In this position the jaws *o o o*, or such others as for the time may be in use, may be opened and closed as often as desired, and each time will instantly bring the work again to accurate center. See *Rest*.

CENTERING INDICATOR. In centering quickly on the universal head, this tool is indispensible. It will also be found valuable for other work. It is not kept by dealers, and will have to be made by the watchmaker. The body of the indicator is made of sheet brass, and should be about five inches long by two inches in width at the larger end. The shank *C*, is made to fit in rest holder, and is either riveted or soldered to the body; *R* is steel or copper wire sharpened to a fine point, and balances on a pivot at 1; *B* is a clock hand pivoted to the body

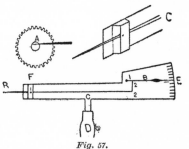

Fig. 57.

at 1; 2 and 2 are pivot joints only, and do not go through the body; fig. *C* will perhaps give a better idea of the end *R*. To center with this tool, unscrew your rest and remove it, then place the shaft *C*, fig. 57, in rest holder and adjust it till the needle point *R* touches the top of hole as

shown in fig. 2.   The index hand will then note the variations as the
head revolves.   If too low, the hand will point above center and if high,
vice versa.

CENTERING TOOL.   A small, steel point used for accurately

Fig. 58.

locating centers.   Figure 59 illustrates the O. K. centering tool, which is
made to fit any tailstock spindle or taper chuck.

CENTER PUNCH.   A punch having a sharp point, for marking

Fig. 59.

the center of work swung in a lathe, so that it may readily be removed
and replaced without the trouble of finding the center each time.

CENTER OF GRAVITY.   That point of a body about which all
its parts are balanced, or which, being supported, the whole body will
remain at rest, though acted upon by gravity. *Webster.*

CENTER OF GYRATION.   That point in a body rotating around
an axis, at which, if a given force were applied, it would produce the same
angular velocity in a given time as it would if the whole mass of the body
were collected at that point.   *Webster.*   Britten says that a circle drawn
seven-tenths of its radius on a circular rotating plate of uniform thickness
would represent its center of gyration.   The moment of inertia, or the
controlling power of balances varies as their mass, and as the square of
the distance of their center of gyration from their center of motion.
Although not strictly accurate, it is practically quite near enough in the
comparison of balances to take their weight, and the square of their
diameter.

CENTER OF MOTION.   That point which remains at rest while
all the other parts of a body revolve around it.

CENTER OF OSCILLATION.   That point at which, if the whole
matter of a suspended body were collected, the time of oscillation would
be the same.   In a long cone suspended from its apex, the center of oscillation is at four-fifths of its length from the apex, and in a bar suspended
from one end that point is at two-thirds of its length.   A pendulum

being irregular in form it is difficult to calculate its center of oscillation, but it always is situated below its center of gravity. The following explanation may aid the student in locating the center of oscillation:

All know that a simple theoretical pendulum is one where the whole weight is centered in one point, suspended from, and oscillating about, a fixed point, or center of suspension. A sphere of platinum, suspended by a fibre of silk, would probably be the nearest approximation to a perfectly simple pendulum. A compound pendulum is one where the weight is not centered in or about one point, but is extended for some distance up and down the rod. Suppose there are fixed upon the fibre, at equal distances, three platinum balls. From the well-known fact that a short pendulum vibrates quicker than a long one, the upper or short pendulum will *endeavor* to make its vibrations in the short time due to its length as a pendulum. The middle ball will *endeavor* to make its oscillations in the time its length of support demands, and the lower and longest will attempt the slow and regular vibrations of the long pendulum. Suppose that these three balls, representing three pendulums of three different lengths, be drawn aside from the perpendicular 5° and suddenly released, the consequence will be that the upper one will have made its full excursion by the time the middle one has descended to the perpendicular, and before the lower one has arrived there; the momentum of the three balls bending the fibre of silk into such a curve as will accommodate the *tendencies* of the three balls.

If the silk fibre be replaced by an inflexible rod, and the now rigid compound pendulum be drawn aside as before, the upper ball will *endeavor* to hasten forward the middle one to its own speed, and the middle and upper one will both combine to hasten the lower one. So also, the middle one will retard somewhat the rapidity of the upper one, and the slow-moving lower one will do its best to restrain the haste of both those above it, and the consequence of all these tendencies will be that the lower one will be somewhat accelerated, and the upper one proportionally retarded; the whole assuming a vibration which is the mean (middle ball) of the two extremes, provided the three masses are equal, thus compelling the whole to oscillate as a pendulum whose length is that of the middle ball. But if the lower ball be the largest, its control over those parts above it will be in proportion to its mass and the time of its vibrations will nearly coincide with those made by its center of gravity.

Suppose, again, the largest amount of matter to be in the upper ball, then will its influence be more potent toward forcing the lower and longer pendulums to accommodate their rate to that of the upper one, and their vibrations will be thereby increased to a degree which will approximate the normal vibrations of that short pendulum. Thus you see the difficulty of exactly fixing upon the exact length of any compound pendulum by simple computation. Every particle of matter from the top of the rod to the lower extremity, which differs in its distance from the point of suspension, has its own time for making an oscillation about that point; and the greater the number of particles that have an equal distance from that point, the greater influence they possess in determining the time of vibration; in this case, as in republics, the mass rules. To obviate these counteracting influences that are constantly at work in the oscillations of the compound pendulum, it becomes necessary to concentrate, as far as possible, all the matter of the pendulum at such a distance from the point of suspension as will produce the number of vibrations desired, and this center of oscillation will always fall in a line produced through the center of gravity and the point of suspension, and will always be below the center of gravity.

The center of oscillation and suspension are convertible points; that is, a pendulum inverted and suspended from the center of oscillation will vibrate in the same time. Huygens, the Dutch scientist, discovered this remarkable fact, and it affords a ready means of determining experimentally the length of a compound pendulum, which may be measured by means of a platinum or lead ball, suspended by a fibre of silk from the same point, and in front of the pendulum to be measured, and of such a length that the vibrations will perfectly coincide in time. The distance from the point of suspension to the center of the ball (which is also the center of oscillation) is nearly the length of that compound pendulum.

It should be remembered that the *center of oscillation* is the point to be affected in all compensations for temperature. The difficulty in producing a perfect compensation pendulum is to harmonize and bring into coincidence the antagonistic tendencies of the center of gravity, center of oscillation and moment of inertia, all of which are properties and peculiarities of compound pendulums, and must be taken into consideration by those who are experimenting upon them with the expectation of producing any arrangement in advance of those in use at present.

CENTER SECONDS. See *Sweep Seconds*.

CENTER WHEEL. The wheel whose staff carries the minute hand.

CENTER STAFF. The arbor, attached to the center wheel, which carries the minute hand.

CENTRIFUGAL FORCE. The tendency that revolving bodies have to fly from the center. Britten says that when balances are made too thin in the rim, they alter in diameter from this cause, in the long and short vibrations.

CHAIN HOOK. A small hook which is attached to each end of a fusee chain, to fasten the chain to the barrel and fusee.

CHALK. To prepare chalk for use for cleaning gilding, etc., pulverize it thoroughly and then mix it with clean water, in proportion of two pounds to the gallon. Stir well and then let it stand about two minutes. In this time the gritty matter will have settled to the bottom. Slowly pour the water into another vessel, so as not to stir up the sediment. Let stand until entirely settled, and then pour off as before. The settlings will be prepared chalk, ready for use as soon as dried. Spanish whiting, treated in the same way, makes a very good cleaning or polishing powder. Some watchmakers add a little crocus; it gives the powder a nice color at least.

CHAMFER. To groove. To cut a channel in. To cut or grind in a sloping manner anything originally right-angled. To bevel.

CHAMFERING TOOL. A tool for cutting a bevel or chamfer. A tool for cutting a furrow or channel is also known as a chamfering tool.

CHAMOIS. A soft leather used by watchmakers and jewelers, and so called because first prepared from the skin of a species of antelope known as chamois.

Chamois, to Clean. Many workshops contain a dirty chamois leather, which is thrown aside and wasted for want of knowing how to cleanse it. Make a solution of weak soda and warm water, rub plenty of soft soap into the leather, and allow it to remain in soak for two hours, then rub it until quite clean. Afterward rub it well in a weak solution composed of warm water, soda and yellow soap. It must not be rinsed in water only, for then it will be so hard, when dry, as to be unfit for use. It is the small quantity of soap left in the leather that allows it to separate and become soft. After rinsing, wring it well in a rough towel, and dry quickly, then pull it about, and brush it well, and it will become softer and better than most new leathers. In using a rough leather to touch up highly polished surfaces, it is frequently observed to scratch the work; this is caused by particles of dust, and even hard rouge, that are left in the leather, and if removed by a clean brush containing rouge, it will then give the brightest and best finish, which all good workmen like to see on their work.

CHARIOT. A brass bar screwed to the pillar plate of a cylinder watch to carry the lower pivot of the cylinder, and to afford a seat for the balance cock. Slight alterations in the intersection of the cylinder and the escape wheel are made by shifting the chariot.

CHIMES. A set of bells musically tuned to one another and sometimes attached to tower clocks, especially in Europe, such clocks being known as quarter clocks, or chiming clocks.

CHIMING BARREL. The cylinder in a chiming clock which raises the hammer in the chiming train, by means of projections upon its surface.

CHOPS. Two metal plates which bind the ends of the pendulum suspension spring.

CHRONOGRAPH. A recording time piece. In modern usage the term is applied to watches having a center seconds hand (driven from the fourth wheel), which generally beats fifths of a second. The hand is started, stopped or caused to fly back by manipulating a push on the side of the case.

CHRONOMETER. A portable time piece of superior construction, with heavy compensation balance, and usually beating half seconds; intended for keeping very accurate time for astronomers, watchmakers, etc. See Fig. 60.

Marine Chronometer. A chronometer hung in gimbals, for use at sea in determining longitude.

Pocket Chronometer. A pocket watch with chronometer escapement.

Fig. 60.

CHRONOMETER ESCAPEMENT. An escapement in which the escape wheel is locked on a stone carried in a detent, and impulse is given by the teeth of the escape wheel to a pallet on the balance staff once in every alternate vibration. The French claim the honor of the invention of the detached detent, or chronometer escapement, for Pierre Le Roy, while the English claim it for John Arnold. The first chronometer escapements were made with the small spring, or gold spring, attached to the roller on the balance staff. F. Berthoud made the escapement after this fashion, but Arnold transferred it to the detent. The detent, as made by Arnold, worked on a pivoted arbor, having a spiral spring around it to bring it back into position after it was released by the pallet. Earnshaw improved upon Arnold's construction by doing away with the arbor and making the detent and spring in one piece, as shown in Fig. 61. He also improved upon the escape wheel made by

Arnold, whose wheel was made so that the unlocking took place inside the wheel, the acting curves of the teeth being raised from the plane of the wheel. Earnshaw made the teeth flat, and also changed the direction of the pressure during locking.

Saunier says of the chronometer escapement, that its mode of action is simple, but it does not admit of any error in the application of its principles, nor any inferior workmanship. It absolutely requires an isochronal balance spring and a compensation balance, and should never be employed in ordinary watches. Nevertheless, the chronometer escapement is adopted wherever the most reliable time is required, and among the best manufacturers in the world the good chronometer is considered as their finest production. Britten says of the

ACTION OF THE ESCAPEMENT.

A tooth of the escape wheel is at rest on the locking pallet. The office of the discharging pallet is to bend the detent so as to allow this tooth to escape. The discharging pallet does not press directly on the detent, but on the free end of the gold spring, which presses on the tip of the detent.

The balance, fixed to the same staff as the rollers, travels in the direction of the arrow around the rollers, with sufficient energy to unlock the tooth of the wheel which is held by the locking pallet. Directly the detent is released by the discharging pallet, it springs back to its original position, ready to receive the next tooth of the wheel. There is a set screw to regulate the amount of the locking on which the pipe of the detent butts. This prevents the locking pallet being drawn further into the wheel. It is omitted in the drawing for clearness. It will be observed that the impulse roller is planted so as to intersect the path of the escape wheel teeth as much as possible, and by the time the unlocking is completed the impulse pallet will have passed far enough in front of the escape wheel tooth to afford it a safe hold. The escape wheel, impelled by the mainspring in the direction of the arrow, overtakes the impulse pallet and drives it on until the contact between them ceases by the divergence of their paths. The wheel is at once brought to rest by the locking pallet, and the balance continues its excursion, winding up the balance spring as it goes, until its energy is exhausted. The balance is immediately started in its return vibration by the effort of the balance spring to return to its state of rest. You will notice that the nose of the detent does not reach to the end of the gold spring, so that the discharging pallet in this return vibration, merely bends the gold spring without affecting the locking pallet at all. When the discharging pallet reaches the gold spring, the balance spring is at rest; but the balance does not stop, it continues to uncoil the balance spring until its momentum is exhausted, and then the effort of the balance spring to revert to its

Fig. 61.

CHRONOMETER ESCAPEMENT.

a. Escape Wheel.
b. Impulse Roller.
c. Impulse Pallet.
    (The Discharging Roller is underneath
    the Impulse Roller, and is indicated
    by means of dotted lines.)
d. Locking Pallet.
e. Foot of Detent.
f. Spring of Detent.
g. Blade of Detent.
h. Horn of Detent.
i. Gold Spring.

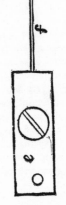

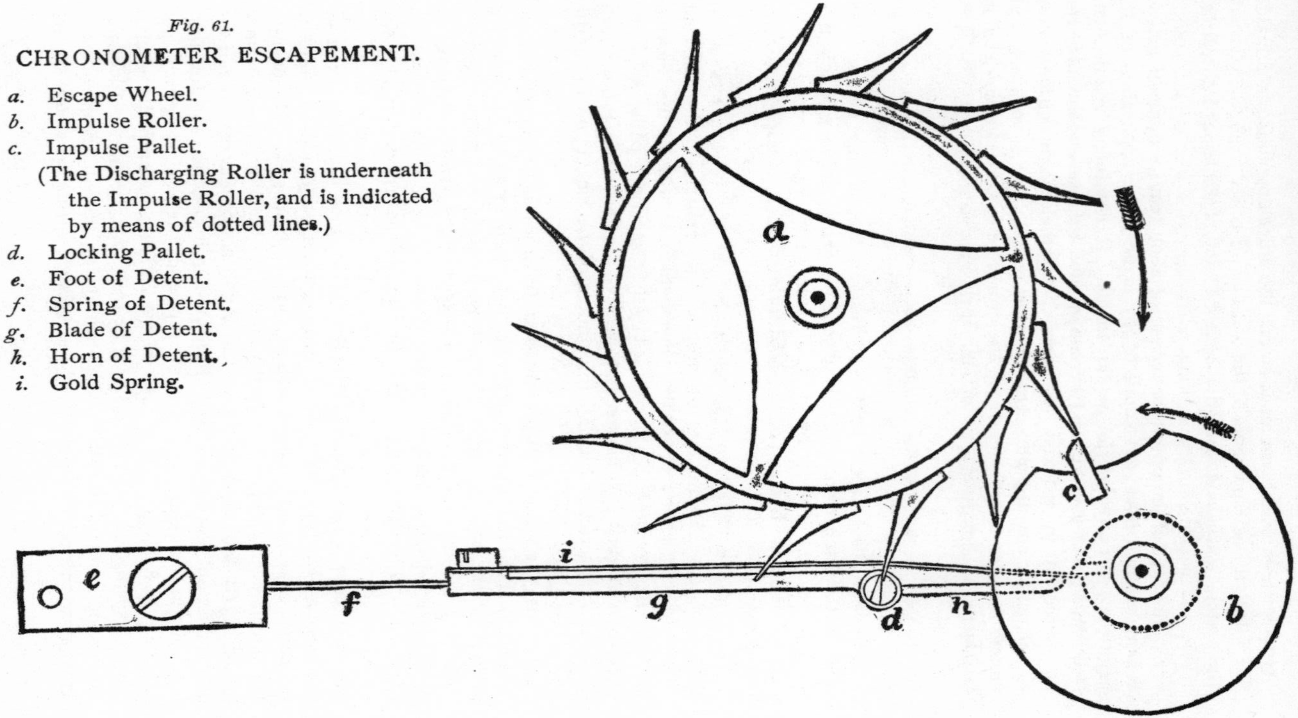

normal state induces another vibration; the wheel is again unlocked and gives the impulse pallet another blow.

Although the balance only gets impulse in one direction, the escape wheel makes a rotation in just the same time as with a lever escapement, because in the chronometer the whole space between two teeth passes every time the wheel is unlocked.

By receiving impulse and having to unlock at every other vibration only, the balance is more highly detached in the chronometer than in most escapements, which is a distinct advantage. No oil is required to the pallets and another disturbing influence is thus got rid of. If properly proportioned and well made, its performance will be quite satisfactory as long as it is not subjected to sudden external motion or jerks. For marine chronometers it thus leaves but little to be desired, and even for pocket watches it does well with a careful wearer; but with rough usage

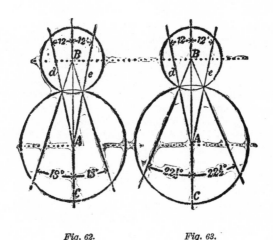

Fig. 62.   Fig. 63.

it is liable to set, and many watchmakers hesitate to recommend it on this account. It is much more costly than the lever, and would only be applied to very high-priced watches, and in these the buyer naturally resents any failure of action. Its use in pocket pieces is therefore nearly confined to such as are used for scientific purposes, or by people who understand the nature of an escapement, and are prepared to exercise care in wearing the watch. There is another reason why watchmakers, as a rule, do not take kindly to the chronometer escapement for pocket work. After the escapement is taken apart, the watch does not so surely yield as good a performance as before. In fact, it is more delicate than the lever.

CONSTRUCTION AND PROPORTION OF THE ESCAPEMENT.

For the ordinary 3-inch, two-day, marine chronometer movements, three sizes of escape wheels are used—viz.: .54, .56, and .58 of an inch in diameter; for eight-day marine chronometer, the sizes are .48, .50 or .52 of an inch. The escape wheel has fifteen teeth, and the diameter of the impulse roller is half that of the escape wheel. The roller is planted as close between two teeth of the escape wheel as possible, so that theoretically the roller intersects the path of the teeth for 24° of the circumference of the wheel. This gives theoretically a balance arc of 45°.* Practically it is less; there must be clearance between the roller and wheel teeth; an allowance must also be made for the side shake of the pivots. In Fig. 61, the impulse pallet is just opposite a tooth of the escape wheel when the discharging pallet is resting on the end of the gold spring. The balance moves through about 5° to accomplish the unlocking, and by the time that is done the impulse pallet will be 5° in advance of the tooth and the tooth will drop through this space and more before it reaches the pallet, because after the wheel is unlocked it takes some time to get into motion at all, and at first its motion is slower than the motion of the pallet, which had not ceased to travel. The drop must be enough to allow the pallet to safely intersect the path of the tooth, and is arranged generally as shown, so that the pallet is 5° in advance of the tooth when the unlocking is completed. But many authorities insist on even more drop, so as to give the impulse more nearly on the line of centres. It is argued that the drop is not all mischievous loss of power, as it is in the lever, escapement, for with a greater amount of drop the wheel attains a greater velocity when it does strike the pallet. However, most makers adhere to the 5°, although it may in some instances be advisable to vary it. If there is fear of over-banking, the arc of vibration may be reduced by giving more drop; and if the vibration is sluggish and the drop can be safely reduced the vibration will be increased thereby.

The body of the escape wheel is thinned down to about one-half for lightness. The fronts of the wheel teeth diverge about 20° from a radial line so that the tips, being more forward, draw the locking stone safely

---

*The balance arc is the amount that the edge of the impulse roller intersects the path of the wheel teeth, and is measured from the center of the balance staff. Figures 62 and 63 show a method of determining the relative size of the escape wheel and impulse roller for a given balance arc, which is taken from a report in the *Horological Journal*, of a most excellent lecture on the chronometer escapement by Mr. Nelson. Figure 62 (36° of balance arc) is an example of a usual proportion for pocket, and Fig. 63 (45° of balance arc) a usual proportion for marine chronometers. Through A B, the given centres of escape wheel and balance, draw the line c. From A set off, by means of a protractor, 12° (half the distance between two teeth of the escape wheel) on each side of the centre line and draw D E. From B set off on each side of the centre line half the amount of the given balance arc and draw two other lines, as shown. The circles representing the tips of the escape wheel teeth and the impulse roller are drawn to cut the intersections of these four lines.

in. The locking face of the stone is also set at a sufficient angle to ensure perceptible draw. The edge of the impulse roller acts as a guard to prevent the wheel teeth passing in the event of accidental unlocking at the wrong time. There is a crescent-shaped piece cut out of the roller to clear the teeth of the wheel. It should be very little behind the pallet and less than the distance between two teeth of the escape wheel in front of it, to avoid the danger of running through, or passing two teeth, when such accidental unlocking occurs. It is important to see that there is enough cut out in front of the pallet to clear the wheel tooth at all times. When the balance is traveling very quickly—i. e., with an unusually large vibration—the pallet gets a long way in front of the tooth before the tooth starts, and then if the crescent is not cut far enough beyond the face of the pallet, the tooth would butt on the roller.

The radius of the discharging pallet is a trifle less than one-half that of the impulse pallet. If made too small the locking stone cannot return quick enough to catch the tooth.

The detent is made very light, and of about the proportion shown in the drawing. The spring of the detent is thinned down so that when the root is fixed and it stands out horizontally, one pennyweight hung from the pipe deflects it about a quarter of an inch. If the spring is made too thin, it will cockle and give trouble. The detent may very easily be made too long from the point where it bends to the locking pallet, and would then be too sluggish and allow the wheel to trip by not returning quick enough after the unlocking to receive the next tooth of the wheel. A very good rule is to have the distance from the shoulder of foot to pipe equal to the diameter of the wheel.

The escape wheel is of hard, hammered brass, the rollers of steel. The detent of steel, carefully tempered, with the point of the horn left softer to allow of bending. The pallets are all of sapphire or ruby, fastened in with shellac. A brass plug is fitted in to occupy the space in the pipe of detent not filled by the locking pallet. The gold spring is hammer-hardened.

POCKET CHRONOMETER.

The escape wheel for pocket chronometers varies from .28 to .35 in diameter. The impulse roller is made larger in proportion to the escape wheel than in the marine chronometer, so as to lessen the tendency of the escapement to set. If the chronometer escapement is brought to rest by external motion just as the unlocking is taking place, *it must set*, for the balance spring is then quiescent. In the lever escapement the tooth of the escape wheel is in the middle of the impulse plane of the pallet when the balance spring is quiescent, and in this respect the lever has the advantage. If the velocity of the balance in a chronometer is much reduced when the unlocking is completed, then a large impulse roller is of great assistance to the wheel in overcoming the inertia of the balance.

As the diameter of the roller is increased, the balance arc, and also the intersection of the path of the wheel teeth by the impulse pallet, is decreased. The velocity of the edge of the roller, too, more nearly approaches the velocity of the wheel tooth, so that less of the power is utilized. It is, therefore, not prudent to adopt a much less balance arc than 28° or 30°.

The tendency of pocket chronometers to set is also lessened by adopting a quick train; 18,000 is the usual train, but they are occasionally made with 19,200 by having sixteen teeth in the escape wheel instead of fifteen. This seems to be an objectionable way of getting the quick train. The teeth of the escape wheel being closer together, a smaller roller must be used to get the same intersection, and as there is less time for the detent to return there is great danger of mislocking.

For the convenience of getting the seconds hand to jump half-seconds, a 14,400 train is sometimes adopted in pocket chronometers. In this case the escape wheel has twelve teeth, the numbers of the rest of the train remaining the same.

The other parts of the pocket chronometer escapement are similar to those of the marine chronometer.

TO EXAMINE THE ESCAPEMENT.

See that the wheel is true and the teeth smooth and perfect, and that the rollers properly fit the staff. See that the end shakes and side shakes are correct. See that the " lights " between the wheel teeth and the edge of the roller are equal on both sides when the wheel is ;locked. If they are not, the foot of the detent must be knocked a trifle to or from the center of the roller till the lights are equal. If the light is more than sufficient for clearance the roller must be warmed to soften the shellac, and the impulse pallet moved out a little. If the light is excessive there will be too much drop on the locking after the wheel tooth leaves the impulse pallet, and with a large drop there is danger of tripping.

To ensure safe locking the detent should be set on so that when the banking screw is removed, and the locking pallet is free of the wheel teeth, it will just spring in as far as the rim of the wheel.

In pocket chronometer escapements it is especially necessary to see that the face of the locking stone is angled so as to give perceptible draw. Many pocket chronometers fail for want of it.

The gold spring should point to the center of the roller. Bring the balance around till the discharging pallet touches the gold spring preparatory to unlocking, and notice how far from that point the balance moves before the gold spring drops off the face of the pallet. Then reverse the motion of the balance, and see if the same arc is traveled through from the time the *back* of the pallet touches the gold spring until it releases it. If not, the horn of the detent must be bent to make the action equal.

Bring the discharging pallet on to the gold spring, and let it bend the detent so that the locking stone is as much outside the wheel as it was within when the wheel was locked. The gold spring should then drop off the discharging pallet. Make it to length, sloping off the end from the side on which the pallet falls to unlock, and finish it with great care The gold spring should be thinned near its fixed end as much as possible, and the detent spring thinned if it is needed. The judgment of the operator must determine the proper strength in both cases. The nose of the detent horn should be nicely flattened and the corners rounded off.

The locking pallet should not be perfectly upright. It should lean a little from the center of the wheel, and a little toward the foot of the detent, so that the locking takes place at the root of the stone, and then the action of locking and unlocking does not tend so much to buckle the detent. The face of the impulse pallet, too, should be slightly inclined so that it bears on the upper part of the wheel teeth. By this means the impulse pallet will not mark the wheel in the same spot as the locking pallet.

Try if the escape wheel teeth drop safely on the impulse pallet by letting each tooth in succession drop on, and after it has dropped, turn the balance gently backward; you can then judge if it is safe by the amount the balance has to be turned back before the tooth leaves the pallet. If some teeth do not get a safe hold, the impulse roller must be twisted round on the arbor to give more drop.

If the escapement is in beat, the balance, when the balance spring is at rest, will have to be turned around an equal distance each way to start the escapement. When the balance spring is in repose, the back of the discharging pallet will be near the gold spring, and if the balance is moved around until the gold spring falls off the back of the pallet and then released, the escapement should start of itself; and in the other direction also, if the balance is released directly the wheel tooth leaves the face of the impulse pallet, the escapement should go on of itself.

Munger's Improved Chronometer Escapement. In this escape-ment, which is illustrated in Fig. 64, the detent and staff are in one piece, with a notch in the head to hold the locking jewel. The detent arm has a hole through it to receive the detent staff, fitting friction tight, so that the detent and arm can be set at the proper angle to each other, and then the staff driven down to the shoulder. These should not fit so tightly that they cannot be separated without danger of breaking, but so firmly as not to be moved out of proper position to each other by use or handling, etc. Figure 64 shows the escape-ment and impulse pallet of the usual construction. The diameter of the pallet should not be less than six-tenths (.6) the diameter of the escapement, or larger than two-thirds the size of the wheel. $A\,a$ shows the line of centers of the escape wheel and balance; $b\,b$ the circle of depthing of the escapement and detent from the balance holes; $c\,c$ extends from the intersection of the periphery of the wheel with the line $a\,a$, and the point of the third tooth of the wheel across the circle $b\,b$.   At the intersection of the lines $b\,b$ and $c\,c$ is the point of location of the detent pivots (a slight variation from this point is not important). The discharge, or unlocking pallet, shown by the dotted lines, is a light bar or arm with a notch at one end to hold its jewel, and is the same length or diameter as the impulse pallet (or nearly so).   In planting the escapement, first mount the wheel on its pinion and top it just enough to have it round. Then use a temporary brass or steel disc, the size required for the impulse

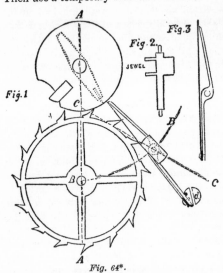

Fig. 1

Fig. 2.

Fig. 3

JEWEL

Fig. 64*.

pallet, place it on the balance staff, and adjust the depth of it and the wheel in the depth tool, and mark the circle $b\,b$. Locate the escape wheel and detent pivots the distance apart indicated by the drawing, and pivot them in, as also the balance, in their proper positions.   In the brass disc cut a notch large enough to allow the escape-wheel tooth to pass through as in escaping.   As the detent jewel is too long to allow of the proper locking of the wheel, let a tooth of the wheel rest on the lock-ing face of the detent (the notch in the disc allows this), and the distance of the entrance tooth from the disc readily shows about how much of the detent jewel has to be ground off before beginning to polish its locking face.   Two or three trials will bring it so near that the final polishing will make the locking correct.   All this really takes but a few minutes to do.

To obtain the adjustment of the detent use a special tool.   The spindle is hollow, and the front end reamed out to take in a small brass taper

*Fig. 1 represents a plan, or face view, of the escapement, showing the method of locating the relative positions of the balance, escape wheel and detent pivots.

Fig. 2 is an elevation of the detent, detached from the detent arm.

Fig. 3 is a plan view of the detent arm and gold spring attached to it. D, eccentric banking screw to adjust the position of the detent arm and depth of locking the escape wheel. The distance of the detent pivot from the escape wheel can be determined and laid out with sufficient accuracy as one-fifth to one-fourth of the distance shown in the drawing.

that also fits a chuck in your lathe-spindle; this small taper is drilled out, with as large a hole as convenient, from the back end to within about one-eighth of an inch of the front. It is then put in the lathe-spindle and the front end turned small enough to be out of the way of the lap, and carefully centered and drilled through into the large hole, and broached out just enough to hold the detent staff firmly by friction, while grinding and polishing the locking surface; and it is readily removed from the taper to try the detent for the correct locking.

In making this adjustment, the arbor carrying the polishing lap should be held firmly, (by means of a loose button on the front end of the spindle) against the adjusting screw *r*, and this screw turned a little at a time, as the length of the detent jewel is shortened, so that the locking face will be a true circle from the pivots; for if the locking corner is much rounded off, or beveled, the pressure of the wheel against it would push the detent out, and cause it to trip or unlock at the wrong time. If the circle is true from the pivots, no amount of pressure of the wheel against the detent can push it out or release it.

With the size of discharge pallet used, the unlocking action can begin, if desired, from ¼ to ⅓ of the whole motion of the detent arm before the line of centers, and is adjusted by the eccentric banking screw *d*. The relative position or angle of the detent to the arm is then so adjusted as to give the right amount of locking to the escape wheel, (which can be very shallow). The gold spring is then shortened, so that it will be released from the discharge pallet when the escape wheel tooth and impulse jewel are about on the line of centers; if the gold spring is too short, the detent will return too soon, so that the inside face of the locking jewel will strike the point of the tooth of the escape wheel, and the wheel drag along the face of the jewel until the detent arm rests against the banking screw *d*. This must be avoided.

The discharge pallet, of course, must be set so as to unlock at the right position of the impulse pallet, but less drop is required in this escapement than in the usual construction.

The spiral return spring on the detent staff, under the arm, should have tension enough to return the detent to its banking, when it is moved a trifle, with all the pressure on it from the train that the mainspring can give. Use five or six coils for the return spring, and put on the spring so that it opens when the detent is moved to unlock, as this gives a trifle quicker action to start the detent on its return. The detent, all complete, is so very light that there is no recoil as it strikes the banking, and no jarring or outside motion will cause it to trip, as all others are liable to do.

The extreme lightness of the detent with its locking so near the pivot, lessens the friction so greatly that the discharge pallet can be of the same diameter as the impulse pallet, and thus greatly lessen the angle or extent of motion required to start it going; and it also admits of very shallow locking, without the least danger of tripping, and requires much less strength of mainspring than any other detached escapement.

CHRONOSCOPE. A clock or watch in which the time is indicated by the presentation of numbers through holes in the dial.

CHUCK. A mechanical contrivance for holding work in a lathe. True chucks are the most important adjuncts to a watchmaker's bench. A good lathe and untrue chucks will result in inferior work, while a cheap lathe with true chucks will permit of some good results. Chucks hold the work truest that come the nearest fitting the hole in them. Trying to hold work too large or too small, will soon get them out of true, and often make the workman dissatisfied with his chucks, his work, himself

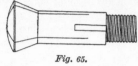

Fig. 65.

and his lathe. Wax is the only sure thing for fine staff and pivot work, although there are many substitutes that do very well, and with the aid of them a good workman can turn out a very fine job. With a good lathe, true chucks and sizes to suit, and a reasonable amount of practice, first class work can be done with split chucks. One chuck or tool of any kind seldom does all kinds of work and does it well.

Fig. 65 is a good example of the modern split wire chuck, such as is furnished to go with all American made lathes.

The table of American wire chucks on page 79 will prove useful to those persons who contemplate purchasing chucks for lathes of foreign manufacture.

Adjustable Chuck. The Hopkins patent adjustable chuck, shown in Fig. 66, is designed to grip and hold firmly and accurately any size of work from the smallest staff to the largest pinion, watch wheels of all sizes, mainspring barrels and other large work, and can be adjusted to any make of lathe by simply placing it friction tight, on a plug chuck fitted properly to the lathe. In using this chuck for staffs, pinions, wire, etc., fasten a V piece 7, of proper size, in the hole in attachment 6, taking care that both the V and the seat in which it rests are free from chips, dirt, etc. Then lay your work in the V and fasten it there by means of the sliding jaw above it. This done, place the

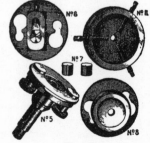

Fig. 66.

attachment on the face of the chuck body, with the disc slipped under the heads of the two spring bolts, and then spin the work to center, same as when using wax. After centering thus, fasten the disc to place by tightening the nuts on the back ends of the spring bolts.

DIMENSIONS OF AMERICAN CHUCKS.

NAME OF CHUCK.	DIAMETER OF BODY IN INCHES.	DIAMETER OF BODY IN MM.	LENGTH OF CHUCK IN INCHES.	ANGLE OF SHOULDER.	PITCH OF THREAD.	LARGEST HOLE CLEAR THROUGH IN MM.	SIZE OF LARGEST HOLE IN MM.
Moseley, No. 1	.240	--	1.28	25°	Eng. 48	38	47
Moseley, 1 x 2	.3135	--	1.34	20°	Eng. 40	50	65
Moseley, No. 2	.3135	--	1.58	20° Con.	Eng. 40	50	65
Moseley, No. 3	.400	--	1.82	20° Con.	Eng. 36	65	75
Whitcomb, No. 1	.197	5	$1\frac{5}{16}$	20°	Eng. 50	30	35
Whitcomb, No. 1½	.256	6½	$1\frac{3}{16}$	20°	Eng. 40	40	50
Whitcomb, No. 2 or W. W.	.315	8	$1\frac{3}{8}$	20°	Eng. 40	50	60
Hopkins, No. 1	.2285	--	$1\frac{1}{16}$	25°	Eng. 48	28	42
Hopkins, No. 3	.2635	--	$1\frac{1}{16}$	25°	Eng. 40	37	50
Hopkins, 3 x 4	.3355	--	$1\frac{15}{32}$	25°	Eng. 40	52	66
Kearney & Swartchild	.300	--	$1\frac{9}{16}$	25°	Eng. 44	48	57
Elgin or Triumph	.275	--	$1\frac{5}{16}$	25°	Eng. 50	45	52
Rivett	.300	--	$1\frac{11}{32}$	20°	Eng. 40	47	57
Geneva	.1965	6	$1\frac{7}{32}$	20°	Met. 14	34	45
Stark, No. 1	About .1875 or $\frac{3}{16}$	--	--	--	Eng. 48	23	30
Stark, No. 2	About .2205	--	--	--	Eng. 48	28	42
Stark, No. 3	.245	--	--	--	Eng. 48	28	45
Stark, E.	.300	--	$1\frac{3}{32}$	20°	Eng. 40	50	57

For holding work by the web of the wheel, place the wheel under the screw cap on the face attachment 8 and screw the cap down firmly on it, with the staff or pinion projecting outward through the center hole. This done proceed the same as when using No. 6.

For mainspring barrels and like work, use attachment 11, and place a bit of broken mainspring between the work and the ends of the three binding screws, and tighten the screws down on that instead of directly on the work.

Arbor Chuck. A screw chuck on the end of which is a threaded

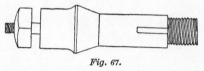

Fig. 67.

arbor for the reception of saws, laps, etc., which are clamped in position firmly by means of a nut or thumb screw as shown in Fig. 66.

Bezel Chuck. The Snyder patent Bezel Chuck, shown in Fig. 68, was originally intended for holding bezels only, but it is now made so that it will hold watch plates, coins, etc., and is adjustable to any size. It can be fitted to any lathe and requires but very little practice to use it, as it is extremely simple and any one who uses a lathe can make or repair bezels in a workmanlike manner. It holds the work as in a vise, and no amount of turning or jarring will loosen the jaws, while it may be opened and closed instantly by simply turning the milled nut behind the face plate, thus enabling the operator to turn and fit a bezel perfectly,

by trying on the case as many times as necessary. It holds the bezel by either groove, so that the recess may be turned out when too shallow or too small for the glass, or the bezel may be inverted and turned away when it rests too hard on the dial. It will be found especially useful in turning out the inevitable lump of solder from the recess in the bezel, after soldering and in fitting to case, as the process of soldering generally makes the bezel shorter; and consequently it will not fit on the case.

Fig. 68. It also renders the operation of polishing bezels after soldering, but a few minutes' work. In turning out the recess for glass in bezels, especially heavy nickel bezels, it will prove a friend indeed, when for instance, you look through your stock of flat glasses and find none to fit, but have one that is just too large. All watchmakers know that if the groove in the bezel is imperfect it is apt to break the glass. The chuck is also useful as a barrel closer, holding work while engraving, and many other uses that will present themselves to the watch or case repairer.

Cement Chuck. The Spickerman patent cement chuck, shown in Fig. 69, is a very handy device, as it holds and centers accurately any wheel in a watch while drilling, polishing or fitting new staffs or pinions,

Fig. 69.

and all danger of injuring wheels is obviated. It fits all kinds of American or Swiss lathes. The holder shown in Fig. 70 at a, is turned down to nearly the size of the screw for the lathe and the screw cut so the holder will set as close as possible to the lathe. The face of the holder is then turned perfectly true. Put wheel to be centered in cap c, as near to center as convenient and screw on b. Then place cement face of chuck b against face of holder a on the lathe and with a lamp, warm the cement between the surfaces, holding the chuck

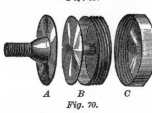

A   B   C
Fig. 70.

with a stick against the pivot of wheel in the cap, and it will move to an exact center as soon as warmed sufficiently. New cement should be added occasionally between the surfaces, as it hardens and burns away and does not center as well as when new. Fig. 69 shows chuck with wheel inside ready for drilling. See also *Cement Brasses.*

Chuck Stepping Device. In this device, shown in Fig. 71, A rests in chuck slightly less than diameter of work. B tightens in rear end of draw-in-spindle. Turning c regulates depth of step.

By the use of this tool any wire chuck will accurately serve as a step chuck. It is a device of great service to the watchmaker when used and understood. It enables him to make a step in any wire chuck of any depth he may wish, and will push out the work if desired. It is very useful many times for a stop for marking or cutting off when you want a number of pieces of the same length or kind. Many object to the stepped chuck for general use, objections which this device obviates.

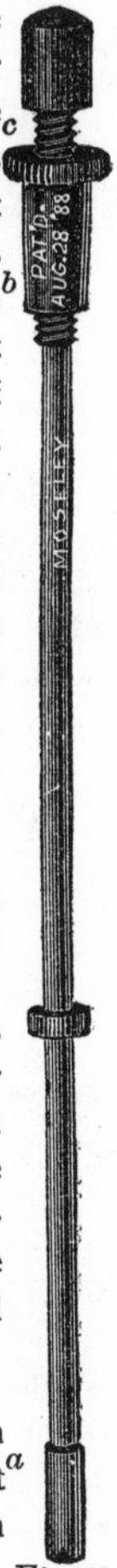

Conoidal Chuck. A wire chuck which has a conoidal shape in lieu of the shoulder usually left on wire chucks for the bend in the lathe head. Fig. 72 illustrates the usual form of conoidal chucks.

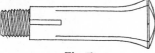

Fig. 72.

Fig. 71.

Crown Chuck. A chuck for holding watch crowns while undergoing repairs of various kinds. Figure 73 illustrates the Dale chuck, which is made on the lines of the ordinary split wire chuck, a large recess being

Fig. 73.

turned in the end for the reception of the crown. The draw-in of the chuck holds the crown firmly in place. Fig. 74 illustrates the Johanson chuck, which is intended to hold all sizes of crowns, from the smallest to the largest. The figure clearly shows the adjustment of parts. This chuck is manufactured in two styles, one like Fig. 74, which is ready to insert into a number 40 wire chuck of an American lathe, while the other style is mounted on a regular chuck and is always ready to insert into the lathe head, the same as an ordinary split chuck.

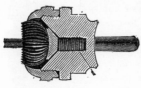

Fig. 74.

Dead Center Chuck. By the use of this chuck, shown in Fig. 75, the work can be run on dead centers as well as by the bow or verge lathe, and the motion will be continuous.

Drill Chuck. A small chuck

Fig. 76.   *Fig. 75.*

for holding drills, made to fit in tail-stock spindles or taper chucks. Fig. 76 illustrates the Gem Pivot Drill Chuck.

Jeweling Chuck. The Hutchinson Jeweling Chuck, which is shown in Fig. 77, is intended as a substitute for wax, when manipulating jewels. The cut represents a full size chuck, which is made similar to the ordinary split chuck, but has an adjustable center which can be moved backward or forward by means of the screw in the rear, and is used to support the jewel while in place in the chuck. They are made in three sizes. Another form of jeweling chuck is shown in Fig. 78, and is known as the Deuss Chuck. It is a self-centering chuck which will hold all sizes of jewels and fits the wheel or step chucks of all American lathes.

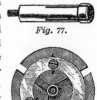

Fig. 77.

Fig. 78.

Pivoting Chuck. The Gem patent pivoting chuck, shown in Figs. 79 and 80, is intended as a substitute for wax for pivoting and like work.

By the means of the ball b, placed between the two sliding sockets c c, with the several other parts as represented in Fig. 79, a combination of sliding and ball and socket movements in connection with a spring pump center, is obtained. A set of ten or more, supplementary chucks g, with different sizes of center holes, and attachment n, for all sizes of wheels, are furnished with each chuck. The supplementary chuck g, in the form

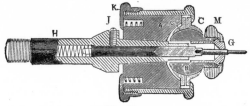

Fig. 79.

of a small split chuck, is made to fit into a hole with taper mouth in the center of the ball b, and is drawn into place and the work fastened firmly in it by means of the binding nut m, which screws on to a projection extending outward from front side of the ball.

To use this chuck proceed as follows: Remove the nut m, and give freedom to the working parts by loosening the large back nut k. Then to bring the hole through the ball b, into line, spin the ball to center, first at the base of the projecting screw and then at the mouth of the hole through it, and in this position again fasten the parts, by tightening the nut k. Then give freedom to the pump center by slightly loosening the set screw j. When doing this, hold your finger against the front of the chuck, to prevent the center rod from shooting out of its place when

Fig. 80.

freed. Then having placed a supplementary chuck g, of proper size, in its place in the chuck, and your work in it, with its back end resting properly in the countersink in the end of the pump center, fasten it there by screwing the cap m down snugly over it, using a small lever pin when necessary for this purpose, but not with nndue force. Then again loosen the nut k and spin the work to center at its outer end; and then tighten both the nut k and set screw j. In tightening the set screw j, make sure it is so tightened as to prevent the pump center from slipping from place

when working. If from tightening the screw j, it is found that the work
has been thrown in any degree away from true center, loosen the nut k,
leaving the pump center fast, and again spin to center, and fasten as
before. All of which after a little practice may be done, and the work
be brought to absolute truth in a few moments.

In using attachment n for wheels, the nut m and chuck g are removed,
and n substituted therefor; the work being held on the face of the attachment by flat headed screws that grip the arms of the wheel. For cylinder escape wheels a special attachment n is furnished. The best thing
to use when spinning work to enter in the chuck, is a bit of peg wood of
wedge shape at one end. The countersinks in the ends of the pump
center should in all cases be carefully tested, and if need be trued up in
the lathe in which the chuck is to be used. In doing this, use a good,
fine-pointed sharp graver, and make sure the countersink is perfectly
true. The same rules in regard to truth in the countersink, and having
the work rest properly in it, are to be observed in using this chuck as
when using wax.

Screw Chuck. A solid chuck having a threaded hole in the end for
the reception of cement brasses, laps, etc., as shown in Fig. 81.

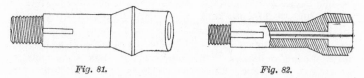

Fig. 81.　　　　　　　　　　　Fig. 82.

Shoulder Chuck. A chuck having a large opening in the end with
square shoulders for the work to rest upon as shown in Fig. 82.

Step or Wheel Chucks. These chucks are usually made in sets of
five, each chuck having nine steps, giving forty-five different sizes.
These chucks are very useful in holding main spring barrels, to fit in the

cap of the barrel, should it become
out of true. They are also valuable
in truing up barrels of English lever
watches, that are damaged owing to
the breakage of a main spring. They
are also very useful in holding almost
any wheel in a watch, but particularly
convenient in fitting a center wheel
to a pinion, or in making sure that
the hole in the wheel is in the center.

Fig. 83.

These chucks are made by the various lathe manufacturers and are all
similar to Fig. 83, and will hold wheels from .5 to 2.26.

Taper Chuck. A solid chuck having a large opening for the reception of tapers, centers, laps, etc., as shown in Fig. 84.

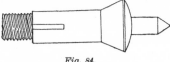

Fig. 84.

CHUCK BOX. A circular box with lid, for holding chucks. They are usually made of cherry or mahogany. By keeping your chucks in a

Fig. 85.

box similar to that shown in **Fig.** 85, you can find a chuck of the desired size in a moment and the chucks are less liable to be damaged than when kept in a drawer with miscellaneous tools.

CIRCULAR ERROR. In a pendulum clock the difference of time caused by the pendulum following a circular instead of a cycloidal path.

CLAMPS. Movable pieces of brass, lead, leather or cork attached to the jaws of a vise while holding objects that would be injured by the vise jaws.

CLEANSING, PICKLING AND POLISHING.

To Clean Pendulums. Brass pendulum bobs are often found with black stains upon them that prove very obstinate to remove. Heat the bob moderately, touch the stains with a brush dipped in nitric acid, rub with a linen rag and again heat moderately.

To Clean Silver. Articles of silver, either solid or plated, are quickly and easily .cleaned by dipping in a moderate concentrated solution of potassium cyanide and then thoroughly rinsing in water. Jewelers will find it very convenient to have three stone jars, with tight fitting covers, to exclude all dirt. Label the jars "Cyanide," "1st Water" and "Second Water.' In these, large pieces of silverware can be cleaned with ease by dipping into the cyanide, then into jar number one and then jar number two. Dry with a soft linen rag and the articles will be found free from all stains.

To Clean Nickel. The nickel plates of watches are sometimes found to have rust stains upon them. These can be removed by rubbing the spot with grease, allowing them to stand for a few days, and rubbing thoroughly with a cloth moistened with ammonia. In obstinate cases, repeat the operation or touch the stains with dilute hydrochloric acid and rub thoroughly. Rinse in clean water and polish. A mixture of fifty parts of rectified alcohol and one part of sulphuric acid is also valuable for cleaning nickel plates. Immerse for ten or fifteen seconds, no longer, rinse in alcohol, and dry in sawdust.

To Clean Brass. To clean old brass, especially small figures, paper knives, etc., immerse them in a mixture of one part of nitric acid and half part of sulphuric acid. Allow them to remain a short time, rinse thoroughly in cold water, dry in sawdust and polish with Vienna lime, when they will appear like new.

Pickling of Metals. Metals are pickled for the purpose of removing the oxide and producing a lustrous surface. An excellent pickle for brass consists of ten parts of water and one of sulphuric acid. Dip into this pickle, wash, dry, and immediately dip into a second pickle consisting of two parts of nitric acid and one of sulphuric acid and rinse thoroughly. This dissolves the zinc from the brass, and gives the metal a brilliant surface. All pickling operations with either hot or cold pickle should be carried on in the open air or in the draft of a well drawing chimney, as the vapors arising from the acids are very injurious. In order to retain the luster, a good transparent varnish should be applied.

Pickle for German Silver. To twelve parts of water add one part of nitric acid; immerse the article in this, quickly remove, and place in a mixture of equal parts of sulphuric and nitric acid, rinse thoroughly in water and dry in sawdust. In all cases of pickling it is essential that all traces of acid be removed by frequent washings in clean water.

Pickle for Gold Alloys. Gold alloys, especially those containing copper, assume an unsightly dark brown exterior, owing to the copper oxide generated by the repeated glow heating necessary during work. In order to remove this the object must be pickled, and either highly diluted sulphuric or nitric acid is used for the purpose, according to the color the article is designed to have.

If working with an alloy consisting only of gold and copper, either sulphuric or nitric acid may be used indifferently, since gold is not attacked by either of these acids, while copper oxide is easily decomposed thereby, and after having been pickled, the article will assume the color of pure gold, because its surface is covered with a layer of the pure metal.

If the alloy is composed of pure gold and silver however, only nitric acid can be employed, and the article is left immersed in it only for a short time; this acid dissolves a very small portion of the silver, and the article also assumes the color of pure gold.

When working with an alloy which, besides the gold, contains both copper and silver, the process of pickling may be varied in accordance with the color desired to be given to the article. If the pickling is performed in sulphuric acid, the copper alone is dissolved, the article assuming a color corresponding to a gold-silver alloy, which now constitutes the surface of the article.

If nitric acid is used it will dissolve the silver as well as the copper and in this case a pure gold color is produced.

Pickling is done by first feebly glow-heating the article and cooling it; this operation is for the purpose of destroying any fat from the hands or other contamination adhering to the article. If it was soldered with some easily-flowing solder, this glow-heating must be omitted, but it may be cleansed from impurities by immersing it at first into very strong caustic lye, and rinsing it with water; it is then laid into the acid.

The acids are employed in a dilute state, taking forty parts water to one part concentrated sulphuric or nitric acid. If more articles than one, they had best be laid beside each other in a porcelain or stoneware dish, the diluted acid is poured over them, and some article is lifted out from time to time to watch the course of proceedings, whether it has assumed a yellow color.

When to satisfaction, they are rinsed with clean water and dried. While pickling for the purpose only of causing the color peculiar to gold to appear, the process of coloring has for its object to lend the appearance of very fine gold to an article of an indifferent alloy. Various mixtures may be employed for the purpose, and we give two receipts below which are very appropriate:

Mix two parts saltpeter, 1 part table salt and six parts alum with 6½ parts water, and place in a porcelain dish for heating. As soon as you notice that the mixture begins to rise, add 1 part of muriatic acid, raise the whole to boiling and stir with a glass rod.

The article to be colored, and previously treated with sulphuric acid, as specified, is suspended to a hook, either of sufficiently thick platinum wire or glass; it is then introduced into the rather slow boiling bath, and moved around in it. It is to be taken out in about three minutes, and rinsed in clean water, inspecting its color at the same time. If not to satisfaction, it is returned to the bath, and this withdrawing it or introducing is repeated until the desired color is obtained. By the latter immersions the article is left only one minute at a time in the fluid.

When sufficiently colored the article, after rinsing, will be of a high yellow and mat color; it is washed repeatedly in water to remove the last traces of the bath, and then dried in hot boxwood sawdust.

In place of drying in sawdust the article may also be dipped in boiling water, leaving it in for a few seconds; the adhering water will evaporate almost instantaneously.

The second coloring method consists in pouring water over a mixture of 115 parts table salt and 230 nitric acid, so that the salt is dissolved; it is then to be heated until a dry salt residue is again present. This residue is mixed with 172 parts fuming muriatic acid and heated to boiling for which purpose a porcelain vessel is to be used.

As soon as the pungent odor of chlorine gas begins to evolve, the article to be colored is immersed, and left for about eight minutes in the fluid for the first time; in other respects, a similar treatment as specified above, is also used for this method; if the article colored was polished previously, a subsequent polishing is unnecessary.

On account of the vapors evolved by the coloring baths, which are very dangerous to health, the operations should be performed either under a well-drawing flue, or what is still better, in open air.—*Goldsch Miedekunst.*

Polishing Agents. Various polishing agents are used by watchmakers, jewelers, gold and silversmiths, a few of which are here described. Where the article will admit of it, the best results are obtained by polishing in the lathe. For this purpose the watchmaker should not use his regular lathe, but should have for the purpose what is known as a polishing lathe, fitted with its various attachments in the shape of scratchbrushes, buffs, etc.

Ferric Oxide. This material is used in its natural state and also prepared artificially under various names, such as crocus, red stuff and rouge

It is used for polishing fine articles of steel, gold, silver, copper and bronze.

Tin Putty is an artificial compound prepared from glowing oxalate of tin, which is obtained by decomposing tin salt with oxalic acid.

Tripoli. A gray-white or yellowish powder, which is made from the shells of microscopic organisms. It is used for polishing soft metals, first with oil, and then dry.

Lime. This material is used in the burned and unslaked state. A popular variety is known as the Vienna lime. See that heading.

Belgian Polishing Powder. This powder is used for polishing articles of silver and silver plated ware. It consists of a mixture of 250 parts of whiting, 117 parts elutriated pipe-clay, 62 parts white lead, 23 parts white magnesia, and 23 parts rouge.

English Silver Soap. This mixture, which is used for polishing silverware, is prepared as follows: Dissolve 2 parts of castile soap in 2 parts of soft water over a fire; when melted remove and stir in 6 parts of fine whiting, pour into moulds and allow it to cool. A little rouge may be added as coloring matter if desirable.

English Silver Paste. Three parts of perfumed vaseline, 5 parts of whiting, 1 part of burnt hartshorn, and one of pulverized cuttle bone. Stir well and put up in tin boxes.

Gold Polishing Powder. Mix together 4.3 parts of alumina, 17.4 of chalk, 4.3 of carbonate of lead, 1.7 of carbonate of magnesia, and 1.7 of rouge.

Polishing Paste for Brass. Dissolve 15 parts of oxalic acid in 120 parts of boiling water and add 500 parts of pumice powder, 7 of oil of turpentine, 60 of soft soap, and 65 of fat oil.

The polishing agent is usually mixed with oil, alcohol or water to prevent scattering, and is then applied by the polishing tool in the shape of cloth and leather buffs, polishing files, etc. Either the work or the tool should revolve with great velocity in order to secure good results. Many articles are brought to a high degree of polish by the use of the burnisher, after subjecting them to the action of the ordinary polishing agents. See *Burnisher*, also *Buff*.

Scratch Brushing. Articles in relief which do not admit of the use of the burnisher are brightened by the aid of the scratch brush. The shape of the brush varies according to the article to be operated upon. Hand scratch brushes are sometimes made of spun glass, with fibres of extreme fineness and elasticity, and are used for scouring only very deli-cate objects. They are also made of numerous wires of hardened brass and are prepared in similar form to the glass brushes, except when purchased the ends of the wires are not cut off, the operator being expec-ted to do so before using them. The object in leaving the wires con-nected being to prevent them becoming damaged. Circular scratch brushes, in which the wires are arranged radially, are used for scouring articles which will admit of their use. They are attached to the spindle of a polishing lathe, and the wires consequently all receive a uniform motion in the same direction. Scratch brushes are seldom, if ever, used dry, the tool and the work being constantly wet with a decoction of soap-root, marshmallow, cream of tartar, alum or licorice root. With small articles the scratch brush is held as you would a pencil, and is moved over the articles with a backward and forward motion. The brushes must be carefully looked after and the wires kept straight and in good order. If they become greasy they are cleansed in caustic potash, and if they become rough they are sometimes dipped into nitric acid. With circular brushes it is well to reverse them occasionally in order to change the direction of the wires. Dirty polishing leathers should be cleaned by soaking them for an hour or two in a weak solution of soda in warm water, first rubbing the leather thoroughly with soap. Rinse thoroughly and wash in soap and water. The soap in the water will keep the leather soft and pliable. Dry it in a towel and rub it thoroughly and your leather will be much better than any new one you can buy.

CLEAT. A narrow or thin piece of metal used to fasten two pieces of metal together by the aid of solder, screws or rivets.

CLEMENT, WILLIAM. A London clockmaker, who in 1680, laid claim to the invention of the long or royal pendulum.

CLEPSYDRA. A water clock. A machine used anciently for measuring time by means of the discharge of water through a small aperture. The Egyptians divided the space between sunrise and sunset into twelve hours, known as day, and between sunset and sunrise into twelve others, known at night. The days and nights therefore varied according to the seasons, so that the artificial divisions varied in like pro-portions, rendering the task of inventing a mechanism capable of being retarded or accelerated quite a formidable one for the mechanic of that day. The clock illustrated in Fig. 86 was so constructed that its aperture was adjusted as the year advanced by the attachment of an index to the sun's place in an ecliptic circle. It consists of a reservoir, *A*, at the top of which will be seen a waste pipe, to carry off the superfluous water

and thus keep the level the same at all times. From this reservoir projects a pipe, B, which connects with the rim of a drum, M, N, on the
front of which is a circle with the signs of the ecliptic engraved upon its
dial. Fitting inside this large drum is a smaller one, O F, having an
index attached to it. This drum has a groove or slot, a b, cut through it,
tapering in breadth both ways to a point. This tapering groove, when
the parts are in their places, comes just under the end of the pipe leading
from the reservoir. This smaller drum turns upon the pipe F, which is
continued within and has a funnel attached for receiving the water as it
drops through the groove in the drum. The index or hand is double,
L for day and O for night, and it will be evident that as it is turned the

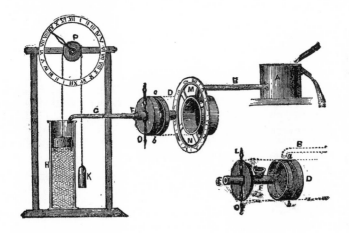

Fig. 86.

capacity of the orifice is altered and the water is regulated to pass more or
less rapidly through the pipe. The ecliptic being properly divided, the
hand was set to the proper sign in which the sun then was and was
altered as it shifted around the ecliptic. The water, after passing through
the regulator and the pipe C, dropped into the cylinder H, in which was
a float I, connected by a chain passing over a pulley on an arbor P, and
having a counter-poise weight K attached to its other end. To the pulley was attached a hand which pointed to the hour on the circular dial.

A water clock, made by Ctesibius, is illustrated in Fig. 87. The water
dropped into a funnel A, and was conveyed to the reservoir by means of
the pipe M. In this cylinder was located a float, to which was attached
a light pillar, on top of which was a figure pointing to the hour upon
a column opposite. Attached to the bottom of the water cylinder was a
small pipe, bent in the form of a syphon, as shown at E B F. As the

water rose in the cylinder it also rose in the small pipe until it reached the top, when it flowed over the bend, thus filling the syphon, and by a well-known law it quickly emptied the cylinder, the float and figure falling as the water receded. In order to overcome the obstacle of hours of a varying length, the inventor very cleverly drew the divisions on the column out of horizontal, so as to vary in their distance on different sides of the column. As the water came from the syphon it fell into receptacles in a wheel, shown at *K*, which, turning with the weight, as each compartment filled, caused the cylinder to revolve by the action of

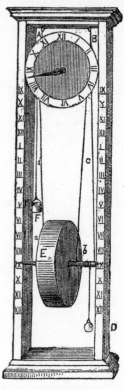

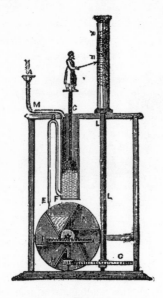

Fig. 87.   Fig. 88.

the pinion on its axis, taking into the contrate wheel *I*, which by another pinion *H*, turned the wheel and shaft *G* and *L*. In this way a variable scale of divisions was presented to the index, the space being regulated by the number of teeth in the wheels. Authorities differ as to the date of the revival of the clepsydra, one authority placing the date at 1646, while another gives it as 1693. A clepsydra of the seventeenth century is illustrated in Fig. 88. It consisted of an oblong frame of wood, *A B C D*, to the upper part of which two cords *A a*, *B b*, are fixed at their superior extremities and at their inferior are wound around the axis of the drum *E*. This drum was divided into several water-tight compartments, as

shown in Fig. 89. The cord was wound around the axis until the drum
was elevated to the top of the frame and it was then left to obey the force
of gravity. A hole was pierced near the bottom of each compartment, allowing the water to slowly ooze from
one compartment to the other, thus causing
the drum to revolve with a certain degree of
accuracy. The rate of motion was regulated
by altering the size of the apertures. The
hours were indicated in two ways; one by the
axis pointing out the hours on the side of the
frame as it revolved, and another by passing
a cord, $c d$, over a pulley attached to an arbor,
having an index or hand to point out the
hours on a dial, a weight, F. being fastened to
the other end of the cord.

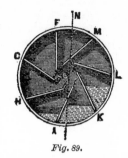

Fig. 89.

CLERKENWELL. One of the great watch and clock centers of
England. It is one of the parishes of London, and within its limits
every branch of the watch trade is carried on.

CLICHE. The forming of metal objects by means of forcing a die
into heated metal.

CLICK. A pawl or dog which falls into a ratchet wheel and prevents it from turning backward, and is usually held in position by means
of a spring, known as the click spring. A ratchet wheel with click is
fixed to the barrel arbor of watches and clocks to maintain the mainspring after being wound.

Click Spring. The spring which holds the click in position on a
ratchet wheel's tooth.

To Mount a Click Spring. When the old click spring has been
taken down from the bridge, find a new one, which, in length from click
to foot, into which the holes are drilled for fastening, is suited to the
shape and length of the bridge. With three claws fasten this latter in
an uprighting tool, placing the centering center into the screw hole of
the bridge, which serves for screwing on the click spring. When the
bridge has in this manner been mounted well upon the plate of the
uprighting tool, raise up the centering center and lay the new click spring
exactly as it is to be located in its place upon the bridge, carefully preventing the claws from covering that part of the bridge to which the
spring is fastened. The upper face of the spring must, by so much as
will be lost afterwards in grinding and polishing, protrude beyond the
surface of the barrel bridge. Then retain the spring in its place by

applying a finger, and lower the point of the uprighting tool upon the click spring, making a dot by applying a gentle pressure exactly at the true spot. This dot is enlarged by punching, and a hole is then drilled exactly to suit the size of the screw. The burr is next removed, and the spring finished suitable to shape and length. If the bridge contains a foot-pin hole, bush it by firmly driving into it a brass pin, file off its projecting part level with the bridge, and screw the spring in place. Then drill, as closely as possible, to the extreme end of the spring, a small hole for the pin, clear through into the bridge. Harden the spring, anneal it, chamfer and polish the edges, grind and polish the surface; fit the foot pin.

CLOCKS. It has been a matter of no small dispute as to who first invented clocks employing a weight for the motive power. Pacificus, Archdeacon of Verona, is said to have constructed a clock in 850 A. D., which marked, besides the hours, the days of the week, the phases of the moon, etc. Bailly, in his history of Modern Astronomy, argues very forcibly in favor of Pacificus, saying that he was the inventor of an escapement, in which the inertia of a balance was employed to retard and regulate the movement of a train of wheels moved by a weight. Father Alexandre, the author of a treatise on clocks, decides against Pacificus as the inventor of the weight clock, and Berthoud is of the same opinion. Nelthropp, in his treastise on watch work, says that it is more than probable, almost certain, that to the Moors of Spain the world is indebted for the great advance in clock work, and that from Cordova, Granada and Barcelona went forth the ideas which gave birth to the weight as a motive power, instead of water. Nelthropp is of the opinion that the inventor of the weight clock was one Gerbert, who was born in 920, A. D., in the village of Belliac in Auvergne. Certain it is that in 996 he made a clock for Madgeburg, which writers agree in stating had a weight for the motive power. After various ups and downs he became Pope, under the name of Sylvester II., in the year 999.

According to Stowe, a clock was erected near Westminister Hall, out of a fine of 800 marks imposed upon Ralph de Heugham, Chief Justice of the King's Bench, in 1288, A. D. In 1292 a clock was erected in Canterbury Cathedral, by Henry, the Prior. In 1317, a clock was erected in Exeter Cathedral. In 1326, Richard Wallingford, Abbot of St. Albans, constructed for the abbey a clock, which, Leland says, showed the course of the sun, moon and planets, and the rise and fall of the tides. In 1344 a clock was constructed for Padua by a workman named Antoine, after the designs of Jacques de Dondis. In 1348, a clock was constructed for Dover Castle, with wheels and frame of wrought iron; escapement, a crown wheel acting on pallets fixed to a verge, the upper end of which was suspended to a cock by a piece of cord, so as to hang perpendicular; lower end, a pivot working into a kind of stud attached to frame;

balance, an iron bar, each end terminating in an elbow, to which a weight was attached in order to produce an equilibrium.

The first Strasburg clock was begun in 1352, and completed two years after, by John Bishop, of Lichtenberg. The second clock was begun in 1547, by Dr. Michael Heer, Nicholas Bruckner and Christian Herlin, professor of the University of Strasburg, and one of the most distinguished mathematicians of his time. Owing to the death of the Colleagues of Herlin, the work was not completed until 1574. In 1570,

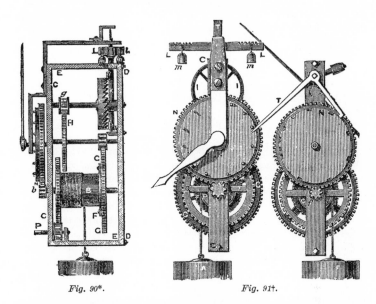

Fig. 90*.   *Fig. 91†.*

Conrad Dasypodius, a disciple of Herlin, reconstructed it on a larger scale. The mechanical work was performed by Isaac and Josiah Habrecht, clock-makers of Schaffhausen, Switzerland. This clock, which was restored in 1669, by Michael Isaac Habrecht, grandson of Dasypodius, one of the original makers, and a second time restored by James Straubharr, in 1732, ceased to act in 1789. The present Strasburg clock was commenced June 24, 1838, and started running on October 2, 1842.

In 1370, Charles V., King of France, caused to be made at Paris, a large

---

**Side view of Time Train.* B, Barrel; C, D, E, Plates; F, Ratchet and Click; G, Great Wheel; P, O, Winding Pinion and Wheel; H, Second Wheel; *g*, Escape Pinion; *b*, Pinion driving Hour Wheel; N. Hour Wheel, the arbor of which carries the hand.

†*Front view of Time and Striking Train.* K, Verge; L, Balance; *m*, Shifting Weights for adjusting the Clock to time; N, Count Wheel or Locking Plate; T, Lever for letting off Striking Work.

turret clock, by one Henry de Vick, (sometimes spelled De Wyck), a clockmaker of Wurtemburg. He took eight years to complete the work. John Jouvance cast the bell on which the hammer of the clock struck the hours. It was on this bell the signal was given for the massacre of Saint Bartholomew, 1572.

The escape wheel of this clock was a crown wheel which acted on pallets attached to a vertical rod or axis, moving on two pivots; the balance, a heavy bar of iron, was fixed to the upper part of this verge, and had weights placed at corresponding distances on each arm by means of a number of equidistant notches, in order to regulate its vibrations. The upper end of the verge was suspended by a small cord, to a cock fixed to the larger cock, in which the pivot hole was pierced, for the purpose of keeping it perpendicular and decreasing the friction of the lower pivot.

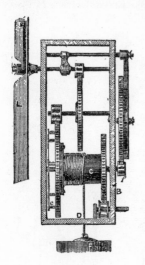

Fig. 92*.

In 1391, a clock was constructed for the Cathedral of Metz. In 1401, a clock was constructed for the Cathedral of Seville.

In the National Horogical Museum, at Nuremburg, Germany, is a clock which was presented to the museum by Gustav Speckhart, the court watchmaker. Speckhart estimates that it was made between the years 1400 and 1420, and is therefore the oldest clock in the city of Nuremburg. It was originally located upon the clock-tower of the St. Sebaldus Church, and indicated the hours to a watchman, who thereupon announced them to the inhabitants of the city by striking upon a bell in the tower. The hammer used weighed 120 pounds, and was introduced at the same time as the great bell Benedicta, in the year 1392. This clock is constructed entirely of iron, and is 15¾ inches high. The dial, which is also constructed of iron, is 11 inches in diameter. The clock when first discovered had a painted dial with twelve hours upon it, but Speckhart was aware that this was not the original dial because on the outer circumference of the dial, he found sixteen nails, one with a sharp pointed head, corresponding to the figure 12 and fifteen with round heads. On carefully removing this paint, he found another dial with twelve hours recorded, and on removing this he came upon the original dial which was painted with sixteen Roman figures of a gothic form. The original division of the day and night was into 16 hours, since the

---

Side view of Striking Train. F, Weight; A, B, Plates; C, Barrel; *c*, Pins for raising the hammer tail; L, Fly; *f*, Pinion for driving Count Wheel.

longest day, as well as the longest night, has sixteen hours. It is supposed that the nails were used by the watchman in determining the hour without the use of a light, and that he first sought the nail with the point, then felt downwards, counting the others, until he arived at the nail above which the hand rested. When the day was divided into twice twelve hours, about 1560-1580, the old hour wheel was removed and

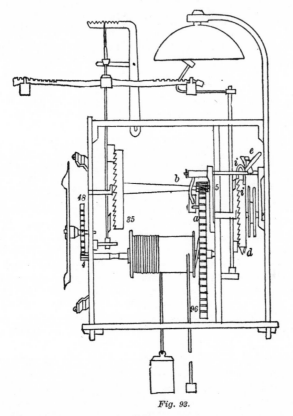

Fig. 93.

replaced by a new one, and the dial was repainted to correspond. The clock has no striking work proper, but as shown in Fig. 93 is provided with a kind of alarm, which after each hour, rattles the hammer to and fro on a bell, to call the attention of the watchman. The motion work consists of a barrel wheel with ninety-six teeth; a vertical wheel with thirty-five teeth, and a five-leaf pinion. The barrel wheel has a four-leaf pinion, seizing into forty-eight teeth of the hour wheel. In the former division of sixteen hours the hour wheel had sixty-four teeth.

The verge is suspended by a cord, and in lieu of a balance, is provided with a horizental toothed bar, on the ends of which hang two small weights, for regulating purposes. The winding part is peculiar, because, while the cord with the heavy weight descends, another cord with a small weight winds up in an opposite direction, and it is only necessary to draw down the small weight in order to wind up the heavier.

A pin *a* is inserted in the barrel wheel, which makes one revolution every hour; this pin unlocks the lever *b* and actuates the alarm; but since it was thought necessary to prolong the alarm for about one-quarter of a minute, the following arrangement was introduced: While the lever *b* on the movable part *c*, is raised up by the pin *a*, it liberates the wedge *d*, which, when the alarm is at rest, leans on the lever arm *e*, so that the alarm wheel, with one winding, sets the hammer into activity. Ordinarily it would take some time for the pin *a*, with its movable part *c*, to pass the lever *b*, and the alarm would in consequence run down with the first ringing. To prevent this, the angle *i* is riveted to the circumference of the alarm wheel, opposite to the wedge *d*, which after a half revoluion of said wheel, still lifts up a part of the lever arm *e*, so that the part *c* falls downward by its own weight, and leaves the pin *a* free, so that the lever arm *e* again assumes its place upon the face of the alarm wheel, and the wedge *d*, in its further half revolution, places itself against it in order to place the alarm into repose, until the performance is again repeated.

An astrological clock, bearing the date 1525, is in the museum of the Society of Antiquaries, London. It was made by one Jacob Zech, of Prague, and Nelthropp, after investigation, is of the opinion that it was once the property of Sigismund the First, King of Poland. The wheels of this clock are made of iron. It is fitted with a powerful expansive spring, coiled in a drum or barrel, and has a hand-made fusee for equalizing the variable power. The balance consists of an iron bar carrying a screw at each of the ends, with tapped weights of lead. At present the barrel is connected with the fusee by a chain, but there is every reason to believe that in the original construction a catgut or cord was used. The escapement is of the verge and crown wheel type.

In 1532, Henry, the Eighth, presented to Anne Boleyn, on their marriage, a clock of beautiful construction which is now in Windsor Castle. There is a clock at Hampton Court Palace bearing the date 1540, and the initials N. O.

There is a clock at Berne, Switzerland, constructed by Gaspard Brunner, a locksmith, but improved and repaired by Angely, a French clockmaker, in 1686.

In 1758 James Ferguson invented what was known as the "Simple Clock." Fig. 94 illustrates the dial and wheel work of this clock. It showed the hours, minutes and seconds, by means of only three wheels and two pinions. The great wheel contained 120 teeth and turned around in twelve hours, and on its axis was the plate on which the twelve hours were engraved.   This wheel turned a pinion of ten leaves and the minute hand was on the axis of this pinion.   On this axis was also a wheel of 120 teeth which geared into a pinion of six leaves, and on the axis of this pinion was a wheel of 90 teeth, going around in three minutes and keeping a pendulum in motion that vibrated seconds, by

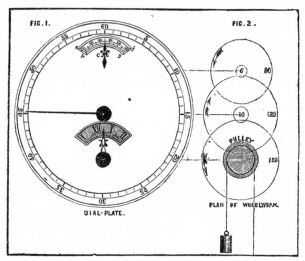

Fig. 94.

pallets, as in a common clock, where the scape wheel has thirty teeth and revolves in a minute.   As this wheel only revolved in three minutes it was necessary, in order to show the seconds, that a thin plate be fastened to the axis and divided into 180 equal parts, and divided as shown in the illustration, 10, 20, 30, 40, 50, 60 ; 10, 20, 30, etc.

Annual and 400 Day Clocks.   These clocks are made to run much longer than usual with one winding, by simply interposing a number of gears and pinions between the barrel and the usual train, and using a longer and stronger spring to overcome the increased friction in the train.   These clocks are usually provided with torsion pendulums.   They are made chiefly as curiosities.

Astronomical Clock.   A clock having twenty-four hours shown on the dial and a pendulum of such length as to show stellar time, which is three minutes, fifty-six seconds shorter than the mean solar day.   Also called sidereal clock.

2. A clock, or orrery, showing the comparative motion of the heavenly bodies, by means of concentric discs, rotating proportionately on a central arbor which also carries the ordinary clock hands.

Calendar Clock.   A clock which shows the progress of the calendar. In a simple calendar the mechanism has to be adjusted at the end of all months having less than thirty-one days.   In a perpetual calendar the correct indications during short months and leap years are performed without adjustment.

Carriage Clock.   A European term for a clock having a balance instead of a pendulum, so as to be readily portable.

Chiming Clock.   A clock which plays tunes, or runs through musical notes periodically.   Church clocks strike these notes on a chime, or series of bells; mantel clocks operate a music box placed in the case.

Clock Watch.   A watch which strikes the hours in passing, as distinguished from a repeater, which strikes the hours and minutes on pushing a lever.

Electric Clock.   A clock operated by a weight or spring and having a pendulum, which is controlled by electrical currents transmitted automatically by a master clock.   2.   A clock in which the winding is performed by electricity, by means of a motor placed in the case.

Equation Clock.   A clock invented about the end of the seventeenth century, which contained a device for partially rotating the dial, so as to make the length of the day indicated by the clock, coinicide with that of the solar day.

Equatorial Clock.   A clock for driving an equatorial telescope.

Locomotive Clock.   A clock adapted to be carried in the cab of a locomotive, and so constructed as to withstand the jarring and heat variations of the temperature.   They are usually made with detached lever escapement, jeweled, like a watch, and compensated for temperature.

Master Clock.   A clock which is carefully regulated and used to correct others, by electricity or otherwise.   2.   The original clock model from which others are made.

Pneumatic Clock.   One of a series of clocks governed by pulsations of air, sent to them at regular intervals through tubes which are controlled and operated by a master clock.

Repeating Clock.   The mechanism by which a clock or watch may be made to strike the hours and minutes by pulling or pushing a cord or rod, so as to tell the time without looking at the dial, was invented in in 1676, by a Wm. Derham. It immediately became popular, and the idea was taken up by many English, French and German horologists. It was at first applied only to clocks, but was subsequently put into watches as well, and forms the origin of the repeating watches of the present day.

Watchman's Clock. A clock having a paper dial, which is used to control the movements of a watchman by means of keys fastened to short chains at various portions of his beat. The various keys operate variously shaped punches which perforate the dial, and thus show the time of his presence at any particular station.

Cleaning and Repairing Clocks. In taking down clocks, prior to cleaning, it is a good plan to mark where the teeth of the wheels engage with the pinion leaves, for if there should be any slight inaccuracy the teeth may not gear so well if altered; and in striking trains the lifting pins and the run after warning will then be correct when the clock is again put together, that is assuming they were right beforehand. In many French clocks there is already such a mark, one leaf of the pinion being sloped off and a dot being made on the wheel tooth that corresponds with it. All the parts may be placed in a bath of kerosene, which forms as good a detergent as any and as they are taken out, brushed with a moderately hard clock brush; clean the pivot holes by twirling a pointed peg in each one. Tarnished gilt plates, and polished ones, if not much stained, may be restored by immersing in a cyanide bath. Badly stained polished plates may be repolished with rotten-stone used on a willow polisher or soft brush.

For the ordinary run of clocks the following course of examination may be followed with advantage: After taking the movement from its case, remove the hands, dial, minute cock, and bridge, to try the escapement with some power on, and note any faults there. Next remove the cock and pallets, and if it is a spring clock, put a peg between the escape wheel arms to prevent it from running down, and let down the spring. Here sometimes is a difficulty; if the spring has been set up too far, and the clock is fully wound, it may not be possible to move the barrel arbor sufficiently to get the click out of the rachet. In many old clocks there will be found a hole drilled at the bottom of, and between the great wheel teeth, directly over the tail of the click; so that you can put a key on the fusee square and the point of a fine joint pusher through the hole, release the click, and allow the fusee to turn gently back until it is down. Having let down the spring, try all depths and endshakes and all pivots for wide holes; if it is a striking clock, do the same with the striking train, paying particular attention to the pallet pinion front pivot to see if it is worn and the rack depth made unsafe thereby, also seeing that none of the rack teeth are bent or broken. Having noted the faults, if any, take the clock to pieces, look over all the pivots, and note those that require repolishing. Finally take out the barrel cover, and see to the condition of the springs; if a spring is exhausted or soft, several of the inner coils will be found lying closely round the arbor.

Pallets. In most cases some repairs will be required to the pallets, as these nearly always show signs of wear first; if they are not much cut, the marks can be polished out, and for this purpose a small disc of emery about three inches in diameter, mounted truly on an arbor, and run at a high speed in the lathe, will be of great assistance; finishing off with iron or steel polisher and sharp red stuff. If you have to close the pallets to make the escape correct, see that the pallet arms are not left hard, or you may break them. After making any alterations in the pallets, it may be necessary to correct the depth; should it only require a slight alteration, it will be sufficient to knock out the steady pins in the cock, and screw it on so that it can be shifted by the fingers until you have got the depth correct, then screw it tight and broach out the steady pin holes, and fit new pins. If much alteration in the depth is required, it may be necessary to put in a new back pallet hole; this can be made from a piece of hollow bushing, broached out and turned true on an arbor. It is not safe to rely on the truth of this bushing, unless it is turned on an arbor first. The hole in the plate is now drawn in the direction required with a round file, and opened with a broach from the inside until the bushing enters about half way. Of course, in finishing broaching the hole, you will roughen the extremities to form rivets. Drive the bushing in, and rivet it with a round-faced punch from the outside; reveres it, and resting the bushing on the punch, rivet the inside with the pene of the hammer; remove any excess of brass with the file, chamfer out the oil sink, and stone off any file marks; finally open the hole for the pivot to the proper size.

Making New Pinions. Freqently one meets with an escape pinion that has become so badly cut or worn as to be useless, and if a new one cannot be purchased it will be necessary to make it from pinion wire. In sectoring the pinion wire to the wheel, bear in mind that it will become slightly smaller in filing up. Considerable practice is required to make good-shaped pinions quickly and well. A piece of pinion wire of a slightly greater diameter than the pinion is to be when finished, is cut about one-eighth of an inch longer than required, and the position of the leaves or head marked by two notches with a file. The leaved portion of the wire that is not required, is filed down on a filing block, taking care not to remove any of the arbor in so doing; a center is then filed at each end true with the arbor, and then projected through a hole in a runner and turned.

Get the pinion head quite true, by straightening the arbor if necessary, and turn the arbor and faces of the pinion square and smooth. The pinion is now filed out true, using a hollow-edged bottoming file for the spaces, and a pinion-rounding file for the sides of the leaves. The file marks are taken out with fine emery and oil; the polishers may be pieces of oak, about a quarter of an inch thick, five inches broad, and six inches long, used endwise of the grain. One end is planed to a V shape to go between the leaves, and the other cut into grooves by rubbing it on the sharp edges of the pinion itself, which speedily cuts it into grooves to fit. The pinion is rested while polishing in a groove cut in a block of soft wood, which allows it to give to the hand, and keeps it flat. When the file marks are all out, the pinion is ready for hardening. Twist a piece of stout binding wire around it, and cover it with soap; heat it carefully in a clear fire, and quench it in a pail of water that has been stirred into a whirlpool by an assistant, taking care to dip it vertically. When dried, it is covered with tallow and held over a clear fire until the tallow catches fire; it is allowed to burn for a moment, and then blown out and left to cool. The leaves are polished out with crocus and oil in the same way that they previously were with emery. Now, if the pinion is put in the centers and tried, it will probably be found to have warped a little in hardening. This is corrected in the following manner. The rounding side of the arbor is laid on a soft iron stake, and the hollow side stretched by a series of light blows with the pene of the hammer, given at regular intervals along the curve. Having got the leaves to run quite true by this means, turn both arbors true, and polish them with the double sticks—these are simply two pieces of thin boxwood, about three-eighths of an inch wide and three inches long, hinged together at one extremity and open at the other; between these the arbor is pinched with oil and fine emery, and they are traversed from end to end, to take out the graver marks. The brass for the collet, to which the wheel is rivited, is now drilled, broached and turned roughly to shape on an arbor. The position on the pinion arbor is marked with a fine nick, and the collet soldered on with soft solder and a spirit-lamp taking care not to draw the temper of the arbor when doing so. Wash it out in soda and water, and polish the arbor with crocus, turn the collet true and fit the wheel on. If the pinion face is to be polished, it is now done, the facing tool being a piece of iron about one-sixteenth of an inch thick, with a slit in it to fit over the arbor with slight fredom, used with oil-stone dust first, and then sharp red stuff.

Sometimes cut pinions are used for the centers, and then the body of the arbor is sufficiently large to allow the front pivot to be made from the solid arbor, but if the center pinions are made from pinion wire in the manner just described, the leaves are beaten together on an anvil to form a solid mass for the front pivot. This piece should project sufficiently far through the pivot hole to allow it to be squared to receive the friction spring which drives the motion work. In cases where this pivot is much cut, it may be turned down and have a steel tube soldered on to form a new one; as these pinions are very long and flexible, some difficulty will be experienced in turning this pivot unless a backrest is used to support the arbor, and prevent it springing from the graver.

Worn Pinions. In common clocks, where both third and escape pinions are worn by the wheel teeth, if the pivots are still in good condition, the third pinion leaves can be turned back from the outer end rather more than the thickness of the center wheel, the pivot shoulder also turned back the same distance, the pivot re-made, burnished and shortened. Then the pivot hole in the front plate is opened with a broach to about twice its original size, and a bushing with a good large shoulder is turned true on an arbor and riveted into the plate. The thickness of the shoulder of this bushing will depend on the amount the arbor was shortened, and must be such as just to give correct end shake to the pinion. By shifting the third wheel and its pinion thus, a fresh portion of both the third and escape pinions is brought into action, and as good results will be obtained as by putting in two new pinions.

Escape Wheel. Often, in old clocks, the escape wheel is so much out of truth that anything like close escaping is out of the question, as so much drop has to be given to enable some teeth to escape, that nearly all the power is lost; in such a case a new wheel is a necessity, and if you want to get a good hard wheel you must make the blank yourself. Take a piece of hard sheet brass, about twice as thick as the wheel is to be when finished, and cut from it a square sufficiently large for your wheel; then with a hammer with a slightly rounded face, reduce it to nearly the thickness you require. In hammering go regularly over the surface, so that no two consecutive blows fall on the same spot; and when one side is done turn it over, and treat the other in the same way. File one side flat, find the center and drill a hole nearly as large as required for the collet; cement it with shellac to a flat-faced chuck in the lathe, and center it true by the center hole. Mark with the graver the size of the weeel, and with a narrow cutter remove the corners; face the blank with the graver, and turn it to size, leaving it slightly larger than the old wheel; knock it off the chuck and reverse it, bringing the turned face next the chuck, turn that face flat and to thickness, and it is ready for cutting. After it is cut, remove any burs with a fine file, and mark a circle to show the thickness of the room, and on that circle divide it into the number of arms it is to have; mark also a smaller circle slightly larger than the collet on which it is to be rivited, draw lines through the divisions in the outer circle and the center of wheel to mark the center of the arms. Drill a hole between each of the arms to enable you to enter the file, which, to begin with, should be a coarse round one, then follow with the crossing file, holding the wheel between a piece of thick card in the vice; finish by draw-filing the arms and crosses with a very smooth file, followed by a half-round scraper used as when draw-filing. This leaves the surface smooth and ready for the burnisher, of which tool two different shapes will be required, one oval, and the other half-round. These tools, when in use, require to be repeatedly cleaned on a piece of leather, and passed over the palm of the hand, to prevent tearing up the surface of the metal. The wheel teeth are now polished out with a short-haired brush and fine crocus and oil; then take out the file marks from both sides of the wheel with a good stone and oil, and it is ready for riveting on. Take a slight chamfer out of the front of the wheel-hole, and roughen the surface of it with a graver; turn the collet down to fit in tightly, and rivet it on with a half round punch, taking care to strike light blows and keep the wheel turning while riveting. It is then ready for stoning off and polishing with a flat wood polisher and fine crocus and oil. In crossing out a small delicate wheel, it is a good plan to fasten it with shellac to a flat plate of brass, having a hole in it rather larger than the inside of the rim of the wheel. In this way all danger of bending a tooth of the wheel accidentally is avoided, and the crossing can be finished without removing it from the plate.

Striking Work. The parts most frequently found to require repair in the striking train of clocks, are the pivots of the upper pinions, especially those of the fly, pin wheel, and pallet wheel. If a pivot is only slightly cut, it can be re-turned and repolished, and a new hole put in; but if to entirely remove the marks the pivot would have to be much reduced in diameter, a new pivot is the only resource.

New Pivots. In putting in a new pivot, the arbor may be centered in the lathe. A short stiff drill should be used, ground to cut in one direction only, rather thin at the point, and for a short distance behind the cuttings quite parallel. The drill should be left quite hard, or if a soft arbor is to be drilled, it may be tempered to a light straw color, and the rest of the shank rather softer. If this is lubricated with either turpentine or benzine, but little difficulty will be found in drilling the arbor; the hole should be rather deeper than the pivot is long, and in size rather larger than the pivot is to be. A piece of staff steel is now centered, hardened and blazed off, and turned down true to fit the hole, and very slightly tapered; if too tapered, the arbor will split in driving it in; when it fits half-way in, draw-file it carefully, and cut it to length, filing the end off square. A few blows of a light hammer will fix it firmly in position, then the extreme end of the pivot can be turned to a center, through a hole in the lantern runner. The pivot can now be turned down to size, polished, burnished, and the end rounded up. Should the pallet wheel front pivot require repairing, a center may be cut with the graver in the end of the square, then a male center can be used, and the pivot turned and polished in the usual manner.

Gathering Pallet and Rack. In many old clocks, particularly in long case striking-clocks, the rack and gathering pallet are frequently found in a very bad condition; the pallet perhaps fitting the square very badly, thus making its depths with the rack uncertain. In the absence of a proper forging, a pallet may be made from a square bar of steel, thick enough to give the requisite length of boss. Mark the length of the tail of the pallet, and file it down to almost the required thickness; file also the opposite face of the bar smooth and flat, Mark the position of the hole, and drill it at right angles to the face; the diameter of the hole will be the same as the small end of the square on the pallet pinion, measuring across the flats, of course. Start the corners of the square in the position required with a good square file; then take a piece of broken square file of rather a coarse cut, and of the same taper as the square on the pinion; oil it, and drive it in with a few light blows of the hammer, turn the pallet over and knock it out again, turning it a quarter round each time you withdraw it. In a few minutes you can thus form a good square straight hole, and fit it accurately to pinion-square. Put it on an arbor and turn the ends square and to length; see that the tail is at right angles to the hole, also file the boss to form and shape the lip; this is usually made straight and the back sloped off, consequently it scrapes the rack teeth with its extreme end only, and wears quickly. As the pallet is in reality a pinion with only one leaf, its durability is increased by curving the face similiar to a pinion leaf cut in half. The end of the tail of the pallet should be rounded and finished off smoothly at right angles to its face, its length such that it is well free of the pin in the rack when gathering the last tooth but one, and rests fairly on the pin when the rack is up. If the tail of the pallet were left quite straight, and the end filed off square, there would be a danger of the rack being held up by the pallet, particularly when the pin in the rack is planted lower down than it should be, its proper position being rather above the top of the the teeth. The tail of the pallet is therefore curved to just throw the rack off.

If any of the rack teeth are damaged at the points, it may be necessary to slightly top all the teeth and file them up again; only the backs or curved sides of the teeth, should be filled, finally taking the burr off with the oil-stone slip. To make the depth correct again, the rack arm is hammered a little, to stretch it; care must be taken to keep the teeth truly in circle, also to see that they are well free of the boss of the gathering pallet, not only when it is in position resting on the rack pin, but also when it has moved into the position that it would be in when the clock has warned. If the boss of the pallet is not perfectly concentric, it may be just foul of the rack teeth in this position, although free when tried with the pallet resting on the stop pin.

Run. Clocks are occasionally met with in which the hammer begins to lift as the clock warns, with a lot of useless run after the hammer has fallen. This is just the reverse of what should be the case, as the more run before the hammer begins to lift, the less probability there will be of the clock failing to strike when the oil gets thick.

Rack Tail. A frequent source of trouble in some old clocks is the spring tail to the rack; it is intended to allow the hands to set forward without allowing the clock to strike. If the spring is weak and the rack spring strong, it sometimes gives a little and allows the rack to fall lower than it should, consequently a wrong hour is struck; an excess of end-shake to the hour wheel will also cause this fault, if the snail is mounted on the hour-wheel pipe. This is, of course, easily corrected by a thicker collet in front of the minute hand.

Pendulum Suspension Spring. This in ordinary clocks gets but little attention. The best material is straight lengths of steel, to be obtained from the mainspring maker, of various thicknesses. The chops at the top of the spring are usually made either by folding a piece of brass over to form both sides, or by cutting a slit in a piece of brass of suitable thickness, and closing the slit down with the hammer upon the spring until it fits it. A much better plan is to make the chops of two pieces of brass, and rivet them together; the bottom edges should be slightly rounded off to prevent any chance of the spring breaking at that point, as it sometimes does if the edges are left sharp. Most suspension springs err in being too thick, but it is not always advisable to substitute a much thinner spring, especially should there be but little room for the pendulum to vibrate in, as the arc may be so much increased as to cause the pendulum to strike the sides of the case, rendering it necessary to substitute a lighter weight or a weaker mainspring. The slit in the top of the pendulum is also generally cut with a thin saw, and then closed in; but there is no certainty of keeping it straight this way, and it is better to file a true slot and fit a slip of brass to fill it up to the proper size, thus keeping the spring true with the rod.

Mainsprings. In selecting a new mainspring it is often not safe to accept the thickness of the old one as a guide. Mainsprings now are made more elastic and of a better surface than formerly; and with a pin pallet escapement, having but little recoil, a stronger mainspring may cause the pins to bottom in the escape wheel, or, if there is but little room in the case the pendulum may strike the sides. This latter diffi_culty is also likely to arise with a half-dead escapement.

When a spring of proper length is broken close to the eye it will be sufficient to soften the inner end, punch a fresh hole for the hook, and carefully bend round another eye.—*Britten.*

CLOCKMAKERS' COMPANY. In 1631 the clockmakers residing within the liberties and suburbs of the city of London petitioned the crown for a charter incorporating all the clockmakers, both free and foreign, who practiced clockmaking in the city of London, and ten miles compass, by the name of the Master, Wardens, and Fellowship of the art or mystery of clockmaking of the City of London, constituting them one body corporate and politic in deed and in name, to have and continue forever. By this charter, power was granted to elect a master, three wardens and ten assistants; to make laws for the government of all persons using the art within the city of London; and also to regulate the manner in which all persons using the art throughout England and Wales shall carry on the same, with power to fine and punish offenders against their laws. All apprentices were to be bound to some free brother of the company of clockmakers for the term of seven years. They were empowered to seize and break work if unlawfully made, or made of bad materials, or to cause the same to be amended and made perfect. Faulty and deceitful work could be seized in the King's name. Persons who imported clocks, watches, sun-dials, or cases for the same, were compelled to bring them to the company's hall to be examined and marked, upon pain of forfeiture. They were empowered to search for such imported work, not Hall-marked, to seize the same and prosecute the offenders. In compliance with the Act of Parliament of 1632, the acts and ordinances made by the officers and fellows, were accepted, ratified and approved, on August 11, 1632. The following were named in the Royal Charter to be the first officers: Master, David Ramsay; Wardens, Henry Archer, John Wellowe and Sampson Shelton; Assistants, James Vantrollyer, John Smith, Francis Forman, John Harris, Richard Morgan, Samuel Lynaker, John Charlton, John Midnale, Simon Bartram and Edward East.

The first meeting of the company was held October 12, 1632. Strange to relate, says Nelthropp, the company has never possessed a hall, but its meetings have been regularly held in some city tavern, even to the present time.

CLUB TOOTH. The form of tooth shown in Fig. 95 and for lever escape wheels, having a part of the impulse angle on the tooth. See *Lever Escapement.*

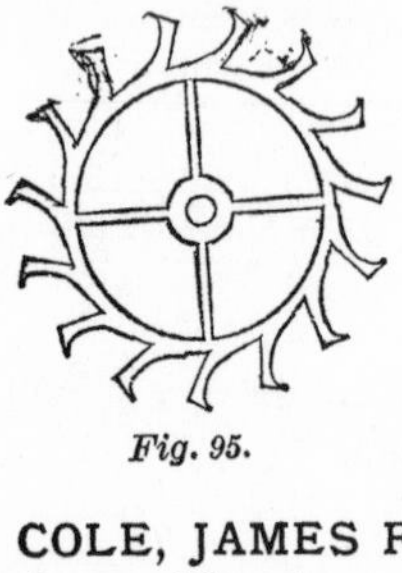

Fig. 95.

CLUTCH. A mechanism for connecting two shafts with each other, or with wheels, in such a manner that they may be readily disengaged.

COCK. The horizontal bracket which holds the end of a staff. A vertical or hang-down bracket is called a potance. See *Balance Bridge.*

COLE, JAMES FERGUSON. An able watchmaker and expert springer of London. He devoted considerable attention to the lever escapement, and devised several forms of it. He was born in 1799 and died in 1880.

COLLET. A collar or band of metal.   2. A small collar fitted friction tight to the balance staff, and which is slotted to receive the lower end of the hairspring.   3. The part of a ring in which a stone is set.   4. The under side of a brilliant cut stone.

COLLET WRENCH. A tool for twisting a hairspring collet to position, which consists of a metal handle, hollow at the extremity for the reception of the pivot, and having a minute wedge-shaped projection from its face, which enters the slit in the collet, allowing it to be turned readily.

COLORING GOLD ARTICLES.   See *Cleansing, Pickling and Polishing.*

COMPASS. An instrument consisting of a magnetized needle turning freely on a point, used to determine horizontal directions in reference to the cardinal points.

COMPASSES. An instrument for measuring figures, describing circles, etc., consisting of two pointed limbs usually pivoted together at the top.

COMPENSATION The correction of the effect of variations of temperature on the vibrations of the balance or pendulum. The first person, says Nelthrop, who seems to have observed that metals changed their length, by changes of temperature, was Godfroi Wendelinus, Canon of Conde, in Flanders, about the year 1648.   John Ellicott, a watchmaker of London, invented a pyrometer, for testing the expansions and contraction of metals, about 1740.   About the year 1715, Graham endeavored to make a pendulum rod that should counteract the effect of heat and cold, but did not succeed.   In 1722 he made a clock with a mercurial pendulum, or rather, instead of a metal bob he used a vase filled with mercury which he attached to the end of the rod, which proved quite successful and was the first attempt at compensation.   In 1726, Harrison completed his gridiron pendulum, and there is little doubt that he was the first to apply compensation to the balance of a watch, which he did in 1749; but as there is no written evidence, the honor was claimed by F. Berthoud, who in 1766 made a watch with compensation balance, for Pinchbeck, a London watchmaker, for his majesty George III. Nelthrop thus describes it: The compensation piece was made of brass and steel pinned together; one end was fixed to the fore-plate, the other was made to act on a short arm projecting from a movable arbor; a longer arm, having the curb pins in it, moved nearly in the circle of the outer coil of the spiral spring. Mudge invented a compensation for heat and cold, which he applied to his time keepers. His system was more simple than that invented by Berthoud, but acted in the same manner on the spiral spring. He applied it in 1774 to a watch. Abraham Breguet invented and applied to his watches a V-shaped compensation curb, made to correspond in a great measure with the circumference of the balance. Nelthrop describes it as a curb being made of brass and steel, the brass being inside, and so arranged, by being screwed on to the extremity of the regulating index, that the balance-spring vibrated between one end of it, formed into a heel, and a fixed pin. The action was simple: in cold weather the space between the heel of the compensation curb and the pin, became enlarged, through the contraction of the compound laminæ; consequently the balance-spring had more room to vibrate in. In warm weather the laminæ expanded, thereby reducing the space, and contracting the expansion of the spring. The defect in this curb was the difficulty of adjustment, which caused it to be abandoned.

Arnold had recourse to various experiments in order to obtain compensation, and finally adopted a system totally different from any of the preceding ones. He placed the compensation in the balance alone, as will

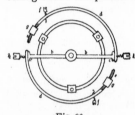

Fig. 96.

be seen by the diagram, judging that it would not be desirable to interfere with the pendulum spring, but better to allow it perfect freedom, as there would then be greater probability of its performance being good. Fig. 96 illustrates this balance. Let *b, b* represent the arms of the balance, which is screwed upon a collet fixed to the end of the axis. At extremities of these arms are two shoulders, *c, c,* against which, by means of two screws, are fixed the expansion or compensation pieces, *d, d.* These expansion pieces are each composed of two laminæ, the outside being of brass, the inside of steel. At *e, e* the steel laminæ are rounded off and tapped to receive the brass weights *g, g ; f, f* are small screws designed to adjust for small differences. At *h, h* are screws to regulate the mean time.

The next important improvement in balances was made by Earnshaw in 1802. His balance was practically the same in construction as Arnold's, except that one balance rim only was used; he omitted the inner ring altogether.

COMPENSATION BALANCE. A balance for a watch or chronometer which compensates the effect of variations of temperature on the vibrations of the balance. See *Balance.*

Berthoud, in 1773, tabulated the effect of temperature on one of his marine watches. He reckoned that in passing from 32° to 90° (Fahr.) it lost per diem by—

    Expansion of the Balance ---- -------------- 62 secs.
    The loss of Spring's Elastic Force------------312 "
    Elongation of the Spring------------------- 19 "

                            393, or 6m. 33s.

Doubtless Berthoud's observation was correct as far as the total amount of the temperature error goes, but there appears to be no warrant for assuming that a part of the loss was due to elongation of the spring. Mr. Wright, of the London Horological Institute, first pointed out the fallacy in this reasoning of Berthoud's in 1882, although the statement appears to have been accepted by all authorities for so many years. Mr. Wright called attention to the fact that the thickness and the width of spring would be increased in precisely the same proportion as the length, and as the strength of a spring varies as the cube of its thickness, the spring would be absolutely stronger for a rise of temperature if the relative dimensions only were considered.

Sir G. B. Airy, by experiment in 1859, showed that a chronometer with a plain uncompensated brass balance lost on its rate 6.11 secs. in 24 hours for each degree of increase in temperature.

COMPENSATION PENDULUM. A pendulum in which the effect of changes of temperature on the length of the rod is so counteracted that the distance of the center of oscillation from the center of suspension remains invariable.

COMPENSATION CURB. A bar composed of two metals, usually brass and steel, free to act at one end but retained at the other, the free end carrying the curb pins that regulate the acting length of a hairspring. Not used in American watches and found only in old watches of European make.

CONCAVE. The internal surface of a hollow rounded body. The reverse of convex.

CONICAL PENDULUM. A pendulum whose bob moves in a circle. See *Pendulum.*

CONICAL PIVOT. A pivot whose shoulders are of conical form used only in pivots having end stones. Fig. 97. See *Balance Staff.*

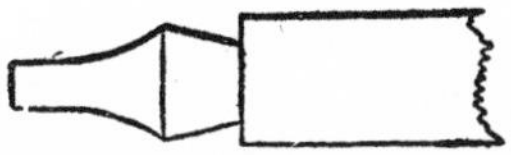

Fig. 97.

CONOIDAL. Having the form of a cone.

CONTRATE WHEEL. A crown wheel. A wheel whose teeth are set at right angles to its plane and used ordinarily as a gear wheel for transmitting power from one shaft to another, standing at right angles to it. The escape wheel of the verge escapement.

CONVERSION. A term in watch-making signifying that a change of escapement is made, as a movement originally having a duplex escapement is changed to a lever escapement.

CONVEX. Rising or swelling into a rounded body. The reverse of concave.

CONVEXO-CONCAVE. Convex on one side and concave on the other.

CONVEXO-CONVEX. Convex on both sides.

COPPER. A metal of a reddish color, malleable, ductile and tenacious. It fuses at 2,000° Fah. and has a specific gravity varying from 8.8 to 8.9. It has a breaking strain of 48,000 lbs. per square inch. In horology it is employed as a backing for enameled watch dials; in the construction of gridiron compensation pendulums; in the manufacture of compensation balances, etc. When mixed with tin it forms bell-metal and bronze and with zinc it forms brass and other alloys. See *Alloys.*

CORUNDUM. The earth alumina, as found native in a crystalline state, including sapphire, which is the fine blue variety; the oriental ruby or red sapphire; the oriental amethyst, or purple sapphire. It is the hardest known substance next to the diamond. The non-transparent variety, dark-colored and granular is known as emery. See *Carborundum.*

CORUNDUM-WHEELS. Wheels faced with corundum, (emery) or made of a composition of corundum and cement. See *Emery Wheels.*

COUNTER BALANCE. A mass of metal placed on the opposite side of a wheel to that to which a crank is attached to compensate for the weight of the latter.

COUNTERMARK. A mark attached to gold and silver-ware of English make to attest its standard. See *Hall Mark.*

COUNTERSHAFT. A short shafting mounted on two uprights, used extensively by American watchmakers. It is indispensable in using milling tools, wheel cutters, and pivot polishers.

Fig. 98.

Fig. 98 illustrates one of several patterns of countershafts used by watchmakers. In some of the patterns the uprights extend through the top of the bench and are held firmly in place by means of nuts or thumb screws. The pattern shown in the illustration is mounted on a solid metal base which can be fastened to the bench by means of screws. The advantages of using a countershaft are three fold: first, you are able to regulate your speed perfectly; second, your belt is carried to the back of the bench where it is out of the way instead of coming down in front of the head; and third, you obviate the necessity of having holes in your bench on each side of the lathe, that small articles may drop through.

COUNTERSINK. To enlarge the outer end of a hole for the reception of the head of a screw, bolt, etc. A tool used to turn out or

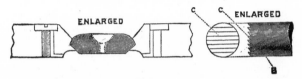

Fig. 99.

countersink. Fig. 99 illustrates Happersberger's patent, flat-bottomed countersinks, which are designed for making or deepening flat bottomed countersinks for screw heads of any kind. The screw-thread or hole will not be injured in using these tools. Fig. 100 illustrates a set of

Fig. 100.

wheel countersinks made with cutters on one end and burnishers on the other. Countersinks are also made from steel in the form of drills and from emery in the form of a cone with metal handle for revolving. The emery countersink will be found very useful for large holes and for trimming the edges of holes in enamel dials.

CRANK. The bent portion of an axis serving as a handle or connection for communicating circular motion, as the crank on a steam engine. To twist or distort, as applied to metals.

CREMAILLERE. The winding rack of a repeating watch.

CRESCENT. The concave formed in the roller of the lever escapement to allow the passage of the safety pin.

CROCUS. Sesquioxide of iron used with oil for polishing brass and steel work. Crystals of sulphate of iron are subjected to a great heat, and then graded into polishing powders of various degrees of fineness. The more calcined part is of a bluish purple color, coarser and harder than the less calcined and is known as crocus The less calcined and finer portion is of a scarlet color and is known as rouge.

CROWN-WHEEL. A wheel whose teeth are set at right angles to its plane. A contrate wheel. The escape wheel of the verge escapement is a crown wheel.

CRUCIBLE. A melting pot capable of enduring great heat, without injury and used for melting metals. It is made of clay or clay compounded with black lead and other materials.

CRUTCH. A wire fixed to the pallet staff arbor of a clock. The free end of it communicates impulse to the pendulum. It either passes into a longitudinal slit in the pendulum rod, or is formed into two fingers to embrace it. The pendulum rod is sometimes fitted with a flat piece of brass to work in the crutch. Should this be very closely fitted and the pendulum spring a little twisted, the clock will stop, a fault occasionally overlooked. Where the crutch is in contact with the pendulum rod it should be very slightly oiled.

CRYSTAL. A term applied to the glass of a watch case. Crystals for watches were first used between the years 1615 and 1620.

CUMMING, ALEXANDER. A celebrated clockmaker of England, who was born about 1732 and died at Pentonville in 1814. He was the author of a book called "Elements of Clock and Watch Work," which he published in 1766. There stands in Buckingham Palace to-day a clock made by Cumming for George III., which registers the height of the barometer every day throughout the year. He was paid $10,000 for this clock, and received $1,000 per annum for looking after it.

CURB PINS. The two brass pins that stand on either side of the hairspring near its stud attachment, and are attached to the regulator. They effect the time of the vibration of the balance according as they are shifted by means of the regulator to or from the point of attachment of the spring. Some authors advise timing in positions by the curb pins. This should never be attempted. The regulator should always stand as near the center of the index as possible. The curb pins should never be far from the stud and should be just wide enough apart to let the spring move between them and no more. Instead of disturbing the curb pins when timing in positions, add to or take from the weight of the balance. See *Balance Screw Washers.*

CUSIN, CHARLES. A watch manufacturer of Autun, Burgundy, who in consequence of the great persecutions which protestants had to endure, went and settled in Geneva in 1587, where, it is claimed, he was the first to establish the watch trade.

CUSTER, JACOB D. The third maker of American watches, Jacob D. Custer, was born in Montgomery County, Pa., in 1809. In 1831 he went to Norristown, Pa., and began the manufacture of "Grandfather" clocks. In 1840 he began the first of a series of twelve watches. The writer has in his possession one of these watches, which is numbered 5 and bears the date February 4, 1843. It is a three-quarter plate, lever escapement, and about 14 size. It has a fuzee evidently of English make, as is also the dial. The balance bridge is made of steel and is countersunk into the plate so that it is flush with the surface of the upper plate. The rest of the movement was undoubtedly made by Custer, including the case, which is of silver and of the old English type of boxed cases. The gilding is extremely thin. In 1842 Prof. Bache, of the U. S. Coast Survey asked him to make an estimate on clocks to propel lights in the government light houses. His estimate was $200, and he subsequently furnished several hundred of them. He had little or no educational advantages, and never learned a trade, and his sole knowledge of mechanics was acquired by associating with those who learned a mechanical trade and the knowledge gained by years of experience and experiment. He built several large clocks, one of which may still be seen in the Norristown Court House. He died in 1879.

CYCLOID. A curve generated by a point in the plane of a circle, when the circle is rolled along a straight line, keeping always in the same plane.

The path through which a pendulum travels, to secure uniformity in the time of its vibration, through arcs different in extent, should be cycloidal.

CYLINDER ESCAPEMENT. The cylinder escapement was invented by George Graham about 1700, and was an improvement upon and a development of an idea conceived by Tompion, who had prior to this time, in 1695, invented an escapement somewhat similar. It is a frictional dead beat escapement as distinguished from a detached escapement. It was, at the time of its introduction, considered of but little value, as its principles were not thoroughly understood, it was difficult to manufacture, and above all the tendency to excessive wear of the acting surfaces. The Swiss solved the problem by making both the cylinder and escape wheel of steel and hardening them.

The balance with this escapement is mounted on a hollow cylinder large enough in the bore to admit a tooth of the escape wheel. Nearly one-half of the cylinder is cut away where the teeth enter, and impulse is given to the balance by the teeth, which are wedge-shaped, rubbing against the edge of the cylinder as they enter and leave. The teeth of

Fig. 101*.

the verge escapement lie in a vertical plane in the plan of a watch, and the term horizontal, therefore, fairly distinguished the cylinder escapement when it was introduced, but now that all the escapements in general use answer to the title, "cylinder escapement" appears to be the more suitable description.

ACTION OF THE ESCAPEMENT.

Fig. 101 is a plan of the cylinder escapement, in which a point of a tooth of the escape wheel is pressed against the outside of the shell of the cylinder. As the cylinder, on which the balance is mounted, moves around in the direction of the arrow, the wedge-shaped tooth of the escape wheel pushes into the cylinder, thereby giving it impulse. The tooth cannot escape at the other side of the cylinder, for the shell of the cylinder at this point is rather more than half a circle; but its point rests against the inner side of the shell until the balance completes its

---

* *a.* Escape Wheel.
   b. Cylinder.

f. Tooth removed, showing Stalk on which Teeth are supported.

vibration and returns, when the tooth which was inside the cylinder escapes, and the point of the succeeding tooth is caught on the outside of the shell.

The teeth rise on stalks from the body of the escape wheel, and the cylinder is cut away just below the acting part of the exit side, leaving only one-fourth of a circle in order to allow as much vibration as possible. This will be seen very plainly by examining Fig. 102, which is an elevation of the cylinder to an enlarged scale.

PROPORTION OF THE ESCAPEMENT.

The escape wheel has fifteen teeth formed to give impulse to the cylinder during from 20° to 40° of its vibration each way. Lower angles are as a rule used with large rather than with small sized watches, but to secure the best result either extreme must be avoided. In an escapement with very slight inclines to the wheel teeth, the first part of the tooth does not work, as the tooth drops

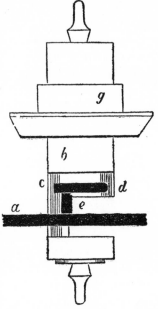

Fig. 102.*

into the lip of the cylinder some distance up the plane. On the other hand, a very steep tooth is almost sure to set in action as the oil thickens. The diameter of the cylinder, its thickness, and the length of the wheel teeth are all co-related. The size of the cylinder with relation to the wheel also varies somewhat with the angle of impulse, a very high angle requiring a slightly larger cylinder than a low one. If a cylinder of average thickness is desired for an escapement with medium im-

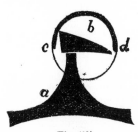

Fig. 103†.

pulse, its external diameter may be made equal to the extreme diameter of the escape wheel × .115.

Then to set out the escapement, if a lift of say 30° be decided on, a circle on which the points of the teeth will fall is drawn within one

---

*Elevation of Cylinder and One Tooth of Escape Wheel therein.

†Plan of Cylinder and One Tooth of Escape Wheel therein.

a, Escape Wheel; *b*, Cylinder; *c*, Entering Lip of Cylinder; *d*, Exit Lip of Cylinder; *e*, Passage for Escape Wheel; *g*, Collet for Balance.

representing the extreme diameter of the escape wheel at a distance from
it equal to 30° of the circumference of the cylinder. Midway between
these two circles the cylinder is planted. (See Fig. 104). If the point
of one tooth is shown resting on the cylinder, a space of half a degree
should be allowed for freedom between the opposite side of the cylinder
and the heel of the next tooth. From the heel of one tooth to the heel
of the next = 24° of the circumference of the wheel $(\frac{360}{15})$ = 24), and
from the point of one tooth to the point of the next also

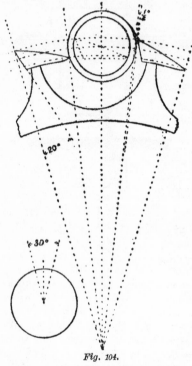

= 24°, so that the teeth may
now be drawn. They are
extended within the inner-
most dotted circle to give
them a little extra substance,
and their tips are rounded a
little, leaving the points of the
impulse planes the most advanced. The backs of the
teeth diverge from a radial
line from 12° to 30° to give
the cylinder clearance; a high-
angled tooth requiring to be
cut back more than a low one.
A curve, whose radius is about
two-thirds that of the wheel,
is suitable for rounding the
impulse planes of the teeth.
The internal diameter of the
cylinder should be such as to
allow a little freedom for the
tooth. The acting part of the
shell of the cylinder should
be a trifle less than seven-
twelfths of a whole circle,
with the entering and exit
lips rounded as shown in the

Fig. 104.

enlarged plan, Fig. 103, the former both ways, and the latter from the
inside only. This rounding of the lips of the cylinder adds a little to
the impulse beyond what would be given by the angle on the wheel
teeth alone. The diameter of the escape wheel is usually half that of
the balance, rather under than over.

EXAMINATION OF THE ESCAPEMENT.

See that cylinder and wheel are perfectly upright. Remove the balance spring, and put the cylinder and cock in their places. Then with a
little power on, and a wedge of cork under the balance to check its

motion, try if all the escape wheel teeth have sufficient drop, both inside and out. If the drop is sufficient inside with none outside, the wheel is too small; if the reverse, the wheel is too large—that is, provided the cylinder is planted the correct depth. If some of the teeth only are without necessary freedom, make a hole in thin sheet brass of such a size that one of the teeth that has proper shake will just enter. Use this as a gauge to shorten the full teeth by. For this purpose use either steel and oil-stone dust, or a sapphire file, polish well with metal and red stuff, and finish with a burnisher. Be careful to operate on the noses of the teeth only, and round them both ways, so that a mere point is in contact with the cylinder. If the inside drop is right, and there is no outside drop with any of the teeth, although it would indicate a wheel too small, it may be prudent to change the cylinder for one of the same inside diameter, but thinner, rather than remove the wheel, for it often happens that a larger wheel would not clear the fourth pinion.

If the teeth of the escape wheel are too high or too low in passing the opening of the cylinder, the wheel should be placed on a cylinder of soft brass or zinc small enough to go inside the teeth, with a hole through it, and with a slightly concaved faced. A hollow punch is placed over the middle of the wheel while it is resting on the concave face of the brass or zinc cylinder, and one or two light taps with a hammer will bend the wheel sufficiently. In fact, care must be taken not to overdo it. It rarely happens that the wheel is free neither of the top nor bottom plug, but should this be the case sufficient clearance may be obtained by deepening the opening with a steel polisher and oil-stone dust, or with a sapphire file. A cylinder with too high an opening is bad, for the oil is drawn away from the teeth by the escape wheel.

If a cylinder pivot is bent, it may very readily be straightened by placing a bushing of a proper size over it.

When the balance spring is at rest, the balance should have to be moved an equal amount each way before a tooth escapes. By gently pressing the fourth wheel with a peg this may be tried. There is a dot on the balance and three dots on the plate to assist in estimating the lift. When the balance is at rest, the dot on the balance should be opposite to the center dot on the plate. The escapement will then be beat, that is, provided the dots are properly placed, which should be tested. Turn the balance from its point of rest until a tooth just drops, and note the position of the dot on the balance with reference to one of the outer dots on the plate. Turn the balance in the opposite direction until a tooth drops again, and if the dot on the balance is then in the same position with reference to the outer dot, the escapement will be in beat. The two outer dots should mark the extent of the lifting, and the dot on the balance would then be coincident with them as the teeth dropped when tried in this way; but the dots may be a little too wide or too close, and it will, therefore, be sufficient if the dot on the balance bears the same *relative* position to them as just explained; but if it is found that the lift is unequal from the point of rest, the balance spring collet must be shifted in the direction of the least lift until the lift is equal. A new mark should then be made on the balance opposite to the central dot on the plate.

When the balance is at rest, the banking pin in the balance should be opposite to the banking stud in the cock, so as to give equal vibration on both sides. This is important for the following reason: The banking pin allows nearly a turn of vibration, and the shell of the cylinder is but little over half a turn, so that as the outside of the shell gets around toward the center of the escape wheel, the point of a tooth may escape and jamb the cylinder unless the vibration is pretty equally divided. When the banking is properly adjusted, bring the balance around until banking pin is against the stud; there should then be a perceptible shake between the cylinder and the plane of the escape wheel. Try this with the banking pin, first against one and then against the other side of the stud. If there is no shake the wheel may be freed by taking a little off the edge of the passage of the cylinder where it fouls the wheel, by means of a sapphire file, or a larger banking pin may be substituted at the judgment of the operator. See that the banking pin and stud are perfectly dry and clean before leaving them; a sticky banking often stops a watch. Cylinder watches and timepieces, after going for a few months, sometimes increase their vibration so much as to persistently bank. To meet this fault a weaker mainspring may be used, or a larger balance, or a wheel with a smaller angle of impulse. By far the quickest and best way is to very slightly top the wheel by holding a piece of Arkansas stone against the teeth afterward polishing with boxwood and red stuff. So little, taken off the wheel in this way as to be hardly imperceptible will have great effect.

Fitting New Cylinder and Plugs. In most cases of broken cylinders the upper half is left while the lower and most important part is missing. Take total length over all first, the same as in replacing staff, which can be done by the use of the Staff Length Gauge, (see *Gauges*), and then measure the length of the old cylinder from the under side of the hub to the end of the top pivot, and the difference between the two measurements will give the length of the lower part of cylinder and pivot, and this will serve as a guide in selecting an unfinished cylinder of proper length. The cylinders and also cylinder plugs can be purchased from material houses so cheaply that it will scarcely pay the watchmaker to make them. See *Cylinder Plugs*. Having selected a cylinder proceed to center it in the lathe in a finely centered chuck, leaving the lower end exposed. Turn the lower pivot first; then finish off the lower plug, and if necessary, turn off any surplus body of shell from the lower part of the cylinder as occasion demands. For obtaining the requisite measurements for the work, the little tool shown in Fig. 19 and the Staff or Cylinder Height Gauge shown under *Gauges* will be found useful. Saunier advocates the use of experimental cylinders, and suggests that the workman will do well to make two or three different sizes during his leisure moments. They can be made from the cylinders kept in stock by material dealers. The cylinder and lower plug are better to be in one piece to increase the strength; the slot shallow and in different positions, (for the position of the banking slot is the most difficult to ascertain), and the cylinder only perforated where the top plug is inserted. The top plug should be removed, the hole tapped, and a new plug, somewhat longer, screwed in. The action of this tool is similar to the Staff Height Gauge mentioned above.

After the lower end is finished the wax is turned away and the cylinder turned true and finally cut off at the proper length, preserving as fine a center as possible, after which the cylinder is reversed and finished.

In pivoting, it is very seldom necessary to drill the cylinder, as the upper and lower pivots are generally the extremity of plugs closely fitting in each end. In most cases the top pivot may be replaced by resting the cylinder on a stake, the hold of which is of a sufficient diameter to allow of the entrance of the plug, and too small to allow the cylinder to pass through. A knee punch and a few light taps of a hammer are generally sufficient to drive the plug out far enough to admit of the turning of a new pivot. The lower plug must be driven out entirely (being too short to admit of turning a new pivot) and a new plug inserted. The plugs must be made to fit tightly without taper, as with a taper plug there is great danger of splitting the cylinder. Should the plug be very tight and difficulty is encountered in driving it out, a few light taps all around the cylinder will generally stretch it enough to remove the plug easily.

CYLINDER HEIGHT TOOL. See *Gauge.*

CYLINDER PLUGS. Steel plugs fitted to the ends of a cylinder and on the ends of which the pivots are formed. Cylinder plugs can be obtained ready made from material dealers; assorted sizes in neat boxes.

DAMASKEEN. To decorate a metal by the inlaying of other metals, or by etching designs upon its surface. The embellishment of the surface of metals with rings or bars is snailing and is not damaskeening, although improperly called so by watchmakers and watch factory employees particularly. See *Snailing, also Electro Plating, Bronzing and Staining.*

DAY. The whole time or period of one revolution of the earth on its axis.

Solar Day. The period during which the sun is above the horizon or shines continuously on any given portion of the earth's surface. Also called astronomical day, since the length of this day is continually varying, owing to the eccentricity of the earth's orbit and the obliquity of the ecliptic, a mean solar day is employed which is the average period of one revolution of the earth on its axis, relative to the sun considered as fixed. In astronomy and navigation the day is reckoned from noon to noon, but the civil day is reckoned from midnight to midnight. The mean solar day is uniformly equal to twenty-four hours.

Sidereal Day. The interval between two successive transits of a given star. It is uniformly equal to 23 hours, 56 minutes, 4.099 seconds, or 3 minutes, 55.901 seconds less than the mean solar day.

DEAD BEAT ESCAPEMENT. An escapement in which, except during the actual impulsion, the escape wheel remains stationary and does not recoil. See *Graham Escapement*.

DECANT. To pour off a liquid from its sediment; as the decanting of diamond powder, prepared chalk, etc. Saunier advises the watchmaker to prepare all his smoothing and polishing materials by decantation, as he will by this means free them from hard or large particles and obtain a uniform grain. At the present time the watchmaker can, however, obtain diamond dust, prepared chalk, etc., ready for use, that are supposed to have been properly decanted. There are, however, many poor concoctions that have not gone through the proper treatment, and if the watchmaker is desirous of doing fine work and having reliable materials always at hand, it is well to decant these preparations, even though they be labeled "prepared." The operation is a very simple one and takes but little time. The material, being reduced to a powder, is placed in a vessel filled with water, oil, or other liquids, according to the nature of the material to be operated upon, and after being thoroughly stirred it is allowed to partially settle. The liquid is then poured into another vessel, the heavy portion remaining in the bottom of the first vessel. This residue is only fit for use in the very coarsest work. The liquid is then stirred, allowed to settle partially again and is then poured into another vessel. The powder left should be labeled 1. By successive operations, each time increasing the interval of time allowed for settlement, finer deposits can be obtained, which may be labeled respectively, 2, 3, 4, etc. In decanting diamond power or oil-stone dust, oil should be used; for tripoli, rottenstone, or chalk, water; and for hartshorn and some other materials, alcohol is used. Diamond powder, as purchased from the material dealer, can rarely be improved upon by manipulation unless the operator is expert.

DEMAGNETIZER. A machine or tool used to remove magnetism from parts of watches. There are several demagnetizers upon the market. In some of these machines the arc and incandescent electric light wires are attached to generate the magnetism, while in the Ide demagnetizer it is generated by the use of horseshoe magnets.

The Greaves demagnetizer, shown in Fig. 105, is intended to be used

either with a battery or electric light wire.

Fig. 106 shows the Berlin Demagnetizer; it is constructed on a principle similar to the Greaves, and like it, gives the best results when used with electric light wires. Pro-

Fig. 105.

cure an attachment plug and fasten to the end of the flexible cord accompanying machine. Insert a lamp receptacle and turn on the current. Press down the key and turn the handle of commutator, about 150 revolutions a minute. Insert the watch or part to be demagnetized into the opening of the magnet, and revolve very slowly, keeping it in a straight line with the center of the magnet until at a distance of two

Fig. 106.

or three feet. Keep turning commutator at regular speed. Release key before ceasing to turn. It is not necessary to remove the movement from the case nor to let it remain in the magnet. While the current is on and the handle being turned with key down, insert the watch into the opening and proceed as above.

DENISON, E. B. A barrister of London, who was requested by the government to draw up, in conjunction with the Astronomer-Royal, specifications for the construction of a large clock for the Victoria Tower of the Houses of Parliament. Vulliamy and other leading clockmakers, who were invited to tender for the work, all demurred to a stipulation that the clock should be guaranteed to perform within a margin of a minute a week, which they declared to be too small. Mr. Denison would not yield, and the clock makers were equally firm. Eventually it was decided to entrust the work to Mr. Dent, who was to make a clock from designs to be furnished by Mr. Denison. Mr. Denison's temerity was justified by his success. The Westminster clock, says Britten, turned out to be the finest timekeeper of any public clock in the world. The double three-legged gravity Escapement was invented for it, besides a new maintaining power and a novel arrangement for letting off the hours to satisfy another of the conditions, which required the first blow of the hour to be given within a second of the true time. Mr. Denison was elected President of the British Horological Institute in 1868, and succeeded his father as baronet, taking the title of Sir Edmund Beckett in 1874. In 1886 he was called to the House of Lords under the title of Baron Grimthorpe.

DENNISON, AARON L. The father of the American watch factories. The first person to apply the interchangeable system to the manufacture of watches. This he did in 1850. He was the son of a shoemaker of Freeport, Me., and was born in the year 1812. He was apprenticed to James Carey, a watchmaker of Brunswick, Me., in 1830. In

Aaron L. Dennison.

1839 he was engaged in a general watch and jewelry business in Boston and also carried a line of watchmakers' tools and materials. Invented the Dennison Standard Gauge in 1840. In the fall of 1849 he began to build machinery for the manufacture of watches on the interchangeable system, having associated himself with Messrs Howard, Davis and Curtis. In 1850 he completed the model for the first watch which was 18 size, with two barrels, and was made to run eight days. The watch, however, was not a success, and its place was filled by a one-day. At this time the company was known as the American Horologe Company. In 1851 the name was changed to the Warren Manufacturing Company, and the first one hundred watches bore that name. The first watches were placed on the market in 1853. The next six hundred watches bore the name Samuel Curtis and the name of the company was then changed to the Boston Watch Company. In 1854 the factory was removed from Boston to Waltham, the company then making about five watches per day, and employing ninety hands. After the removal the movements were engraved Dennison, Howard and Davis. In 1857 the company assigned, and the property was purchased by Mr. Royal E. Robbins for $56,000. Mr. Dennison was then employed as superintendent and filled that position until 1862. In 1864, he with others, organized the Tremont Watch Company. He retired from this company in 1866, the name of the company having in the meantime been changed to the Melrose Watch Company, and the factory removed from Boston to Melrose, Mass. Prior to the removal, the barrel, plates and minor parts were made in the Boston factory, while the trains, escapements and balances were made in Zurich, Switzerland, Mr. Dennison having charge of the latter factory. In 1868 this company failed and Mr. Dennison was deputized to sell the factory, which he did, to the English Watch Company, of Coventry, Eng. Mr. Dennison then went to Birmingham, Eng., and embarked in the manufacture of watch cases. In this he was quite successful and he is still carrying on a very profitable business there, the firm being known as Dennison, Wigley & Co.

DENT, E. J. Born in 1790, and died in 1853. Builder of the great Westminister Clock, London.

DEPTH. The contact point between a wheel and pinion.

DEPTHING TOOL. A mechanical device for transferring the depthing of a wheel and pinion to a plate. Britten advises that before using a new depthing tool, the centers be turned end for end, also transposed, and ascertaining after each change if there is any deviation in a circle described by the points, in order to test the truth of the tool. The tool should be held in the left hand, with the adjusting screw pointed to the right. Place the pinion in the centers on the left, and the wheel on the right, first opening the tool sufficiently for the teeth of the wheel to clear the teeth of the pinion. The teeth of the wheel and pinion are then brought into contact by means of the regulating screw, shown at

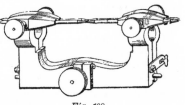

Fig. 108.

the bottom in Fig. 108. When the pinion and wheel are in right contact the tool may be secured with the screws furnished for that purpose. Then hold the tool so that you may observe the contact of wheel and pinion. After you are satisfied that the depthing is correct, and that the teeth do not butt, the depth may be marked off by loosening the binding screws, taking the wheel and pinion out of the tool, and while one center is kept tight and inserted in the hole from which the depth is to be taken, the loose center is brought down until it touches the plate. If the tool is found to be perfectly upright, and all is satisfactory, tighten the loose center and mark the plate where the wheel or pinion is to be planted. The mark can then be made permanent by the use of a center punch or graver.

DERHAM, WILLIAM. An eminent English divine, and one of the early writers on practical horology. He was born at Stourton, near Worcester, in 1657, and died in 1735. He was the author of "The Artificial Clockmaker," a treatise on watch and clock work, showing the art of calculating numbers for all sorts of movements; the way to alter clock work, to make chimes and set them to musical notes, and to calculate and correct the motions of pendulums. It was published about 1700. He was also the author of a work, entitled, " Philosophical Experiments and Observations of Dr. Robert Hooke, F. R. S." and another, called " The Antiquity of Clock-work."

DETACHED ESCAPEMENT. The escapement of a time piece in which the balance, or pendulum, is detached from the train, during a portion of its vibration.

DETENT. That which locks or unlocks a movement; the piece of steel that carries the stones that lock and unlock an escape wheel.

DE VICK, HENRY. A celebrated German watchmaker of the fourteenth century and the builder of the famous clock belonging to Charles V., of France. Also claimed, by some writers, to be the inventor of the Verge escapement. See *Clocks.*

DIAL. The graduated face of a time piece. Dials were first enameled by Paul Viet, of Blois, in 1635.

The greater majority of American dials are what are known as enamel dials, which consist of a copper plate for a base and an enameled face. The process of making these dials, as carried on in our factories, is as follows: The copper is shaped and holes punched in one operation. The feet are then brazed on, after which the enamel is applied to both the back and face, after which it is fired. After smoothing they are again fired, and, if perfect, they are sent to the painter. For many years after most of the other work in our factories was done by machinery; the painting of dials was hand work. The Waltham Company, after experimenting for a number of years, finally brought to perfection a process, by means of which the dials are lettered, and the numerals, minute and second marks are printed by photography. Various processes are used in other factories, among them being the transfer process, which is effected by rubbing the enamel paint into a steel plate into which the lettering of the dial is countersunk, taking an impression from this plate upon a rubber platen and then transferring this impression to the dial. After painting, the dials are again fired.

Dials of gold, silver and other metals are extensively used, particularly in the Spanish-American countries.

To Drill an Enamel Dial. Select a piece of soft copper wire of the diameter you wish the hole, file off the end perfectly flat and hammer into the copper a small quantity of fine diamond powder. This form of drill will be found to perforate the enamel of a dial quite rapidly. Broaches made in the same manner give excellent results. These tools can be used either by revolving in the fingers or in the lathe. Emery countersinks will be found very useful for trimming the edges of holes in enamel dials.

To Remove a Name From Dial. Apply a little fine diamantine to the end of your forefinger, and gently rub the name until it disappears. The finish can be restored by polishing the place carefully with a small quantity of diamantine mixed with oil, and applied by means of a small piece of cork. An agate burnisher is also used for the same purpose.

To Remove Stains From Enamel Dials. Enamel dials sometimes have black or cloudy stains upon their faces, caused usually by the tin boxes in which they are shipped. These can be removed with a piece of soft tissue paper previously dampened with nitric acid. Wipe the stained places, carefully avoiding the painted portions as much as possible, for in some very cheap dials the painting is not well fired, and may be injured by the acid. Wash the dial thoroughly in clean water and dry in sawdust.

To Reduce the Diameter of a Dial. Rest the dial in an inclined position and file the edge with a half-smooth file, dipping the file in turpentine occasionally, and finish with a fine emery stick.

To Repair a Chipped Dial. Gently heat the surface of the dial and fill the hole with a compound of white lead and white resin, heated over the flame of a spirit lamp. It is better to heat the blade of a knife rather than the wax, and run no risk of discoloring the wax. Cut off a small piece of the wax and press firmly into the hole, allowing it to project a little above the dial. When cold, scrape down even with the dial, and finish, by holding it close to the flame, when the patch will gloss over nicely. Be careful and do not get it too close to the flame, or you may turn the enamel yellow. A mixture of white lead and white wax applied and polished by friction is also used, but it is not as handy and is not as capable of a high polish.

To Clean Metal Dials. Silver and gold dials can be restored by gently heating the back over a spirit lamp and dipping the dial in diluted nitric acid. If the figures are painted however, they will be removed, and it will be necessary to repaint them, but if they are enameled on, the enamel will not be injured. If the figures are painted the dial may be cleaned by brushing with powdered cream of tarter either dry or in the form of a paste mixed with water. Avoid all the painted portions and work the paste in between the painted portions with a pointed peg wood. Wash with warm water and dry by carefully patting with a soft linen rag.

To Grind Enamel from the Back of Dial. It is sometimes necessary to remove a portion of the enamel from the back of a dial to allow room for the motion work, etc. The most convenient method is to grind the back with emery, preferably in the shape of a wheel. Water should be applied to the work from time to time to prevent heating.

Luminous or Phosphorescent Dial. A dial covered with varnish or a solution of white wax in turpentine, over which is dusted powdered sulphide of barium. Such a dial is luminous in the dark so that it can be read without a light. It loses its phosphorescence after a time, but this may be restored by exposing it to sunlight or to the flame of magnesium wire.

DIALING. The art of constructing dials. The science which explains the principles of measuring time by the sun dial.

DIAL WORK. The motion work of a watch between the dial and the movement plate.

DIAMANTINE. This polishing agent is used extensively for polishing steel, and is a preparation of crystallized boron. It is not applicable to brass or copper work. Rubitine and Sapphirine are similar chemical preparations; they act quicker, but do not yield as good results.

DIAMOND DRILLS. Pieces or copper wire, in the ends of which are embedded fragments of diamond in the shape of triangular prisms and held in place with shellac. They are used for drilling jewels, etc. They may be obtained from material dealers.

DIAMOND GRAVERS. These are very similar to diamond drills and are mounted in the same manner, but usually consist of larger, though shorter and stronger diamond fragments, and are used for shaping jewels, etc. They may also be obtained from material dealers.

DIAMOND LAPS OR MILLS. These are of two kinds, one for grinding and the other for polishing. The grinding mills are copper discs, from an inch to an inch and a half in diameter, into the surface of which diamond powder of various grades has been hammered or rolled. The polishing mills are made of box-wood, vegetable ivory, etc., and the powder is applied to their surfaces in the shape of a paste mixed with olive oil. These mills are useful for cutting or polishing ruby-pallets, and other hard stones, for flattening stones to be used as jewels and for manipulating hard steel.

DIAMOND FILES. Strips of copper into the face of which diamond powder of various degrees of coarseness has been hammered or rolled. Used for working ruby-pallets and other hard stones and hard steel.

DIAMOND POWDER. A cutting and polishing agent prepared from the crushed chips from the diamond cutter's table, black, brown, and other inferior stones, known as bort, and small diamonds. After pulverizing thoroughly, the powder is decanted in olive oil to various degrees of fineness. To be had of material dealers generally. Used for charging the face of mills or laps for grinding and polishing hard stones, etc. It is also used for drilling by being applied to the end of a small taper piece of steel, flattened on the end for the reception of the powder, which is moistened with olive oil.

DIPLEIDOSCOPE. An instrument invented by J. M. Bloxam, in 1843, used for determining the time of apparent noon. It consists of two mirrors and a plane glass disposed in the form of a prism, so that, by the reflection of the sun's rays from their surfaces, two images are presented to the eye, moving in opposite directions, and coinciding the instant the sun's center is on the meridian.

DIVIDING PLATE. See *Index*.

DOG. A clutch. An adjustable stop to change the motion of a machine tool.

DOG SCREWS. The screws with half heads by which a movement is held in its case.

DOUBLE ROLLER ESCAPEMENT. A form of the lever escapement in which a separate roller is employed for the guard action.

DOUBLE SUNK DIAL. A dial having two sinks, one for the hour and another for the seconds hand.

DOUZIEME. A unit of measurement indicating, $\frac{1}{12}$ of a line or $\frac{1}{144}$ of an inch. See *Gauge*.

DRAW. The angle of the locking faces of the pallets, as in the lever escapement.

DRAW PLATE. A plate of very hard steel for drawing wire of various shapes and diameters. They are made for drawing round, half-round and square wire. The plates are sometimes formed of jewels for working steel wire, etc. These plates are very handy for readily reducing wire to any desired diameter, and may also be employed for reducing the diameter of bushings.

DRIFTING TOOL. A tool for punching holes in mainsprings, etc. It consists of a frame to be held in the vise, through which a screw passes, and to the end of which a handle is attached. It is used but little in this country, as the mainspring punch has superceded it, being simpler and quicker to operate.

DRILLS AND DRILLING. Drilling may be effected in two ways, by rotating the drill and holding the work stationary, or *vice versa*. The most satisfactory results, however, are obtained by revolving the work and gradually bringing the drill into contact with it. Although it is not always possible to do this, owing to the shape of the article to be drilled. A drill of the shape shown in Fig. 109 is preferable for drilling hard steel, while the shape shown in Fig. 110 is best suited for drilling soft steel, brass, etc. Oil or glycerine diluted with alcohol is the best lubricant for the softer metals, but when drilling hard steel turpentine should be used. Drills of the form shown in Fig. 111, are used for drilling

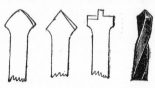

Fig. 109. Fig. 110. Fig. 111. Fig. 112.

flat bottomed holes, for countersinking screw heads, etc. See also *Countersinks.* The twist drill shown in Fig. 112 is desirable when drilling deeply, as this form of drill heats slowly and the particles are carried to the surface of the work. Pivot drills, like those shown in Fig. 113, can be purchased from material dealers, mounted on cards and ready for use, at such small cost that it will scarcely pay the watchmaker to make them.

Drills of a form indicated by Fig. 114 are recommended highly by Saunier and are known as semi-cylindrical drills. They are made from cylindrical steel rods, rounded at their ends and filed down to a trifle less than half their thickness. The length of the point should be greater or less according to the nature or the metal to be operated upon, but under no circumstances must the point itself be sharp. This form of

drill should be sharpened on the round side and not on the flat surface. It possesses, says Saunier, the advantages that when placed in a drill-chuck it can be turned exactly round, of the required diameter and finish; so that whenever replaced in the chuck, one can be certain beforehand

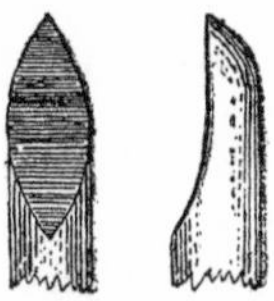

Fig. 113.

Fig. 114.

that the hole drilled will be of a definite diameter. With such a drill the hole is smoothed immediately after it is made by one or the other cutting edges.

DRILL REST. In using the lathe for drilling, a great saving in both time and drills can be effected by using a drill rest similar to that shown in Fig. 115. It is well to have a half dozen different sizes, starting at $\frac{1}{4}$ inch and increasing by $\frac{1}{8}$ inch, for various classes of work. These rests are not kept by material dealers, but can be made by the watchmaker. Saw from a piece of rolled sheet brass, say 1-16 inch thick, the circles required, leaving metal enough to finish nicely Place a steel taper plug in the taper chuck of your lathe and turn down a recess, leaving a shoulder on the taper. Drill a hole through the brass plate to fit the steel taper tightly. Place the end of the taper on a lead block

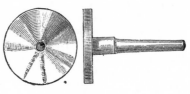

Fig. 115.

and proceed to rivet the brass plate on the taper, making sure that it is true. Replace the taper in the lathe-chuck and proceed to turn the face and edge of the brass plate perfectly true and to the proper size. Those who have tried to drill a straight hole through an object by holding it in the fingers know just how difficult it is to do, but by placing one of these drill rests in the spindle of the tail stock, placing the article to be drilled against it and bringing it up against the drill, you can drill the hole perfectly upright and avoid all danger of breaking the drill.

DRILL STOCK. A tool used for holding drills, the more modern variety having a small chuck on one end for centering and holding the drill.

DRILLING LATHE. A lathe, used for centering and drilling staffs and pinions, The plate has various sizes of conical holes for supporting the arbor, and can be turned upon its center.

DROP. The distance which the escape wheel travels before touching on the pallet.

DRUM. The barrel of a turret clock on which the driving cord is wound. There is a variety of escapement, known as the Drum Escapement, which is met with but little in this country. Britten says this variety of escapement is a continual source of trouble to English repairers. It receives impulse at every other vibration only, and the idea of the escapement appears to be, that by providing a long frictional rest on one of the pallets, the extra pressure of the escape wheel tooth, when the mainspring is fully wound, will be sufficient to prevent any considerable increase in the arc of vibration of the pendulum. Clocks with this escapement, however, often stop from the diminished power when the spring is nearly run down, again, when it is fully wound, because the small and light pendulum has not the energy to unlock the pallet.

DUPLEX ESCAPEMENT. An escapement invented by Pierre Le Roy about 1750. As first constructed, this escapement had two escape wheels (from whence its name is derived), one used for giving impulse, and the other to lock or check the wheel when the impulse tooth escaped from the pallet. This form was afterwards simplified by changing to that shown in Fig. 116. Britten says of this escapement, that like the Chronometer, it is a single beat escapement, that is, it receives impulse at every other vibration only. The escapement has two sets of teeth. Those farthest from the center lock the wheel by pressing on a hollow ruby cylinder, or roller, fitted around a reduced part of the balance staff, and planted so that it intercepts the path of the teeth. There is a notch in the ruby roller, and a tooth passes every time the balance, in its excursion in the opposite direction to that in which the wheel moves, brings this notch past the point of the tooth resting on the roller. When the tooth leaves the notch, the impulse finger, fixed to the balance staff, receives a blow from one of the impulse teeth of the wheel. The impulse teeth are not in the same plane as the body of the wheel but stand up from it so as to meet the impulse finger. There is no action in the return vibration. In the figure the detaining roller, traveling in the direction of the arrow, is just allowing a locking tooth of the wheel to escape from the notch, and the pallet is sufficiently in front of the tooth from which it will receive impulse to insure a safe intersection.

The balance is never detached, but the roller on which the wheel teeth rest is very small and highly polished, so that there is but very little friction from this cause, and the alteration in its amount, is, therefore, not of such consequence as might be imagined. A very usual proportion is for the diameter of the roller to be one-fifteenth of the diameter, of the largest part of the escape wheel, which it intersects about 30°

measured from the center of the roller. The impulse teeth should have considerable drop on the pallet. Ten degrees is not an unusual amount. The scape wheel is made as light as possible, of hard hammered brass of very fine quality. The points of the impulse teeth are usually two-thirds the distance of the points of the locking teeth from the center of the wheel. The impulse pallet is sometimes jeweled.

The staff requires to be planted with great exactness, and one of the most frequent causes of derangement of the Duplex Escapement is the

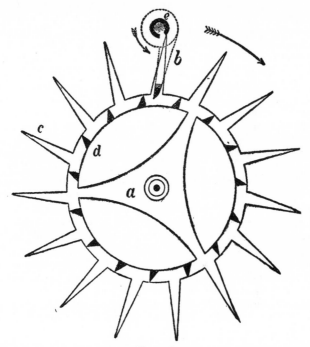

Fig. 116.*

wearing of the balance pivots. In such cases, the pivots having been re-polished, new holes, or at all events a new bottom hole, should be put in. See also that the point of each locking tooth is smooth and nicely rounded, and that every impulse tooth falls safely on the pallet; if some are shallow, twist the impulse pallet round so as to give more drop. Or if the roller depth is also shallow, carefully make the teeth of equal length by topping, and then, supposing it to be a full-plate watch, very

a. Escape Wheel.	*d.* Impulse Teeth.
b. Impulse Pallet.	*e.* Ruby Roller.
c. Locking Teeth.	

slightly tap the cock and the potance towards the wheel until the escapement is made safe. In a three-quarter plate the recess for the jewel setting may be scraped away on one side and rubbed over on the other. The extra amount of intersection of the impulse pallet in the path of the wheel teeth thus made can be easily corrected by polishing off the surplus amount, if any.

It is of the utmost consequence in this escapement that all the jewel holes should fit accurately, and that the balance staff should have very little end shake, otherwise the pivots will be found to wear away very quickly.

A loose roller is occasionally the cause of stoppage. The staff and roller should be carefully cleaned from oil, which would prevent the shellac from sticking, and if the staff is polished where the roller fits, it may be grayed for the same reason. Then warm the roller and fix with shellac.

It sometimes happens that the impulse pallet, in running past, just catches on the impulse tooth, and when the balance leans toward the escape wheel, the continual recurrence of this, causes the vibration to fall off, and gradually stops the watch. If the locking teeth are already the right depth, the fault should be corrected by polishing a very little off the corner of the pallet, with a bell-metal polisher, if the pallet is of steel, or with an ivory polisher and the finest diamond powder if it is jeweled. But the greatest care must be taken not to overdo it.

A small drop of oil should be applied to the notch and nowhere else except to the pivots.

When the escapement is in beat, the notch in the roller is between the locking tooth resting on it and the line of centers, or a little nearer the latter; out of beat is a cause of stoppage.

The idea of this escapement is seductive; it conforms to the requirement of giving impulse across the line of centers, and at one time it was considered an excellent arrangement, but it has proved to be quite unreliable. The best proportion of its parts and the finest work are insufficient to prevent its setting. On the introduction of the lever it declined, and is rarely made now.

DUPLEX HOOK. The impulse pallet in the duplex escapement.

DUPLEX ROLLER. The ruby roller of the duplex escapement.

DUST BANDS. Thin metal bands or guards which are inserted between the upper and lower plates of a movement to exclude all dust.

EARNSHAW, THOMAS. A celebrated watchmaker of London, who was born at Ashton-under-Lyne, Lancashire, in 1749, and died in 1814. He was the inventor of the spring detent escapement and the compensation balance, both substantially as now used in chronometers. He made his improvement in the spring detent in 1781. He presented a petition to the Board of Longitude for aid in 1791, and again in 1797. He received his long-contested reward, Dec. 27, 1805.

EAST, EDWARD. A celebrated watch and clockmaker of London. He was one of the ten original assistants appointed by the Charter of Incorporation of the Clockmakers' Company in 1632. Was Warder in 1638-9, Master in 1645-52, Treasurer in 1637, being the only occupant of the latter office in the history of the company. He was watchmaker to Charles I.

Thomas Earnshaw.

ELECTROPLATING, BRONZING AND STAINING. The first requisite in attempting to do electroplating in a small way is to understand the battery and to select one that will give an electric current of the proper intensity and quantity for the required time, without too much care and attention on the part of the workman. Were he provided with measuring instruments, so that he could readily determine when his current was changing in quantity and power, the choice of a battery would not be of so much importance; but volt meters and ampere meters are too expensive to be possessed by the average man who does plating in a small way, and he is necessarily obliged to depend on theory in arranging his forces and judge of the results by the appearance of his work in the bath. Hence it is important that he should have an understanding of the nature of the action in the battery and be able to maintain the requisite conditions from the appearance of the battery itself.

Without attempting to give too close a definition, electricity may be defined as a force or energy which is the result of a displacement of the normal balance of forces between two elements in close connection with one another. This normal force is called the potential of its element, and if two elements having different potentials, are connected together and placed in a fluid which will produce chemical action upon one or both, the result will be a flowing of energy through the connection to the element having the lowest potential. This will be kept up as long as the chemical action continues and the connection between the two elements remains unbroken. It will be readily seen that, owing to the varying potentials of the different elements, the varying facility of the conductors used to connect them, and the varying intensity of chemical action in the solution employed, the electrical current will vary in strength (or voltage) in different batteries, and in quantity, according to the size of the elements and the freedom with which they are attacked by the solution.

Voltage is the measure of strength or intensity of the current and depends upon the difference of potentials of the elements and the kind of chemical action between them.   It is the same for the same combination, regardless of the size of the elements.   Thus, a battery the size of a thimble has the same voltage as one the size of a door, if the elements and solution are the same.   We have not the space to explain this at length, but will simply state that the volt is the recognized unit of the measurement of strength of electric currents.

The ampere is the unit of measurement of the quantity of currents. Amperage depends on the size of the elements; and the available amperage depends on the size of the conductors and the freedom of action between the elements.   Amperage is consumed by doing work or by the heating of insufficient conductors, or by undue resistance in the battery, just as power is consumed in turning steel, or in running shafting, or overcoming the resistance caused by friction of boxes on a shaft that is run without oil.   Strictly speaking, if the voltage or intensity of the current be sufficient to do the work required, then the amperage is the force used to do the work, and it is destroyed by that work and the chemical or electrical resistance, just as mechanical power is consumed in running a lathe or doing any other work.   From this, it follows, that in order to operate economically, extreme care should be taken that the connections be large enough to carry the current easily ; that the solution be kept in perfect order, both in the battery and the plating vat; and that all joints be kept bright and firm so as to insure perfect contact and offer no resistance to the passage of the current.

The current always flows from the element having the highest potential (called the + or positive pole) along the wire and through the solution in the plating vat, to the other wire, and thence to the negative pole, carrying with it in passing through the solution, particles of metal from the anode and depositing it on the article to be electroplated (called the cathode); hence care should be taken to *always* get the cathode affixed to the *negative* (—) pole of the battery, in order that it may receive the deposit.

Electrical resistance is that property of conductors (wires, solutions, objects, etc.) by which they tend to reduce the intensity of a current passing through them.   The practical unit of resistance is the ohm. The number of amperes of current flowing through a circuit is equal to the number of volts of electro motive force, divided by the number of ohms of resistance in the entire circuit, that is from positive pole clear through wires, solution and battery, back to the starting point.   Thus it will be seen that if the resistance be greater than the voltage of one cell will overcome, no current will flow, and the voltage must be increased to such an amount as will allow the desired quantity of current to pass.   This is done by coupling cells in various ways, which will be explained at length further on.

The resistance of a conducting wire is directly proportional to its length, and inversely proportional to the square of its diameter; hence it follows that the short and large wires cause less loss of current than smaller and longer ones.

In all batteries the resistance increases with the distance between the elements, and decreases when the immersed surfaces are increased. The resistance is also increased by the bubbles of hydrogen liberated at the positive pole sticking to it in great numbers. Hydrogen is a nonconductor and prevents the action of the solution on the metal. When this takes place to such an extent as to stop chemical action altogether, no current will pass and the battery is said to be polarized.

These remarks are intended to aid in the intelligent selection of batteries, etc., those who, having to deal with such apparatus, yet have never had the opportunity to study an electrical treatise. We are often asked: What is the best battery? We can only answer: There is no best battery; that is, no battery is suited to all kinds of work. That which is best in one case may be worst in another. The suitability of a battery for any special purpose depends on what is called its constants, i. e., electro-motive force and internal resistance. In order to be really perfect a battery should fulfill the following conditions:

1. It electro-motive force should be high and constant.

2. Its internal resistance should be small.

3. It should give a constant current and must therefore be free from polarization, and not liable to rapid exhaustion, requiring frequent renewal of material.

4. It should consume no material when the circuit is open.

5. It should be cheap and of durable materials.

6. It should be manageable and, if possible, should not emit corrosive fumes.

No single battery fulfills all these conditions, however, and, as we have already intimated, some batteries are better for one purpose and some for another. Thus, for telegraphing through a long line of wire, a considerable internal resistance is of no great consequence, as it is but a small fraction of the total resistance in circuit. For electric gas lighting or other low resistance circuits, on the other hand, much internal resistance would be, if not absolutely fatal, certainly a positive disadvantage. The most reliable batteries for electroplating work are the Daniel, Gravity, Bunsen, Smee and Carbon, which we will accordingly describe in their order.

The Daniell, Fig. 118, consists of a glass or stoneware jar, containing a cylinder of copper surrounding a porous clay cup, in which stands a cylinder of zinc. At the upper part of the copper sheet is a pocket of perforated copper, which is filled with crystals of sulphate of copper. The object of the pocket is simply to hold the sulphate up to the top of the solution, so that it will dissolve more readily, and any other method would do as well. In charging this battery, the glass vessel and the porous cup are filled with water, and crystals of sulphate of copper are put in the pocket. If wanted for immediate use, a small quantity of sulphate of zinc may be dissolved in water and added to the porous cup; if not wanted immediately, the battery may be short circuited by connecting the zinc and copper elements by a piece of copper wire, and it will attain its full strength in ten or twelve hours. A little sulphuric acid dropped in the porous cup will answer just as well, if sulphate of zinc is not on hand. The chemical action of this battery is as follows: The zinc decomposes the water, forming oxide of zinc and liberating the hydrogen. The oxide of zinc attacks the sulphate of vitriol, depriving it of the acid, which forms sulphate of zinc, and leaving it as oxide of copper; the oxide of copper is thereupon attacked by the hydrogen, which combines with the oxygen and forms water, while the metallic copper falls to the bottom as a fine powder. It will thus

Fig. 118.

be seen that action is simple and continuous, no fumes are given off, and all that is required to maintain the action is a regular supply of copper sulphate to keep the fluid in the outer jar, near the point of saturation. The most prominent fault of this battery is the tendency of the copper to fill the pores of the cup, and thus decrease the action of the battery. It can be partially prevented by coating the bottom and about a quarter of an inch of the sides of the porous cup with wax, and brushing off the deposit as fast as it is formed. The battery should not be allowed to stand on open circuit without the zinc element being removed, and the sulphate of zinc solution in the cup should not be heavier than 25° B, nor lighter than 15° B. If these precautions are observed, the battery should give a constant and free current as long as any zinc remains. Its electro-motive force is about 1.07 volt, and a gallon cell will give about one-half ampere, when in good order, on a short circuit. Its internal resistance varies, but should not be allowed to exceed three to five ohms.

The Gravity Battery. In consequence of the trouble caused by the precipitation of the copper on the porous cell in the Daniell battery, Cromwell F. Varley, in 1854, while experimenting, found that the difference in specific gravity between solutions of sulphate of copper and sulphate of zinc was sufficient in itself to entirely separate them, the copper solution lying at the bottom of the cell, and the zinc solution remaining superposed upon it. He accordingly dispensed with the porous cup, placed his copper element at the bottom, and the zinc near the top of a glass jar, and thus originated the gravity battery of to-day. It is the simplest, most reliable and constant form known, and has displaced all others for closed circuit work, requiring a low voltage, such as telegraphing, etc. Its voltage, when first set up, is 1.07, running down under constant work to .90, and a gallon cell will give one-half ampere on short circuit. The form of cell shown in Fig. 119 is known as the " crowfoot," on account

Fig. 119.

of the manner in which the zinc (positive) element is spread out, to expose a large surface of zinc to the solution. It is the form used for telegraphing, and, therefore, can be readily attained anywhere. Of course, other forms, shapes and sizes can be made at the option of the workman. To set up this battery, the copper strip, being unfolded so as to form a cross, is placed at the bottom of a jar, the zinc is suspended from the top as shown, and clean water, containing one-tenth of a saturated solution of sulphate of zinc is added, until it nearly touches the zinc. Sulphate of copper crystals are then added one by one until, if the battery is meant to be continually used, they nearly cover the top of the copper strip. If the battery is not intended for continual use, it will be fonnd more advantageous to use but a few ounces of sulphate of copper, as the more concentrated the solution, the greater is the tendency to local action. The sulphate of zinc may be dispensed with if the battery is not required for immediate use; in this case, the latter should be short circuited, and left so for several days. The need of blue vitriol will be indicated by the discoloration of the lower stratum of the liquid. It is best to keep the line marking the two solutions about halfway between the zinc and copper. Should the sulphate of zinc become too concentrated, a portion of it should be removed by means of a syringe or cup, and its place supplied by water. To determine when this is necessary, a hydrometer may be used. Below 15° the solution is too weak; above 25° it is too strong, and should be diluted. If the battery is taken care of from month to month, it should not require a thorough cleaning more than once a year When this is done the deposits formed upon the surface of the zinc should be scraped off, the jars washed and the liquids renewed as in the beginning.

If, however, the batteries are in constant use, care must be taken to keep the zincs clean and the solutions as indicated above. If the sulphate of zinc is allowed to become saturated, it will crystalize on the zinc and on the edge of the jar, gradually creeping over the edge. This should be wiped off with a damp cloth and a little oil or fat smeared over the top of the jar to prevent creeping.   The jars should not be disturbed, as this would cause the two solutions to mix, and they should be kept in a dry, even temperature, (60° to 80° F).   Freezing would stop the action of the battery.

The Bunsen, or Carbon Battery.   Fig. 120, consists of a glass jar containing a hollow zinc cylinder, slit on one side to allow a free circulation of the solution; within this stands a porous cup containing a bar of carbon.   To charge this battery, the amalgamated zinc is placed in the glass jar, the porous jar in the center of the zinc cylinder and the

carbon in the porous jar.   In the outer jar is sulphuric acid, diluted with twelve times its weight of water and in the porous jar electropoion fluid. (See *Electropoion Fluid*, page 143).

The voltage of this battery is 2.028; its amperage cannot be given, as it depends largely upon the care which is given the battery, the size of the cell and the condition of the porous cups, which vary greatly in porosity and conducting power.   It emits fumes of hydrogen and sulphurous acid if not in good condition, and should not be used in the same room with fine tools or metal work that is liable to injury.   It soon runs

Fig. 120.   down, requiring recharging every day when in constant use, but is simple to handle when understood and is generally furnished in small outfits for nickel plating, etc., on account of its high voltage and the quantity of current given off when in good order.   The zincs must be kept well amalgamated or they will polarize very rapidly and destroy the current; care should also be taken that no sediment be allowed to accumulate in the porous cup and fill its pores, thus stopping the action.   It is more expensive to run than the gravity, as the zincs are eaten by the acid much faster, especially if not kept well amalgamated; but it will deliver a greater quantity of current in a given time than a gravity cell of equal size.   The internal resistance of a new cell is about one-half an ohm.   The plates should be removed and cleaned when the battery is not in use.

The Smee Battery.   Fig. 121, consists of two plates of amalgamated zinc, between which is placed a silver plate coated with platinum, the object of the platinum being to fill the surface of the plate with inumerable fine points which aid in discharging the bubbles of hydrogen which would cling closely to it if the plate were smooth and thus polarize the battery.   This battery is charged with a solution of one part sulphuric acid to seven of water.   The plates are connected to the clamp and placed in jar. In this battery, above all, the precaution of amalgamating the zinc should never be neglected. With an unamalgamated zinc the results are very unsatisfactory.

The voltage of the Smee, when not in action, .s 1.09 volts; when in action it runs down to .482 volts; this is caused by the hydrogen clinging to the plate as described. This was the form of cell generally used before the introduction of dynamos for electrotyping and other heavy work, and it is still used to a large extent. It emits fumes of hydrogen when in action, but it is a single fluid battery and when working in large sizes, plates 12x12 inches in size are suspended in a large tank of acidulated water, first a plate of zinc, then a plate of platinized silver, then another of zinc and so on alternately, zinc and platinum, to the end.

This gives great facility in handling, as any number of plates to suit the work may be placed in the tank. As there is but one tank and the plates may be placed close together or far apart as required, the resistance may be easily made to balance that in the depositing tank, and thus the work will be performed under the most favorable conditions.

In working the Smee, or any other battery for that matter, large tanks are better than small ones, provided that the plates are kept close together so as to reduce internal resistance of the battery. In the large Smee, if plates 12x12 are worked in a tank say

Fig. 121.

15x15x30, it will not be long before the sulphate of zinc, which forms and falls to the bottom, will soon commence to rise in the tank, thus shutting off the acid from a portion of the plates and reducing the quantity of current. If the same plates were worked in a tank 24x24x30, the tank might be permitted to become half full of zinc sulphate before the action would be impaired at all, and thus a much more even and constant current would be maintained; this is generally done in practice. In a gravity battery, however, the tank ought not to be deep, because the two elements should not be more than eight inches apart on account of the increased resistance caused by the separation. The tank, however, may be made large enough in length and width to contain elements of the desired size, or a number of standard zincs and coppers, if such an arrangement seems desirable, either to increase the facility of handling or to reduce the cost of a large number of jars, wires, connections, etc. We have seen a number of tanks made of wood, lined with lead, 10x10-x60 inches, in which a single large copper element was placed at the bottom and a number of zincs hung as required from an insulated copper bar across the top. It seemed to work well and was convenient.

A few words as to coupling batteries may be of service. It should be born in mind that the quantity of current flowing in any circuit is the quotient resulting from dividing the voltage by the total resistance in that circuit and that the resistance may be increased or diminished by increasing or dimishing the distance between the elements of the battery and between the anode and cathode in the plating vat; also that the resistance varies inversely, as the surface of the elements immersed. Thus a plating surface of one square foot in the plating vat will offer four times as much resistance as four square feet. It thus becomes possible by increasing or diminishing the voltage of a current to keep the

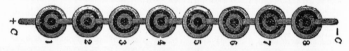

Fig. 122.

current flowing in the desirea quantity, and by keeping the resistance in the battery about equal to that in the vats the highest economy is obtained.

For example, let us take eight cells, having a voltage of 1, and giving say ½ ampere per cell on short circuit. If we now couple then —, +, —, +, —, +, —, +, we shall have the voltage of 8 and the amperage of one cell of the same size with a voltage of eight, in other words, the same amount of current and eight times the strength of the single cell, as in Fig. 122.

This is termed coupling in series, and would be used in solutions having a high resistance and small amount of surface immersed. If, on the other hand, the solution had a low resistance and large surface exposed, so that the voltage of one cell was ample to force the current

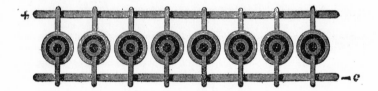

Fig. 123.

through the circuit, they should be connected +, +, +, +, +, +, +, +, and —, —, —, —, —, —, —, —, giving the quantity of eight cells and the voltage of one, which amounts to nearly the same thing as if a single battery having eight times the surface of the single cell were used. This is termed coupling in multiple, Fig. 123. Similarly, if they were coupled +, —, +, —, +, —, +, — and +, —, +, —, +, —, +, and those two were joined as in Fig. 124, we should have the equivalent of a bat. tery possessing a voltage of four, and elements twice the size of the single cell. This would be spoken of as a battery of eight cells in series of four. Also four multiples, in series of two, might be arranged to give a voltage of two and quantity due to cells of four times the size of a single cell, as shown in Fig. 125. As the amperes of current passing per second depends upon the voltage, divided by the number of ohms resistance, in the circuit, it will be seen that the current can be controlled by coupling and by manipulating the resistance.

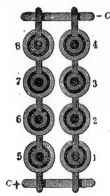

Fig. 124.

To Amalgamate Zincs. This may be very well done by first immersing the zincs in a solution of dilute sulphuric acid and then in a bath of mercury. A brush or cloth may be used to rub them, so as to reach all points of the surface. Where a large quantity is to be amalgamated, the following will be found to be a good method: Dissolve eight ounces of mercury in a mixture consisting of two lbs. of hydrochloric and one lb. of nitric acid; when the solution is complete, add three lbs. more of hydrochloric acid. The zinc is amalgamated by immersing it in this solution for a few seconds, quickly removing to a vat of clear water and rubbing it, as in the first case, with a brush or cloth. If the solution is kept in a covered vessel it may be used a number of times.

In all batteries in which acids are used the zincs should be kept well amalgamated and should be removed from the solution when not in use. This is very important and should not be overlooked.

Improved Electropoion Fluid. Add one part (by volume) of sulphuric acid to 10 parts of water. Of 10 pounds (or pints) of the dilute acid,

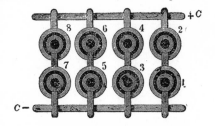

Fig. 125.

add from 1 to 2 pounds of chromic acid, according to the strength of current desired. Where constant action over a long time is desired, rather than maximum energy, omit part or all of the sulphuric acid.

Bichromate of potash is no longer used for batteries by intelligent workers. It owes its virtues to a small amount of chromic acid which can be obtained from it by reaction. Pure chromic acid is cheaper for the same work, and is free from many of the difficulties attendant on the use of the bichromate.

Connections. Having a knowledge of the theoretical action of the battery, the next question is the connections. Cleanliness cannot be too strongly insisted upon in making joints, etc. The plater should make it an invariable rule to see that all surfaces of wires, screws, etc., through which the current must pass, be kept bright on the surfaces, through which electrical contact is made. When joining wires they should be brightened with a file, or with emery cloth, and then twisted firmly together with a pair of pliers; all permanent connections should be carefully soldered and the holes and the ends of screws in binding posts should be kept bright; and if for permanent use all conducting wires should be of pure copper, well insulated. The following table shows in the last column the loss of current in wires carrying an economical amount of current; if the wire be too small this loss is rapidly quadrupled until the wire burns. The economy of using large and short connections will be apparent after a slight study of this table.

Table showing the Weight, Carrying Capacity and Loss in Volts of different sizes Copper Wire.

Brown & Sharpe's Gauge No.	Diameter in Thousandths of an inch.	Pounds per 1000 feet bare wire.	Approximate weight Underwriters' Insulation, per 1000 feet.	Safe Current in Amperes.	Loss in Volts per Ampere per 100 feet of line (2 Wire.)
0000	.46	640.5	825 lbs.	312.	.0098
000	.40964	508.5	610 lbs.	262.	.0123
00	.3648	402.8	458 lbs.	220.	.0155
0	.32495	319.6	385 lbs.	185.	.0196
1	.2893	253.4	308 lbs.	156.	.0247
2	.25763	201.0	249 lbs.	131.	.0311
3	.22942	159.3	201 lbs.	110.	.0392
4	.20431	126.4	163 lbs.	92.3	.0495
5	.18194	100.2	133 lbs.	77.6	.0624
6	.16202	79.46	109 lbs.	65.2	.0787
7	.14428	63.01	90 lbs.	54.8	.0992
8	.12849	49.98	74 lbs.	46.1	.125
9	.11443	39 64	62 lbs.	38.7	.158
10	.10189	31.43	52 lbs.	32.5	.199
11	.090742	24.93	43 lbs.	27.3	.251
12	.080808	19.77	36 lbs.	23.	.316
13	.071961	15.68	30 lbs.	19.3	.399
14	.064084	12.43	25 lbs.	16.2	.503
15	.057068	9.86	21 lbs.	13.6	.634
16	.05082	7.82	18 lbs.	11.5	.799
17	.045257	6.20	15 lbs.	9.6	1.088
18	.040303	4.92	13 lbs.	8.1	1.271

No matter what battery be used, there are several preliminary conditions that must be complied with in order to produce satisfactory results, i. e. that the deposition may adhere firmly and take place uniformly. It is absolutely necessary that the pure metallic surface of the article be exposed, and that it be perfectly free from grease. The articles to be plated, if lustrous surfaces are desired, must first be ground and polished. The grease must be removed from the surface by boiling in potash or caustic soda, and this is followed by scouring with freshly burnt lime, pulverized thoroughly and free from all grit. If the article will not stand heat, cleanse with benzine. In order to free the surface of non-metallic substances, if the article be of iron, steel or silver, dip it in a mixture of 1 part by weight of sulphuric acid, to 15 of water; if copper or brass, the articles are first dipped in dilute sulphuric acid, and then in a mixture of 100 parts, by weight, of nitric acid, 50 of sulphuric acid, 1 of common salt and 1 of soot. As soon as the surface of the article assumes a bright appearance, it is washed in clean water once or twice, avoiding handling with the fingers or greasy cloths. Wooden plyers, kept clean, serve well for handling.

Avoid the injurious fumes produced by the acids, by operating in the open air or in the draft of a chimney. In order to determine whether the article is entirely free from grease, dip it into water, and if all grease is removed, the water will adhere uniformly; if, however, lines and spots appear, the article is not thoroughly clean, and must again be put through the cleasing process.

Copper. Perhaps the most useful solutions for the plater are the cyanide copper solution, and the cyanide brass or bronze solution. The acid copper solution generally used, which is merely sulphate of copper dissolved in water, is easily made and used, but has numerous disadvantages when compared with the cyanide. It will deposit faster, but leaves a rough and crystalline surface, and cannot be used on steel, as the latter metal is electrically opposed to copper in the presence of sulphuric acid, and sets up a local action which throws off the deposit in scales as fast as it is formed.

The cyanide solution deposits a smooth, even and firm coating, takes equally well on steel, brass or other surfaces, and is capable of so many variations that it may be regarded as the basis of all brass, bronze and copper plating. It is also the only sure means of making a firm deposit of silver or gold on steel. Articles of iron or steel should first be given a light coating of copper, and then the gold or nickel will be held firmly, evenly and smoothly, so that lighter coatings of the more expensive metals will wear longer and look better than a thicker deposit directly on the steel.

The old formulæ for cyanide of copper solutions, all recommend mixing acetate of copper with carbonate and bisulphite of soda, and then adding potassium cyanide to the carbonate of copper thus formed. This encumbers the bath with a number of useless secondary reactions, and makes it liable to get out of order. It is much better to buy carbonate of copper from a dealer in platers' supplies. It is cheaper than the acetate, and does not put anything in the solution which is unnecessary

To make the solution, use to each gallon of water:

Carbonate of copper_____ _____7 ozs.
Carbonate of soda_____2 ozs.
Cyanide of potassium (chemically pure)_____8 ozs.

Dissolve about nine-tenths of the cyanide of potassium in a portion of the water, and add nearly all of the carbonate of copper, previously dissolved in a portion of the water; then add the carbonate of soda, also dissolved in water, slowly stirring until thoroughly mixed. If you have a hydrometer, make your solution to 16° B., then put in a small article and test your solution, adding cyanide or copper, or both, until the solution deposits freely and uniformly.

This may be regarded as a stock solution, and if much work is done, it is best to use it as a basis and make others from it, keeping them separate.

Brass. Brass solutions of any desired color may be made by adding carbonate of zinc, in varying proportions, to the above solution. One part of zinc and two of copper carbonates will give a beautiful golden yellow brass, and should be used with an anode of the same color. If, however, the plater desires to match colors on repairing jobs, etc., he can get any desired color from this bath by varying his current; a strong current will deposit more zinc than copper, giving a paler color of brass in the deposit; and a weaker current will deposit more copper than zinc, giving a redder deposit. In this way most repair jobs can be matched in color, although it is better, when doing new work, to make your solution of the color desired, and use an anode of the same color, as by doing so you put the two metals into the solution in the same proportion as you are taking them out. If you are using copper anodes, it is best to buy the electrically deposited anodes from a dealer in platers' supplies, as they cost no more, are always pure, and deposit much freer and smoother than the hard rolled copper for sale at metal houses. The same thing also applies to anodes of brass, gold or silver, but in less degree.

Management. Those who have never used the cyanide bath may desire some additional particulars regarding its management. The anodes in such a bath generally carry a slight greenish coating, consisting of copper cyanide. This is soluble in the free cyanide that is in the bath, and only traces of it should appear on the anodes. When the cyanide is used up, this green coating thickens up rapidly, and the bath, shortly afterwards, stops depositing. In such case, add cyanide (dissolved in water) very slowly, in order not to get in too much.

If too much cyanide is in the bath, bubbles of hydrogen will come from the objects to be coated, but no copper will be deposited, and the remedy is adding carbonate of copper.

If either of the above does not give a rapid and even coating, the bath needs more metal, and you are likely using too small an anode and stripping your bath. The remedy is, of course, found in adding more carbonate and using a larger anode.

Gold Baths. Both warm and cold baths are used, the former being preferable, as they yield denser depositions, require less strength of current, and need not be so rich in gold as cold baths. Many platers prepare gold baths by dissolving 3½ ounces of chemically pure cyanide of potassium in a quart of distilled water, and connecting two cells of Bunsen battery with two gold anodes, and working it until the solution contains 32 grains of gold to the quart of water, which can be told by weighing the anodes from time to time. It does not give as bright a color, however, as dissolving an equivalent quantity of chloride of gold in the cyanide, owing to the presence of silver and copper in the gold anodes, and consequently in the bath. In purchasing your chloride of gold, where possible get the brown neutral variety, as it is preferable to others, as it contains less acid.

A good warm bath is prepared as follows: Neutral chloride of gold, 7 pennyweights; 99 per cent potassium cyanide, 33 grains; water, 1 quart. Dissolve the potassium cyanide in one-half of the water and the chloride in the other half, mix both solutions, and boil for half an hour, replacing the water lost by evaporation. The solution will last indefinitely if the anode used is large enough to make up for the gold used. When the anode is covered with a slight coating in the bath, it shows a want of cyanide of potassium, which is best added by dissolving an ounce of chemically pure cyanide in a pint of water, and adding a little at a time, until the bath works all right again. Too much free cyanide in the bath gives an ugly, pale color and irregular deposit.

A cold solution will give a pale color; increasing the temperature to 140° gives a reddish color; 120° to 130° gives a fine yellow. The reason of this is that heat hastens the chemical reactions in the bath, and the gold deposits much more rapidly, so the operator should look out not to deposit more gold than he wants, and thus strip his solution. The anode surface should also be less with the hot solution.

Changes of color can also be made by increasing the current and anode surface in a cold solution, by putting in some sort of resistance in the circuit for the paler colors, and withdrawing it for the redder ones. As anodes, it is best to use sheets of fine gold, which gradually dissolve, and thus convey fresh metal to the bath. The current must not be so strong that a formation of bubbles is perceptible; it is best to use a current of such strength only that deposition takes place slowly, a coating of the greatest density being thus obtained. Avoid using cheap and inferior chemicals, as the difference in price is more than offset by the time and damage that often results from inferior grades. To obtain good results, always use as pure water as possible, filtered rain water being the most desirable. The best temperature for cold baths is 66° F. Care should also be taken to see that the baths are covered with cloths to exclude dust, and where it does penetrate, the baths should be skimmed off.

Only copper, brass and bronze can be directly gilded; other metals must first be coppered or brassed; this applies to good work. In gilding parts of watches, gold is seldom directly applied upon the brass; there is generally a preliminary operation called graining, by which a slightly dead appearance is given to the articles. They are thoroughly finished, all grease removed as described above, threaded upon a brass wire, cleansed in the compound acids for a bright luster, and dried in sawdust. The pieces are fastened upon the flat side of a piece of cork by means of brass pins, and the parts are thoroughly rubbed over with a clean brush dipped in a paste composed of fine pumice stone powder and water. The brush is moved in circles, in order to rub evenly. Thoroughly rinse in clean water in order to remove every particle of pumice stone, both from the article and the cork. Place the whole in a weak mercurial solution, composed of nitrate of mercury, 4 grains; water, 9 quarts; sulphuric acid, 1 dram; which will slightly whiten the brass. Pass quickly through this solution and then rinse. After the parts are grained in the manner described, they may be gilded the same as ordinary work.

Carat Baths. The plating baths of a large establishment are made up to have the same alloy in them as is intended to be used in the anode, that is, 18k, 16k, 14k, etc., by adding cyanide of copper and cyanide of silver, or chloride of silver, to the gold bath above described. Or it may be made by battery, as described above, and any article intended to receive a certain quality of plate is put into its appropriate bath, weighed from time to time, and when it has received the allotted number of pennyweights, is given to the finishers.

Red Gold. A solution of copper cyanide in potassium cyanide is added to the gold bath in small proportions, until it assumes the color desired.

Green Gold. Add cyanide or chloride of silver to the gold bath, until it assumes the desired color; or suspend silver anodes beside the gold anodes.

Coloring is always done with pure gold, and the best workmen take especial pains to see that no silver or copper is allowed in the solution. They do this by using only the best chemicals, and frequently evaporating their baths and parting out the silver with nitric acid. By this means they obtain an immense advantage over others, in the brightness and thinness of the coating of gold deposited.

The durability of gold plating does not depend altogether on the time it is in the solution. If the current is about two to three volts (about equal to a Bunsen cell, or two Smee cells connected, for intensity) and the quantity is proportioned to the work in the bath, then if the solution be worked at 120° to 130°, which also deepens the color of the deposit, it is possible to get a coat inside of five minutes that will last for several years.

It is always best, when other conditions are all right, to keep the work moving, and immerse the gold anode gradually, to suit the surface of the work that is being plated; care should be taken not to allow the work and anode to touch each other, as a black or burned spot will be left on the work wherever the anode touches it.

After getting the first slight coat of gold, the work should be scratch brushed with a fine brass scratch brush (wire about .003 inch), letting a little soap suds drip on the brush. This lays down the first coat of gold, which should be sufficient to cover the article entirely. The scratch brush acts as a burnisher. After this it is thoroughly cleaned of the soap suds in hot water, and again placed in the solution. The time it remains will have to be governed by experience, but generally five minutes will give a sufficient coat to stand burnishing.

Burnishing may be done with steel and agate burnishers, same as with silver, or the articles may be polished with a soft cotton flannel wheel, run at 2,500 revolutions per minute, and bearing a very little of the finest rouge, mixed with alcohol. If you run your wheel too slow the layers of cotton will not stand up, and you will not get a polish; 2,500 to 3,000 revolutions is about right, and the pressure should be light and even.

Silver Baths. For ordinary plating 7 pennyweights of fine silver (11 pennyweights of nitrate of silver, or 9 pennyweights of chloride of silver), is dissolved in a solution of 33 grains of 98 per cent potassium cyanide in 1 quart of water. For heavy silvering of knives, forks, etc., a stronger bath is used: 17½ pennyweights of fine silver (1 oz., 4 pennyweights of chloride of silver, or 1 oz. 15 grains of cyanide of silver,) is dissolved in a solution of 1 oz. 15 pennyweights of 98 per cent potassium cyanide in 1 quart of water. No accurate statement can be made in regard to the quantity of potassium cyanide in the bath, as it depends on the strength of the current used. With a very weak current, and consequently slow precipitation, somewhat more potassium cyanide may be used than with a stronger current and more rapid precipitation. The anodes, for which fine silver is used, will indicate by their appearance whether the bath contains too much or too little potassium cyanide. They should become gray during silvering, and gradually resume their white color after the interruption of the current. If they remain white during silvering, the bath contains too much potassium cyanide, and, if they turn black, and retain this color after the interruption of the current, potassium cyanide should be added.

The article to be silvered should be moved constantly to avoid the formation of streaks. Before silvering the metals must be prepared by amalgamation. This is done by dipping the articles, previously freed from grease, as explained above, in a dilute solution of mercurous nitrate (30 to 150 grains per qt.) allowing them to remain in the solution only long enough to become uniformly white. Rinse them in water, brush off with a clean soft brush, and immediately place in the striking bath.

Silvering of iron and steel is best accomplished by using a striking solution made as follows: ¾ of an oz. of C. P. chloride silver, 6 oz. C. P. cyanide of potash, 1 gallon water. After thoroughly cleaning hang the articles for a few minutes in the solution, using a large silver anode surface. The hydrogen gas should escape freely from the surface of work and as soon as covered with a yellowish deposit of silver, which is very adhesive, transfer to the standard solution, which can be made from the concentrated solution. From this no gas should escape, and the anode surface should be about the same as surface of work. A Bunsen or three Smee batteries connected for intensity can be used for the striker, and one Smee cell for standard solution, zinc surface of same equalling that of work.

The articles remain in the bath from ten to fifteen minutes, when they show a uniformly white surface; they are then taken out, scratch-brushed with a brass brush to see that the deposit adheres, all grease removed, and then placed in the bath. After the current is shut off, the articles should be left in the bath a few seconds to prevent the deposit from turning yellow.

If the articles are not to be burnished, but are to be left with a mat as they come from the bath, they must be thoroughly rinsed in water without coming in contact with the fingers or the sides of the vessel, then dipped in clean hot water and hung up to dry. They then should be coated with a colorless laquer to prevent turning yellow. If the articles are to have a polished surface, they are to be finally scratch-brushed with frequent moistening with soap-root, dried in warm sawdust and burnished with a steel or stone burnisher.

Nickel Baths. Iron and steel must be prepared by immersing in a hot solution of caustic soda or potash, thoroughly brushed, rinsed in

water and dipped in a pickle of 1 part sulphuric acid, 2 parts hydrochloric acid and 10 parts of water, again rinsed, thoroughly rubbed with
fine well washed pumice stone or Vienna lime, again rinsed and put in
the bath. If finely polished tools, they may be brushed with whiting or
tripoli instead of pumice stone. Copper wire should be tightly wound
around all metal articles. Small articles may be suspended from copper
hooks. The battery or dynamo is placed in action before immersing the
articles, which remain in the bath until they have acquired a white
appearance, which will be in from five to thirty minutes, depending on
the strength of the current and the size of the article. In case the article
assumes a gray or black color, or feels rough and gritty, the current is
too strong, or if it assumes a yellowish white appearance, it is too weak.
The simplest nickel bath consists of a solution of pure double sulphate
of nickel and ammonium 8 to 10 parts by weight in 100 parts of distilled
water. Boil the salt in a corresponding quantity of water, say 8 to 10
parts of nickel-salt to 100 of water, depending on the temperature.
With this bath cast nickel anodes and a strong current should be used.
When a pure white deposit is required on unpolished surfaces the addition of 2 oz. of pure chloride of nickel to each gallon of the above solution is recommended. On an article of iron, steel, lead or its alloys a
previous slight deposit of copper from a cyanide solution is advisable. It
adds scarcely anything to the cost and insures a uniform coating which
is not always apparent in a deposit on a light colored metal. The article
after its removal from the bath should be dipped for a few seconds in
boiling water, drained and dried in warm sawdust. They may then be
polished, but cannot be burnished. The luster on nickel-plated objects
depends greatly on the polish given them before plating. The composition of nickel baths depends greatly upon the metals to be operated on,
which can best be determined by experiment. The anodes should be
suspended by strong hooks of pure nickel wire, and the articles should
be placed at a distance of from 3¾ to 4¾ inches from them. If the
article is to receive a thick deposit, it should be turned in the bath from
time to time, from end to end, so that those portions which were down
come up. Small articles which cannot be suspended are placed in a
sieve, it being preferable to use a heated bath for the purpose. Iron,
steel, copper, brass and bronze are usually nickeled directly, but Brittan-
nia ware, zinc and tin are coppered or brassed before nickeling. In case
a freshly prepared bath yields a dark deposit it can generally be rem-
edied by working the bath for two or three hours.

Doctoring. This term is applied to plating defective places which
occurred either by accident or negligence on the part of the operator.
It is equally applicable to gold, silver or nickel plated articles. Take a
piece of the anode, be it gold, silver or nickel, about the size of your
little finger and connect it with the positive pole by a thin copper wire.

Around this anode wrap a piece of ordinary muslin several times; hold the defective article on the top of the positive pole, and after dipping the anode in the solution until the muslin is thoroughly soaked, move it to and fro over the defective place, and a coating is thus formed.

Recovery of Gold from Bath. To recover gold from bath evaporate the bath to dryness, mix the residue with litharge and fuse the mixture. A lead button is thus formed in which all the gold is contained. Dissolve the button in nitric acid, and the gold will remain behind in the form of small flakes. Filter off and dissolve the flakes in aqua regia.

Recovering Gold from Coloring Bath. Dissolve a handful of sulphate of iron in boiling water, and add to it your "color" water; it precipites the small particles of gold. Now draw off the water, being very careful not to disturb the auriferous sediment at the bottom. You will now proceed to wash the sediment from all traces of acid with plenty of boiling water; it will require three or four separate washings, with sufficient time between each to allow the water to cool and the sediment to settle, before passing off the water. Then dry in an iron vessel by the fire and finally fuse in a covered crucible, with a flux.

Recovery of Silver from a Bath. To recover silver from cyanide bath; evaporate the bath to dryness, mix the residue with a small quantity of calcined soda and potassium cyanide and fuse in a crucible, and the metal will be found in the form of a button in the bottom of the crucible.

Antique Green. An imitation of antique bronze can be applied to new articles by the following process: Dissolve 3 parts of common salt, 1 part of sal-ammoniac and 3 parts of powdered tartar in 12 parts of boiling water. Add 8 parts of a solution of cupric nitrate, and coat the articles with the liquid.

Black Bronze for Brass. 1. Dissolve one oz. of copper carbonate in 8¾ fluid ounces of spirit of sal-ammoniac. Add one pint of water and stir constantly. The articles to be colored should be suspended in the liquid by means of brass or copper wires for a short time. The coating adheres better if the articles are polished with coarse emery paper.

2. Brush the brass with a solution of nitrate of mercury, and then several times with a solution of liver of sulphur.*

Blue Bronze. Cleanse the metal from all grease by dipping in boiling potash lye and afterwards treat it with strong vinegar. Wipe and

---

* Fused sulphuret of potassium, so called from its resemblance to liver in color.

dry the article thoroughly, and rub it with a linen rag, moistened with hydrochloric acid. Allow the coating to dry for a quarter of an hour, and then heat the article on a sand bath, until it assumes the desired color, when it should be removed.

Bronze for Small Brass Articles. Oxide of iron, 3 parts; white arsenic, 8 parts; hydrochloric acid, 36 parts. Clean the brass thoroughly and apply with a brush until the desired color is obtained. Oil well and finish by varnishing or lacquering.

Bronze Liquid. Dissolve sal-ammoniac 1 oz.; alum, ½ oz.; arsenic, ¼ oz.; in strong vinegar, 1 pt. The compound is immediately fit for use, and, where the metal is good, is seldom found to fail.

Bronze for Medals. The following process of bronzing is carried on in the Paris mint. Powder and mix 1 pound each of verdigris and sal-ammoniac. Take a quantity of this mixture, as large as a hen's egg, and mix into a dough with vinegar. Place this in a copper pan (not tinned), boil in about 5 pints of water for 20 minutes, and then pour off the water. For bronzing, pour part of this fluid into a copper pan; place the medals separately in it upon pieces of wood or glass, so that they do not touch each other, or come in contact with the copper pan, and then boil them in the liquid for a quarter of an hour.

Bronze for Steel. Methylated spirit, 1 pint; gum shellac, 4 ounces; gum benzoin, ½ ounce. Set the bottle in a warm place, with occasional agitation. When dissolved, decant the clear part for fine work, and strain the dregs through muslin. Now take 4 ounces powdered bronze green, varying the color with yellow ochre, red ochre and lamp black, as may be desired. Mix the bronze powder with the above varnish in quantities to suit, and apply to the work, after previously cleansing and warming the articles, giving them a second coat, and touching off with gold powder, if required, previous to varnishing.

Brown Bronze. Brown bronze is prepared the same as blue bronze but the blue bronze is finally rubbed over with a linen rag saturated with olive oil, which will change the blue color into brown.

Brown Stain for Copper. To produce a dark-brown color upon copper, take the white of an egg, beat it into froth, add a little boiled or rain water, and add to this mixture *caput mortuum* (red oxide of iron); rub them well together in a mortar, and sufficiently thick until the color covers, and may be applied. The copper articles are to be pickled and simply washed; no sand must be used, else the color adheres badly. The latter is next applied with a brush until it covers the surface it is then dried by a fire, the article is gently rubbed with a soft rag and *caput mortuum* powder, and finally hammered with a hammer with polished face.

Brown Stain for Gun Barrels. Mix 12 parts of a solution of sulphate of iron, 16 parts of sulphate of copper, 16 parts of sweet spirit of nitre and 12 parts of butter of antimony. Let the mixture stand in a well corked bottle for twenty-four hours and then add 500 parts of rain water. Thoroughly polish and clean the barrels, wash with fresh lime water, dry thoroughly and apply the mixture evenly with a piece of cotton. After drying for twenty-four hours, brush with a scratch brush and repeat the coating. Do this twice, the last time using leather moistened with olive oil in lieu of the scratch brush, rubbing thoroughly. After standing for ten or twelve hours, repeat the polishing with sweet oil and leather until a beautiful polish is obtained.

Chinese Bronze. Small articles bronzed by this process possess a peculiar beauty, and lose none of their luster, even when exposed to atmospheric influences and rain. Powder and mix thoroughly 2 parts of crystalized verdigris, 2 parts of cinnabar, 2 of sal-ammoniac, 2 of bills and livers of ducks, and 5 of alum. Moisten the mixture with water or spirit of wine, and rub into a paste; cleanse the article to be bronzed thoroughly, and polish with ashes and vinegar. Then apply the paste with a brush. Heat the article over a coal fire, and wash the coating off. Repeat this operation until the desired brown color is obtained. By adding blue vitriol to the mixture, a chestnut brown color is produced, while an addition of borax gives a yellowish shade.

Gold Bronze for Iron. Dissolve three ounces of finely powdered shellac in 1¼ pints of spirit of wine. Filter the varnish through linen and rub a sufficient quantity of Dutch gold with the the filtrate to give a lustrous color to it. The iron, previously polished and heated, is brushed over with vinegar and the color applied with a brush. When dry the article may be coated with copal lacquer to which some amber lacquer has been added.

Gold Tinge to Silver. A bright gold tinge may be given to silver by steeping it for a suitable length of time in a weak solution of sulphuric acid and water, strongly impregnated with iron rust.

Gold-Yellow Color on Brass. A gold like appearance may be given to brass by the use of a fluid prepared by boiling for about 15 minutes, 4 parts caustic soda, 4 parts milk sugar, and 100 parts of water, after which 4 parts concentrated solution of sulphate of copper is added with constant stirring. The mixture is then cooled to $79°$ C., and the previously well cleaned articles are for a short time laid into it. When left in it for some time they will first assume a blueish and then a rainbow color.

Gray Stain for Brass. Many black and gray pickles possess the defect that they give different colors with different copper alloys, while in the case of certain alloys they refuse to act altogether. For instance, carbonate of copper, dissolved in ammonia, gives to brass a handsome, dark-gray color, while it does not whatever attack various other alloys; therefore it is little suitable for instruments. A dark-gray pickle, which almost indiscriminately stains all copper alloys a handsome gray, resembling in color the costly platinum, is composed by dissolving 50 grams arsenic in 250 grams hydrochloric acid, and adding to the solution 35 grams chloride of antimony and 35 grams finely pulverized hammer scales. The articles to be pickled are rinsed in a weak, warm soda solution, prior to as well as after immersion, to be followed by continued rinsing in water. The recipe is simple, and has been repeatedly tested with uniformly good results.

Green Bronze for Brass. Add to a solution of 8 ½ drachms of copper in one ounce of strong nitric acid, 10 ½ fluid ounces of vinegar, 3 ½ drachms of sal-ammoniac, and 6 ¾ drachms of aqua-ammonia. Put the liquid in a loosely corked bottle, and allow it to stand in a warm place for a few days, when it may be used. After applying it to the articles, dry them by exposure to heat, and when dry, apply a coat of linseed oil varnish, which is also dried by heat.

Imitation of Antique Silver. The article is dipped in a bath of water containing about 10 per cent of sulphide of ammonium, and then scratch brushed with a brush made of glass threads or bristles. When afterwards burnished with an agate tool its surface becomes a beautiful dark brown color.

Oxidizing Silver. 1. Place the silver or plated articles in a solution of liver of sulphur diluted with spirit of sal-ammoniac. They are then taken out, washed, dried and polished. This produces a blue-black tint, while a solution of equal quantities of sal-ammoniac and blue vitrol in vinegar gives a brown shade.

2. Sal-ammoniac, 2 parts; sulphate of copper, 2 parts; saltpeter, 1 part. Reduce these ingredients to a fine powder, and dissolve in a little acetic acid. If the article is to be entirely oxidized, it may be dipped for a short time in the boiling mixture; if only in parts, it may be applied with a camel-hair pencil, the article and the mixture both being warmed before using.

3. There are two distinct shades in use, one produced by chloride, which has a brownish tint, and the other by sulphur, which has a bluish-black tint. To produce the former it is only necessary to work the article with a solution of sal-ammoniac; a much more beautiful tint, however, may be obtained by employing a solution composed of equal parts of sulphate of copper and sal-ammoniac in vinegar. The fine black tint may be produced by a slightly warm solution of sulphate of potassium or sodium.

Silvering for Copper or Brass. Mix 1 part of chloride of silver with 3 parts of pearl ash, 1½ parts common salt, and one part whiting; and well rub the mixture on the surface of brass or copper (previously well cleaned), by means of a piece of soft leather, or a cork moistened with water and dipped in the powder. When properly silvered, the metal should be well washed in hot water, slightly alkalized, then wiped dry.

2. Mix three parts of chloride of silver with 20 parts finely pulverized cream tartar, and 15 parts culinary salt. Add water in sufficient quantity, and stir until the mixture forms a paste, with which cover the surface to be silvered by means of blotting paper. The surface is then rubbed with a rag and powdered lime, washed, and rubbed with a piece of soft cloth. The deposited film is extremely thin.

Silvering Small Iron Articles. The small iron articles are suspended in dilute sulphuric acid until the iron shows a bright clean surface. After rinsing in pure water, they are placed in a bath of mixed solution of sulphate of zinc, sulphate of copper, and cyanide of potassium, and there remain until they receive a bright coating of brass. Lastly they are transferred to a bath of nitrate of silver, cyanide of potassium, and sulphate of soda, in which they quickly receive a coating of silver.

Silver Plating Without a Battery. 1. The process consists in exposing the article, which has previously been well cleansed with a potash solution and dilute hydrochloric acid, to the operation of a silver bath, which is prepared in the following manner: Form a solution of 32 grams (1 oz., 13.8 grains) nitrate of silver, 20 grams silver (12 dwts., 20.6 grains) in 60 (1 oz., 18 dwts., 13.9 grains) grams nitric acid. The silver is precipitated as silver oxide with a solution of 20 grams solid caustic potash in 50 grams (1 oz., 12 dwts., 3.6 grains) distilled water, carefully washed, and the precipitate taken up by a solution of 100 grams (3 oz., 4 dwts., 7.2 grains) cyanide of potassium in 500 grams distilled water. The fluid, distilled through paper, is finally diluted with distilled water to 2 liters (4½ pints). The thus prepared silver bath is gently warmed in the water bath, and the article to be silver plated laid in it and kept in motion for a few minutes, and after taking out it is dried in sawdust, and then polished with Vienna chalk for giving luster.

2. For rapid silver plating, prepare a powder of 3 parts of chloride of silver, 20 parts carefully pulverized cream of tartar, and 15 parts pulverized cooking salt; mix it into a thin paste with water, and rub it upon the well cleaned metallic surface with blotting paper. After you are certain that all parts of the article have been touched alike, rub it with very fine chalk or dust upon wadding or other soft cloth. Wash with clean water and dry with a cloth.

3. Dissolve 1 oz nitrate of silver, in crystals, in 12 ozs., soft water; then dissolve in the water 2 ozs. cyanide of potash, shake the whole together, and let it stand until it becomes clear. Have ready some half-ounce vials, and fill half full with Paris white, or fine whiting, and then fill up the bottles with the liquid, and it is ready for use. The whiting does not increase the coating power, it only helps to clean the article, and save the silver fluid.

4. Make a solution of 4 ounces lunar caustic (equal to a solution 2½ ounces silver in 7½ ounces nitric acid); the silver of this solution is precipitated as an oxide of silver by the addition of a solution of 2½ ounces of caustic potash in 6½ ounces distilled water; and the precipitate, after being washed, is added to a solution of 12½ ounces of cyanide of potassium in one quart of water. This solution is then filtered and water added to bring it to 4 quarts. In this solution, which is heated on the water bath, the pieces to be silvered are left for a few minutes. Being agitated, they are taken out, and put to dry in fine sawdust and then polished.

Steel-Blue on Brass. Dissolve 1½ drachms of antimony sulphide and 2 ounces calcined soda in ¾ pint of water. Add 2¾ drachms of kermes, filter, and mix this solution with another of 2¾ drachms of tartar, 5½ drachms of sodium hyposulphite and ¾ pint of water. Polished sheet brass placed in the warm mixture assumes a beautiful steel-blue.

To Give Copper a Durable Luster. Place the copper articles in a boiling solution of tartar and water for fifteen minutes. Remove, rinse off with cold water and dry.

ELLICOTT, JOHN. A celebrated London clockmaker. He was born in 1700, was elected a fellow of the Royal Society in 1738, and published a work on pendulums in 1751. He invented a compensation pendulum in 1753, in which the bob rested on the longer ends of two levers, of which the shorter ends are depressed by the superior expansion of a brass bar attached to the pendulum rod. The invention, however has not proved of any practical value. He died in 1772.

EMERY. The dark colored and non-transparent variety of corundum. See *Corundum*.

Emery Countersinks. See *Countersinks.*

Emery Files, Pencils and Sticks. Emery files are to be had ready made from all material dealers and consist of wooden handles to which emery cloth is glued. Emery pencils are kept by some dealers and will be found very useful for grinding the inside of metal objects, and also on small work of various kinds, being easy to handle, clean and light. Emery sticks are of two kinds, solid square sticks and round and square sticks of wood to which emery paper or cloth is glued. Emery paper and cloth may be had from most material dealers, varying from 0000 to No. 4.

Emery Wheels. Wheels of solid emery or wooden wheels, to the surface of which emery paste has been applied. The best wheels for watchmakers' use are the solid wheels in which vulcanite is the cementing medium. They may be had from material dealers generally or from dental supply houses, in sizes varying from ½ x ⅛ in. to 3½ x ¾ in. A set of three or more of these wheels will prove very valuable

Fig. 126.

adjuncts to the watchmaker's bench for grinding dials to allow freedom of motion for wheels in fitting new dials; for grinding milling cutters, drills, gravers, etc. As purchased from dealers these wheels have a central hole, by means of which they can be mounted for use by the watchmaker as follows: Turn down a piece of No. 30, Stubbs' steel wire, to the size of the opening in your wheel and rivet your wheel firmly upon it, as shown in Fig. 126. It can then be used in your lathe very handily, either with or without water. The best sizes for watchmakers use are ½ in., 1 in. and 1½ in. diameter.

END STONE. The small stone disc on which a watch pivot rests, applied principally to escapement and balance pivots. Jewels with end stones are known as capped jewels.

ENGINE TURNING. The wavy, curved lines used as decorations for watch cases. See *Rose Engine.*

ENGRAVING BLOCKS. A mechanical device for holding coins, jewelry, silverware, etc., while engraving. Fig. 127 is the usual form given to engraving blocks and is known as the flat base variety. Fig. 128 has what is known as the cannon-ball base, but the holding devices are similar to the flat base. Various attachments are furnished for holding rings, spoons, coins, etc.

EPICYCLOID. A curve generated by a point in the circumference of a movable circle, as it rolls upon another circle. The teeth of driving wheels are usually of this form.

<table>
<tr><td>Fig. 127.</td><td>Fig. 128.</td></tr>
</table>

EQUATION OF TIME. The difference between mean and apparent, or solar, time.

ESCAPEMENT. The mechanical device in a watch or clock by which the motion of the train is controlled so that the power may be distributed uniformly. Saunier divides escapements into three principal classes: Recoil, Dead Beat and Detached. 1. Recoil escapements are so classed, because at a certain period of this action, the wheel moves backward or recoils in a manner more or less marked. The verge escapement in watches and certain forms of the anchor in clocks, may be used as examples.

2. Dead Beat escapements are so called because except during the actual impulsion, the wheel remains stationary, a point being supported either against the axis of the balance itself, or against the accessory piece, concentric with this axis, which catches it in its movement of rotation. The cylinder and duplex escapements in watches and the pin and Graham escapements in clocks are examples of this class.

3. Detached escapements may be called Dead Beat escapements, but their principal characteristic consists in the fact that the balance performs its vibration in absolute independence of the wheel, except during the very brief periods of impulse and unlocking. The wheel, then, does not rest on the axis of the balance, but on an intermediate and distinct piece. The lever escapement in watches, the detent escapement in chronometers, as well as several forms of escapements employed in clocks, come under this head. See *Anchor, Chronometer, Cylinder, Dead Beat, Duplex, Graham, Pin Pallet, Pin Wheel and Verge.*

ESCAPE PINION. The pinion on the escape wheel staff.

ESCAPING ARC. Twice the angular distance a pendulum has to be moved from its point of rest, in order to allow a tooth of the escape wheel to pass from one pallet to another.

EYE GLASS. Eye glasses for watchmaker's use are mounted in many different styles. Some have horn, others have vulcanite and still others cork mountings. The vulcanite mounted glass with a light spring attached to sustain it in place is very popular with apprentices. The Clark patent glass, shown in Fig. 129, is becoming very popular in this country. It is provided with an annular reflector, with a central opening and corrugations, and so seated in the outer end of the glass as to reflect the rays of light falling on the outside of it in front of the glass, and concentrating them upon the object being viewed. It is especially useful in examin-

Fig. 129.

ing the inside of watches, as it often occurs that it is difficult to get light sufficient to do so.

FACIO, NICHOLAS. A native of Geneva, who discovered the art of piercing holes in rubies, garnets and other stones. He first went to Paris and from there, in 1700, went to London, and there with the brothers Peter and Jacob de Beaufre carried on the business of watch jewelling. A patent on his process of piercing jewels was granted to him in England in May, 1704.

FERGUSON, JAMES. A celebrated astronomer and mechanician. He was born in the year 1710, a few miles from Keith, a little village in Banffshire, in the north of Scotland. Ferguson can hardly be classed among horologists, although he made many improve-

James Ferguson. ments in the clocks of his day and many inventions in this line. In the year 1750 Ferguson invented and made his celebrated machine, known as the "Mechanical Paradox." This curious machine was made for the purpose of silencing a London watchmaker who did not believe in the doctrine of the Trinity. The paradox, which is illustrated in Fig. 131, is described by Ferguson as follows: "A is called the *immovable* plate, because it lies on a table whilst the machine is at

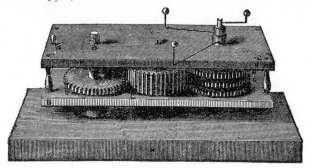

Fig. 131.

work; B C is a moveable frame to be turned round an upright axis *a* (fixt in the centre of the immoveable plate) by taking hold of the nob *u*.

Fig. 132.

On the said axis is fixt the immoveable wheel D whose teeth take into the teeth of the thick moveable wheel E, and turns it round its own axis as the frame is turned round the fixt axis of the immoveable wheel D and in the same direction that the frame is moved. The teeth of the thick wheel E take equally deep into the teeth of the three wheels, F, G and H, but operate on these wheels in such a manner, that whilst the frame is turned round, the wheel H turns *the same way* that the wheel E does, the wheel G turns *the contrary way*, and the wheel F *no way at all*." Fig. 132 illustrates what Ferguson termed "a one-wheeled clock." The drawing he made in 1774 and there was no description accompanying it, simply these few words: "The number of wheels in a clock reduced to one, by means of a double 'scapement." This is a problem for the ingenious watch or clock maker to solve. James Ferguson died Nov. 16, 1776.

FERRULE. The small pulley or wheel around which the string of a bow is wound when giving motion to a piece of work. See also *Collet*.

FETIL, PIERRE. A noted French Watchmaker, born at Nantes in 1753, and died at Orleans May 18, 1814.

FILES. Files for watchmakers' use are made in every conceivable shape, and in sizes from that of a fine cambric needle to 1 x ⅛ in. The various styles are known as flat, pillar, joint, three-cornered, knife, round, half round, oval, square, smooth cut, barrette, warding, conical, slitting, pivot, ratchet, screwhead, escapement, etc. Escapement files are usually put up in sets of twelve assorted shapes. The average American has a tendency to be extravagant, and in no trade or calling is this extravagance better exemplified than in that of the watchmaker and particularly in the matter of files. Many watchmakers' benches will be found, in the drawers of which, from one to two dozen files will be found, and out of all that number, not to exceed six will be in anything like respectable shape for good work. This is not occasioned by the poor quality of the goods used in this country, because eight out of every ten files used by watchmakers are of French, Swiss or English manufacture, and cost the American more money than his European brother, but rather from a careless handling of these tools, from a want of training. The skilled European watchmaker serves a long apprenticeship to a master who insists that he first becomes proficient in the use of the file, then the graver, etc., before he is allowed to work upon a clock or watch. In this way he acquires a proficency in the use of tools which the average young American watchmaker is a stranger to. The American watchmaker will employ a new file upon steel work, whereas, the European first employs a new file in working brass or copper and even then handles it very carefully. He would no more think of using a new file upon steel work than he would of flying. A new file, if carefully used, and gradually advanced from a soft to a hard metal, will at the end of six months, be a much better file for steel work than a new one, and will last four times as long. When the surface of a file becomes chocked with particles of steel, iron or brass, Saunier advises that it be cleaned as follows: Place the file for a few seconds in hot potash and water, and on withdrawal, dry it before the fire and brush the surface with a stiff brush. If the file has a tendency to fill up, slightly oil the surface by means of a linen rag.

FILING BLOCK. A contrivance made to take the place of the

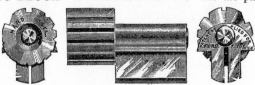

Fig. 133.

filing rest, which was made of boxwood or bone. It consists of a cylinder

of hardened steel rivetted upon a staff which in turn enters a split socket.
The surface of the steel cylinder is grooved with various sizes of grooves
for the different sizes of wire, or to suit any work, as shown in Fig. 133.
The cylinder is revolved until the desired size groove is brought uppermost, when the split socket is placed between the jaws of a vise, and the
vice closed, thus holding the cylinder in the desired position. Fig. 133
illustrates Mr. Ide's patent block which is well made and of superior
material.

FILING FIXTURE OR REST.   These rests will be found very
convenient in squaring winding arbors, center squares, etc.   There are
several makes of these tools, but they are all built upon the same principle, that of two hardened steel rollers on which the
file rests, and Fig. 134 is a fair example.   One pattern
is made to fit in the hand rest after the T is removed,
while the other is attached to the bed of the lathe in
the same manner as the slide rest.   The piece to be
squared is held in the split or spring chuck in the
lathe, and the index on the pulley is used to divide
the square correctly.   Any article can be filed to a
perfect square, hexagon or octagon as may be desired.   The arm carrying the rollers can be raised or lowered as required for adjustment to
work of various sizes.

Fig. 134.

FLUX.   A mixture or compound to promote the fusion of metals;
used in assaying, refining and soldering, as alkalies, borax, etc.

FLY OR FAN.   A fan having two blades, used for preserving the
uniformity of motion, as in music-boxes and the striking mechanism of
clocks.   The resistance of the air on the fan blades prevents the train
from accelerating.

FOLLOWER.   Where two wheels are toothed together the one that
imparts the power is known as the driver, and the one receiving the
power is called the follower.

FOOT WHEEL.   In the selection of a foot wheel the workman
must be governed by his own experience and taste, for, like cigars, the
variety that exactly suits one person is very distasteful to another.
Some workman prefer a treadle having a heel and toe motion, while
others prefer a swing treadle like that shown in Fig. 135.

FOURTH WHEEL.   The wheel that imparts motion to the escape
pinion, the second hand being attached to the wheel.

FRICTION.   The resistance which a moving body meets with from
the surface of the body on which it moves; is caused by the unevenness

of the surfaces, combined with some other causes, such as natural attraction, magnetism, etc. It varies as does the weight or pressure applied and is independent of surfaces in contact, but if the surfaces are disproportionate to the pressure, rapid abrasion will be the result, which in its turn produces uneven surfaces and tends to increase the friction.

Fig. 135.

In order to prevent the abrasion of the surface a lubricant is applied, either in the shape of oil or plumbago which, spreading itself over the surfaces of the bodies, interposes a film between the two acting surfaces, and this film, especially in light bodies, has a greater retarding influence than mere friction itself. In such cases the acting surfaces are made very minute, as in balance staff pivots, etc. In these pivots the resistance arising from the lubricant is usually greater than that of the friction proper, and it gradully increases as the lubricant becomes viscid. For this reason plumbago is advocated as a lubricant in large machines, as it does not become viscid and is an excellent lubricant. It is not applicable, however, for watch or clock work. From the above it is apparent that a light bodied or thin lubricant is desirable on small bearings, such as balance pivots, while as the barrel or power is approached and larger surfaces used the lubricant should be of a heavier body, or thicker. The nearer that a revolving surface is to its center of motion the less the friction. It is therefore essential where extra surface is desired that the surfaces be *increased in length*, and that the *diameter* of a pivot be *not increased* for if the *diameter* be doubled the resistance is doubled, as the acting surface is twice the distance from the center of motion.

FRICTIONAL ESCAPEMENTS. Those escapements in which the balance is never free or detached from the escapement. In contradistinction to the detached escapement. The duplex, cylinder or verge are examples of frictional escapements.

FRODSHAM, CHARLES. A skillful and successful watchmaker of London and the author of several valuable works on watchmaking. He was born in 1810 and died in 1871.

FROSTING. The matted or rough surface sometimes given to work before gilding or silvering. See *Electro-Plating*, *Bronzing and Staining*. The gray surface produced on steel work of watches is also known as frosting, though more commonly called graying.

FULL PLATE. A term applied to movements having a full top plate and the balance above the plate.

FUZEE. A brass cone, as shown in Figure 136, having a spiral groove cut on it to hold the chain, and interposed between the barrel and center pinion of a watch for the purpose of equalizing the pull of the mainspring and converting it into a constant pressure at the center of the pinion, for the pull of the mainspring is greater when wound around the barrel arbor than when it has expanded to the circumference

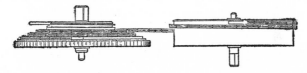

Fig. 136.

of the barrel. The principle of its construction is that by winding the fusee chain upon its cone the mainspring is wound, and the greatest pull comes upon the smaller end of the cone, and as the pull becomes less by the unwinding of the mainspring, the leverage (by means of the chain unwinding from a smaller to a larger cone) increases, and the rate of its increase constitutes a perfect adjustment of the mainspring. The fuzee chain was first introduced by Gruet of Geneva in 1664. The fuzee is held in great esteem by English watchmakers, and possesses many excellent points, although not employed in any American-made watch.

Repairing Watch Fuzee Top Pivot. First file up and re-polish the square, taking off the corners sufficiently to prevent them standing above the pivot when it is repolished. Put the square into an eccentric arbor and get the fuzee quite true. Now put a screw ferrule on to the fuzee back arbor, and place the whole piece in the turns with the eccentric in front, using the bow on the ferrule at the back. If the pivot is much cut it should be turned slightly with the point of the graver. Polish first with steel and coarse stuff, afterwards with bell-metal and fine stuff, and finish with the glossing burnisher.

To Put in a Watch Fuzee Top Hole. Put the pillar plate in the mandrel and peg the bottom hole true, then turn out the top hole to the required size for stopping. The stopping (a hollow one) should be small, and no longer than just sufficient to form the rivet. If there be danger of bending the plate, the stopping should be softened slightly (the hammering will re-harden it), and the ends turned hollow to facilitate the riveting. The top hole is now to be turned to nearly right size for the pivot, testing it frequently for truth with the peg, as much broaching is especially to be avoided. In finishing the stopping use polished cutters, take off the corners of the hole, and polish the cup or chamfer for the oil with the peg and redstuff. The same procedure is to be followed with ¾-plate fuzee, and it will be found best to finish the stopping in fuzee piece before screwing the steel on to the brass. Be careful to give the fuzee but little end shake; if it be at all excessive the stop work and the maintaining work will become uncertain, and either or both may fail

GALILEO. A celebrated mathematician, born 1564, who discovered the use of the pendulum about the close of the sixteenth century. It

Fig. 137.

is related that he was studying medicine and philosophy, when one morning he was in church and saw a lamp which was suspended by a silken cord from the ceiling, swinging to and fro after having been carelessly struck by one of the attendants. He noticed the regularity of the swing, comparing it with his pulse, and concluded that, by reason of its regularity, a simple pendulum might become a valuable agent in the measurement of time. In 1639, he published a treatise on the use of the pendulum in clocks, but there is no record of his having made one. The credit of actually putting a pendulum in a clock has been claimed for Richard Harris, of London, 1641; Vincent Galileo, son of the philosopher, 1649; and Huyghens, 1657. The weight of the evidence seems to be in favor of Huyghens as being the first to apply the Galilean theory in practice, but it is beyond dispute that the invention of the pendulum belongs to Galileo.

GAS HEATER. This heater, shown in Fig. 138, is to take the place of a forge in heating and tempering small articles. With a full pressure of gas, a piece of steel half an inch in diameter can be heated sufficiently to harden in about six minutes. It does not heat to a degree that will injure the quality of steel; which makes it very valuable for heating small pieces. Watchmakers will find in its use great convenience as well as economy of time and fuel; and also, that tools heated by it will be tougher than when heated in a forge in the usual way.

Put on sufficient gas to prevent the flame from descending into the tube. For heating larger pieces the flame should be nearly three inches wide. The upper ends of the curved side pieces should not be more than one-quarter of an inch apart. The article to be heated should be held in the upper part of the flame above the central blue part and parallel with it. The larger the piece to be heated the further it should extend into the flame. The heater should be located in a dark place, and supports may be provided for greater convenience in heating heavy articles.

Fig. 138.

GAUGE. An instrument for determining dimensions or capacity. The watchmaker cannot be too careful in the selection of his measuring instruments, as accuracy and perfection in watchmaking are essential elements to success. Accuracy is more essential than finish, though both are desirable; still a movement that is accurate may be a fine time-keeper, although it may be lacking in finish and not artistic to look upon. Measuring instruments of all kinds should be handled with care, and in the more delicate ones cleanliness also plays an important part. You cannot expect accurate results from a fine Vernier caliper that is recklessly thrown into a heap of other tools upon the bench. It should be carefully handled, and when you are through using it you should carefully wipe it and place it in some drawer in your bench, where it will not be mutilated by being jammed against other tools.

Douzieme. A measuring tool having two limbs hinged together similar to a pair of scissors. One of the limbs terminates in a pointer that indicates upon a scale the extent to which the jaws are opened. The true Douzieme gauge has a scale divided into twelfths, though some patterns are now made that have a scale divided into tenths and hundreds of an inch, and again there are others that measure the fractions of a millimeter. This tool is useful for taking measurements of

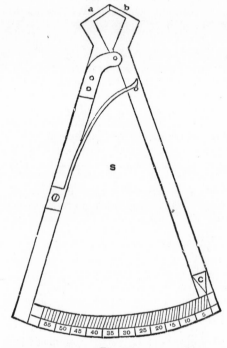

Fig. 139.

all kinds. For example, we will suppose that the watchmaker is putting in a new balance staff; we will take it for granted that the upper part of the staff is entirely finished and that he is ready to find the total length that the staff should be. He takes the top plate with the balance cock and potance attached, and measures the distance from the top of the cock hole jewel to top of potance hole jewel by means of this gauge. He places the jaw *a* on potance jewel and *b* on cock jewel, and notes the number on the scale that the pointer is opposite, which is generally 30 for an 18 inch size full plate American movement.

Micrometer Caliper. Fig. 140 is a full size cut of the Brown & Sharp Mfg. Co.'s micrometer caliper. It measures from one-thousandth of an inch to one-half inch. It is graduated to read to thousandths of an inch, but one-half and one-quarter thousandths are readily estimated. This instrument is also graduated to the hundredths of a millimeter, but when so graduated the table of decimal equivalents is omitted. They are also made to read to ten-thousandths of an inch. The edges of the measuring surfaces are not beveled, but are left square, as it is more convenient for measuring certain classes of work. It will gauge under a shoulder or measure a small projection on a plain surface.

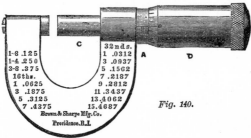

Fig. 140.

Watchmakers will especially appreciate micrometers of this form. This tool will be found very useful for gauging mainsprings, pinions, etc. In the caliper, shown by cut, the gauge or measuring screw is cut on the concealed part of the spindle C, and moves in the thread tapped in the hub A; the hollow sleeve or thimble D is attached to the spindle C and covers and protects the gauge screw. By turning the thimble, the screw is drawn back and the caliper opened.

The pitch of the screw is 40 to the inch. The graduation of the hub A, in a line parallel to the axis of the screw, is 40 to the inch, and is figured 0, 1, 2, etc., every fourth division. As the graduation conforms to the pitch of the screw, each division equals the longitudinal distance traversed by the screw in one complete rotation, and shows that the caliper has been opened 1-40th or .025 of an inch. The beveled edge of the thimble D is graduated into 25 parts, and figured every fifth division 0, 5, 10, 15, 20. Each division, when passing the line of graduation on hub A, indicates that the screw has made 1-25th of a turn, and the opening of the caliper increased 1-25th of 1-40th, or a thousandth of an inch.

Hence, to read the caliper, multiply the number of divisions visible on the scale of the hub by 25, and add the number of divisions on the scale of the thimble, from zero to the line coincident with the line of graduations on hub. For example: As the caliper is set in the cut, there are three whole divisions visible on the hub. Multiply this number by 25, and add the number of divisions registered on the scale of the thimble, which is 0 in this case, the result is seventy-five thousandths of an inch. (3x25=75+0=75). These calculations are readily made mentally.

Differences between Wire Gauges in Decimal Parts of an Inch.

No. of Wire Gauge.	American or Brown & Sharpe.	Birmingham or Stubs'.	Washburn & Moen Manufacturing Co., Worcester, Mass.	Trenton Iron Co., Trenton, N. J.	New British.	Old English from Brass Mfrs. List.	No. of Wire.
000000	-----	---	.46	-----	----	-----	000000
00000	-----	---	.43	.45	----	-----	00000
0000	.46	.454	.393	.4	.4	-----	0000
000	.40964	.425	.362	.36	.372	-----	000
00	.3648	.38	.331	.33	.348	-----	00
0	.32495	.34	.307	.305	.324	-----	0
1	.2893	.3	.283	.285	.3	-----	1
2	.25763	.284	.263	.265	.276	-----	2
3	.22942	.259	.244	.245	.252	-----	3
4	.20431	.238	.225	.225	.232	-----	4
5	.18194	.22	.207	.205	.212	-----	5
6	.16202	.203	.192	.19	.192	-----	6
7	.14428	.18	.177	.175	.176	-----	7
8	.12849	.165	.162	.16	.16	-----	8
9	.11443	.148	.148	.145	.144	----.	9
10	.10189	.134	.135	.13	.128	-----	10
11	.090742	.12	.12	.1175	.116	-----	11
12	.080808	.109	.105	.105	.104	-----	12
13	.071961	.095	.092	.0925	.092	-----	13
14	.064084	.083	.08	.08	.08	.083	14
15	.057068	.072	.072	.07	.072	.072	15
16	.05082	.065	.063	.061	.064	.065	16
17	.045257	.058	.054	.0525	.056	.058	17
18	.040303	.049	.047	.045	.048	.049	18
19	.03589	.042	.041	.039	.04	.04	19
20	.031961	.035	.035	.034	.036	.035	20
21	.028462	.032	.032	.03	.032	.0315	21
22	.025347	.028	.028	.27	.028	.0295	22
23	.022571	.025	.025	.024	.024	.027	23
24	.0201	.022	.023	.0215	.022	.025	24
25	.0179	.02	.02	.019	.02	.023	25
26	.01594	.018	.018	.018	.018	.0205	26
27	.014195	.016	.017	.017	.0164	.01875	27
28	.012641	.014	.016	.016	.0148	.0165	28
29	.011257	.013	.015	.015	.0136	.0155	29
30	.010025	.012	.014	.014	.0124	.01375	30
31	.008928	.01	.0135	.013	.0116	.01225	31
32	.00795	.009	.013	.012	.0108	.01125	32
33	.00708	.008	.011	.011	.01	.01025	33
34	.006304	.007	.01	.01	.0092	.0095	34
35	.005614	.005	.0095	.009	.0084	.009	35
36	.005	.004	.009	.008	.0076	.0075	36
37	.004453	---	.0085	.00725	.0068	.0065	37
38	.003965	---	.008	.0065	.006	.00575	38
39	.003531	---	.0075	.00575	.0052	.005	39
40	.003144	---	.007	.005	.0048	.0045	40

Pinion and Wire Gauge. The jewelers' gauge shown in Fig. 141, will be found very useful in measuring pinions, wire or flat metal. The

Fig. 141.

DECIMALS EQUALING PARTS OF AN INCH.

$\frac{1}{64}$ =	.0156	$\frac{11}{64}$ =	.1718
$\frac{1}{32}$ =	.0312	$\frac{3}{16}$ =	.1875
$\frac{3}{64}$ =	.0468	$\frac{13}{64}$ =	.2031
$\frac{1}{16}$ =	.0625	$\frac{7}{32}$ =	.2187
$\frac{5}{64}$ =	.0781	$\frac{15}{64}$ =	.2343
$\frac{3}{32}$ =	.0937	$\frac{1}{4}$ =	.2500
$\frac{7}{64}$ =	.1093	$\frac{17}{64}$ =	.2656
$\frac{1}{8}$ =	.1250	$\frac{9}{32}$ =	.2812
$\frac{9}{64}$ =	.1406	$\frac{19}{64}$ =	.2968
$\frac{5}{32}$ =	.1562	$\frac{5}{16}$ =	.3125

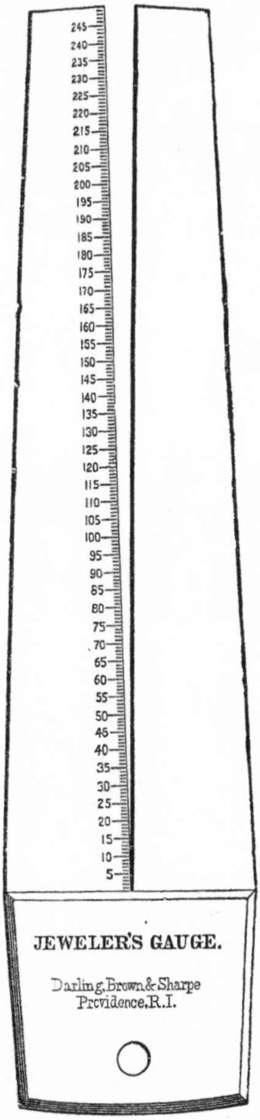

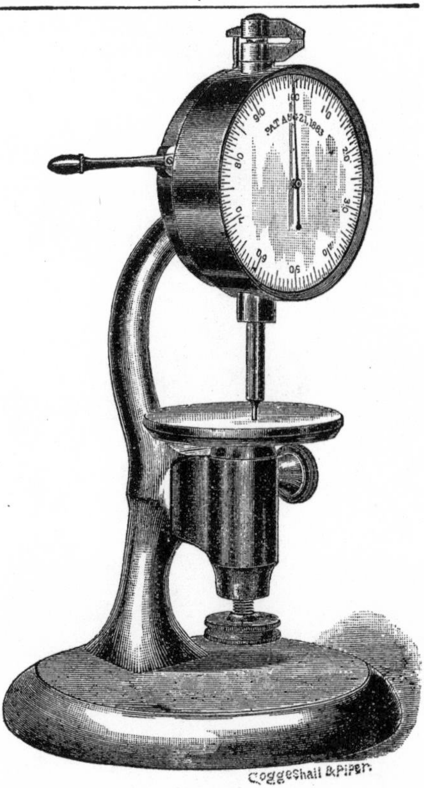

Fig. 142.

slot is graduated to thousandths of an inch. If in measuring a pinion it passes down the slot to number 70, then the pinion is $\frac{70}{1000}$ of an inch in diameter.

Registering Gauge. The registering gauges shown in the illustrations are two of the best examples of this class of tools. They are manufactured by A. J. Logan, Waltham, Mass., and are very accurate and nicely finished. Fig. 142 is an upright and jaw gauge, and Fig. 143 is designated as a jaw and depth gauge. They are both made to gauge one one-thousandth of a centimeter or one one-thousandth of an inch.

Fig. 143.

Fig. 143 shows the piece of work marked A, being gauged, while B represents a stationary spindle to get the depth of a hole or recess or the thickness of any piece of work which will be indicated on the dial.

Another form of registering gauge is shown in Fig. 144. It is an English gauge and but little used in this country. The principle of its construction however is good and any ingenious watchmaker can make it. The back of the dial is recessed and arranged as in Fig. 145. One

limb is fixed; the other is pivoted, and has a few rack teeth taking into
a center pinion. The pinion carries the hand, which should make a

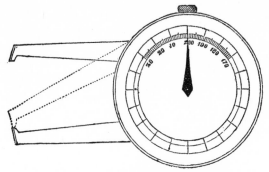

Fig. 144.

revolution in closing the calipers. The spiral spring attached to the
pinion is to keep it and the hand banked in one direction for shake.
The spring *s* is to keep the jaws open. The milled headed screw and
the clamp *c* are to fix the jaws in case it is required to do so. A cover
is snapped into the recess, and takes the back pivot of the pinion.

Staff Gauge. The tool shown in Fig. 146, the invention of Mr. E.
Beeton, is designed for measuring the height of the balance staff from
the balance seat to the end of the top pivot. The illustration is enlarged
to give more distinctness.

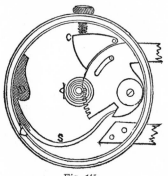

Fig. 145.

E E' is a piece of curved steel
about $\frac{1}{20}$ of an inch thick, and $\frac{1}{15}$ of
an inch wide. On the lower side
from *E'* to the end the arm is filed
down in width and thickness to
correspond to an ordinary balance
arm; *C* is a slot in the upper arm *E*,
which allows *A*, *B*, *D*, *A'* to be
moved backward and forward. *D D'*
is a round brass post drilled and
tapped, the part *D'* has a thread cut
on it, and the part shown in the slot
C fits with easy friction. *B* is a lock-
nut, drilled and tapped to fit the thread on *D'*. It is for the purpose of
clamping *D D'* against the arm *E*. *A A'* is a small steel screw with
milled head, and is made to fit the tapped hole in *D D'*.

Mr. Beeton describes his method of using this tool as follows: Take
your measurement of the distance *the balance seat is to be from the end of
the top pivot*, as follows: remove the end stone in balance cock, and

screw the cock on the top of the top plate, (18-size full plate movement) then taking the plate in your left hand, and tool (shown in Fig. 146) in your right, place H in position, so that the end of the screw A' rests on the jewel in the balance cock, and notice the position of the arm E' which corresponds to the balance arm, between the top plate and under side of balance cock. If the distance between the arm E' and end of screw A' is too great, the arm E' will be too low and touch the plate; if not enough, it will be too high and touch the regulator pins. Therefore, all that is necessary to do is to move the screw $A A'$ up or down as the

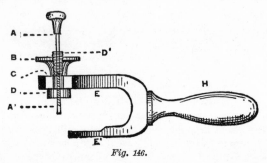

Fig. 146.

case may be, sufficiently to ensure that the arm E' will assume the position the *arm of the balance* is to have. Take an 18-size balance with oversprung hairspring, the arm is at the bottom of the rim; in that case, when measuring, the screw A' is adjusted so as to bring the arm E' close to the plate, when A' is resting on the balance jewel; if the balance is old style with undersprung hairspring, the balance arm is at top of rim, in which case A' is adjusted so that the arm E' is close to the balance cock; if the balance arm is in the center of the rim, as in some English and Swiss balances, the screw A' is adjusted so that the arm E' is midway between the plate and cock.

The reason the part A, B, D, A', is arranged to move laterally in slot C is, because all balance shoulders are not the same distance from the center, and where, in some cases, the screw A' would be in a line with the center of the staff when the arm E' was resting on the balance seat, in other cases it would reach past the center, of course, short of it; and, therefore, it is made adjustable to suit all cases.

Staff Length Gauge. Another form of staff gauge, which is very simple, and which any watchmaker can manufacture is made as follows: Procure a small tube of steel, or make one from steel wire, thread it on the inside, and screw into each end a small steel plug as shown in Fig. 147, until the ends of the plug meet, cut off the outer end of plugs so as to leave the total length that of a short staff; harden, draw to a blue, place in a split chuck, plugs and all, and turn a pivot of good length on each plug. Flatten the sides of the plugs at the base of the pivots, so that they may be readily turned in or out by the aid of tweezers. By

Fig. 147.

inserting this tool in the place of the balance, and screwing the plugs to the right position, screwing bridge down, and adjusting until the right endshake is obtained, you can ascertain in a moment the exact length that the staff should be over all, which can easily be transferred to calipers and thence to the new staff.

Staff or Cylinder Height Gauge. The obvious advantage of this tool, which is shown at Fig. 148, is the automatic transfer of the measurement so that it may be readily applied to the work in hand. The tool, as the illustration shows, consists of a brass tube terminating in a cone-shaped piece. To the bottom of this cone is attached a disc through which a needle plays. Around the upper end of the tube is a collar upon which is fixed a curved steel index finger. A similar jaw, which is free to move, works in a slot in the tube. The movable jaw is tapped and is propelled by a screw that terminates in the needle point. This tool is very useful in making the necessary measurements required in putting in a staff. To use it in this work, set the pivots of the gauge through the foot hole, and upon the end-stone project the needle such a distance as you wish the shoulder to be formed above the point of the pivot. Next set the gauge in the foot hole as before, and elevate the disc to a height that shall be right for the roller, which is done by having the lever in

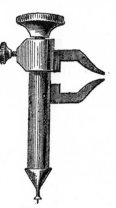

Fig. 148.

place, the little disc showing exactly where the roller should come. Finish the staff up to that point; then take the next measurement from the end-stone to where the shoulder should be, for the balance to rest upon. This point being marked, the staff can be reversed and measurements commenced from the upper end-stone, by which to finish the upper end of the staff. Distances between the shoulders for pinions and arbors can be obtained with the same facility, a little practice being the only requisite.

Twist Drill and Steel Wire Gauge. This gauge, which is shown in Fig. 149 will be found very useful in determining the diameter of twist drills and steel wire, and is very accurately and nicely made.

Vernier Caliper. Fig. 150 is an illustration of the Vernier Caliper, a light, convenient and valuable instrument for obtaining correct measurements. The side represented in the illustration is graduated upon the bar to inches and fiftieths of an inch, and by the aid of a Vernier is read to the thousandths of an inch, (see description below). The opposite side is graduated to inches and sixty-fourths of an inch. The outside of the jaws are of suitable form for taking inside measurements, and when the jaws are closed, measure two hundred and fifty thousandths of an inch in diameter.

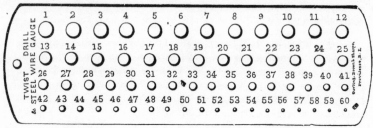

Fig. 149.

These instruments can be furnished with millimeters (in the place of sixty-fourths of an inch), and provided with a Vernier to read to one-fiftieth of a millimeter.

On the bar of the instrument is a line of inches numbered 1, 2, 3, each inch being divided into tenths, and each tenth into five parts, making fifty divisions to one inch. Upon the sliding jaw is a line of divisions, (called a Vernier, from the inventor's name), of twenty parts, figured 0, 5, 10, 15, 20. These twenty divisions on the Vernier correspond in

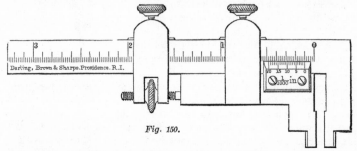

Fig. 150.

extreme length with nineteen parts, or nineteen-fiftieths on the bar, consequently each division on the Vernier is smaller than each division on the bar, by one-thousandth of an inch. If the sliding jaw of the caliper is pushed up to the other, so that the line 0 on the Vernier corresponds with 0 on the bar, then the next two lines to the left will differ from each other one-thousandth of an inch, and so the difference will continue to increase one-thousandth of an inch for each division till they again correspond on the twentieth line on the Vernier. To read the distance the caliper may be open, commence by noticing how many inches, tenths and parts of tenths the zero point on the Vernier has been moved from the zero point on the bar. Then count upon the Vernier the number of divisions until one is found which coincides with one on the bar, which will be the number of thousandths to be added to the distance read off on the bar. The best way of expressing the value of the divisions on the bar is to call the tenths one hundred thousandths (.100) and the fifths of tenths, or fiftieths, twenty thousandths (.020). Referring to the accompanying cut it will be seen that the jaws are open one-tenth of an inch, which is equal to one hundred thousandths (.100). Suppose now, the sliding jaw was moved to the left, so that the first line on the Vernier would coincide with the next line on the bar, this would then make twenty thousandths (.020) more to be added to one hundred thousandths (.100), making the jaws then open one hundred and twenty thousandths (.120) of an inch. If but half the last described movement was made, the *tenth line on the Vernier* would coincide with a line on the bar, and would then read, one hundred and ten thousandths (.110) of an inch.

GERBERT. By some authorities accredited with the invention of the escapement and the application of the weight as a motive power for clocks. He was born in Belliac, in Auvergne, in 920 A. D. He was educated in a monastery, and served successively as Monk, Bishop, Archbishop and finally as Pope, being better known under the name of Sylvester II. He died May 12, 1003.

GILDING. (See *Electro-Plating.*)

GIMBALS. A contrivance for securing free motion and suspension of a ship's chronometer, compass, etc., so that it may not be affected by the motion of the ship. It is virtually a universal joint. It was invented by Cardan and first applied to timepieces by Huyghens.

GODDARD, LUTHER. One of the earliest manufacturers of American watches. In 1809 he opened a small shop in Shrewsbury, Mass., and commenced to manufacture watches of the verge pattern, as shown in Fig. 151, in somewhat larger quantities than had been attempted before. He could not compete in price, however, with the cheap foreign watches which were then being imported in large quantities, and accordingly he retired

Fig. 151.

from the business in 1817, having manufactured about 500 watches. This was the greatest number of watches ever made by any one manufacturer in America up to this time.

GOING BARREL. A barrel having teeth around its circumference for driving the train. All American watches are of the going barrel type.

GOING FUSEE. A fusee having the maintaining power attachment. All modern fusees have a maintaining power which drives the train while the fusee is being wound. Examples of old fusees are, however, occasionally met with which have no maintaining power and the watch is stopped during the operation of winding.

GOLD ALLOYS. (See *Alloys.*)

To Distinguish Genuine from Spurious Gold. Genuine gold dissolves in chlorine water and the solution has only a slightly yellowish color. Hence chlorine is a safe agent to distinguish genuine from spurious gold. To test the genuineness of gilt articles, rub a tiny drop of mercury on one corner of the surface to be examined; it will produce a white, silvery spot if the gold is pure, or if there is gold in the alloy. If this silvery spot does not appear there is no gold in the surface exposed. To prove the correctness of this result a drop of the solution of nitrate of mercury can be dropped on the surface, when a white spot will appear if the gold is counterfeit, while the surface will remain unaltered if the gold is genuine. After the operation, heating the article slightly will volatize the mercury and the spots will disappear. Pure gold can be distinguished from its alloys by a drop of chloride of gold or of nitrate of silver. If the gold is pure there will be no stain, but if mixed with other metals the chloride of gold will leave a brownish stain upon it and the nitrate of silver a gray stain. The simplest means of distinguishing genuine gold from a gold-like alloy consists in running the article to be tested against an ordinary flint until a lustrous metallic coloring remains upon the latter. Now hold a strongly sulphurated burning match against the coloring; if it disappears from the flint the article is not gold.

GOLD SPRING. A very thin spring made of gold, attached to the detent of a chronometer escapement. *See Chrono meter Escapement.*

GRAHAM, GEORGE. Born in Cumberland, England, in 1673 and died in 1751. He was buried in Westminister Abbey. He was the inventor of the mercurial pendulum (1715), the dead beat escapement for clocks, and is credited with being the inventor of the cylinder escapement.

George Graham.

GRAHAM ESCAPEMENT. A dead beat escapement, or one in which the escape wheel does not recoil. It was invented by George Graham early in the eighteenth century, and is used in regulators and fine clocks. For regulators and other clocks with seconds pendulum, says Britten, this escapement, which is shown in Fig. 153, is the one most generally approved. The only defect inherent in its construction is that the thickening of the oil on the pallet will affect the rate of the clock after it has been going some time. Notwithstanding this it has held its own against all other escapements on account of its simplicity and certainty of action. The pallets of the Graham escapement were formerly made to embrace fifteen teeth of the wheel, and until recently ten, but now many escapements are made as shown in the drawing, with the pallets embracing but eight. This reduces the length of the impulse plane and the length of run on the dead face for a given arc of vibration, and consequently the relative effect of the thickening of the oil. The angle of impulse is kept small for the same reason. There is not much gained by making the pallet embrace a less number of teeth than eight, for the shake in the pivot holes and inaccuracies of work cannot be reduced in the same ratio, and are therefore greater in proportion. This involves larger angles and more drop. It is purely a practical question, and has been decided by the adoption of eight teeth as a good mean for regulators and fine clocks where the shakes are small. For large clocks of a rougher character, ten teeth is a good number for the pallets to embrace.

TO SET OUT THE ESCAPEMENT.

Draw a circle representing the escape wheel to any convenient size, and assuming the wheel to have 30 teeth and the pallets are to embrace eight of them, set off on each side of a centre line, by means of a protractor, 45°. Lines drawn from the centre of the escape wheel through these points will pass through the center of impulse faces of the pallets; thus, 360 (number of degrees in the whole circle) divided by 30 (proposed number of teeth) = 12, which is the number of degrees between one tooth and the next. Between 8 teeth there are seven such places and 12 x 7 = 84, and 84 + 6 (half of one space = 90), the number of degrees between the centers of the pallets. The proper position for the pallet staff center will be indicated by the intersection of tangents to the wheel circle drawn from the centers of the pallets. But it happens that a tangent of 45° = the radius, and, therefore, the practical method adopted is to make the pallet arms from the staff hole to the center of impulse face equal to the radius of the escape wheel. If we take the radius of wheel to be = 1, it will be found that with the pallet arms this length, the height of the pallet staff hole from the center of the wheel will be 1.41, and the horizontal distance between the impulse faces of the pallets will be 1.41 also.

The width of each pallet is equal to half the distance between one tooth and the next, less drop, which need not be much if the escape wheel teeth are made thin as they should be. The dead faces of the pallets are curves struck from the pallet staff hole. The escaping arc, which equals 2°, is divided into $1\frac{1}{2}^\circ$ of impulse and $\frac{1}{2}^\circ$ of rest; $1\frac{1}{2}^\circ$ of impulse is quite enough if the encapement is properly made, and if increased beyond 2°,

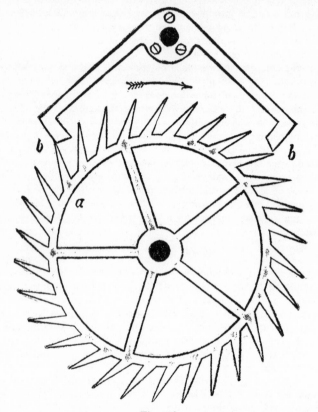

Fig. 153*.

it will be at the cost of the time keeping properties of the clock, from the effect of the thicking of the oil already referred to.

From the center of the wheel set off two radial lines barely 3° on each sides of the radial lines already drawn, to mark the center of the pallets. Then strike the curved dead faces of the pallets just touching the radial lines last drawn.

---

* *a.* Escape Wheel. *b.* Pallets.

Now from the pallet center draw lines through the spot where the curved locking face of each pallet cuts the wheel circle. If you look at the engraving you will see that a wheel tooth is resting on the left-hand pallet. The amount of this rest is $\frac{1}{2}°$, as already stated. Mark off this $\frac{1}{2}°$, which gives the position of the locking corner of the pallet, and then set off another line $1\frac{1}{2}°$, below it, which will mark the spot for the other corner of the pallet. On the right-hand pallet, the line already drawn marks the extreme corner, and it is only necessary in order to get the locking corner, to set off a line $1\frac{1}{2}°$ ABOVE it.

The wheel teeth diverge from a radial line about $10°$, so that only their tips touch the dead faces of the pallets.

For escaping over ten teeth, the distance between the center of the wheel and the center of the pallet staff should be equal to the diameter of the wheel; with this exception the preceding directions are applicable for setting out.

The wheel is of hard hammered brass, and for regulators is made from an inch and a half to two inches in diameter, and very light. The pallets are usually of steel, nicely fitted to the arbor, and, in addition, screwed to a collet thereon as shown. In the best clocks the acting faces are jeweled. Sometimes the pallet arms are cast of brass, and the pallets formed of solid jewels. Many good clockmakers put two banking pins in the plate, one on each side of the crutch, to prevent the pallets from being jammed into the wheel by careless handling.

The Graham escapement requires a heavy pendulum, especially if the train is comparatively rough. The clock weight must be sufficient to overcome increased resistance arising from inaccuracy of work; consequently, when the train runs freely, so much extra pressure is thrown upon the dead faces of the pallets that a light pendulum has not enough energy to unlock, and the clock stops. For clocks with shorter than half-seconds pendulums the pallets are generally made "half dead," that is the rests, instead of being curves struck from the pallet staff hole, are formed so as to give a light recoil to the wheel.

GRAVER. A steel cutting tool used for engraving, turning, etc. The "Guaranteed" gravers, shown in Fig. 154, are unique from the fact that they cut at both ends; the handle (which is patented) is so adapted that it will accommodate the reverse ends of innumerable sizes and shapes of gravers. The various angles of points of the gravers are very excellent and cover the entire field as used both for turning and engraving.

Use of the Graver.* The beginner should first practice on hard wood, then brass, iron, steel and hardened and tempered steel, progressing

---

* The directions apply to the use of the graver as a turning tool only. For directions for engraving on gold, silver, copper, etc., the reader is referred to an excellent work by G. F. Whelpley, entitled "General Letter Engraving," George K. Hazlitt & Co., Publishers, Chicago.

ing from one material to the other as his ability warrants. He should turn for a long time with the *point* of a square or lozenge-shaped graver, the end of which is ground off on a slope; this is the only possible method of learning to turn *true*, and it enables the workman to acquire great delicacy of touch. Owing to carelessness, or to the fact that when first beginning they were set to work on metal that was too hard or rough, most beginners turn with gravers that are ground to very blunt points; as the graver bites less, they are obliged to apply a proportionately increased pressure, and only succeed in tearing the metal away, subjecting it to a kind of rolling action and rendering the hand heavy. If a pupil will not practice turning with the graver point so as to preserve it intact for some time, dependent on the nature of the metal, he will never be able to turn perfectly true. Irregular and sudden depressing of the graver point, or engaging it too deeply, causes its frequent rupture.† When sufficient experience has been gained in turning with the graver point and a trial is made with the cutting edge, do not attempt to take off much at a time by pressing heavily, but take the metal sideways, so as to remove a continuous thread, using all the points of the edge in succession. The metal will thus be removed as a thin ribbon or shaving. When the hand has had some experience, it will be found easy to remove long strips.

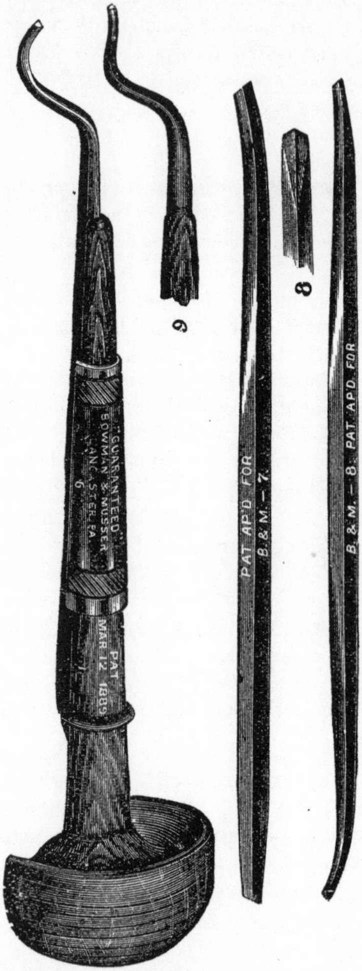

Fig. 154.

Hardened steel that has been drawn down to a blue temper requires certain precautions. If the graver is found not to cut cleanly, it must at once be sharpened, and no

† See illustrations and directions for holding graver, under heading *Making Balance Staff.*

attempt should be made to remove more metal by increasing the pressure of the hand, because the steel will burnish and become hard under a point or edge that is blunt, and the portions thus burnished are sometimes so hard as to resist the best gravers. The only way of attacking them is to begin at one side with a fine graver point, which must be sharpened frequently; at times it becomes necessary to temper the metal afresh before it will yield. It is well to moisten the point of the graver with turpentine.

Apprentices, and even watchmakers themselves, are frequently careless as to the proper sharpening of their gravers, and think they can hasten their work by application of considerable pressure; in this way they sometimes produce bright spots that require several hours' work before they can be removed. A majority of the Swiss workmen turn with the right or left hand indifferently. This is a very useful accomplishment, easily acquired when young.

GRAVIMETER. An instrument for ascertaining the specific gravity of liquid or solid bodies.

GRAVITY. The tendency which a body has towards the center of the earth.

Specific Gravity. The ratio of the weight of a body to the weight of an equal volume of some other body taken as the standard or unit. This standard is usually water for solids and liquids, and air for gases. Thus 19, the specific gravity of gold, signifies that gold is 19 times heavier than water.

GRAVITY CLOCK. This is a large glass clock dial, with a stud fixed in the center on which revolve two hands, as shown in Fig. 155, without any visible power to operate them. Hung in a jeweler's window so that it can be inspected from both sides without anyone discovering the source of power, it forms a great attraction to the curious and so becomes a durable and valuable advertisement. Take a plate of glass two feet square and lay out and gild a clock dial upon it, avoiding all ornament, in order to give the observer as little to see and as much to guess as is possible; cement, drill or otherwise fasten a stud in the center of the dial, projecting from the rear side so as to give facility for adjustment and certain exhibitions, which will be mentioned later. This stud must be perfectly hard and very finely polished in order to reduce the friction, which is considerable. The hands should be made of cedar, perfectly dry pine, or some other extremely light wood, left about a half inch thick, so that they can be nicely counterbalanced with lead, and will appear to the observer to be merely wooden hands. The circular discs at the inner extremities of the hands are hollowed out to receive two watch movements, and the boxes are closed with a cover fitting closely enough so that it cannot be perceived by ordinary inspection. Each side of the hands is perfectly jeweled with large English fusee jewels, so as to revolve on the stud with as little friction as possible. The two watch movements must be regulated to run as closely together as possible and to keep exact time. Two half circles of lead are attached to the movements in such a way that their rotation in the hollow discs will change the center of gravity of the hands and so cause them to rotate on the stud of the dial. The lead half-circle for the minute hand is attached to the minute arbor of its movement and that of the hour hand to the hour pipe on its movement. If the wooden hands are nicely gilded it will add to the deception, as the disc for the movement may then be made of tin and be much smaller and more symmetrical. When finished, the clock is hung in the window, suspended by chains from holes bored in the corners. We will suppose that you have the clock finished

Fig. 155.

and running nicely, and that the time shown is 2:20; take hold of the hands, bring them together and send them twirling around the dial; when they stop they will show the correct time, say 2:21. Suppose the hands show 9:45 or 2:45, bring both hands to 12 or 6 and they will immediately assume the correct position. Take off the minute hand and lay it on the bench for five or six minutes; put it on again, give it a twirl, and it will stop at the correct time. Various other tricks will suggest themselves for the astonishment and mystification of the jeweler's patrons, and considerable benefit can be derived from the curiosity of an excited town.

GRAVITY ESCAPEMENT. An escapement in which the train raises a lever a constant distance, and the weight of the lever when returning to position gives impulse to the pendulum. The double three-legged variety was invented by E. B. Denison in 1854. Gravity escapements are particularly applicable to turret clocks.

GREAT WHEEL. The wheel on the fusee arbor which drives the center pinion. The largest wheel in a watch or clock.

GRIGNION, THOMAS. A well-known watch and clockmaker, of London, who died in 1784. His son Thomas, also a clockmaker, claimed for him the honor of bringing to perfection the horizontal principle in watches and the dead beat in clocks.

GROSSMANN, MORITZ. A celebrated horologist, author and linguist. Though born and raised in Saxony, he was very conversant with the French, Italian and English languages, and contributed to many technical journals throughout the world. He was a member of the

British Horological Institute, the Galileo Galilei, Milan, Italy, and the Polytechnic Society of Leipzig. It was while in the hall of the latter society, and just after delivering a lecture on horology, that he was stricken with apoplexy, which resulted in his death Jan. 23, 1885. He received his training as a watch-maker under the best masters of Saxony, Switzerland, France and England. He located in Glashutte, Saxony, in 1854, and began the manufacture of

Moritz Grossman.   fine watches, tools and metric gauges, and later on large sized models of the various escapements. His first essay, "The Detached Lever Escapement," was written in 1864 and was awarded first prize by the British Horological Institute. In 1869 he took the first prize offered by the Chambre de Commerce, Geneva, on the subject of "The Construction of a Simple and Mechanically Perfect Watch." In 1878 he published a translation of Claudius Saunier's "Modern Horology."

GUARD PIN.   See *Safety Pin.*

GYRATE.   To revolve around a central point.   See *Center of Gyration.*

HAIR SPRING.   The spring that determines the time of vibrations of the balance. The term hair spring is distinctively American, as all other nations use the more fitting appellation of Balance Spring. The hair spring was invented by Dr. Robert Hooke in 1658, and first applied to a double balance watch for Charles II., on which was inscribed "Robt. Hooke, Inven: 1658. T. Tompion, fecit, 1675." The spring was nearly straight. In 1660 Dr. Hooke altered the form by making it spiral. The different forms of hair springs are illustrated in Fig. 157. The most common form is the volute or spiral spring, shown at A. B is a helical spring used in chronometers. C is a Breguet spring, which is a flat spiral with its outer end bent up above the plane of the body of the spring, and carried in a long curve towards the center, near which it is fixed. The advantage of the Breguet spring is that it distends when in action, on each side of the center, thus relieving the balance pivots of the side pressure which the ordinary flat spring tends to give, and it also offers opportunities of obtaining isochronism by varying the character of the curve.   Glasgow says that a hair spring, of whatever form, to be isochronous must satisfy the following conditions: its center of gravity must always be on the axis of the balance, and it must expand and contract in the vibrations concentrically with that axis.   Immish contends that mere length of spring has nothing to do with isochronism.   Mr. Glasgow contends that the whole question of isochronism resolves itself into the adoption of a spring of the correct length, and recommends for a lever watch fourteen turns if a flat, and twenty turns if a Breguet spring is used, if a cylinder watch use from eight to twelve turns.   He argues that if a spring is too short, the short vibrations will be fast and

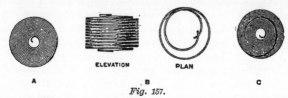

ELEVATION   PLAN

A   B   C

Fig. 157.

the long vibrations slow, and that all bending and manipulation of the spring with a view to obtaining isochronism are really only attempts to alter the effective length of the spring.   Mr. Britten contends that the position of the points of attachment of the inner and outer turns of a hair spring in relation to each other has an effect on the long and short vibrations quite apart from its length.   For instance, a very different performance may be obtained with two springs of precisely the same length and character in other respects, but pinned in so that one has exactly complete turns, and the other a little under or a little over complete turns.   He argues that a short spring as a rule requires to be pinned in short or complete turns, and a long one beyond the complete turns.

Fig. 158.

In duplex and other watches with frictional escapements, small arcs of vibration and short springs, it will be found that the spring requires to be pinned in nearly half a turn short of complete turns.

HAIR SPRING STUD INDEX.
Wathier's Self-adjusting Hair Spring Stud Index, shown in Fig. 158, is a very useful device, and by its use the watchmaker can save much time and can obtain better results than by following the regular methods of determining when a movement is in beat.   Place the lower part of balance staff in round cleat A.   Turn balance until ruby pin comes over oblong hole at

B. Now let the balance down until roller table rests on steel center plate. The balance will then be ready for the spring. Place the hair spring on the staff, with the stud in exact line with the line on the index corresponding in name with the movement you wish to put in beat. Now fasten the hair spring collet on the staff, and you will find movement in beat. At a glance, the watchmaker may be lead to believe that this tool is only applicable to the fourteen movements shown on the index, but in reality it serves for almost every movement that comes into the hands of the repairer. For example, the line marked E. Howard & Co., not only serves for that make of watches, but also for Waltham 14 and 16 sizes. Directions accompany each tool.

Fig. 159 shows a hair spring stud index recently placed on the market by A. W. Johanson. The engraving shows the full size of the tool,

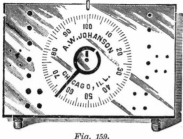

Fig. 159.

which consists of a steel plate mounted on feet, and pierced with a number of holes for the reception of screws, when taking down a watch. In the center of the index is a hole for the staff, and an oblong slot for the reception of the roller jewel. To get any American movement in beat proceed as follows: In front of No. 100 is a small spring, push same towards No. 10, then place the balance on top of the stand, with staff in center and roller jewel in the oblong hole, let the spring back gently, the balance will then take its own position. Set degree hand in front of the desired degree, as per directions on index table, place hair spring stud in front of degree hand, and push on the collet.

INDEX TABLE FOR HAIR SPRING STUDS.

Size.	Degree.	Size.	Degree.
Columbus....18	Open Face Breguet..23	Hampden....16	
Columbus.... 6	Open Face Breguet..	Hampden..... 6	Hunting...............50
Elgin........18	Open Face Breguet..66	Howard 18	Old Model........... 5
Elgin........16	Open Face Breguet..52	Howard 18	New Model...........23
Elgin........16	Flat Hair Spring....52	Howard 16	
Elgin........10	Flat Hair Spring....50	Howard 6	
Elgin...6 and 8	Flat Hair Spring....50	Rockford 18	
Elgin........ 0	Flat Hair Spring....	Rockford 6	
Illinois.......18	Open Face Breguet..33		27
Illinois.......18	Hunting..............84	Waltham....18	Key Flat Hair Spr'g.48
Illinois.......18	Open Face Flat.....89	Waltham....18	O. F. Hair Spring...61
Illinois.......16		Waltham....18	Breguet...............50
Illinois....... 6	Hunting..............52	Waltham .14-16	42
Illinois....... 4		Waltham ..4- 6	50
Hampden....18	Dueber Hunting.....80	Waltham 1	42
Hampden....18	Open Face...........75	Seth Thomas 18	Open Face...........50
		Seth Thomas 18	Hunting..............52

HALF PLATE. A watch in which the top pivot of the fourth wheel pinion is carried in a cock, so as to allow of the use of **a** larger balance than could otherwise be used.

HALL MARK. The stamp placed upon articles of gold and silver after being assayed by government officials. The United States government does not employ hall marks, but articles can be assayed by the proper officers, and a certificate of their standard given upon payment of a small fee. The hall marking of watch-cases is not compulsory in Switzerland, unless they contain some stamp indicating their quality, and the English and other hall marks are recognized. In Great Britain, with few exceptions, the hall marking of jewelry is optional with the manufacturer, but all gold or silver cases made in Great Britain or Ireland must be marked. The hall marks for Switzerland are shown in

| 18k or .750. | 14k or .583. | Sterling or .935. | .800. |
| GOLD. | | SILVER. | |

Fig. 160.

Fig. 160. Hall marks are not alone useful for determining the quality of goods, but are also a great aid in determining the age of watches, etc. The hall mark of Great Britain consists of several impressions in separate frames or shields; the quality mark, the office mark (which designates where it was stamped), year mark, and if duty is chargeable, the head of the reigning sovereign. The standard or quality mark for London and Birmingham is, for gold, a crown, as shown in Fig. 161, and 18 or some other figure to designate the caiat. The standard mark for 22 carat

Fig. 161.

gold prior to 1845 was a lion passant, which is now used as the quality mark for sterling silver. The quality mark for 15k. gold is 15 or .625, for 12k. is 12 or .5 and for 9k. is 9 or .375. The decimals indicate the proportions of pure gold of 24k. in the alloys. The office or location mark for London is a Leopard's head in a shield, as shown in Fig. 161. The leopard's head was crowned prior to 1823. Watch cases have been exempt from duty in Great Britain since 1798, . but all foreign cases are stamped, the die for silver being an octagon with the word foreign and for gold a cross. These dies also contain a mark to show where marked, that of London having a sun or full moon.

Fig. 162.

In Great Britain, from 1697 to 1823, the standard mark for silver was a Lion's head, and the office mark a figure of Britannia, but from the latter date to the present time, a lion passant and a leopard's head have been used. The date marks shown in Fig. 162, will prove very valuable in fixing the dates of watches made in Great Britain as in most cases, the case was made at a date coinciding pretty closely with the manufacture of the watch.

HAND. An index or pointer used in indicating minutes and hours on a watch, clock or similar dial.

HAND REMOVER. The style of watch hand remover shown in Fig. 163 is a very nice pattern and can also be used as a roller remover

Fig. 163.

and for several other purposes. The action of the tool can be readily understood by examining the illustration. The threaded wire in the center extends through the entire tool and is raised or lowered by the milled nut at the end of the handle. This tool can also be used for holding hands while broaching the hole, or the tool shown in Fig. 164, and known as the nine-hole sliding tongs, and many

Fig. 164.

other patterns, for sale by material dealers, may be used for the same purpose. Fig. 165 shows a second hand holder, with the hand in position ready to broach. This tool can also be used as a screw head tool. In order to broach out a new hand, if the boss of the old hand has been preserved, place a small slip of cork upon the end of the broach and insert it in the old hand

Fig. 165.

as far as it will go, and the new hand may then be broached until the cork is reached before trying it for a fit. The holes in the hands may be closed by forcing them into a conical hole in a steel plate, first turning off the metal around the edge of the hole, so that it is left rather thin, or it may be contracted after reducing the edge, by means of the stake.

HARRIS, RICHARD. A clockmaker of London. Comparatively little is known [of this clockmaker, except that a friend of his, one Thomas Grignion, authorized his son to make known that Richard Harris was the person who first applied a pendulum to a clock, eight years before Vincent Galileo laid claim to having made a clock regulated by a pendulum. There is no evidence, however, to prove that Harris was the inventor of the pendulum.

HARRISON, JOHN. This celebrated horologist was born at Faulby, Yorkshire, England, in 1693. In 1700 the family moved to Barrow, in Lincolnshire, where he carried on the business of repairing watches and clocks. In 1735 he went to London with a timekeeper of his own invention and construction, and through the interest taken in him by Graham and Halley, he was allowed, in 1736, to take it on board a king's ship to Lisbon. In 1761 he made another chronometer which was thought sufficiently correct to enable him to claim the government reward offered in 1714. The government offered £20,000 to anyone who would make a chronometer

John Harrison. that would determine the longitude to within half a degree. He received the reward in 1767. He is credited with being the inventor of the going fusee and the gridiron pendulum. He died in 1776.

HAUTEFEUILLE, JOHN. An ingenious mechanic born at Orleans in 1764. He was the first person to apply a small steel spring to regulate the vibrations of the balance. Huyghens applied for a patent on the invention, but was refused, on the ground that Hautefeuille had laid his invention before the Academy of Sciences in 1694, some years before. In 1722 he invented what was known as the rack lever escapement.

HENLEIN, PETER. A clockmaker of Nuremberg, to whom some authorities give the credit of the invention of the pocket watch. It is claimed that he made pocket watches or clocks, soon after the year 1500. He was born in 1480, and died in 1542.

HOOKE, ROBERT. He was born at Freshwater, Isle of Wight, on the 18th of July, 1635. In 1658 he invented the hairspring and applied it to a watch for Bishop Wilkins in 1661. About the same time he invented the circular or conical pendulum, which was in 1663 shown in the Royal Society. In 1664 the Royal Society gave him an annuity of £30 for his work as director of experiments. He invented anchor pallets in 1666. In 1655 he invented a wheel cutting engine and rounding-up tool for watch and clockmakers. He was also the inventor of the hydrometer and leveling instrument, and the author of the axiom on the compression and extension of springs and other elastic bodies "as the tension is so is the force." In 1677 he was elected Honorary Secretary of the Royal Society. He died March 3, 1702, and was buried in St. Helen's church, London.

HORIZONTAL ESCAPEMENT. (*See Cylinder Escapement.*)

HOROLOGICAL BOOKS. The following list of books published on horology and kindred subjects from 1639 to 1850 inclusive, may prove of value to those who have a horological library or who contemplate such a step. Works on horology have become so numerous since 1850 that the space at command will not admit of their mention.

L'usage du Cadran ou de l'Horloge Physique universel. Galileo, Paris, 1639.

Nuova Scienza di Horologi a Polvere.   Angelo Maria P. Radi, 4to, Rome, 1665.

Instructions concerning the use of Pendulum Watches for finding the Longitude at Sea. Christian Huyghens, Phil. Trans., London, 1669.

Horologium Oscillatorium, sive de motu pendulorum ad Horologia aptato. F. Muguet, Paris, 1673.

Horologium Oscillatorium, sive de motu Pendulorum. Christian Huyghens, Paris, 1673.

Factum touchant les Pendules des Cloches. John Hautefeuille, 4to, Paris, 1675.

Horological Dialogues in three parts, shewing the nature, use and right managing of Clocks and Watches. John Smith, London, 1675. This was, beyond doubt, the first work on horology printed in the English language.

On Portable Watches. Godfrey William de Leibnitz, Phil. Trans., London, 1675.

A new invention of a Clock descending on an Inclined Plane. M. de Gennes, Phil. Trans., London, 1678.

Concerning a movement that measures Time after a peculiar manner; being a Clock descendant on an Inclined Plane. Rev. Maurice Wheeler, M. A., Phil. Trans., London, 1684.

Horological Disquisitions concerning the Nature of Time, etc. John Smith, 12mo, London, 1694. A second edition, London, 1708.

The Artificial Clockmaker. Wm. Derham, D. D., F. R. S., 8vo, London, 1696. A second edition, 1700. Fourth edition, with large emendations, 12mo, London, 1734. New edition, 12mo, London, 1759.

The antiquity of Clockwork. Wm. Durham, London, 1700.

Philosophical Experiments and observations of Dr. Robert Hooke, F. R. S., Wm. Derham, London, 1700.

Balance Magnetique. John Hautefeuille, 4to, Paris, 1702.

Reasons of the English Clock and Watchmakers against the Bill to Confirm the pretended new Invention of using precious and common Stones about Watches, Clocks and other Engines. London, 1704.

Règle Artificielle du Temps, Henry Sully. Paris, 1717. A second edition 1717, with additions by Julien LeRoy.

Description abrégée d'une Horloge d'une nouvelle construction, pour la juste mesure du Temps sur mer. Henry Sully, Paris, 1726.

A contrivance to avoid the Irregularities in a Clock's Motion, occasioned by the action of Heat and Cold on the Pendulum Rod. Phil. Trans., London, 1726.

Letter asserting his right to the Curious and Useful Invention of making Clocks to keep time with the Sun's Apparent Motion. Joseph Williamson, Phil. Trans., London, 1726.

Observations on the Going of a Clock in Jamaica. Colin Campbell, Phil. Trans., London, 1734.

Traité Général des Horloges, Jacques Alexandre (R. P. Dom), Paris, 1734.

Experiments on the Vibrations of Pendulums. Wm. Durham, D. D., F. R. S., Phil. Trans , London, 1736.

Traité d'Horlogerie. M. Thiout, 2 vols., Paris, 1741.

Of the True Inventor of the Contrivances in the Pendulum of a Clock to Prevent Irregularities of its motion from Heat or Cold. James Short, F. R. S., Phil. Trans. London, 1751.

Description of two methods by which the Irregularities in the motion of a clock, arising from the influences of heat or cold on the Pendulum, may be prevented. John Ellicott, London, 1753.

Account of the Influence of two Pendulum Clocks on each other. John Ellicott, 4to, London. No date. 1754?

Traité d'Horlogerie. J. E. Lepaute, Paris, 1755.

L'Art des Conduire et de Regler les Pendules et les Montres. F. Berthoud, Paris, 1760.

Concerning the going of Mr. Ellicott's clock at St. Helena. Jas. Short F. R. S., Phil. Trans., London, 1762.

Observations on a clock of Mr. John Shelton, made at St Helena. Nevil Maskelyne, Phil. Trans., London, 1762.

Mechanicus and Flaveus; or the Watch Spiritualized. 8vo, London, 1763.

Les Quatres Parties du Jour.   Charles Francis de Saint-Lambert Paris, 1764.

Etudes Chronometriques.   Pierre Le Roy, Paris, 1764.

Account of the Proceedings in order to the Discovery of the Longitude at Sea, subsequent to those published in the year 1763.   John Harrison, 8vo, London, 1765.

Supplement à l'Essai sur l' Horlogerie.   F. Berthoud, Paris, 1765.

Thoughts on the Means of Improving Watches, and particularly those for use at sea.   Thos. Mudge, Jr., London, 1765.

Elements of Clock and Watch Work adapted to practice.   Alexander Cumming, 4to, London, 1766.

Remarks on a Pamphlet lately published by Dr. Maskelyne.   John Harrison, 8vo, London, 1767.

The Principles of Mr. Harrison's Timekeeper; with plates of the same on India Paper, Published by order of the Commissioners of Longitude. 4to, London, 1767.

The Mensuration of Time.   John Harrison, London, 1767.

An account of the going of Mr. Harrison's Watch, at the Royal Observatory, from 6th May, 1766, to March 4th, 1667, with the original observations and calculations of the same.   Nevil Maskelyne, D. D., F. R. S., 4to, London, 1768.

Memoirs for the Clock-makers of Paris, ent Etrennes Chronometriques. Treatise on the Labours of Harrison and Le Roy for the discovery of the Longitude at Sea, and of the proofs made of their works. English translation from the French of Peter Roy, 4to, London, 1768.

Select Mechanical Exercises,showing how to construct different Clocks, Orreries and Sun dials on plain and easy principles.   James Ferguson, F. R. S., 8vo, London, 1773.

Traité des Horloges Marine.   F. Berthoud, 4to, Paris, 1673.

An Introduction to the Mechanical part of Watch and Clock Work, Illustrated with 18 copper plates.   Thomas Hatton, 8vo, London, 1774.

Les Longitudes par la Mesure du Temps.   F. Berthoud, 4to, Paris, 1775.

Eclaircissements sur l'Invention des Nouvelles Machines proposées pour la détermination des Longitudes en Mer, par la mesure du temps. F. Berthoud, 4to, Paris, 1775.

Clock work and Music.   John Harrison, 8vo, London, 1775.

A letter from Mr. Christian Meyer, Astronomer to the Elector Palatine, to Mr. N. N., on the going of a New Pendulum Clock, made by Mr. John Arnold, and set up in the Elector's Observatory, at Manheim. From the German, 4to, London, 1781.

La Mesure du Temps Appliquée à la Navigation. F. Berthoud, 4to, Paris, 1783.

Essai sur l'Horlogerie. F. Berthoud, 2 vols., 4to, 1763. Reprinted 1786.

De la Mesure du Temps. F. Berthoud, 4to, Paris, 1787.

Narrative of Facts Relating to some Timekeepers Constructed by Thos. Mudge. Thos. Mudge, Jun., London, 1792.

Answer to a pamphlet, entitled, A Narrative of Facts, lately published by T. Mudge, Jun., relating to some timekeepers constructed by his father, Mr. Thos. Mudge. Nevil Maskelyne, 8vo, London, 1792.

Investigations, founded on the theory of Motion, for determinating the Times of Vibrations of Watch Ballances. George Atwood, Phil. Trans., London, 1794.

Histoire de la Mesure du Temps par les Horologes. F. Berthoud, 2 vols., 4to, Paris, 1802.

Pocket Watches. ——Parr, London, 1804.

Essai sur l'Histoire abrégée de l' Horlogerie. M. Perron, Paris, 1820.

Account of Experiments to determine the Figure of the Earth by means of the Pendulum vibrating seconds in different Latitudes; as well as on other subjects of Philosophical Inquiry. Captain Sabine, 4to, London, 1825.

An Appeal. Thos. Earnshaw, 8vo, London, 1836.

Historical Treatise on Horology. ——— Henderson, 8vo, London, 1836.

Results of Experiments on the Vibration of Pendulums with different Suspending Springs. J. W. Frodsham, 4to, London, 1839.

A Treatise on the Management of Public Clocks, etc., Francis Abbot, London. No date. About 1840. Three editions.

Eiffe's Improvements in Chronometers and Molyneux's Specification of Patent for Improvement in Chronometers. 4to, London, 1842.

On the Construction and Management of Chronometers. E. J. Dent, 8vo, London, 1842.

Traité d'Horlogerie. Louis Moinet, Paris, 1843.

Railroad Clocks. B. L. Vulliamy, 8vo, London, 1845.

Treatise on Clock and Watch Making, Theoretical and Practical. Thomas Reid. 8vo, Edinburgh, 1826. Reprint, Philadelphia, 1832. Reprint, London, 1847.

Time and Time Keepers. Adam Thompson, 12mo., London, 1847.

Clock and Watchmaking. E. B. Denison, M. A., 12mo, London, 1848.

HOUR GLASS. An instrument for measuring the hours, consisting of a glass vessel having two cone-shaped compartments, from the uppermost of which a quantity of sand, water, or mercury occupies an hour in running through a small aperture into the lower.

HOUR WHEEL. The wheel which turns on the cannon pinion and carries the hour hand.

HOURIET, F. A noted Swiss watchmaker of the eighteenth century. He worked for nine years in Paris with such men as F. Berthoud, Romilly and Le Roy. He afterwards returned to Neufchatel, and much of the rapid progress made by the watchmakers of that canton was credited to his efforts.

HOWARD, EDWARD. The veteran watch and clockmaker of Boston. He was born in Hingham, Mass., Oct. 6, 1813. He served an apprenticeship of seven years as a clockmaker. At the age of twenty-nine he embarked in the business of clockmaking on his own account, his partner being D. P. Davis, and the firm being known as Howard &

Edward Howard.

Davis. The firm manufactured a very superior line of clocks and regulators, and their goods soon gained a world-wide reputation. In 1849 Mr. Howard, together with A. L. Dennison, Samuel Curtis, a Boston capitalist, and D. P. Davis organized a company for the manufacture of watches. This company was separate and distinct from that of Howard & Davis, and was known as the American Horologe Company. This company was the first in the world to undertake the manufacture of watches on the interchangeable system. The first watches were made to run eight days and had two barrels. They proved a failure, however, and were soon abandoned. The factory was situated directly opposite to the Howard & Davis shop. The name of the company was changed subsequently to the Warren Manufacturing Company, and later to the Boston Watch Company. In 1854 the location of the factory was changed to Waltham. In 1857 the company made an assignment, and the property, consisting of real estate, the factory, and numerous other buildings, machinery, steam engine, etc., was offered at public auction and was bid in for $56,500 by Royal E. Robbins, for himself and the firm of Tracy & Baker, case makers of Philadelphia, who were creditors of the defunct company. After the failure of the Boston Watch Company, Mr. Howard returned to Roxbury and continued with his clock business in connection with Mr. Davis. In 1858 he again began manufacturing watches in the old factory of the Boston Company, in Roxbury, and placed on the market the first quick train movements ever made

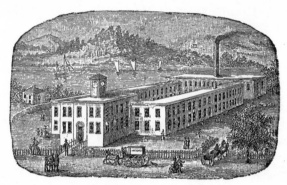

Factory of Boston Watch Co., 1857.

in this country. Even in those early days of American watchmaking, the Howard watches were noted for their superior qualities as time keepers, a reputation which followed them up to the present time. In 1861 the Howard Clock and Watch Company was organized with a capital of $120,000. In 1863 the name was changed to the Howard Watch and Clock Company and in 1881 it was again changed to the E. Howard Watch and Clock Company. In 1882 Mr. Howard severed his connection with the watch company and retired from all active business. Mr. Howard invented many labor saving devices in the horological line, among which may be mentioned the swing rest.

HUYGHENS, CHRISTIAN. A Dutch mathematician and author of a work on pendulums. He was born at the Hague on 14th of April, 1629. In 1665, Louis XIV. invited him to Paris for the purpose of founding a Royal Academy of Science. He resided in Paris from 1666 to 1681, when he returned to Holland. In the year 1656, he first conceived the idea of applying a pendulum to a clock, and at once set to work at his task. On the 16th of June, 1657, he presented to the States of Holland his first pendulum clock. In 1658 Adrian Ulaag, of the Hague, published for him in Dutch, a short description of this new clock. In 1673, finding that Vincent Galileo and others claimed the merit of the adaptation he authorized F. Muguet, of Paris to publish for him a valuable work entitled "Horologium oscillatorium, sive de motu pendulorum ad Horologia aptato," wherein he gave the construction of his clocks, with drawings, and the theory (useless in practice), of the cycloidal checks, as a means of rectifying the variations in the length of the arcs of vibration of the pendulum. Galileo claimed to have adapted a pendulum to a clock as early as 1649, but there appears to be no authority to be relied on, to prove his having done so. Dr. Hooke was another of the claimants

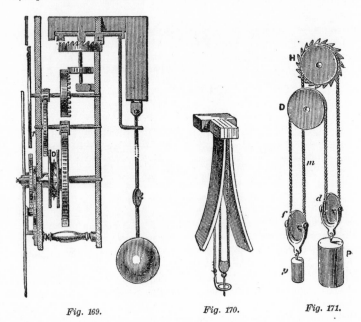

Fig. 169.   *Fig. 170.*   *Fig. 171.*

for the honor of the first application of the pendulum to a clock, but Nelthropp, after reviewing the question says: But it may without much fear of contradiction be here asserted that to the careful searcher after truth, the following conclusions only can be arrived at. First—That credit ought to be given to Huyghens for being the first to apply the discovery of Galileo to a clock. 2nd. That Dr. Hooke can justly lay claim to having brought the whole matter to perfection by the invention of his anchor escapement, which enabled him to use a long pendulum with a heavy bob, thereby rendering the arcs of vibration shorter, and necessitating much less motive power.

Huyghens' clock is shown in Fig. 169. The upper part of the pendulum is a double cord hanging between two cyloidal checks, to give a cycloidal path to the bob. Fig. 170 gives a better idea of the device, which was no doubt of advantage with the long arcs required by the Verge Escapement. Another feature of Huyghens' clock is the maintaining power. The driving weight, P, Fig. 171, is supported by an endless cord passing over the pulley D, attached to the great wheel, and also over the pulley H, which is provided with ratchet teeth and pivoted to the inside of the clock case. The cord *m* is pulled down to wind the clock, and the ratchet wheel H then runs under its click. So that while winding, as in going, one-half of P minus one-half of *p* is driving the clock. The pulleys D and H are spiked to prevent slipping of the cord.

When this ingenious maintaining power is applied to a clock with a striking train, the pulley with the ratchet is attached to the great wheel of the striking part, one weight thus serving to drive both trains. A chain is preferable to a cord, owing to the dust which accumulates in the clock through the wearing of the latter.

HYPOCYCLOID. A curve generated by a point in the circumference of a circle when it is rolled within another circle. The proper shape for the teeth of the wheels that are driven by others having epicycloidal addenda. If the tracing circle is half the diameter of the one within which it rolls, the hypocycloid will be a radial line.

ICE BOX. A box or chamber used when adjusting chronometers and fine watches for temperature. It is usually built in the form of a double box, the ice being placed between the two boxes and both boxes hermetically sealed, so that the movement may not come in contact with damp air. The outer box is provided with a drain pipe for carrying off the water and plate glass is inserted in the front of each box, so that the movement may be viewed without removing it from the box. The cover of the inner box should not be removed for at least two hours after it has been removed from the ice chamber in order to protect the steel work from rust caused by the condensation of the air in the cold metal.

IDLER. 1, An idle wheel. 2, A wheel for transmitting motion from one wheel to another, either by contact or by means of belts, as the wheel on a countershaft, or overhead fixture. 3, An intermediate wheel used for reversing motion. Figs. 172 and 173 illustrate two forms of idlers, sometimes called overhead fixtures. The supports for the idlers are adjustable in all directions. They are especially valuable for use on slide rest tools, such as polisher, milling attachments, etc., to give a vertical direction to the belts. The rods are about 20 inches long and the pattern shown in Fig. 172 has a ball and socket joint where it is screwed to the bench. The radial arms which hold the pulleys may be adjusted to any position on the rod by means of a thumb screw, and the pulleys have a lateral play of ¾ of an inch to aid in maintaining

greater freedom of the belt during the travel of the tool on the slide rest. The idlers shown were designed by A. W. Johanson, and have hard rubber pulleys 1¾ inches in diameter, having brass bushings. The style shown in Fig. 173 is intended to be clamped on the swiveled bearing of the counter shafts which are supported on standards.

IMPULSE PIN. The ruby pin of the lever escapement which, entering the notch of the lever, unlocks the escape wheel and then receives impulse from the lever and passes out at the opposite side.

INDEPENDENT SECONDS. A movement having a seconds hand that is driven by a separate train.

INDEX, The small curved plate with divisions on its face, over which the regulator arm passes. The circular plate at the back of a lathe head, having holes drilled around its margin for the reception of a pin, for dividing a wheel or other object placed in a chuck. Sometimes called a dividing plate.

Fig. 172.   Fig. 173.

INERTIA. That property of matter by which it tends when in rest to remain so, or when set in motion to continue so.

INGOLD FRAISE. A pinion-shaped cutter used for correcting inaccuracies in the shape of wheel teeth, invented by Ingold, a Swiss watchmaker. This consists really of a hardened pinion with square, sharp points. The fraise is gradually brought into depth, in a specially arranged depth tool, with a wheel whose teeth are incorrect, and rotated the while by means of a ferrule and bow. The fraises do not supercede the rounding up tool, but may often be used after it with advantage, for if a wheel contain any thick teeth they would not be corrected in the rounding up tool, which also of necessity leaves the teeth slightly hollow. The fraises cut the teeth in the direction they move on the pinion in working, and, therefore, leave a surface which works with the least friction.

A fraise for any particular wheel should be chosen so that, when placed upon the wheel, the fraise does not bottom, but just touches the sides and almost closes over the middle one of the teeth engaged, at the same time just making contact with the teeth right and left.   If the fraise chosen is too large, it will cut a jagged and uneven tooth; and, if too small, will leave a ridge or shoulder on the tooth; in this, as in everything else, practice makes perfect.   As a guide at first, it will be prudent to use the sector to ascertain the most suitable fraise for use; thus—place the wheel to be operated upon in the sector, and choose a fraise of such size as will correspond, not to the size indicated by the number of its teeth, but to *two teeth less.*

INVOLUTE.   The curve traced by the end of a string wound upon a roller or unwound from it.   This was a favorite shape for wheel teeth at one time, but was abandoned because it was found that the pressure on the pivot was increased by it, and it is now entirely superceded by the epicycloidal.

ISOCHRONAL.   Uniform in time; moving in equal time.   When the long and short arcs of a balance are caused to be performed in the same time by means of a hairspring, that spring is said to be an isochronal one, or isochronous.   When the vibrations of a pendulum are all of the same duration, no matter through what extent of arc the pendulum moves, the vibrations are isochronal.

JACOT PIVOT LATHE.   A tool used but little in this country, the American lathe and its attachments having superceded it.   It is used for reburnishing and dressing up pivots.

JANVIER, ANTIDE.   He was celebrated for his skill in representing planetary movements by the aid of mechanism.   He was a profound mathematician.   He was born at Saint-Claude-du-Jura, in 1751, and died in 1835.

JAPANESE CLOCKS.   The Japanese use a clock which divides the day into twelve hours, and an attempt is made to follow the variations of the solar day, so that the period from sunrise to sunset shall be divided into six equal portions, which vary in length according to the season.   These clocks are of three kinds.   The first has a dial, on which the hours are printed, which turns with a varying speed, according to the season, while the time is denoted by means of a fixed index.   The second has a dial rotating with a constant rate, but the points indicating the hours approach automatically nearer to the center when the season calls for shorter hours.   The third has no dial, but instead uses a vertical scale which is traversed by an index attached to the weight; see Figs. 174 and 175.   The works consist of the drum, B, around which the cord winds from two other wheels, and a verge balance with spiral spring.   Three thousand eight hundred vibrations are produced for each revolution of the drum. The weight is composed of the striking works and carries the index A, which points to the hours as the weight descends. The striking works consist of a barrel *b*, Fig. 176, with spring and a train of four

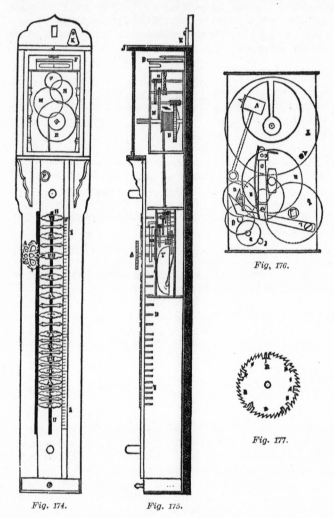

Fig. 174.　　Fig. 175.

Fig. 176.

Fig. 177.

wheels, ending with a lone pinion. The first wheel, *a*, carries pins which control the hammer to strike the gong T; the second wheel, *c*, carries an elbow which stops the train and raises the bascule L with one end, while the other end impels the wheel R at each revolution. The weight strikes against the pins h, b, Fig. 175, as it descends. These pins act successively on the arm L, Fig. 176, turning the bascule G and liberating the hammer, which strikes the gong. The wheel R, Fig. 177, has three cuttings that allow but one stroke of the hammer, and three others that allow two strokes, the remainder being divided so as to give 4, 5, 6, 7, 8 and 9 strokes respectively.

JEROME, CHAUNCEY. Mr. Jerome was one of the earliest clockmakers of America and at one time was one of the largest manufacturers. He was born at Canaan, Conn., June 10, 1793. In 1816 he

Chauncey Jerome.

went to work for Eli Terry, then the largest manufacturer of clocks in America. In 1817 he started in the business of clockmaking for himself in a small way. He put up the first circular saw ever used in Bristol, in 1822. In 1824 he organized a company for the manufacture of clocks. In 1838 he put the first brass clock upon the market. In 1842 he introduced these brass clocks in England, being the first American manufacturer of clocks who succeeded in establishing a trade with England. In 1850 he organized the Jerome Manufacturing Company, which carried on the large clock business of its time. Owing to poor management the company failed in 1855, and Jerome, although a very rich man at one time, was hopelessly ruined by this failure. This company was succeeded by the New Haven Clock Company.

JEWEL. In watch work, a stone having a hole pierced in it for the reception of a pivot. To Nicholas Facio, a native of Genoa, is attributed the invention of piercing stones for this purpose, early in the eighteenth century. See *Facio*.

JEWEL HOLDER. This tool, which is shown in Fig. 179, is intended for holding jewels when cleaning and manipulating, and is far superior to the ordinary tweezers as it holds the jewel firmly and there

PAT. OCT. 13. 91.

Fig. 179.

in no danger of it snapping out as with tweezers. The jaws being made of boxwood it will not injure the finest setting. The metal parts are of German silver.

JEWELING. The act of fitting in jewels for pivots to run in, to diminish wear of the acting parts. Sapphires and rubies are used in the better class of work, while in cheaper watches garnets are substituted. In escapement holes, where endstones are used, as in Fig. 181, the jewel

Fig. 180.

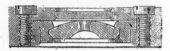

Fig. 181.

in a loose setting is fitted into a recessed hole, and upon it the end-stone, also set in metal, is laid, and the whole secured by two small screws. In cheaper movements the jewel is rubbed in, as shown in Fig. 180. *

JEWELING TOOL. Fig. 182 illustrates Hutchinson's Automatic Jeweling Tool. To cut a setting for a jewel, place tool in tail-stock and taper in head of lathe, and see that corner of cutter E comes to center. If it does not, turn screw D back or forward until it comes to the center. Now drill hole half as large as the jewel you wish to set; then place jewel in slot A, and bring index finger over until jewel is tight in slot A, being careful to have jewel in center of slot

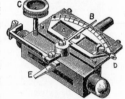

Fig. 182.

and not to one side. Now turn set screw C up tight and tool will cut setting exact size.

JEWELING AND STAKING TOOL. Hopkins' patent jeweling and staking tool, shown in Fig. 183, is an ingenious device, and one that will be found very useful to the watch repairer. As the spindle, or handle, to which the cutters and burnishers P. P. P. are attached, is sustained in upright position when in use, by the long bearings through which it passes in the upright F. independently of the lower center, the hole to be cut may be centered either from below or above as preferred ; and the depth to which it is desired a cutter shall work is regulated by adjustment of the sliding collar E, and this being a correct uprighting, as well as jeweling tool, with it a pivot hole, or a jewel setting the correct center (upright) of which has been lost, may readily be corrected, or its true center again found, and, what in some cases would be a very desirable consideration, by careful manipulation with the cutter, which is under perfect control of the operator, the position of jewel settings may be so changed so as to alter the depth of locking of the wheels to any desired

* For full directions in regard to making and setting jewels the reader is referred to Watch and Chronometer Jeweling, published by Geo. K. Hazlitt & Co., Chicago.

extent. To regulate the depth to which it is desired a cutter shall work
below the surface of a plate, lower the spindle **D** till, when moved out
sufficiently far, the end of the cutter will rest down on the top of the
plate to be operated upon, and fasten it there by lightly tightening the
screw **K**; this done, adjust and fasten the collar **E** on the spindle **D**, to the

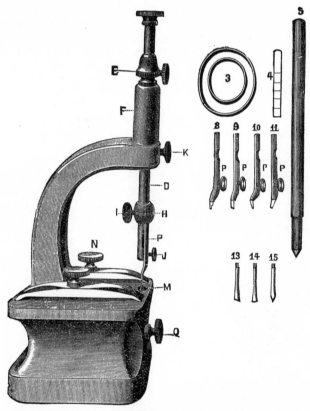

Fig. 183.

same height above the top of the upright **F** as it is desired the cutter shall
work below the surface of the plate on which it now rests. This, when
the spindle **D** has been again set free by loosening the screw **K**, will of
course allow the cutter to sink into the hole to be operated upon to the
exact distance the collar **E** had been set above the top of **F**. In adjusting the collar **E**, the graduated wedge, No. 4, or the jewel to be set, as
preferred, may be used as a gauge. The burnishers, No. 9, are used both
for opening and closing settings; the same burnisher, having chosen one

of proper size, is used for both purposes ; the side being used for opening the setting, and the beveled and rounded end for burnishing it
down again over the jewel. The pieces 13 and 14 are made to fit in the
lower end of the spindle D (the cutter P having been removed), same
as an ordinary drill stock, and are used for burnishing the edges of a
jewel setting down flat over the jewel, countersinking screw heads,
giving end shake to wheels, etc.; and being easily made, any one
owning the tool can make these for himself, of forms and sizes
to suit the particular work in hand. For uprighting purposes,
withdraw the spindle D and substitute No. 5, the rings, No. 3, being
intended for laying the work on, on the tool bed. For upright drilling through watch plates, mark the place to be drilled (prick punch it
slightly) with the cone point of No. 5 ; which done, turn the spindle
No. 5 upside down and rest the upper end of the drill in the countersink
in its end, the drill being operated with a fiddle bow acting on a collet
placed on its shank for the purpose. For cutting off bushings level with
a watch plate, either a cutter of the No. 13 or 14 class, or one of the P
cutters can be used. For staking or riveting wheels upright on their
pinions, lay the stake No. 7 level on the tool bed (the center M having
been fastened down out of the way), and with No 5 center accurately the
hole to be used in the stake, and fasten it there by means of the clamps
N; then remove the cone end of No. 5, and place a punch with hole in
its end of the required size, on the part m, and proceed as in an ordinary
upright staking tool.

JEWELING CALIPER REST.

Fig. 184.

JEWELING CALIPER REST. This tool will be found very
useful for setting jewels in
plates or settings, in countersinking for screw heads, opening wheels for pinions or bushings, turning barrel heads, etc.
The sliding jaws of the calipers should be so adjusted
that when the swinging part
is brought back snugly against
them, the front cutting edge
of the cutter in the sliding
spindle will exactly line with
the center of the lathe spindle.
Then if the calipers are at the
right height, when a jewel or
jewel setting is placed in the
jaws of the caliper it will move
the edge of the cutter outward from the lathe center just half the diameter
of the jewel then in the caliper, and the cutting made at that distance

from the center will exactly coincide with the size of the jewel to be set.
If however, if set and worked as above, it is found that the hole cut is too
large for the jewel, it will indicate that the calipers are too low down, and
should be raised, provision for which is made in the construction of the
tool. If on the other hand, the cutting is found too small to fit, it will
indicate the calipers should be lowered. The final cutting for the jewel
seat should be made by running the center straight inward from the face
of the plate; the adjustable screw stop on the back end of the sliding
spindle serving to gauge the depth of the cutting.

JEWEL PIN. To set a jewel pin in the table roller (of American
watches) correctly, is a difficult task. Where the jewel pin is broken off,
you will often save much valuable time by examining the broken part
with your glass and noting the exact location of the pin before disturbing
it. In some movements the jewel pin will be set as in Fig. 185, occupying about two-thirds of the hole, in another movement the pin will not
occupy much over one-half the space, as shown in Fig 186. By using

care in selecting a jewel pin of
precisely the same size as the
old one and in inserting it in the
same place, nine out of every
ten movements will be found
mechanically perfect and the
balance have a good motion if
the escapement is perfect. Most
watchmakers remove the table
roller from the balance staff, in
case the jewel pin is loose. This
you will find unnecessary if you
will make the following de-

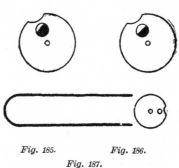

Fig. 185.   Fig. 186.

Fig. 187.

scribed tool and use as directed. Take a piece of copper wire about half
the thickness of a common pin tongue and bend it as shown in Fig. 187,
so that it will be about one and one-eighth inch long. Cut or saw a
groove in the inside of the ends, sufficiently deep to hold on to the table
roller, say one-fourth inch from the end. This can be easily bent to
accommodate all sizes of tables. If you wish to soften the cement, to
tighten or replace a new jewel pin, it is only necessary to slip on the
copper wire, and hold the extreme outer end in the flame of a small
alcohol lamp a few moments and sufficient heat will follow the copper
wire to soften the cement. Care must be exercised to keep the pin in
the proper position, and when sufficiently heated, remove the wire
quickly and allow the table to cool. By use of this little tool there is no
need of removing the table roller, and absolutely no danger of injuring
the finest expansion balance, as the tool need not, and must not touch
the balance. The end of this tool is held in the flame by a pair of

soldering tweezers. Always use shellac for cementing the jewel pin in the table roller.

JEWEL PIN SETTER. Fig 188 illustrates the Logan patent. It is an excellent tool and will save the workman considerable time and

Fig. 188.

much annoyance by its use. Every watchmaker is aware what a difficult and tedious matter it is to set a jewel pin correctly. With this tool the job is accomplished quickly and accurately.

JODIN, JEAN. A clever French watchmaker of the eighteenth century. Author of a work on horology. He was the first to point out that success in the timing of horizontal watches depends on the correct proportioning of all their parts.

JOINT PUSHER. A small piece of tempered steel wire mounted in a wooden handle and used for inserting and removing joint pins.

JURGENSEN, URBAN. He was born at Copenhagen, Denmark, August 5, 1776. His father was a watchmaker to the court, and under him Urban learned the art. At the age of twenty-one he visited Neufchatel, Switzerland, where he remained for eighteen months and afterwards resided for six months in Geneva, being constantly occupied with mathematical and practical work. He afterwards went to Paris and was admitted to the houses of M. Breguet and Ferdinand Berthoud, and for some time worked under the immediate instruction of the former. He spent some time in London and then returned to Paris, and from there went to Geneva and Neufchatel. He returned to Denmark in 1801, and was offered a partnership with a very clever artist, M. Etienne Magnin, who for some years had enjoyed a royal bounty to make longitude-chronometers for the use of ships. Young Jurgensen, however, preferred to enter into partnership with his father, and his younger brother, Frederick, afterwards court watchmaker, was his first pupil. In 1804 he compiled a memoir entitled, "On the Art of Watchmaking," or "Rules for the Exact Measurement of Time," which was published at royal expense. A new and improved edition was published the following year in French. In the same year he received the silver medal of the Royal Society of Sciences, at Copenhagen, for a treatise entitled, "On the best

mode of making and hardening Watch Springs." He resolved, owing
to the scarcity of competent help and his own poor health, to remove to
Switzerland, and accordingly in 1807 he removed to Neufchatel, where
he remained two years. In 1809 he returned to Denmark. In 1815 he
was made a member of "The Royal Society of Sciences." In 1822 he
was made superintendent of all chronometers belonging to the Royal
Navy, and in 1824 he was decorated with the Gold Cross of Dannebrog.
He died on the 14th of May, 1830, being 53 years old.

JURGENSEN, JULES. Son of Urban and one of the most noted
watchmakers of the 19th century. He was
born at Locle, July 27, 1808, during the temporary residence of his parents in Switzerland.   During his youth he worked under
the immediate instruction of his father, but
in 1835 he went to Switzerland, and from
there to Paris and London, where he studied
under the best masters in physics, mechanics
and astronomy.   Later he established a
branch of his father's business in Locle and
devoted his attention to the construction
of pocket chronometers. The result of his
study and experiments was the celebrated

Jules Jurgensen.

Jurgensen watch of to-day. The last years of his life were spent in
Geneva and he died December 17, 1877. His son, Jules F. U. Jurgensen,
succeeded to the business.

KENDALL, LARCUM. A noted watchmaker of London, who
constructed a timekeeper on Harrison's principle, which was given to
Captain Cook, when he commanded the Resolution, in 1776.

KULLBERG, VICTOR. A prominent horologist and successful
chronometer maker. He was born at Wisby, on the Island of Gothland,
in 1824. He went to London in 1851, where he remained until his death.
His chronometers stood at the top of the list in the trials from 1880 to
1890 inclusive. He died July 7, 1890.

LACQUER. The ordinary lacquer of commerce is composed of
spirits of wine and clear shellac in the proportion of 1 oz. of shellac
to a pint of spirit. Heat should not be applied, but the ingredients
placed in a glass stoppered bottle and shaken from time to time until the
shellac is thoroughly dissolved or combined with the spirit. Various
tints may be given lacquer by adding small quantities of aniline colors,
previously well mixed with water and free from lumps.

LANGE, ADOLPH. Adolph Lange was born in Dresden, in 1815, and was apprenticed to a watchmaker of that place. At the expiration of his apprenticeship he went to Paris to perfect himself in the higher branches of horology. He became the foreman in the celebrated workshop of Winnerl. He later returned to Dresden, where he became the partner of his former master. He devoted himself to the manufacture of astronomical clocks, chronometers and fine watches, and soon secured

Adolph Lange.

for himself an enviable reputation. About this time the government of Saxony was in search of some means of bettering the condition of the inhabitants of the mountainous districts of Saxony. The condition of these people was most pitiable, as for generations they had lived there in extreme poverty. Mr. Lange was confident that if the art of watchmaking was introduced into this region the desired result might be achieved. The government looked favorably on his proposition, and in 1845 he, with the assistance of the State, established a watchmaker's school at Glashutte. The populace did not take kindly to the idea, and it was very up-hill work for awhile; but his efforts were finally crowned with success. He taught the youths of the village the art of watchmaking and installed them in his workshop. In less than two years the first watches were marketed, and the success of the enterprise assured. In time his pupils became teachers, and gradually, but surely, the art of horology gained a foothold, until now nearly ihe entire population of Glashutte are engaged in horological and kindred pursuits. He died Dec. 5, 1875, leaving two sons, Richard and Emile, who are still engaged in manufacturing fine watches, chronometers and clocks of precision, in Glashutte.

LANTERN PINION. A pinion formed of two circular brass, or other metal plates, and connected by means of short steel wires.

LAP. A disc used in conjunction with a lathe for polishing or cutting. Laps are made of steel, copper, ivory, etc., and are charged with the cutting or polishing compounds. See *Diamond Laps*.

LATHE. A mechanical device used for shaping articles by causing them to revolve while being brought into contact with cutting tools. Those who contemplate buying a lathe will do well to avoid the cheap imitations of the American pattern, which are made by irresponsible makers in foreign countries, and foisted upon an unsuspecting public, and guaranteed true and "as good as the American." They are usually nicely finished, but inferior both in material and workmanship, their greatest failure being their untruth. If an untrue American lathe, by any possibility is allowed to escape the inspector and finds its way upon the

market, the manufacturer is only too glad to exchange it for a perfect
article, for his reputation is at stake; but who are you going back on in
the event of one of these cheap imitations proving untrue? There are
American made lathes upon the market that are as inferior in many
respects as the imitations, and the watchmaker will do well to do without a lathe until such time as he can afford to purchase one of known

Fig. 191.

reputation. Among the first class American lathes upon the market
may be mentioned the Webster-Whitcomb, Fig. 191; the Moseley, **Fig.**
192; the Hopkins, Fig. 193, and the Rivett, Fig. 194.

An excellent lathe for the heavier work of watchmakers and jewelers,
such as cannot be performed with satisfaction on the watchmaker's lathe,
is the No. 4 Barnes, which is shown in Fig. 195.

Fig. 192.

It is manufactured by the W. F. & John Barnes Company, Rockford,
Ill. For screw cutting, the manufacture of watchmaker's tools, fishing
reels, repairs on tower clocks, in fact, all the heavier work of the trade,
it is admirably fitted.

The American lathe of to-day is a marvel of completeness in its parts, and how many hours, yea months, of study and experiment have been bestowed upon it by its projectors and makers to acquire these points of utility and excellency. What a vast amount of care has been exercised for the production of a perfect lathe! Must this care cease at the moment the lathe passes into the hands of the watchmaker?

It is a very easy matter at any time to wipe off the dust and oil that may accumulate, but does this alone constitute due care? There may be a nice glass case to cover it and keep off the dust, and a very good idea it is, if faithfully used; but if a counter shaft is on the bench, or much lathe work is to be done, it soon falls into blissful desuetude, or finishes its usefulness by being broken. Then, often, a cloth is wrapped about the lathe, which soon gets soiled and looks badly, let alone the poor protection it affords.

Fig. 193.

Dust is omnipresent and the greatest enemy to all active machinery; it insidiously makes its way into every crease and crevice, and if not promptly removed will cause untold damage. We cannot get rid of it and must (like the industrious housewife) wage a constant warfare against it.

The care necessary to be given to a fine lathe differs from most other tools; it is not confined alone to the removal of dust and keeping clean, but the fitting properly of the several parts as used. There should be no overstraining when tightening screws, chucks, etc., or when fitting articles in both wire and wheel chucks, and so on through the list.

The face of the lathe bed when it comes from the makers is (or should be) perfectly true from end to end, in order that head and tail stocks will meet on a direct line of centers, even should they be changed end for end, and a good lathe will meet those requirements. Now, it is obvious to any thinking mind that if this face becomes injured by neglect, whereby the nickling is removed in spots or portions, they will, in all probability become rusty; this rust will then eat away and throw off more, and soon the face presents an uneven surface, which will tend to destroy the line of centers between head and tail stocks.

The head stock, usually occupying one position, causes less wear at this point, or place, while the hand-rest and tail stock are constantly being shifted, so where there is more motion or action there must be

Fig. 194.

more wear, especially if dust, chips, or grit be allowed to accumulate beneath them, and though the wear is seemingly imperceptible, it nevertheless is there, and will sooner or later manifest itself, and this is a signal that the level of the bed is becoming impaired, and, necessarily, the truth. Thus too much care and attention cannot be exercised in guarding against chips and dust when sliding hand rest back and forth on the bed.

At the end of the bed, where the tail stock takes position, many watchmakers have the tail stock off, and this portion is more exposed to atmospheric action, also receiving perspiration from the hands when they come in contact. Again, others let the tail stock remain in position, only removing when it comes in the way. In the former case, it is well to devise some means for the protection of the bed; this is easily done by making a sheath of chamois skin to slip tightly over the bed; it can be removed and replaced readily, and when it becomes soiled, can be washed.

This sheath should be fully two-thirds the length of bed, or reaching from tail end up to hand rest when it is close to head stock. It preserves the bed from dampness, which is considerable in some climates, also the perspiration of the hand and flying chips and dust. In the second case, if the tail stock is allowed to remain on lathe, or, if removed and placed on the bench, it is subjected to all the evils the bed is in the former.

Fig. 195.

Our opinion is, the tail stock should be kept in its compartment in a tight fitting drawer, away from dust and accidental knocks of other tools on the bench; the tail spindle not being nickeled, is more liable to rust if left exposed, and should be kept wrapped in a sheath of oiled paper. This may seem superfluous and too much bother, yet it is taking proper care which tells in the end.

The bottom of tail stock should always be brushed off before placing in position, not only for its protection, but for fear some particle of grit may be adhering, thereby throwing it out of truth, and screwing it down tight only adds injury to the lathe if allowed to remain.

The head stock demands close attention; the spindle should run freely without end shake, and about once a week should be speeded, meanwhile administering oil until it leaves the bearings clean, and then wiped off. A little oil should be added every day. See that the mouth of the spindle is kept bright and clean; thrust a strip of cloth clear through spindle every now and then, that all dust and dirt may be removed.

Wire and wheel chucks should often be washed in gasoline to remove gummy dirt and oil which is constantly adhering, and it is even well each time a chuck is used, to wash off first, then wipe dry. A little dirt on mouth of spindle, or on chuck, often throws it out of truth, and consequently the article fastened therein also.

When fitting head or tail stocks, or in fact any attachment, do so carefully. Do not bang it in place as if you held a grudge against it, and when in position see that they are tightly screwed in place.

Having too much end shake on live spindle, especially in soft lathes, causes uneven wear in its bearings, besides not being reliable for true pivoting or any such work.

When the cost of a lathe is taken into consideration, it goes to prove that it is not easily replaced. Where is the jeweler with a stock of goods who would retire without first seeing his valuables were in the safe, but how many are there who think of giving this protection to their lathes? Some do, but the greater per cent do not. "It is a "pious plan" to see that the head stock, tail stock, and attachments are in the safe, and should a fire break out that endangers the store, and no chance to save it, the feeling of satisfaction is great to know the lathe is safe, that is, the more expensive parts, for the bed can be purchased at a nominal cost compared to the attachments.

A word about chuck blocks or stands. The best kinds are those made to fit in a drawer of the bench and the holes sunk deep enough to let the chuck (wire) drop full length, or to the head, the hole being countersunk to admit the bevel portion. They can easily be picked out with the finger nail. Have the block thoroughly soaked with oil.

To prevent rusting of tools, and especially if the bed shows signs of rust spots, here is a good old remedy: Procure some blue ointment, spread it on a cloth and rub the tools or lathe briskly, then wipe off with a clean cloth, and wipe dry. This ointment leaves a thin coating of mercury which prevents the action of dampness on the tools. This cure need not be resorted to more than once a month, and keep ointment away from gold cases and watch movements. If you find your lathe bed has got in such a condition as to destroy its truth, send it at once to the makers and have it put in first-class condition. Do not trust it, for the sake of saving a little, to some irresponsible firm for repairs.

LEPAUTE, J. A. One of the most celebrated of French horologists. He did much to improve his art, especially in regard to turret clocks. He was the author of a volume on horology, which in its time was a standard authority. He was born at Montmedi in 1709 and died in 1789.

LEPINE MOVEMENT. A bar movement, in which the bar supporting the top pivot of the barrel arbor is straight. Lepine introduced his improvements in 1776 and they consisted of the suppression of the pillar plate, the fuzee and chain and one of the supports to the barrel arbor. The Lepine family resided at Ferney, near Geneva, where Voltaire established a watch factory. Breguet improved on the Lepine system by causing the mainspring to be wound up at the back of the watch through the dome, instead of by a square through the face of the dial.

LE ROY, JULIEN. A celebrated French horologist. He was the inventor of the horizontal mechanism for turret clocks. He introduced improvements in nearly all the branches of horology of his day. He died in 1759

LE ROY, PIERRE. A son of Julien Le Roy and unquestionably the greatest of all French horologists. He was born in 1717 and died in 1785. He was the inventor of the Duplex escapement.

LESSELS, M. A celebrated German clockmaker who worked for a long time with Breguet. He was the maker of a number of excellent astronomical clocks for Swiss, German and Russian observatories. He died in 1849.

LEVER ESCAPEMENT.* George Graham, the English horologist, invented the anchor deadbeat escapement used in clocks, and from it the lever, the favorite watch escapement of to-day, is derived. In order to apply this latter escapement (which only allows of very small arcs of vibration), to the watch, it was necessary, says Saunier, not only to alter its form but also to make the balance independent of the motive force, except during the actual period of lift. Thomas Mudge satisfied these requirements, by producing an escapement in which the two lifts were equal and an impulse was given at each vibration of the balance.

Saunier and other authorities declare that when the modern lever escapement is well made in conformity with the principles of mechanics, and the pallets and pivot holes are provided with jewels, it may be considered to be the best adapted for ordinary use.

Britten declares that, although inferior for time keeping to the chronometer, when made with ordinary care it is so certain in its action that it is generally prefered for pocket watches. Its weak point is the necessity of applying oil to the pallets. However close the rate of the watch at first, the thickening of the oil in the course of time will inevitably affect its going.

The form of escapement presented in Fig. 198, is known as a *right angle* escapement. The *straight line* escapement, which is quite a favorite with Swiss and American watchmakers, is so called because the three

---

*The student will do well to read: The Detached Lever Escapement, by Moritz Grossmann; Modern Horology in Theory and Practice, by Claudius Saunier; Watch and Clock Making, by David Glasgow; The Watch and Clockmaker's Hand Book, by F. J. Britten.

centers of the wheel, the pallets and the balance are in a straight line. It is claimed that there is less friction and shake on the pivots in the straight line than in the right angle form, owing to the direction of the pressures neutralizing each other to some extent.*

In America, Switzerland and France, the "clubbed" tooth is preferred for escape wheels, that is to say, a tooth similar to that shown in Fig. 196, made with a tip of the wheel formed into an inclined plane, thus dividing the impulse between the face of the pallets and the wheel teeth. Saunier, in comparing the two forms of teeth, says: " An escapement with pointed or ratchet teeth has the following objections and advantages: Both the pitch with the locking face and the drop are very nearly doubled; there is therefore an appreciable increase in the resistance opposed to unlocking, especially when the oil is at all thick. Out of the 10° through which the pallet moves, a greater proportion is expended in the unlocking. Lastly, the fine pointed tooth must be made of brass, it is liable to wear and distortion, and is ill-adapted for retaining oil, which must be applied in very small quantities. On the other hand its advantages consist in: 1. The pallets having double width, so that a greater quantity of oil is retained on them. 2. The escapement will go for a considerable time after the oil has become bad or thickened. Some watchmakers, indeed, do not put any oil on either the teeth or pallets when the wheel is made of a particular kind of brass, but the point of the tooth wears in time. 3. The escapement is more easy of construction. When this form is adopted, the escapement can be made with sufficient accuracy by ordinary workmen; for if the planes are inclined to the requisite extent, there will be no time lost in the lift.

As compared with the ratchet toothed wheel, the wheel with clubbed teeth possesses the following qualities: It retains the oil better; the friction occurs at two points of contact instead of one; the impulse commences with a shorter lever and is, therefore, more efficient; no wear or distortion or variation of the acting surfaces need be feared when the wheel is carefully made and of good material; it is possible, within certain limits, to reduce the pitch with the locking faces if necessary, and thus, while diminishing the effect of viscosity on these surfaces, to increase the *real lift* that corresponds to a given apparent lift. Lastly, the drop can be reduced to almost nothing.

It is undoubtedly true that, as a set off against these advantages, it may be objected that this escapement is of a highly scientific character, so that its construction is a matter of some delicacy, and requires the skill of a first-rate workman. In conclusion, Saunier says, that the advantage is on the side of the clubbed tooth.

---

*Saunier does not commit himself on this point; Glasgow and Britten both declare that there is no advantage in the straight line, though the former admits that it may be more handsome to look at, and the latter that it allows of the poising of the lever and pallets with less redundant metal. The principal reason why it is not made in England is that with the fuzee movements it is difficult to find room for it.

Britten says that, on the other hand, English watchmakers maintain that as at some time during each impulse the planes of the wheel and pallet nearly coincide, the increased surface then presented to the varying influence of the adhesion of the oil is a serious evil. Then with

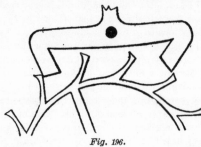

Fig. 196.

clubbed teeth, there is more difficulty in satisfactorily replacing a wheel than with ratchet teeth, for in the former case the planes must be of exactly the same angle and of the same length in the new wheel as in the old one. With brass wheels, the impulse faces on the wheel get cut into ruts, but the Swiss avoid this by using steel wheels, and also much reduce the extra adhesion due to increased surface by thinning the impulse planes of the teeth. Swiss escapements are, as a rule, commendably light, but the levers are disproportionately long. The Germans make an escapement in which the whole of the impulse plane is on the wheel teeth, the pallets being small round pins, as in Fig. 197 Britten thinks this a cheaper and simpler form, but Saunier says of a similar escapement, which was proposed by Perron in 1798, that the simplicity is more apparent than real, for it requires very great care in its construction, or otherwise its accuracy cannot be relied upon.

Britten gives the following very concise description of the action and proportion of the escapement:

ACTION OF THE ESCAPEMENT.

Fig. 199 shows the most usual form of the lever escapement, in which the pallets escape over three teeth of the wheel. A tooth of the escape wheel is at rest upon the locking face of the entering left-hand pallet. The impulse pin has just entered the notch of the lever, and is about to unlock the pallet. The action of the escapement is as follows: The balance, which is attached to the same staff as the roller, is traveling in the direction indicated by the arrow, which is around the roller, with suffi-

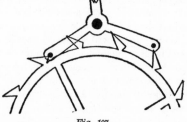

Fig. 197.

cient energy to cause the ruby pin to move the lever and pallets far enough to release the wheel tooth from the locking face, and allow it to enter on the impulse face of the pallet. Directly it is at liberty, the escape wheel, actuated by the mainspring of the watch, moves around the same way as the arrow and pushes the pallet out of its path. By the time the wheel tooth has got to the end of the impulse face of the pallet, its motion is arrested by the exit or right-hand pallet, the locking face of which has been brought into position to receive another tooth of the wheel. When the pallet was pushed aside by the wheel tooth it carried with it the lever, which in its turn communicated a sufficient blow to the ruby pin to send the balance with renewed energy on its vibration. So that the ruby pin has the double office of unlocking the pallets by giving a blow on one side of the notch of the lever, and of immediately receiving a blow from the opposite side of the notch. The balance proceeds on its excursion, winding up the balance spring as it goes, until its energy is expended. After it is brought to a state of rest, its motion is reversed by the uncoiling of the balance spring, the ruby pin again enters the notch of the lever, but from the opposite direction, and the operation already described is repeated. The object of the safety pin is to prevent the wheel from being unlocked except when the ruby pin is in the notch of the lever. The banking pins keep the motion of the lever within the desired limits. They should be placed as shown, where any blow from the ruby pin on to the outside of the lever is received direct. They are sometimes placed at the tail of the lever, but in that position the banking pins receive the blow through the pallet staff pivots, which are liable to be broken in consequence.

PROPORTION OF THE ESCAPEMENT.

The escape wheel has fifteen teeth, and the distance apart of the pallets, from center to center, is equal to 60° of the circumference of the wheel. The pallets are planted as close as possible to the wheel, so that the teeth of the wheel in passing just clear the belly of the pallets. When the tooth is pressing on the locking, the line of pressure should pass through the center of the pallet staff. But as the locking faces of the two pallets are not equidistant from the center of motion, a tangent drawn from the locking corner of one pallet would be wrong for the other, and, as a matter of fact, if a diagram is made it will be found that even when the pallets are planted as close as possible they are hardly as close as they should be for the right-hand pallet. To plant as close as possible is, therefore, a very good rule, and is the one adopted by the best pallet makers; though in setting out the escapement a chord of the width of the pallet is produced to find the center of the staff, as shown in Fig. 200. The width of each pallet is made as nearly as possible half the distance between one tooth of the escape wheel and the next. As the teeth of the wheel must be of an appreciable thickness, and the various pivots must have shake, it is not found practicable to get the pallets of greater width than 10° of the circumference of the wheel instead of 12°, which would be half the distance between one tooth and the next. This difference between the theoretical and actual width of the pallet is called the drop. The lever is pinned to the pallets, and has the same center of motion. The distance between the center of the lever and the center of the roller is not absolute. The distance generally preferred is a chord of 96° of a circle representing the path of the tips of the escape wheel teeth, that is, the distance from the tip of one tooth to the tip of the fourth succeeding tooth. The proportion, as it is called, of the lever and roller is usually from 3 to 1 to 3½ to 1. In the former case the length of the lever (measured from the center of pallet staff to center of the mouth of the notch) is three times the distance of the center of the impulse pin from the center of the roller, and in the latter case 3½ times. The portion of the lever to the left of the pallet staff hole acts as a counterpoise, and should really have the metal in it disposed at as nearly as possible the same distance from the center as that in the other end of the lever, though this is rarely the case.

In this form of the lever escapement, the pallets have not less than 10° of motion. Of this amount, 2° are used for locking, and the remainder for impulse. The amount of locking is to some extent dependent on the size of the escapement. With a large escapement less than 1½° would suffice, while a small one would require rather more than 2°. The quality of the work, too, is an element in deciding the amount of locking. The lighter the locking the better, but it must receive every tooth of the wheel safely, and where all the parts are made with care the escapement can be made with a very light locking.

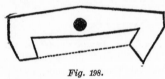

Fig. 198.

Presuming that the staff hole is correctly drilled with relation to the planes, a rough rule used for testing 10° pallets is that a straight edge laid on the plane of the entering pallet should point to the locking corner of the exit pallet, as indicated by the dotted line in Fig. 198. But this is clearly only an approximation, for any variation in the amount allowed for locking alters the direction of the planes.

When, from setting the hands of a watch back, or from a sudden jerk, there is a tendency for the pallets to unlock, the safety pin butts against the edge of the roller. It will be observed that when the ruby pin unlocks the pallets, the safety pin is allowed to pass the roller by means of the crescent which is cut out of the roller opposite the ruby pin. The teeth of the escape wheel make a considerable angle with a radial line (24°), so that only their tips touch the locking faces of the pallets. The locking faces of the pallets, instead of being curves struck from the center of motion of the pallets, as would be otherwise the case, are cut back at an angle so as to interlock with the wheel teeth. The locking face forms an angle of 6° or 8° with a tangent to a circle representing the path of the locking corner. This is done so that the safety pin shall not drag on

ENGLISH LEVER ESCAPEMENT.

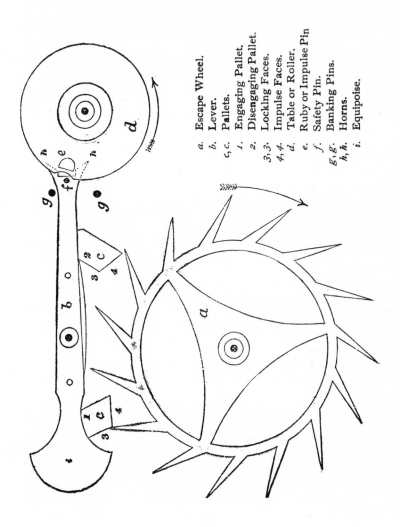

a. Escape Wheel.
b. Lever.
c, c. Pallets.
1. Engaging Pallet,
2. Disengaging Pallet.
3, 3. Locking Faces.
4, 4. Impulse Faces.
d. Table or Roller.
e. Ruby or Impulse Pin
f. Safety Pin.
g, g. Banking Pins.
h, h. Horns.
i. Equipoise.

Fig. 199.

the edge of the roller, but be drawn back till the lever touches the banking pin. When the operation of setting the hands back is finished, or the other cause of disturbance removed, the pressure of the wheel tooth on the locking face of the pallet draws the pallet into the wheel as far as the banking pin will allow. The amount of this "run" should not be more than sufficient to give proper clearance between the safety pin and the roller, for the more the run, the greater is the resistance to unlock. ing. This rule is sometimes sadly transgressed, and occasionally the locking is found to be, from excessive run, almost equal in extent to the impulse. It will generally be found that in these cases the escapement is so badly proportioned that the extra run has had to be given to secure a sound safety action. In common watches the safety action is a frequent source of trouble. The more the path of the safety pin intersects the edge of the roller, the sounder is the safety action, and if the inter. section is small the safety pin is likely to jamb against the edge of the roller, or even to pass it altogether. With an ordinary single roller escapement a sound safety action cannot be obtained with a less balance arc than 33°; 10° pallets with one degree of movement added for run, and with a lever and roller of 3 to 1, give a balance arc of 33°—that is to say, the balance in its vibration is freed from the escapement except during 33°, when the impulse pin is in contact with the lever. Even with a balance arc of 33° the roller must be kept small in the following way to ensure soundness of the safety action. The hole for the ruby pin must not be left round. After it is drilled, a punch of the same shape as the ruby pin—that is, with one-third of the diameter flattened off—should be inserted, and the edge of the roller, where the crescent is to be formed, beaten in. By this means the roller can be turned down small enough to get a sufficient intersection for the safety pin.

It is useful in estimating the balance arc of a watch, to remember if it has a three-armed balance that 30° is one-fourth of the distance between two arms. With a compensation balance a third of the distance between two of the quarter screws is 30°.

A round ruby pin, although it is sometimes used in common watches, gives a bad action and necessitates a very large balance arc.

Fig. 200 is appended as a guide to students in setting out the escapement. A circle representing the extreme diameter of the escape wheel is taken as a basis, and on the left of the center line is set off, by means of a protractor, the middle of one pallet (30°) and its width (10°). The chord of this arc of 10° is then produced till it cuts the center line, and this intersection is taken as the center of the pallet staff. From the pallet-staff center curves, A and B, (representing the paths of the pallet corners,) are drawn. The amount of locking C (say 2°) and impulse D (say 9°) are set off from the chord of the left-hand pallet. The impulse plane is traced through the intersection of

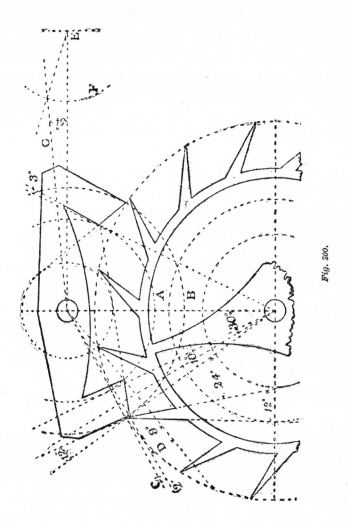

Fig. 200.

the angular lines with the curves A and B, and the line of the plane produced toward the center of the staff as shown. From the center of the staff is described a circle just touching the line so produced. The impulse plane of the other pallet forms a tangent to this circle. In this position of the pallets, a line drawn from the locking corner of the left-hand pallet to form an angle of 12° with the radial line from the center of the wheel, will be required to show the locking face of the pallet, and a similar line forming 3° will answer for the locking face of the right-hand pallet. Mark off the center of the roller (E), and take, say, one–fourth of the distance between this center and the center of the pallet staff for the position of the center of the impulse pin, and describe the arc F to represent its path. The line G, forming with the center line running through the roller an angle equal to half the total angle of the motion of the pallets, or $5\frac{1}{2}$°, will represent the center of the lever. The wheel teeth are set back about 24° from a radial line, so as to bear on their points only, and the rim of the wheel extends to about three-fourths of the whole radius. The remaining parts may be readily filled in from the foregoing remarks on the proportion of the escapement, and a study of Fig. 199.

DOUBLE ROLLER ESCAPEMENT.—THE HORN OF THE LEVER.

Low-angled pallets, says Britten (i. e. pallets having but little motion), and small balance arcs are preferred for fine watches; the low-angle pallets as being less affected by changes in the condition of the oil which is used to lubricate the faces of the pallets than when the motion is greater, and the small balance arc because it allows the balance to be more perfectly detached from the escapement. With a double roller escapement, pallets with from 8° to 9° of motion are generally used, with a lever and roller to give a balance arc of from 28° to 32°. With low-angled pallets, and less than 30° of balance arc, a different arrangement than the usual upright pin in the lever must be made for the safety action. A second roller, not much more than one-half the diameter of the one in which the impulse pin is fixed, is mounted on the balance-staff for the purpose, and a small gold finger, projecting far enough to reach the edge of the smaller roller, is screwed to the lever. The safety roller should not be less than half the diameter of the impulse roller, for the smaller the safety roller, the farther the safety finger enters the crescent before the ruby pin enters the notch of the lever; and, as directly the safety finger enters the crescent, the impulse pin must be within the horn of the lever, the smaller the safety roller, the longer must be the horn. Then, if the horns are excessively long, the extent of the free vibration of the balance is curtailed, because the ruby pin touches the outside of the lever sooner. It will be seen that in the single roller escapement (Fig. 201) the safety pin does not enter the crescent before the ruby pin enters the notch, and, therefore, in the single roller escapement the lever really requires

but the smallest possible amount of horn.   Fig. 201 shows the double
roller arrangement.   Here it will be seen that the safety finger enters
the crescent some time before the ruby pin gets to the notch.   During
this interval, should the hands of the watch be set back, the pallets could
not trip, for the horn of the lever would be caught on the ruby pin.   I

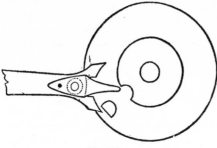

have tried to explain this
fully, because double
roller escapements occa-
sionally fail to give satisfaction owing to the
lever having insufficient
horn.   On the other
hand, the levers of single
roller escapements,
where scarcely any horn
is required, are often
made with long ones.

Fig. 201.

Besides getting a sound safety action with small balance arc, the double roller has three other advantages.   (1) The impulse is given more
nearly on the line of centers, and consequently with less engaging friction.   (2) The safety roller being of a lesser diameter, the safety finger
when in contact with it offers less resistance to the motion of the balance;
and (3) the requisite amount of shake between the safety roller and
banking pins is obtained with less run on the pallets.   Double roller
escapements are sometimes seen with pallets having 10° of motion, and
even more, and with the safety roller nearly as large as the impulse
one.   An escapement made in this way really appears to lose most of
the advantages of the extra roller.   On the other hand, low-angle pallets
are sometimes used with a long lever to get increased balance arc.   This
also is objectionable, for the pallets must have more draw to pull the
longer lever up to the banking, and more draw means harder unlocking.
It is really only to watches of a high character throughout that double
roller escapements with low angle pallets and small balance arcs should
be applied.   For the ordinary run of work, the single roller escapement
with 11° pallets and a balance arc of from 36° to 40° is well suited.

SIZE OF THE LEVER ESCAPEMENT.

Lever escapements are classed, says Britten, into the following sizes:
No. 0 in which the escape wheel is .185 of an inch in diameter.

1	"	"	"	"	.205	"	"	"
2	"	"	"	"	.225	"	"	"
4	"	"	"	"	.245	"	"	"
6	"	"	"	"	.205	"	"	"
8	"	"	"	"	.285	"	"	"
10	"	"	"	"	.295	"	"	"
12	"	"	"	"	.305	"	"	"

No. 1 is the smallest and No. 10 the largest size used in the ordinary run of work. The practice of J. F. Cole was to have the escape wheel three-sevenths of the diameter of the balance, but there is no strict rule for the size of an escapement to a watch, though there has been a disposition of late years to use smaller escapements than formerly, as they are found to yield better results. In course of time a ridge is formed at the beginning of the impulse planes of the pallets, where the wheel teeth fall. This ridge is more marked and farther along the impulse plane when there is much drop and the escape wheel is large and heavy, because the inertia of the wheel which increases in proportion to its weight and the square of its diameter, is so great that the balance after unlocking the pallets, carries them farther before the wheel acquires sufficient velocity to overtake them. Undue shake of the ruby pin in the notch will also cause this ridge to be accentuated. The practice of some of the best London makers is, for 6 and 8 sized movements, No. 2 escapement; for 10 and 12 sized movements, No. 4 escapement; for 14 and 16 sized movements, No. 6 escapement; for 18 and 20 sized movements, No, 8 escapement. Many manufacturers confine themselves to two sizes. "two's" for repeaters and ladies, and "sixes" for gentlemen's watches, A Coventry will be found usually to have a larger escapement than a London watch of the same size.

The escape wheel is of hard, well hammered brass; the pallets are of steel (the practice of rolling the pallet steel to harden it is not a good one, as there is danger of magnetizing it in the operation), wider than the wheel, with the acting parts of ruby in the best, and garnet in the commoner escapements. The pallets are slit longitudinally, and the stones fixed in with shellac. The Swiss generally insert the stones across the pallets so that they are visible. The impulse planes are curved so as to present a smaller surface to the wheel. The ruby pin is fixed in the roller with shellac; the safety pin of gold, and the banking pins of brass. Non-magnetizable watches have the lever and pallets of some other metal than steel, generally aluminium bronze.

In a good lever escapement all the moving parts are extremely light.

In making a new lever it is well to start with it full long, because a deep notch is much easier to polish than a shallow one. When the notch is finished the horns can be filed off as required.

TWO PIN ESCAPEMENT.

As Britten has pointed out in the action of the escapement, the ruby pin performs the double office of unlocking the pallets by giving a blow on one side of the notch of the lever, and of immediately receiving a blow from the opposite side of the notch. George Savage, of London, saw there was a loss of power consequent on this double duty, and also in the unlocking action taking place before the line of centers of the lever and roller, and with a view to avoid this, introduced the escapement shown in Fig. 202. He reversed the order of things by cutting a small notch in the roller, and placing a pin in the lever, in lieu of the ruby pin in the roller, which also answered the purpose of the guard pin. To effect the unlocking, he placed two small pins in the roller in such positions that one of them begins to unlock just before crossing the line of centers. By the time the unlocking is finished, the pin in the lever is drawn into the notch and gives the first portion of the impulse. It then leaves the notch, and the impulse is completed by the horns of the lever striking the second small pin in the roller, which has nearly or quite reached the line of centers by this time.

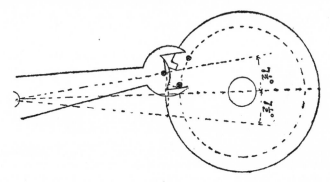

Fig. 202.

In order to get the safety pin well into the notch, says Britten, this escapement requires pallets having 12° to 15° of motion, which is objectionable, and the lever and roller action is besides a very delicate job, and fails if not thoroughly done; so that, although the idea is taking, this form of the escapement has never come much into use, and when it is made one wide stone is generally substituted for the two pins in the roller.

The unlocking nearer the line of centers is also accomplished in what is called the anchor or dovetail escapement, in which the ruby pin is wider than usual, and of a dovetail form. It is open to the objection that, on account of the increased width of the impulse stone and of the lever, banking will occur with a smaller vibration of the balance than with the usual form.

RESILIENT ESCAPEMENTS.

A watch balance in general use, says Britten, rarely vibrates more than a turn and a half, that is, three-quarters of a turn each way; yet occasionally, from pressing on the key after the watch is wound in going-barrel work, sudden movements of the wearer, or other cause of disturbance, the balance will swing round till the impulse pin knocks the *outside* of the lever. If this banking is violent, the timekeeping of the watch is deranged, and a broken pivot may also result if the pivots are small. To obviate the evil of such banking, various plans have been tried. The most usual is to make the banking pins yield to undue pressure, and allow the ruby pin to pass the lever, the wings of which are omitted. Mr. J. F. Cole devised a resilient escapement without any banking pins, in which the teeth of the escape wheel were so formed as to resist the entrance of the pallet into the wheel more than was required for ordinary locking. In the event of overbanking, the pallet compelled the escape wheel to recoil, so that the mainspring was really utilized as spring banking. But in the use of any of these resilient arrangements there is a danger of "setting." When the banking is so violent that the ruby pin drives the lever before it, all is well, but it is sure to happen sometimes, that just as the ruby pin is passing the lever its motion is exhausted, and it jams against the point of the lever and stops the watch. In a recent arrangement Mr. Schoof claims to have overcome this tendency to set by using *very weak* spring bankings. Another objection to spring bankings is that in their recoil they are likely to drive the safety pin against the edge of the roller.

PALLETS WITH EQUIDISTANT LOCKINGS.

The drawing, Fig. 199, shows the pallets at an equal distance from their center of motion, and they are generally made so. But then, although the impulse planes are equal, the locking faces are not the same distance from the center, and the locking resistance is therefore unequal. Pallets are occasionally made having the lockings equidistant. Although advocated by Grossman and other authorities, they are but seldom used. The action of the wheel tooth on the impulse plane of the entering pallet before the line of centers is an engaging action, and on the exit pallet after the line of centers a disengaging action. The friction is therefore greater on the entering pallet, and when an escapement sets on one impulse face, it is nine cases out of ten, the impulse face of the entering pallet. From this it is argued by some that if either pallet should be placed further from the center of motion it should not be the exit, but the entering pallet, so as to give it a more favorable leverage wherewith to encounter the greater friction which undoubtedly exists. But there is really no advantage in the longer arm, for it has to be pushed through a greater distance by the wheel tooth than the shorter one. Arrange the length of the pallet arms how you will, you get but the force of the wheel passing through half the distance between two teeth. As far as the relative adhesion of the oil goes, the advantage is with the shorter arm. But the chief objection to the equidistant lockings is that with them the leaving corner of the exit pallet dips further into the wheel than with circular pallets, thereby requiring more drop to give the requisite freedom. Britten gives the following hints on the

EXAMINATION OF THE LEVER ESCAPEMENT.

See that the balance staff is perfectly upright. See that the wheel is perfectly true on edge and on face, and that the teeth are equally divided and smooth; also by gently turning the wheel backwards, see that the pallets free the backs of the teeth. If the wheel is out of truth, it must be set up in the lathe and re-bored. It can be fixed either with shellac, or in a brass sink bored out the exact size to receive it. If the divisions are unequal, or the wheel has some thick teeth, it should be discarded. It useless to attempt to make the wheel right, and to reduce the corners of the pallet to free the wheel is simply to spoil the escapement for the sake of the wheel. At the same time, it must be left to the operator to judge whether the amount of the inaccuracy is serious. The whole affair is so minute that no rule can be given.

Is the wheel the right size? If the lockings are too light, and the greater part of the shake inside, the wheel is too small, and should be replaced by one larger. Before removing the wheel, gently draw the balance around until the point of the tooth is exactly on the locking corner, and see if there is sufficient shake. If not, it will be prudent to have the new wheel with the teeth a little straighter than the old ones. If the lockings are too deep and most of the drop outside, the wheel is too large and should be topped *

The wheel is so fragile that care is required in topping, which is done by revolving it in the turns against a diamond or sapphire file. A brass collet is broached to fit friction-tight on one of the runners of a depth tool; one side of this collet is then filed away, leaving sufficient substance to avoid bursting into the hole. On this flat a small piece of sapphire file is attached with shellac, taking care that the *face of the file is parallel to the center of the runner*. The escape wheel on its pinion, with a ferrule attached, is placed in the centers of the depth tool *further from the adjusting screw*, and the collet and file on one of the opposite centers, and that center fixed firmly by its clamping screw. A very light hair bow is used to rotate the pinion, and the depth tool laid on its side on the work board—the tool being closed by its screw until the teeth of the wheel *nearly* touch the surface of the file; now if a slight pressure is made by the fingers on the uppermost limb of the tool, at the same time rotating the wheel by the bow, the *spring* of the tool will allow the teeth to be brought into contact very slightly and without fear of bending the teeth; the wheel can be reduced as much as is necessary.

If the wheel is the right size and there is no shake (which try as before directed), the discharging corner of the pallets may be rounded off by

---

*In planting the wheel and pallets it is always best to err, if at all, by making them too deep rather than too light. If they are a shade deep, topping the wheel soon puts matters right.

means of a diamond file, if they are of garnets.   If they are of ruby, they may be held against an ivory mill charged with diamond powder. If the lockings are too light, and there is but little shake, they may be made safe by polishing away the locking face a sufficient quantity.   If one locking is right and one is too light, the one that is too light may be made safe by polishing away the locking face as before, or the pallet may be warmed and the stone brought out a bit.   The locking faces of the pallets should be sufficiently undercut to draw the lever to the banking pins without hesitation.   If they require alteration in this respect, polish away the upper part of the locking faces so as to give more draw, leaving the locking corner quite untouched.   But proceed with great care, lest in curing this fault the watch sets on the locking, as small watches with light balances are very liable to do.   If a watch sets on the lockings, or on one of them, the locking face or faces may be polished away so as to give less draw—i. e. have most taken off the corner of the locking.   If the watch sets on the impulse, the impulse face may be polished to a less angle, if the locking is sufficiently deep to allow of it.   For it must be remembered that in reducing the impulse, the locking of the opposite pallet will also be reduced.   In fact, the greatest caution should be exercised in making any alteration in the pallets.

Sometimes in new escapements, the oil at the escape wheel teeth will be found to thicken rapidly through the pallet cutting the wheel, showing that one or both corners of the pallets are too sharp.   If ruby, the corner may be polished off with a peg cut to the shape of a pivot polisher, and a little of the finest diamond powder in oil; if garnet, diamantine on a peg will do it very well.   Great care should be taken to remove every trace of the polishing material, or the wheel may become charged with it.

See that the pivots are well polished, of proper length to come through the holes, and neither bull-headed or taper.   A conical pivot should be conical only as far as the shoulder; the part that runs in the hole must be perfectly cylindrical.   They must have perceptible and equal side shake, or, if any difference be made, the pallet pivots should fit the closest. Both balance staff pivots should be of exactly the same size.   The end shakes should all be equal.   Bad pivots, bad uprighting, excessive and unequal shake in the pivots, are responsible for much of the trouble experienced in position timing.   With unequal end shakes the pallet depth is liable to be altered owing to the curved form of the pallet faces.   The action of the escapement will also be affected if the end shakes are not equal, by a banking pin slightly bent, a slight inaccuracy in uprighting, and other minute faults.   The infinitesimal quantity necessary to derange the wheel and pallet action may be gathered from the fact that a difference of .002 of an inch is quite enough to make a tripping pallet depth safe, or correct depth quite unsound.

When the wheel and pallets are right, see that the impulse pin is in a line with an arm of the balance, and proceed to try if the lever is fixed in the correct position with relation to the pallets. Gently move the balance around until the tooth drops off the pallet. Observe the position of the balance arm, and see if it comes the same distance on the other side of the pallet hole when the other pallet falls off. If not, the pins connecting pallet and lever are generally light enough to allow of the lever being twisted. When the lever is right with relation to the pallets, see that the pallets are quite firmly fixed to the lever, and that the lever and pallets are perfectly in poise. This latter is an essential point in a fine watch to be timed in positions, but it is often neglected.

See that the escapement is in beat. When the balance spring is at rest, the impulse pin should be on the line of centers, that is, in the middle of its motion. If this is not so, the spring should be drawn through or let out from the stud, if the position of the index allows; if it does not, the roller may be twisted around on the staff in the direction required.

Is the roller depth right? If the safety pin has insufficient freedom while there is enough run, the roller is probably planted too deep. On the other hand, if it is found that, while the safety pin has plenty of freedom, there is no shake between the bankings, the roller depth is probably too shallow. When the impulse pin is led around, there should be an equal clearance all around the inside of the horn, and the pin must fall safely into the notch. If it binds in the horn and bottoms in the notch, it is too deep, and, on the other hand, if with excessive clearance in the horn, the pin when it falls does not pass well into the notch, it is too shallow. The readiest method of altering, is to warm the roller, remove the impulse pin, and using a to-and-fro motion with a wire and oil-stone dust, draw the hole in the required direction. If the pin is deep in the notch and too tight in the roller to give a little, it should be removed and flattened off a trifle more. If too shallow, a triangular pin, or one of some other shape, with the point of contact more forward, can generally be substituted by polishing out the hole towards the crescent. If not, the staff hole in the lever may be drawn to allow of shifting the lever sufficiently; or the recesses for the jewel settings of the balance staff pivots may be scraped away on one side and rubbed over on the other to suit. See, as it passes around, that the impulse pin is free when in the notch.

Just as the safety pin is about to enter the crescent, the impulse pin must be well inside of the horn. In the single roller escapement a very little horn is required, unless the crescent has been made of an unnecessary width. In very common work one occasionally sees a flat filed on the edge of the roller instead of a crescent. There is no excuse for such a piece of bungling.

A fault occasionally met with is that the impulse pin after leaving the notch just touches on some part of the horn in passing out. If a wedge of cork is placed under the lever, so that the lever moves stiffly, it can be readily seen whether or not the impulse pin is free to leave the notch and is free all around the horn when the wheel tooth drops on the locking.

See to the safety action. When the tooth drops on to the locking, the safety pin should be just clear of the roller. If it is not clear, the edge of the roller should be polished down until it is right. If there is more than clearance, the safety pin must be brought closer to the roller. See, upon pressing the safety pin against the roller, that the tooth does not leave the locking, and that the impulse pin is free to enter the notch without butting on the horn of the lever; also that the safety action is sound, so that the pin is in no danger of passing the roller. If the action is not sound, the diameter of the roller should be reduced and the safety pin brought towards it sufficiently to get a sound action, if it can be done; but if the escapement has been so badly proportioned as not to allow of a sound action being obtained in this way, the pin must be shifted forward and the bankings opened to allow more run.

See if the banking pins are so placed as to allow of an equal run on each side. If not they should not be bent, for with bent banking pins a difference in the end shakes of the pivots will cause a difference in the run. The banking pin allowing of the most run should be removed, and the hole broached out to receive a larger pin.

A Lever Escapement Fault. In the lever escapement there are several faults that frequently give trouble, and which are not readily seen nor understood. One of the number is what is called mismatched pallets and escape wheel. In the club tooth this error is very fatal to good rate and is about as represented in Fig. 204. The action between the tooth and the pallet is one attended with friction, under the most favorable circumstances, and the aim should be to keep the friction

at the lowest and to maintain it constant. With the escapement at its best the friction is very little, but to maintain it constant is of the greatest importance. Fully one-third of the low-priced watches have some escapement fault that renders their performance much below the normal standard of the grade, and helps largely to shorten their career and make

Fig. 203.   Fig. 204.

it, while it does last, a terror to the innocent wearer and repairer. Now, to thoroughly explain the fault above mentioned it is necessary to first state it and then call attention to the illustrations. This error is the relative pitch or slant of the impulse plane of the tooth and the pallet. When in a perfect relation, as in Fig. 203, the tooth gets onto the impulse plane of the pallet, with its front corner touching the pallet's plane and so moves about two-thirds of the way across, with only the corner touching, then as it proceeds, the whole face of the tooth touches the plane, shortly after the front corner has left the plane, and thus the escapement is made. With the faulty escapement, as in Fig. 204, the pallet's front corner gets onto the impulse plane of the tooth and thus proceeds a part of the way before the correct relation begins. Now when, as in the first case, the tooth rides over the pallet with its corner, the corner of the tooth cannot cut the plane of the pallet, as the metal will not act on the stone; but as in the second case, when the pallet's corner gets onto the plane of the tooth and so proceeds, the pallet corner will wear the face of the tooth, as the stone will cut the soft metal. This fault is present in a more or less degree in many escapements with the club tooth and when a watch gives trouble by failing to keep its rate after cleaning, as soon as the oil is the least dry on the pallets, it argues that this fault may be looked for. The illustrations of the two actions are purposely exaggerated to clearly illustrate the points under treatment.

LOCKING. That portion of the pallet on which the escape wheel teeth drop.

MAGNETISM. The agent or force in nature which gives rise to the phenomena of attraction, polarity, etc., exhibited by the loadstone, magnet, etc. A watch will become magnetized by too close proximity to a powerful magnetic field, such as is developed in a dynamo electro machine, for producing electric light, or by coming in contact with an ordinary magnet, as well as other sources of magnetic or electro-magnetic influences, and by these means all its steel parts become permanent magnets. Each piece of steel has then assumed definite polarity, so that if it is balanced on a point like a compass, it will, like the latter, indicate the direction of the earth's magnetic poles. The influence of these separate magnets, one on the other, and the influence of the earth's magnetism on the different parts, become very potent disturbers of time, keeping. Hairsprings, balances, and other small steel parts often become magnetized through being handled with magnetized tweezers or being placed near or in contact with other steel tools that have been magnetized.

Mr. B. Frese exemplifies the influence of the separate magnets produced in a watch by its parts becoming magnetized as follows: if we take two compasses and place them side by side, so that the two bearing points of the needles will form a right angle to their direction, neither of them will show any variation from their natural position or the position they are compelled to take by the influence of the earth's magnetism; but by moving one a little to the North or South of this position, we notice a deflection in both, which is caused by the poles of unequal names having been brought near to each other. Besides this main disturbing influence upon accurate time keeping, we must also consider the disturbance caused by direct attraction, which takes place by two magnetized parts when their equal, as well as their unequal, polarities come close together, but when two extremities of equal polarity come close together or in contact, the stronger magnetized piece will cause the weaker to assume its own polarity, so that when the South polarity of a strongly magnetized piece is brought in contact with the South polarity of a weaker, the South of the latter will be changed to North, and the North to South when the two North polarities have been in contact. The largest steel parts in a watch are the mainspring and the case springs, and these are, therefore, the most potent to cause a disturbance in a steel or compensation balance, aside from the earth's magnetism; the balance being the medium by which nearly all the disturbance is caused, as during its vibrations it makes different positions to the polarities of the other steel parts, as well as the earth's polarities, which is the greatest disturber, aside from the mainspring, the polarities of which change in relation to the balance as the watch runs down. The force one magnetized piece exerts on the other multiplies with ſdecreased distance. The fork, pallets and 'scape wheel are too small in bulk to cause much disturbance, either by direct attraction or directive force, unless they are charged to saturation, which very seldom occurs. If a magnetized balance is placed on a poising tool, with the staff in North and South direction, it will appear out of poise, caused by the earth's magnetism, and will maintain its North polarity uppermost. If it is placed in an East direction, it will no longer allow the North polarity to remain uppermost, but will cause the same to move toward the North and indicate the magnetic dip, the amount of which varies in the different latitudes of the globe. If we place the balance in a horizontal position, its north and South polarities will coincide with those of a compass, showing that if the balance were the only part magnetized in a watch, that magnetism causes more complicated variations than a balance out of poise to the same extent. That trying to poise a magnetized balance would be useless, is self-evident, for the reason that in a horizontal and North and South position, no equilibrum can be obtained. The influence of magnetized parts that do change position in a watch, is a constant one, as long as the size of vibration is maintained, and is, therefore, not the cause of serious disturbance. The substituting of new case springs will, therefore, be of little or no benefit.

To detect magnetism, place a pocket compass upon a show case, and place the watch to be operated upon on the table and close to the compass, and to the East and West of it. Before starting the test, stop the watch, and keep it from running by inserting a wedge made from a thin slip of paper beneath the balance. Turn the compass box around until the needle points to zero, before approaching the watch to it. Having placed the watch to the East or West of the compass, proceed to turn the movement, presenting first one figure of the dial and then another to the compass, and at the same time noting the deflection of the compass needle. Note whether the deflection is towards the East or West, i. e., whether it repels or attracts the needle. If the movement is not magnetized, the compass needle will remain stationary. If it is magnetized, the needle will be deflected, and by noting tne spot, you can very readily detect the magnetized part. Magnetism may be removed from small steel parts by placing them in the lathe and revolving them rapidly, and at the same time approaching them with a horseshoe magnet, and then gradually withdrawing the magnet. ˆ It is not good policy, however, to place any magnetized piece in your lathe, as you are liable to magnetize chucks, and they will cause you no end of trouble in the future. Demagnetizers are now to be purchased so cheaply that it will scarcely pay you to experiment with home made substitutes. See *Demagnetizer*.

To Demagnetize Watches. As watches only become magnetized by being brought into too close contact with magnets, dynamos, and the like, it is an utter waste of time to try and demagnetize them by applying heat or cold, or rubbing on decoctions of various kinds. Magnetic influence is the only remedy for the evil. The application of the remedy is effected in various ways. If we suspect that a watch is magnetized, the first thing to do is to prove it. It is well to try all watches for magnetism before starting on repairs, and this can be done in the presence of the customer. Place a fair sized pocket compass on, or gummed to the under side of your show case glass, in such a position that when at rest the needle will point to O. Place the watch a little to the East or West of the compass and revolve it showly, watching the needle of the compass to see if the needle is deflected. Be careful to keep the centers of the watch and compass at a given distance apart. If magnetized, the needle of the compass will deflect to the right and left as the watch is revolved. Note the deflection at a given point, and then proceed to revolve. In this way you can closely approximate the location of the affected part. By taking the movement apart you can in the same manner readily determine the affected part or parts, and they can be demagnetized without much difficulty. All of the steel parts of a watch, except the balance and spring, can be readily demagnetized in the following manner: Place a bar magnet upon a piece of white paper, previously marked with lines, say one-eighth of an inch apart. Lift the affected part with a pair of brass or non-magnetic tweezers, and approach one end of it within one-eighth of an inch of the magnet, then reverse and approach the opposite end to within one-fourth of an inch; reverse and approach first end to within three-eighths of an inch, and so on until you reach a distance where the magnet exerts no influence. Test your piece, as previously described, with a compass, and if the cure is not effected, repeat the operation. The circular form of the balance renders it somewhat more difficult to treat successfully, and it is best demagnetized as follows: Fasten the balance on a large cork, say from one and a half to two inches in diameter, by means of a small brass pin bent at right angles, and mount the cork in your lathe and revolve. Take a ten-inch compound magnet and approach it as closely to the balance as possible, and then gradually withdraw the magnet, keeping the balance revolving meanwhile, thus presenting every portion of it to the influence of the magnetic force. In some cases it will be found impossible to demagnetize the balance, although the operation may be repeated many times. A close examination and test of the balance by means of a compass will show that each arc of the balance has a positive and negative end, and the cross-bar will be found in the same condition. Under such circumstances it is absolutely unnecessary to thoroughly magnetize the balance by applying it to the magnet. You can demagnetize it, as previously described, without difficulty. It is advisable not to use your regular lathe in this operation, but rather to use some old lathe, or a polishing lathe will be found very desirable. See *Demagnetizer*.

MAINSPRING. The ribbon of steel which serves to produce the motive power for a watch, chronometer, or clock. It is said to be the invention of Peter Hele, a clockmaker of Nuremberg, about the year 1500.

It would appear that the mainspring, when first applied to the watch, was not enclosed in a barrel, but the outer end of the spring was bent into the form of a hook and fixed to a winding arbor, together with a ratchet wheel and click. A guard was attached to one of the plates in order to check the outer coil of the spring and prevent it expanding too far. The inner end was made fast to the axis of the great wheel, consequently it was wound up from the center. The re-expansion set the train in motion.

The motive force due to the tension of a spring is more or less variable. The causes of this want of uniformity, says Saunier, are as follows: The elastic reaction of a spring becomes greater as the spring is further wound up. A metallic blade is very rarely homogeneous, and worked with sufficient care to avoid different parts being of variable strength. Its energy alters with time dependent on the duration and intensity of the flexure, and this change nearly always occurs irregularly throughout its length. Its elastic force diminishes slightly on elevating the temperature, and lastly, a spring rubs against the bottom and lid of the barrel in uncoiling. The successive coils also adhere and rub together, either permanently or occasionally. All these resistances are from the nature of the case variable.

Various forms of mainsprings have been adopted from time to time. The cylindrical spring was one in which the central coils were made thicker with a view to diminish the differences in the pull of the spring when wound up to varying degrees, and to increase its energy when nearly run down. The spring, when fully wound up, rubbed together in the central coils, so that the motive force when it was fully wound was neutralized by the friction. These springs are very rarely seen now, as they were expensive to manufacture, and the advantages they possessed were more apparent than real. The taper spring was another form, which is rarely seen now. The thickness of the metal in these springs, gradually diminished throughout its entire length, the effect being to make the coils, when fully wound up, separate, and on this account the spring developed freely. This form was abandoned on account of the cost of manufacture. The third form is the ordinary spring in use to-day, the thickness of whose coils is the same throughout. The development is less uniform than with the tapered spring, as is also the separation of the coils, but it is cheaper of construction, and the variations do not exceed the limits that ordinary escapements can neutralize.

M. M. Roze, in a work on the mainspring, lays down and demonstrates the following theorems:

1. *A mainspring in the act of uncoiling in its barrel, always gives a number of turns equal to the difference between the number of coils in the up and down positions.*

For example, if 17 is the number of coils when the spring is run down, and 25 is the number when against the arbor, the difference between 17 and 25 or 8, will represent the number of turns in the uncoiling.

2. *With a given barrel, spring and arbor, in order that the number of turns may be a maximum, it is necessary that the length of the spring be such that the occupied part of the barrel, (exclusive of that filled by the arbor), be equal to the unoccupied part; in other words, the surface covered by the spring when up or down must be equal to the uncovered surface of the barrel bottom.*

The diameter of the arbor is not an arbitrary quantity, as it depends on the duration of flexure and thickness of the spring, and this depends greatly on the quality of the metal; if it is too small, it is liable to rupture the spring and deprive it of part of its elastic reaction, and if too large, part of this reaction will be wasted. M. Roze demonstrated that the thickness of the spring should be to the diameter of the arbor as 1:26 or 34, according as the rotation of the barrel takes place more or less rapidly. For example, 1:26 is best suited to watches; 1:30 for chronometers; and 1:34 for clocks or time pieces that are expected to go for longer periods.*

Until within a very few years mainsprings were made by a method that had been in use, and never improved on, for years.

About 1885 the American Waltham Watch Company secured the services of foreman Logan, who for years had been engaged in making hairsprings, and was about to carry out a scheme for making mainsprings, which he had long experimented upon and secured patents on.

At the outset, Mr. Logan forsook the old methods of manufacturing springs, and adopted new and novel ways of producing better results at

---

*If the reader is desirous of studying the subject at length, he is referred to Saunier's Modern Horology, pp. 661 to 673 inclusive, and a Simple and Mechanically Perfect Watch, by Moritz Grossman. Geo. K. Hazlitt & Co., Chicago.

less cost. The experiments necessary to such a radical change were costly, but the improvement in the quality and finish of the springs was so gratifying that mechanical appliances in great variety have from time to time been put to work, so that to-day the product is double that of two years ago, while the number of employes necessary is about one-half, owing to automatic machinery.

The steel used is manufactured expressly for springs, and comes in strips varying in length from one hundred to five hundred feet. As may well be supposed the best quality of steel adapted for the peculiar demands of a first-class watch mainspring was not found without much trouble, experimenting and expense. Steel made in England, France, Belgium, and this country were tried. After a series of trials, just the kind of steel desired was obtained. This steel is run through a machine which cuts it into numerous narrow ribbons, of widths suitable for the particular size of spring desired.

These ribbons are simultaneously wound upon bobbins, and are next passed, individually, through specially designed rolls, to bring the steel to a more exact and uniform thickness than can possibly be obtained from steel makers.

The next operation is that of rounding the edges, which is done by a new and unique machine. Following this the flat sides are ground and polished.

Up to this point the steel is in the untempered condition in which it is received at the factory. Hardening and tempering is next in order; these operations are performed by new methods which are almost automatic.

One of the elements which contributes largely to the very successful treatment of the steel in this important but delicate part of spring making is that of the fuel used for heating. In the earlier days of the manufacture a great variety of fuel was tried, but nothing has been found to equal the carefully purified water gas, which is now used.

Next in order the finishing polish is put on the sides and edges of the ribbons. Next the ribbons are cut up into exact lengths for individual springs. The ends are then annealed, preparatory to the punching for the reception of the barrel arbor hook and the tip. After punching follows coiling, when any faults in tempering are made apparent. If the steel has been overheated the severe strain of coiling will cause it to break. Failure to draw the temper sufficiently low will produce the same result, while too low a temper will cause them to "set," and thereby indicate their worthlessness.

Too soft springs are seldom found and the breakage in coiling is less than one-third of one per cent. The springs returned from the finishing department of the American factory for unsatisfactory performance in any direction amount to less than one-half of one per cent.

After the springs have been coiled, the tips riveted on, they are carefully gauged and then oiled to prevent rusting. They are then either

Dimensions of Mainsprings.

Millimeters and Fractions.   Compiled by L. A. Grosclaude, Geneva.

Diameter of Barrel	Diameter of Arbor	Space occupied by Spring when run down	Length of Spring	Thickness of Spring	Length	Thickness	Length	Thickness	Length	Thickness	Length	Thickness	Length	Thickness	Length	Thickness	Length	Thickness	Length	Thickness
No. of turns spring is capable of developing.			5		5½		6		6½		7		7½		8		9		10	
Theoretical No. / Real No.			4½		5		5½		6		6½		7		7½		8½		9½	
No. of coils the Spring makes in the barrel when run down.			8.92		9.81		10.70		11.60		12.49		13.38		14.27		16.06		17.84	
10	3.3	1 23	246	0,138	270	0,125	295	0,115	319	0,106	344	0,090	369	0,092	393	0,086	442	0,077	492	0,069
11	3.7	1.35	270	0,152	297	0,138	324	0,126	351	0,117	378	0,108	406	0,101	432	0,095	487	0,084	541	0,076
12	4.0	1.48	295	0,166	324	0,150	354	0,138	383	0,127	413	0,118	442	0,110	472	0,103	531	0,092	590	0,083
13	4 3	1.60	319	0,179	351	0,163	383	0,149	415	0,138	447	0 128	479	0,120	511	0,112	575	0,100	639	0,090
14	4.7	1.72	344	0,193	378	0,176	413	0,161	447	0,149	482	0,138	516	0,129	550	0,120	619	0,107	688	0,097
15	5.0	1.84	369	0,207	406	0,188	442	0,172	479	0,159	516	0,148	553	0,138	590	0,129	663	0,115	737	0,103
16	5.3	1.97	393	0,221	433	0,201	472	0,184	511	0,170	551	0,158	590	0,147	629	0,138	708	0,123	786	0,110
17	5.7	2 09	418	0,235	460	0,213	501	0,195	543	0,180	585	0,167	627	0,156	668	0,146	752	0,130	836	0,117
18	6.0	2.21	442	0,248	487	0,226	531	0,207	575	0,191	619	0,177	664	0,165	708	0,155	796	0,138	885	0,124
19	6.3	2.34	467	0,262	514	0,238	560	0,218	607	0,202	654	0,187	700	0,175	747	0,163	840	0,146	934	0,131
20	6.7	2.46	491	0,276	541	0,251	590	0,230	639	0,212	688	0,197	737	0,184	786	0,172	885	0,153	983	0,138
21	7.0	2 58	516	0,290	568	0,263	619	0,241	671	0,223	723	0,207	774	0,193	826	0,181	929	0,161	1032	0,145
22	7.3	2.71	541	0,304	595	0,276	649	0,253	708	0,233	757	0,217	811	0,202	865	0,189	973	0,169	1081	0,152
23	7.7	2.83	565	0,317	622	0,288	678	0,264	735	0,244	791	0,227	848	0,211	904	0 198	1017	0,176	1131	0,159
24	8.0	2.95	590	0,331	649	0,301	708	0,276	767	0,255	826	0,236	885	0,221	944	0,207	1062	0,184	1180	0,166
25	8.3	3.07	614	0,345	676	0,313	737	0,287	799	0,265	860	0,246	922	0,230	983	0,215	1106	0,192	1229	0,172
26	8.7	3.20	639	0,359	703	0,326	767	0,299	831	0,276	895	0,256	958	0,239	1022	0 224	1150	0,199	1278	0,179
27	9.0	3.32	663	0,373	730	0,339	796	0,310	863	0,286	929	0,266	995	0,248	1062	0,233	1194	0,207	1327	0,186
28	9.3	3.44	688	0,386	757	0,351	826	0,322	895	0,297	963	0,276	1032	0,257	1101	0,241	1238	0,215	1376	0,193
29	9.7	3.57	713	0,400	784	0,364	855	0,333	927	0,308	998	0,286	1069	0,267	1140	0,250	1283	0,222	1425	0,200
30	10.0	3.69	737	0,414	811	0,376	885	0 345	958	0,318	1032	0,296	1106	0,276	1180	0,259	1327	0,230	1475	0,207
31	10.3	3.81	762	0,428	838	0,389	914	0,356	990	0,329	1067	0,305	1143	0,285	1219	0,267	1371	0,238	1524	0,214
32	10.7	3.94	786	0,442	865	0,401	944	0,368	1022	0,339	1101	0,315	1180	0,294	1258	0,276	1415	0,240	1573	0,221
33	11.0	4.06	811	0,455	892	0,414	973	0,379	1054	0,350	1135	0,325	1217	0,303	1297	0,284	1460	0,253	1622	0,228
34	11 3	4.18	835	0,469	919	0,426	1003	0,391	1086	0,361	1170	0,335	1253	0,313	1337	0,293	1504	0,261	1671	0,234
35	11.7	4.30	860	0,483	946	0,439	1032	0,402	1118	0,371	1204	0,345	1290	0,322	1376	0,302	1548	0,268	1720	0,241
36	12.0	4.43	885	0,497	973	0,451	1062	0,414	1150	0,382	1239	0,355	1327	0,331	1415	0,310	1592	0,276	1770	0,248
37	12.3	4.55	909	0,511	1000	0,464	1091	0,425	1182	0,393	1273	0,364	1364	0,340	1455	0,319	1637	0,283	1819	0,255
38	12.7	4 67	934	0,524	1027	0,476	1121	0,437	1214	0,403	1307	0,374	1401	0,349	1494	0,327	1681	0,291	1868	0,262
39	13 0	4 80	958	0,538	1054	0,489	1150	0,448	1246	0,414	1342	0,384	1438	0,359	1533	0,336	1725	0,299	1917	0,269
40	13.3	4.92	983	0,552	1081	0,502	1180	0,460	1278	0,424	1376	0,394	1475	0,368	1573	0,345	1769	0,306	1966	0,276
41	13.7	5.04	1007	0,566	1108	0,514	1209	0,471	1310	0,435	1411	0,404	1511	0,377	1612	0,353	1813	0,314	2015	0,283
42	14.0	5.17	1032	0,580	1135	0,527	1239	0,483	1342	0,446	1445	0 414	1548	0,386	1651	0 362	1858	0,322	2064	0,290
43	14.3	5.29	1057	0 593	1162	0,539	1268	0,494	1374	0,456	1479	0,424	1585	0,395	1691	0,371	1902	0,329	2114	0,297
44	14.7	5.41	1081	0,607	1189	0,552	1298	0,506	1406	0,467	1514	0,433	1622	0,405	1730	0,379	1946	0,337	2163	0,303
45	15.0	5.53	1106	0,621	1217	0,564	1327	0,517	1438	0,477	1548	0,443	1659	0,414	1769	0,388	1990	0,345	2212	0,310
46	15.3	5.66	1130	0,635	1244	0,577	1357	0,529	1470	0,488	1583	0,453	1696	0,423	1809	0,397	2035	0,352	2261	0,317
47	15.7	5.78	1155	0,649	1271	0,589	1386	0,540	1502	0,499	1617	0,463	1733	0,432	1848	0,405	2079	0,360	2310	0,324
48	16.0	5.90	1179	0,662	1298	0,602	1416	0,552	1534	0,509	1652	0,473	1769	0,441	1887	0,414	2123	0,368	2359	0,331
49	16.3	6.03	1204	0,676	1325	0,614	1445	0,563	1566	0,520	1686	0,483	1806	0,451	1927	0,422	2167	0,375	2408	0,338
50	16.7	6.15	1228	0,690	1352	0,627	1474	0,575	1597	0,530	1720	0,493	1843	0,460	1966	0,431	2211	0,383	2458	0,345
51	17.0	6.27	1253	0,704	1379	0,639	1504	0,586	1629	0,541	1755	0,502	1880	0,469	2005	0,440	2256	0,391	2507	0,352
52	17.3	6.40	1278	0,718	1406	0,652	1533	0,598	1661	0,552	1789	0,512	1917	0,478	2045	0,448	2300	0,398	2556	0,359
53	17.7	6.52	1302	0,731	1433	0,665	1563	0,609	1693	0,562	1824	0,522	1954	0,487	2084	0,457	2344	0,406	2605	0,365
54	18.0	6.64	1327	0,745	1460	0,677	1592	0,621	1725	0,573	1858	0,532	1991	0,496	2123	0,465	2388	0,414	2654	0,372
55	18.3	6.76	1351	0,759	1487	0,690	1622	0,632	1757	0,583	1892	0,542	2028	0,506	2163	0,474	2433	0,421	2703	0,379
56	18.7	6.89	1376	0,773	1514	0,702	1651	0,644	1789	0,594	1927	0,552	2064	0,515	2202	0,483	2477	0,429	2753	0,386
57	19.0	7.01	1400	0,787	1541	0,715	1681	0,655	1821	0,605	1961	0,562	2101	0,524	2241	0,491	2521	0,437	2802	0,393
58	19.3	7.13	1425	0,800	1568	0,727	1710	0,667	1853	0,615	1996	0,571	2138	0,533	2281	0,500	2565	0,444	2851	0,400
59	19.7	7.26	1450	0,814	1595	0,740	1740	0,678	1885	0,626	2030	0,581	2175	0,542	2320	0,508	2610	0,452	2900	0,407
60	20.0	7.38	1474	0,828	1622	0,752	1769	0,690	1917	0,637	2064	0,591	2212	0,552	2359	0,517	2654	0,460	2949	0,414

wound into capsules (from which they can be transferred directly into a watch barrel) or enclosed in packages containing one dozen each.

The product has been increased from sixty-five gross per month in 1886, to two thousand gross per month in 1892. Of this large amount about two thousand springs are required daily for the product of watches at the factory and the remainder are sold to the trade to supply the watch repairers throughout the country.

Cleaning Mainsprings. Workmen have often been seen cleaning a mainspring by seizing it with a rag and then drawing it out pitilessly and unmercifully. No other consequences can follow such treatment than the breakage of the spring on the earliest possible occasion. Cleaning is best done in the following manner: Lay the spring in benzine. As soon as the adhering oil is dissolved, take it out and seize it with a soft linen rag which imbibes the greater part of the adhering benzine. Cover the palm of the left hand with a corner of the rag; put the spring flat upon it and with the index finger of the right hand, around which another part of the rag is wound, press gently upon it, and let it assume a conical shape; by suitable motions of the finger while wiping, the spring will turn, and every part of its blade may easily and thoroughly be cleansed of all impurities. A spring treated in this manner will be freed of all matter, while at the same time its molecular arrangement is not violently interfered with, in a way calculated to injure its elasticity.

MAINSPRING PUNCH. A punch used by watchmakers for perforating mainsprings. It is inserted in a vise when used. These punches are also made in the form of tongs or plyers.

MAINSPRING WINDER. A good mainspring winder is a necessary adjunct to every watchmaker's bench. The Stark patent winder, shown in Fig. 205, is a very superior tool, is simple and durable,

and should last for a life time. The winder is fastened in a vise: the adjustable nut is then turned until the barrel will fit loosely over the jaws; the barrel is then removed and the spring wound on the arbor inside the jaws. Now let the handle turn backward until the arbor is free from the center; pull

Fig. 205.

the arbor back and turn it half round; place the barrel back again over the jaws and spring, and hold it up tightly against the winder with the left hand; at the same time push the arbor forward with the right hand

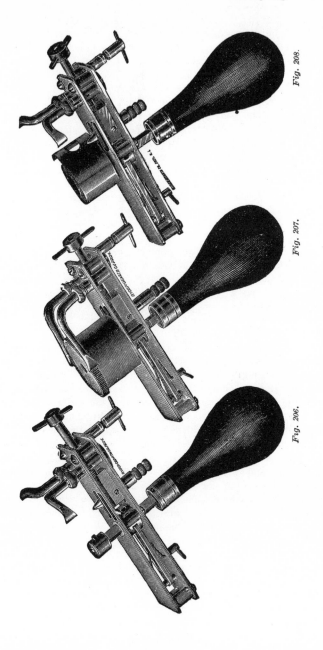

Fig. 208.

Fig. 207.

Fig. 206.

until the barrel and spring are free from the jaws, and the spring will be found to be in its proper place without further operation. There are two sizes of winding arbors, one for small and the other for large barrels. The arbors are easily changed by turning the thumb screw up until it is free, then changing the arbors and screwing the thumb screw down again.

The Vaughan patent mainspring winder, shown in the illustration, is intended for removing and replacing springs in clock barrels. Fig. 206 shows the machine ready for use; Fig. 207 shows the arms adjusted to the teeth of barrel, for holding barrel while spring is being wound. Fig. 208 shows the winder holding the spring after the barrel has been removed, and also as wound, ready to place in the barrel.

The claims made for this device are: It winds either way, as the case may require. Every part is adjustable, so that it will handle any spring, and hold any size barrel. Through the whole operation of removing the spring from the barrel and replacing it, the spring is kept in its natural position. After spring and barrel have been cleaned and barrel polished, they need not be touched with the hands, if the operator chooses to handle them with paper. The spring can be oiled when wound, as in Fig. 208, which carries the oil to bottom of the barrel, and prevents any excess of oil getting on the outside. It does not require a vise, but can be used in one place as well as another. There is no strain on the hands, more than winding the spring after it is in the clock. The plates and all the working parts are made of steel, and though light and neat in appearance, it is strong and durable.

To take the spring out of the barrel, adjust the arms used to hold the barrel, to the right height to meet the teeth of the barrel and swing them wide open, securing them by the thumb screw on the back of the winder. Place the barrel containing the spring over the winding arbor of the machine, and catch the hook on the arbor to the spring. Swing the pawl lever to allow you to wind the way you desire, and turn the handle, allowing the barrel to turn with it, until the hook in the barrel, to which the outer end of the spring fastens, comes to within about one-half inch of the jaws which hold the outer edge of the spring on the machine. Free the arms and swing them into the teeth of the barrel, and with the barrel in the center of the machine, again secure them firmly by the thumb screw. Take the machine in the left hand, which will enable you to hold the arms tightly to the barrel, and the barrel down to the winder, without any danger of their springing away. Wind the spring nearly up, which will free the outer coil from the barrel, and allow you to adjust the jaws to the spring. Crowd the jaws onto the spring as far as possible and fasten them firmly to the spring by means of the thumb screw at the upper end of the winder The spring is now transferred from the barrel to the winder, and the arms can be released and the barrel removed. Reverse the pawl lever and turn the handle up a trifle, when the pawl will change sides, allowing the spring to let down.

To replace the spring in the barrel, wind the spring on the machine, as shown in Fig. 208. Place the barrel over it, with the hook opposite the hole in the spring. Reverse the pawl lever and let the spring down. Release the jaws from the spring, and the work is done. The arms for holding the barrel are only used in taking the spring out.

MAINTAINING POWER. A mechanism for driving a watch or clock while being wound.

MALTESE CROSS. A wheel in the shape of a maltese cross, used in stop works.

MANDREL. A cheap form of lathe, but little used in this country, being superseded by the American lathe. It is known also as the Swiss Universal Lathe. The mandrel is worked by means of a handle, and is

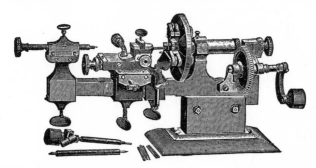

Fig. 209.

usually made with wheel and pinion, although a round belt or gut is sometimes used. It has a face plate, pump center, tail stock and slide rest. This tool is superfluous where the workman has an American lathe with slide rest and universal head; for on a lathe with these attachments, a greater variety of work can be performed in less time and in a better manner.

MASS. The amount of matter a body contains. It must not be confounded with weight, for the mass of a body remains the same, no matter in what part of the world it may be, but its weight would vary in different latitudes.

MATERIAL CUP. This cup will be found very useful to those who keep small material in bottles. The material, being placed in the cup, spreads out over the bottom, and the piece wanted is easily selected. The remainder can then be returned to the bottle through the spout with no danger of losing a piece.

MATTING. The grained or frosted surface given to work before gilding or silvering. See *Electro-Plating*.

MERIDIAN DIAL. An instrument for determining when the sun is on the meridian

MICROMETER. An instrument used for measuring very minute distances with extreme exactness. See *Gauge*.

MILLIMETER. A lineal measure based on the thousandth part of a meter, or about one-twenty-fifth of an inch. It is used principally by French watchmakers.

MILLING CUTTERS. It has been a difficult matter for mechanics

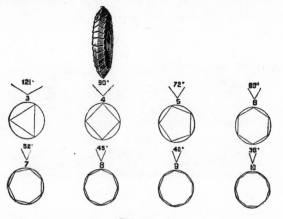

Fig. 210.

to understand the proper angle for a cutter to mill, or burr the stock, so that it will bend into the proper angle and make it a right joint. Fig. 210 will convey a very good idea of the proper shapes or angles for such cutters.

The angle of the cutter depends entirely on the number of sides the article is to have, and can always be determined by rule. The rule is a simple one, which is to divide 360° by the number of sides to the angle, i. e., 360÷4=90.

Fig. 211.

MILLING FIXTURE. This attachment is fitted to the slide rest and holds the wire chuck vertically under the center of the lathe, so that articles held in the chucks can be fed under mills or saws held in the saw arbor.

MITER GEARS. Gears whose shafts are at right angles to each other and whose diameters are equal. All miter gears are bevel gears, but all bevel gears are not miter gears

MOINET, LOUIS. A clever watchmaker and writer of France. He was born at Bourges, in 1768 and died in 1853.

MOMENT OF ELASTICITY of a spring is its power of resistance. It varies directly as the modulus of elasticity of the material, and as the breadth and the cube of the thickness of the spring when its section is rectangular. $Mo = E\dfrac{b\,t^3}{12}$ is Mr. T. D. Wright's formula, E representing the modulus of elasticity, b the breadth, and t the thickness of the spring.

The moment of elasticity must not be confounded with the bending moment. The bending moment is a measure of the resistance a spring offers to bending, and of the amount of bending which has been produced, which varies directly as the angle wound through, and inversely as the length of the spring.

$M = \dfrac{Ebt^3A}{12L}$ is the formula given by Mr. T. D. Wright for ascertaining the bending moment, E being the modulus of elasticity, b the breadth, t the thickness, and L the length of the spring, and A the angle through which it is wound.

This formula also determines the value of the force which has produced the bending, for if the forces are in equilibrium, the moment of the resisting force must be exactly equal to the moment of the bending force.

MOMENT OF INERTIA. The resistance to change of velocity offered by a rotating or revolving body. The moment of inertia, which is generally represented by I, varies directly as the mass, and as the square of the radius of gyration of the body.

MOMENTUM. The amount of motion in a body, which is obtained by multiplying its mass by its velocity.

MOSELEY, CHARLES S. Mr. Moseley has been intimately connected with nearly every watch company in the United States, and as a mechanical engineer and designer of watch machinery, of the automatic type, he has had no superiors and but few equals. Among those that have acquired a world-wide reputation may be mentioned the interchangeable stem-wind mechanism of the Elgin National Watch Company; the dust-band used by the same company, the best and cheapest ever made; the triangular hairspring stud; a patent regulator and the split chuck, an accessory now become universal and indispensable to every watchmaker in the land. He was born at Westfield, Mass., Feb. 28, 1838.

His first connection with watchmaking was in 1852, when he entered the employ of Dennison, Howard & Davis, at Roxbury, Mass. He followed the factory to Waltham and was employed in the capacity of foreman of the machine shop and later as master mechanic. In 1859 he became master mechanic of the Nashua Watch factory, and designed and built the machinery with which that watch was manufactured.

Charles S. Moseley.

In 1864 he joined the Elgin National Watch Company, then just starting, and was made general superintendent, in which capacity he remained with the company until 1877.

MOTEL, H. A French chronometer maker, pupil and successor of Louis Berthoud. His chronometers were remarkable for their close rates and for their beautiful construction. He died in 1859.

MOTION WORK. The wheels of a watch or clock which cause the hour hand to travel one-twelfth as fast as the minute hand.

MOVEMENT. A term usually applied to the mechanism of a watch or clock, independent of a case.

MOVEMENT BOX. A metal box with glass sides, for holding watch movements while timing, etc., before casing. In the Rockford box, shown in Fig. 213, stem wind movements can be wound without fingering or exposure to dust.

Fig. 213.   *Fig. 214.*

MOVEMENT COVER. A glass shade to protect a movement, or portions of a movement from dust and from being lost while undergoing repairs. Fig. 214, illustrates an improved cover, with wooden base divided into compartments for the reception of the various parts, so they may be kept separate and readily picked out.

MOVEMENT HOLDER. A metal frame, as shown in Fig. 215, having three adjustable arms for holding the movement by clamping on to the plate. It is useful in putting a watch together, as it rests upon the bench and leaves both hands free to work with and the plates are kept free from finger marks.

Fig. 215.   Fig. 216.

MOVEMENT REST. A wooden, bone or rubber shell, Fig. 216, similar to eye-glass frames, for holding movements while undergoing repairs, oiling, etc.

MUDGE THOMAS. The inventor of the lever escapement and a maker of marine chronometers. He was born at Exeter, England, in 1715. He was apprenticed to the celebrated George Graham in 1729.

From 1750 to 1771 he was engaged in business in Fleet street, London. In 1765 he invented the lever escapement. In 1771 he removed to Plymouth. In 1777 he was made clockmaker to the king. In 1793 Parliament voted him the sum of £2,500, he having previously received £500, as a reward for his marine time keepers. He devoted the greater part of his life to the improve-

Thomas Mudge. ment of the marine chronometer, and his work in this line was celebrated for finish and correct proportion of details. He died Nov. 24, 1794.

NON-MAGNETIC WATCH. A watch whose parts cannot be polarized in a magnetic field; a watch whose quick moving parts are made of some other metal than steel or iron. Paillard, who has studied non-magnetic metals with great care, makes his balance springs of palladium, and his balances of palladium alloyed with copper, silver and other metals. In some instances he appears to have used a palladium alloy for the inner part, and brass for the outer part of the rim, and in others to have formed both laminæ of different alloys of palladium. Aluminium bronze, which combines strength with lightness, is particularly suited for the lever and pallets. The American Waltham Watch Company have obtained remarkable results in non-magnetic watches, with an alloy of platinum. Steel in its hardened and tempered form, has long been used for the balance springs of watches, but from the fact that it owed its elasticity to the process of fire hardening, it has always been uncertain in its action, and often two springs from the same piece of steel would give very different results when put to the same tests. This, it is claimed, is not true of the alloy used by the Waltham Company. The non-magnetic spring, they claim, is a natural spring; it requires no rolling or hammering to harden or make it elastic. Its elasticity is a property of the alloy, and from nothing mechanical done to it, and that it cannot be annealed, or robbed of its elasticity, can be shown by heating it to a red heat of nearly 1,100 degrees Fahr., with no change of elasticity. At this degree of heat, steal is annealed, or becomes soft, and of no use as a spring.

In the expansion balance of ordinary construction, intended to compensate for temperature, steel is used as the metal of lowest expansion ratio, but in this case never in its hardened and tempered form. Such a balance would be too irregular in its action. No two balances would work alike, and anyone manufacturing such would find a difference of temper or degree of elasticity in each arm of the inside steel laminæ. The greatest controlling factor in the expansion balance, is the brass outside laminæ, and unless it is hammered or rolled it is of no practical use. A good expansion balance of the usual make depends more on the brass than the steel for its action, and it is a well known fact that brass is one of the most uncertain alloys known, and will often, when not in use, deteriorate to such an extent as to have no value for its original purpose. The Waltham non-magnetic balance is said to stand a change of temperature of 400 degrees Fahr., and return to its original form, as shown by guages. The non-magnetic balance metals, while having the expansion ratio required, also have a greater natural degree of elasticity than the brass and steel construction, thus making a balance that, when in use in the watch, retains its shape, and will not get out of poise.

OIL. One of the most essential things to the good performance and durability of a watch or clock is good oil. A little thought given to the subject of oil will show how very essential it is that only the very best attainable be used. The mechanism of a fine watch, and particularly one of a complicated nature, is expected to perform regularly and with little or no variation, although after a thorough cleaning and oiling that mechanism may not fall into the hands of the repairer oftener than once a year, and in the majority of cases it is a longer interval of time. There

are few mechanical contrivances from which so much is expected as a
fine watch or chronometer, and yet there are none that receive, in proportion to their mechanism, so little care and attention. The engineer
carefully wipes and oils his engine at least once a day: the machinist
does the same with the lathes and machines under his care, but the
watch, a mechanism far more complicated and from which much more
is expected in regard to correct performance, does not receive this care
oftener, on an average, than once a year. How essential it is then that
the lubricant be of the finest possible quality.

The essential requisites of an oil that will insure correct performance
of a watch during this time are:

1. It must remain liquid when exposed to severe cold.
2. It must evaporate slowly under intense heat.
3. It must not corrode on metal.
4. It must not become gummy.

What oils best withstand this test? For many years European watchmakers gave the preference to pure olive oil, but experiment has proven
that this oil is wholly unfit for watches and the same may be said of all
vegetable oils, for they invariably become gummy and turn green when
placed in contact with brass. Neat's foot oils were found to possess similar unfitting qualities, and mineral oils are found to evaporate too
quickly.

Nothing then remains but fish oils and those made from a species of
porpoise known as the black fish, are considered the very best. Fine
watch and chronometer oils of this class are prepared from the head
and jaw only, which parts yield a limited quantity of very pure oil,
known as "jaw and melon oil." This oil is carefully extracted without
allowing any flesh or blood to come in contact with it, and after trying is
filtered and retained in its native purity as nearly as possible, no bleach-
ing, either by sun, acids or alkalies being employed. There is a popular
fallacy existing in the trade that oils should be used when fresh, and even
the acknowledged authority, Saunier, says, "do not buy, from motives of
economy, bottles that have laid for years in the shop." This may be
true and probably is, in regard to vegetable and animal oils, which
are likely to become rancid if kept for a long time, but Wm. F. Nye, one
of the largest and most celebrated manufacturers of fine watch and
chronometer oils in the world, declares that black fish oils are improved
by age, and his oils are seldom placed upon the market in the same
year as obtained. We are indebted to the same authority for the statement that oils of this kind are clearer and more brilliant after some years
than fresh oils. The Nye oils are tried at New Bedford, Mass., and in
the following winter are sent to St. Albans, Vt., where it is chilled down
and filtered at an average temperature of 25° below zero, and in some
instances, even as low as 37° below zero. In this manner the specific
gravity and density of the oil is increased, a finer grain and texture are

secured, giving increased resistance to the effects of both heat and cold. The two prominent manufacturers of black fish oils in this country, and we might say in the world, are Wm. F. Nye and Ezra Kelley, both of New Bedford, Mass. The watchmaker should be very careful what oils he uses, as many on the market are of foreign manufacture and are made from the olive, or are combinations of animal and vegetable oils.

OILER. A fine steel wire, mounted in a wooden or bone handle and used for applying oil to the mechanism of a watch or clock. Fig. 218 is a

Fig. 218.

Bullock oiler, made with 14k. gold tip, and has a collet which keeps the point from touching the bench and also prevents oiler from rolling.

OIL SINK. The cavity turned in watch and clock plates and jewels, around the pivot holes. Experience, says Britten, has shown that when the oil sink in chronometers and clocks, where the plates are not gilt, is thoroughly well polished, not only is the oil drawn to the pivot more freely, but it is less decomposed by contact with the metal than when the sinks are rougher. Oil sinks should be deep and small in diameter rather than shallow and wide. Saunier says that care should be taken that the internal faces of the holes in which the shoulders of the axis rest, as well as the external faces, when these holes are provided with end-stones, are hollowed in *tallow drop* form, with a very slight interval between the bottom of the hole and the end-stone. When these precautions are taken, the oil, if not present in too great a quantity, will neither spread nor run down the axis, but will remain partly in the oil sink and partly attached to the shoulders of the axis, and in the case of pivot holes with end-stones, as the oil is exhausted, that spread over the end-stone will be drawn into the pivot hole through capillarity.

OILSTONES. A stone upon which cutting tools are rubbed to give them a fine edge. Oil or some other lubricant is always used with the oilstone. A mixture of one part alcohol and two parts glycerine will be found a much better lubricant for the oilstone, where small tools such as watchmakers use, are sharpened. than will the ordinary oils used. Oilstones often become so saturated with oil as to be almost useless and are often abandoned on this account. Such a stone, if soaked in benzine for a few days, will come out as good as new.

Circular Oilstones. Circular stones will be found much superior to the ordinary flat oilstones commonly used, for sharpening drills, gravers and other cutting tools, where it is desirable to have an exact angle. An Arkansas or Turkey stone dressed down to circular form, and say 1½ inches in diameter, when mounted on a lathe chuck, will be found to be far superior to the common flat stone. Apply a small quantity of watch oil, or what is better, a mixture composed of one-half alcohol and one-half glycerine, and hold your graver or drill at the exact angle you want the cutting edges and turn at a moderate speed. Truer angles and better work can be obtained in this manner than by any other. Emery and corundum wheels mounted in a similar manner will be found very handy accessories to the watchmaker's bench.

OILSTONE DUST. A preparation of powdered oilstone, used for smoothing pivots and other steel parts.

OVERBANKING. When the balance vibrates excessively and causes the ruby pin to push past the lever, it is known as overbanking.

OVERCOIL. The last coil of a Breguet hairspring, where it is bent over the body of the spring towards the center, is called the overcoil.

PACIFICUS. Archdeacon of Verona, and the accredited inventor of the weight clock, in 850, A. D. See *Clock*.

PALLET. That portion of an escapement by means of which the escape wheel gives impulse to the balance.

PALLET STAFF. The staff or axis of the pallets.

PALLET STONES. The stones which form the rubber surfaces of a pallet.

PALLET STONE ADJUSTER. Fig. 219 is a Bullock pallet stone adjuster, which will be found very useful in holding pallets and protecting them from heat, while heating cement in order to adjust stones.

Fig. 219.

PARACHUTE. An invention of Breguet, in which the end stones of the balance staff of a watch are supported on springs, so as to yield to undue pressure. The idea of the parachute is that if the watch is let fall, or subjected to sudden jerks in any other way, the balance staff pivots may be saved from damage by the yielding of the end stones.

PEG WOOD. Small round sticks of wood used for cleaning out pivot holes, etc.

PENDANT. The portion of a watch case to which the bow is attached, and the portion connecting it with the case.

Pendant Bow. The ring of metal by which the chain is attached to the case.

Pendant Bow Tightenèr. Bullock's patent pendant bow pliers, shown in Fig. 220, are very handy for tightening a loose pendant bow or

Fig. 220.

putting a distorted bow into shape again. It is always desirable to have the pendant bow of a watch tight in its place, and turn with considerable friction, though it it is sometimes difficult to tighten a loose bow when the seat is worn deeply.

Pendant Bow Drill. This tool, which is shown in Fig. 221. consists

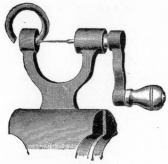

of a loose spindle with a crank and a drill rest, adapted to be used in the vise on the bench. The illustration shows a pendant bow being drilled, and its method of operation will be readily understood from the cut.

PENDULE WATCHES. A name given to watches of early construction, having on one arm, or cross-piece of the balance a representation of the bob of a pendulum and visible to the eye by a portion of

Fig. 221.

the cock being cut away; thus this arm of the balance, at every vibration, would have the appearance as well as regularity of a pendulum.

PENDULUM. A body suspended from a fixed point in such a manner as to swing freely too and fro by the alternate action of gravity and momentum. The theoretical length of a pendulum, to beat seconds, or other time, depends upon its location, for the force that gravity exerts upon a body depends on the distance of the body from the center of the earth. The length of a seconds' pendulum at

The Equator is............... 39   inches
Rio de Janeiro............... 39.01   "
Madras...................... 39.02   "
New York................... 39.1012   "
Paris....................... 39.13   "
London..................... 39.14   "
Edinburgh.................. 39.15   "
Greenland.................. 39.20   "
North and South Pole........ 39.206   "

Galileo's discovery of the law of pendulums was made in 1582 (See *Galileo*.). Observing the regularity of the swinging of a lamp, suspended from the roof of the cathedral of Pisa, he noticed that, whatever the arc of vibration, the time of vibration remained nearly the same. If a slight angular movement be given to a freely suspended pendulum, its oscillations, while gradually diminishing in extent, will occupy periods, which at first sight, Galileo affirmed to be equal. He was mistaken, however, as the difference, although very slight with short arcs, is none the less real, and Huyghens discovered and proved that the oscillations of a pendulum are only isochronal when its center of oscillation describes a cycloidal path. By experiment, Galileo also determined the law of the length of pendulums. He found that by increasing the length of the pendulum the time of vibration increased.

The first application of the pendulum to clocks was made by Huyghens in 1657, although Galileo had some idea of this adaptation, and he even invented an escapement with a view to carrying it out.

Simple Pendulum. A purely theoretical pendulum, having no dimensions except length and no weight except at the center of oscillation. A material point suspended by an ideal line. The nearest approach to a simple pendulum is a heavy weight suspended by a fine silk thread, although this is known as a compound or physical pendulum.

Compound or Physical Pendulum. A heavy weight suspended from a fixed point by means of a slender thread or wire as shown in Fig. 222.

Oscillating Pendulum. A pendulum that moves backward and forward and whose lower extremity traces an arc. This term is used to distinguish an ordinary pendulum (which is an oscillating pendulum), from a conical or torsion pendulum. Fig. 222 is an oscillating pendulum and its path is denoted by the dotted lines.

Fig. 222.

Conical Pendulum. A pendulum which in its swing describes the figure of a cone in the air. A pendulum whose lower extremity

describes a circle as shown by the dotted lines in Fig. 223.   By comparison it will be found that a conical pendulum completes its circular
travel in the same time that an oscillating pendulum requires
to make a complete swing, back and forth.

Torsion Pendulum.   A torsion pendulum is one that
depends for its vibrations upon the twisting and untwisting of
an elastic suspension.   The path of a torsion pendulum is
unlike that of other pendulums, as it does not swing from
right to left, but simply revolves horizontally, the suspension
Fig. 223.   acting as an axis.   The action of a torsion pendulum is very
simple; after turning the bob or weight and releasing it, the elasticity of
the wire or other suspension returns it to the point of rest and the
momentum of the weight carries it forward, twisting the suspension in
the opposite direction, until the weight reaches a point where the
momentum of the weight is overbalanced by the resitance of the suspension, when the suspension again untwists, turning the bob in the opposite direction.   These oscillations, which, within certain limits are
very nearly equal, continue until the force originally applied is exhausted
in friction.   The application of the torsion pendulum to clocks has been
successfully accomplished.   By its use either of two results
may be secured; the time of running may be prolonged in
proportion as the period of the torsion pendulum is longer than
that of an oscillating one, or the number of gear wheels
required in the clock may be greatly reduced.   Ordinary
clocks have been constructed on this principle that would run
a year with a single winding, while others have been constructed that would run a much longer period.   Fig. 224
illustrates a simple torsion pendulum that can easily be con-   *Fig. 224.*
structed for experimental purposes.   It has parallel suspension wires $\frac{3}{8}$
inch apart and 5 feet long, made from No. 30 brass spring wire.   The
bob is formed of a disc of metal, with a series of split lead balls pinched
down upon its edge.   It has a double loop fixed at the center for fastening the suspension wires.   The diameter of the disc is 4 inches and the
total weight of bob 1½ pounds.

Laws of Pendulums.   There are three laws in regard to the
movement of simple pendulums that are well to remember.   1. *The
number of vibrations performed by pendulums in a given time are inversely
as the square roots of the lengths.*   If the bob is displaced from the vertical and released, it will return, and ascend to an equal distance on the
other side in virtue of its weight.   The velocity of movement of the
pendulum is in accordance with the laws of falling bodies for the moving pendulum is no more than a falling body under certain restrictions.
If we assume the pendulum to be displaced laterally until its rod is in a

horizontal position, it will be seen that the distance through which it descends is equal to the length of the pendulum. Hence it follows that the descent of a short pendulum will, in virtue of the laws above referred to, take place in much less time than that of a long one. Thus, consider the case of a short pendulum whose length is a quarter of that of the longer one; the shorter will travel twice as quickly as the longer, or, in other words, it will perform two oscillations while the longer performs one. The lengths are as 1:4 and the square roots of these numbers are 1 and 2; thus the number of oscillations are inversely as these square roots.

The times occupied in the descent, or the periods of the oscillations, are proportional to the square roots of the length. If the longer pendulum fall in 2 seconds, the shorter falls twice as quickly and will therefore reach the vertical in 1 second; and 2 and 1 are the square roots of the length 4 and 1.

3. *The lengths are inversely proportional to the squares of the number of oscillations in a given time.* If we observe that:

> The lengths are_____1 and 4.
>
> The corresponding number of oscillations_2 and 1.
>
> The squares of these number_____4 and 1.

we have some evidence of the truth of this law. These several laws will enable us to determine the length of pendulum for any case that presents itself.

Saunier gives the following method for determining the length of a simple pendulum, the numbers of oscillations being given, or *vice versa.* Let the pendulum be required to perform 7,000 oscillations in an hour. The simple seconds pendulum (at Paris) measures 994 mm. (39.13 in.), and it makes 60 × 60 or 3,600 oscillations per hour; we thus, from the law 3 above given, have the proportion:

$$7,000 \times 7,000 : 3,600 \times 3,600 : : 994 : x$$
$$\text{or } 49,000,000 : \quad 12,960,000 : : 994 : x$$

Dividing the product of the means by the known extreme we obtain:

$$x = \frac{12,960,000 \times 994}{49,000,000} = 262.9 \text{ mm. (10.35 ins.)}$$

If the length of a pendulum be given, say 121 mm. (4.764 ins.), the number of oscillations will be calculated in accordance with law 1:

$$\sqrt{121} : \sqrt{994} : : 3,600 : x \dagger$$
$$\text{or } 11 : 31.525 : : 3,600 : x$$

---

† The radix sign $\sqrt{}$ indicates that the root is to be extracted from the number placed under it.

whence we obtain

$$x = \frac{31.525 \times 3,600}{11} = 10,317, \text{ the required number of oscillations.}$$

From the above it will be seen that it was very easy to find the length of the pendulum for a given number of vibrations, or *vice versa*, although such calculations are quite useless while we have the accompanying table of lengths of pendulums for any number of oscillations. However, it may often be necessary to solve such problems where you do not have access to such tables, and it is therefore valuable to know just how to proceed.

M. Millet gives another method which is rather more simple. Take as a basis for calculation the pendulum that performs *one oscillation in an hour*, the length of which is 12,880,337.93 meters (507,109,080 inches) or in round numbers, 12,880,338 meters; by law 3 we obtain the following proportion:

$$12,880,338 : x \text{ (the length)} :: V^2 \text{ (the velocity)} : 1^2$$

Since the square of 1 is 1, it is only necessary to replace x by the length (if this is given), or V by the number of oscillations in an hour, (if they are pre-determined), and the value of the unknown quantity will be obtained.

Example: How many oscillations will be made by a pendulum measuring 305 mm. (12.008 inches)?

We have the proportion: $12,880,338 : 0.305 :: V^2 : 1$.

Dividing the product of the extremes by the known mean, *

---

* To extract the square root of a whole number, place a point or dot over the units' place of the given number, and thence over every second figure to the left of that place, thus dividing the whole number into several periods. The number of points will show the number of figures in the required root. Find the greatest number whose square is contained in the first period at the left; this is the first figure in the root, and may be ascertained by the aid of the following table;

	Number	1,	4,	9,	16,	25,	36,	49,	64,	81.
Square Root		1,	2,	3,	4,	5,	6,	7,	8,	9.

Subtract the square of the number so determined from the first period and to the remainder bring down the second period. Divide the number thus formed, omitting the last figure, by twice the part of the root already obtained, and annex the quotient to the root and also to the divisor. Then multiply the divisor, as it now stands, by the part of the root last obtained, and subtract the product from the number formed, as above mentioned, by the first remainder and the second period. If there be more periods to be brought down the operation must be repeated, and if, when all the periods have been so brought down, there is a remainder, the given number has no exact square root. If the number be a decimal fraction, or a whole number and a decimal combined, proceed in a similar manner, but observe that a point must always occur over the units' figure and on alternate figures from it on either side to the right and left. A decimal point will be placed in the square root immediately

$$V^2 = \frac{12,880,338}{0.305} = 42,230,616,$$

and V will be the square root of this number, or 6,498 oscillations per hour.

If the dimensions are given in English inches, the numbers 507,109,-080 and 12.008 would be employed thus:

$$507,109,080 : 12.008 : : V^2 : 1 ;$$

$$V^2 = \frac{507,109,080}{12.008} = 42,230,936.$$

The slight difference in the results is due to the non-equality of the two approximate figures given above.   Another example is given in which it will suffice to indicate the several stages of the calculation.

Example: What should be the length of a pendulum to give 4 100 oscillations per hour?

$$12,880,338 : x : : 4,100^2 : 1 ;$$
$$12,880,338 : x : : 16,810,000 : 1 ;$$

$$x = \frac{12,880,338}{16,810,000} = 0.766 \text{ meters (30.158 inches).}$$

---

before bringing down the first decimal period, and in cases where the given number has no exact root, it may be approximated to by bringing down successive pairs of ciphers. *Example:* Extract the square root of 273,529.

$$
\begin{array}{r|l}
 & \overset{\centerdot\ \ \centerdot\ \ \centerdot}{273529}(523 \\
 & 25 \\
\hline
102 & 235 \\
 & 204 \\
\hline
1043 & 3129 \\
 & 3129
\end{array}
$$

Applying the above rule, the square of 5 or 25, the largest contained in 27, is subtracted from the first period, and to the remainder, the second period, 35, is attached. The divisor for the dividend so formed is obtained by doubling the portion of the root already determined (5), and annexing 2 to the 10, since 10 will divide twice into 23, the dividend with the last figure omitted. The 2 is also added to the quotient as forming a figure in the root, and 102 multiplied by it as in ordinary division. The next period, 29, having been brought down to the remainder thus obtained, a similar operation is again gone through, the entire quotient, so far as it has been determined, being each time doubled.

Table Showing the Length of a Simple Pendulum

That performs in one hour any given number of oscillations, from 1 to 20,000, and the variation in this length that will occasion a difference of 1 minute in 24 hours.

Calculated by E. Gourdin.

Number of Oscillations per Hour.	Length in Millimeters.	Variation in Length for One Minute in 24 Hours in Millimeters.	Number of Oscillations per Hour.	Length in Millimeters.	Variation in Length for One Minute in 24 Hours in Millimeters.	Number of Oscillations per Hour.	Length in Millimeters.	Variation in Length for One Minute in 24 Hours in Millimeters.
20,000	32.2	0.04	13,200	73.9	0.10	8,200	191.5	0.26
19,000	35.7	0.05	13,100	75.1	0.10	8,100	196.3	0.27
18,000	39.8	0.05	13,000	76.2	0.10	8,000	201.3	0.27
17,900	40.2	0.06	12,900	77.4	0.11	7,900	206.4	0.28
17,800	40.7	0.06	12,800	78.6	0.11	7,800	211.7	0.29
17,700	41.1	0.06	12,700	79.9	0.11	7,700	217.2	0.30
17,600	41.6	0.06	12,600	81.1	0.11	7,600	223.0	0.30
17,500	42.1	0.06	12,500	82.4	0.11	7,500	229.0	0.31
17,400	42.4	0.06	12,400	83.8	0.11	7,400	235.2	0.32
17,300	43.0	0.06	12,300	85.1	0.12	7,300	241.7	0.33
17,200	43.5	0.06	12,200	86.5	0.12	7,200	248.5	0.34
17,100	44.0	0.06	12,100	88.0	0.12	7,100	255.7	0.35
17,000	44.6	0.06	12,000	89.5	0.12	7,000	262.9	0.36
16,900	45.1	0.06	11,900	91.0	0.12	6,900	270.5	0.37
16,800	45.7	0.06	11,800	92.5	0.13	6,800	278.6	0.38
16,700	46.3	0.06	11,700	94.1	0.13	6,700	286.9	0.39
16,600	46.7	0.07	11,600	95.7	0.13	6,600	295.7	0.40
16,500	47.3	0.07	11,500	97.4	0.13	6,500	304.9	0.41
16,400	47.9	0.07	11,400	99.1	0.13	6,400	314.5	0.43
16,300	48.5	0.07	11,300	100.9	0.14	6,300	324.5	0.44
16,200	49.1	0.07	11,200	102.7	0.14	6,200	335.1	0.46
16,100	49.7	0.07	11,100	104.5	0.14	6,100	346.2	0.47
16,000	50.0	0.07	11,000	106.5	0.14	6,000	357.8	0.48
15,900	51.0	0.07	10,900	108.4	0.15	5,900	370.0	0.50
15,800	51.6	0.07	10,800	110.5	0.15	5,800	382.9	0.52
15,700	52.3	0.07	10,700	112.5	0.15	5,700	396.4	0.54
15,600	52.9	0.07	10,600	114.6	0.16	5,600	410.7	0.56
15,500	53.6	0.07	10,500	116.8	0.16	5,500	425.8	0.58
15,400	54.3	0.08	10,400	119.1	0.16	5,400	440.1	0.60
15,300	55.0	0.08	11,300	111.4	0.17	5,300	458.5	0.62
15,200	55.7	0.08	10,200	123.8	0.17	5,200	476.3	0.65
15,100	56.5	0.08	10,100	126.3	0.17	5,100	495.2	0.67
15,000	57.3	0.08	10,000	128.8	0.18	5,000	515.2	0.70
14,900	58.0	0.08	9,900	131.4	0.18	4,900	536.5	0.73
14,800	58.8	0.08	9,800	134.1	0.18	4,800	559.1	0.76
14,700	59.6	0.08	9,700	136.9	0.19	4,700	583.1	0.79
14,600	60.4	0.08	9,600	139.8	0.19	4,600	608.7	0.83
14,500	61.3	0.08	9,500	142.7	0.19	4,500	636.1	0.86
14,400	62.1	0.09	9,400	145.8	0.20	4,400	665.3	0.90
14,300	63.0	0.09	9,300	148.9	0.20	4,300	696.7	0.95
14,200	63.9	0.09	9,200	152.2	0.21	4,200	730.2	0.99
14,100	64.8	0.09	9,100	155.5	0.21	4,100	766.2	1.04
14,000	65.7	0.09	9,000	159.0	0.22	4,000	805.0	1.09
13,900	66.7	0.09	8,900	162.6	0.22	3,950	825.5	1.12
13,800	67.6	0.09	8,800	166.3	0.23	3,900	846.8	1.15
13,700	68.6	0.09	8,700	170.2	0.23	3,850	869.0	1.18
13,600	69.6	0.09	8,600	173.7	0.24	3,800	892.0	1.21
13,500	70.7	0.09	8,500	178.3	0.24	3,750	915.9	1.25
13,400	71.7	0.10	8,400	182.5	0.25	3,700	940.1	1.28
13,300	72.8	0.10	8,300	187.0	0.25	3,650	966.8	1.31

Table of the Length of a Simple Pendulum,

(CONTINUED.)

Number of Oscillations per Hour.	Length in Meters.	To Produce in 24 Hours 1 Minute.		Number of Oscillations per Hour.	Length in Meters.	To Produce in 24 Hours 1 Minute.	
		Loss, Lengthen by Millimeters.	Gain, Shorten by Millimeters.			Loss, Lengthen by Meters.	Gain, Shorten by Meters.
3 600	0.9939	1.38	1.32	1,900	3.568	0.0050	0.0048
3,550	1.0221	1.42	1.36	1,800	3 975	0 0055	0.0053
3,500	1.0515	1.46	1.40	1,700	4.457	0.0062	0.0059
3,450	1.0822	1.50	1 44	1,600	5.031	0 0070	0.0067
3,400	1.1143	1.55	1.48	1,500	5 725	0.0080	0.0076
3 350	1.1477	1.60	1.53	1,400	6.572	0.0091	0.0087
3,300	1.1828	1.64	1.57	1,300	7.622	0.0106	0.0101
3 250	1.2194	1.69	1.62	1,200	8.945	0 0124	0.0119
3 200	1.2578	1 75	1.67	1,100	10.645	0.0148	0.0142
3,150	1.2981	1.80	1.73	1,000	12.880	0.0179	0.0171
3,100	1.3403	1.86	1 78	900	15.902	0.0221	0.0211
3,050	1.3846	1.93	1.84	800	20.126	0 0280	0.0268
3,000	1.4312	1.99	1 90	700	26.287	0 0365	0.0350
2.900	1.5316	2.13	2.04	600	35 779	0.0497	0.0476
2.800	1.6429	2.28	2 18	500	51.521	0.0716	0.0685
2,700	1.7669	2.46	2 35	400	80 502	0.1119	0.1071
2,600	1.9054	2.65	2 53	300	143.115	0.1989	0.1903
2,500	2.0609	2 87	2.74	200	322.008	0.4476	0.4282
2,400	2.2362	3.11	2 97	100	1,288.034	1.7904	1.7131
2,300	2.4349	3.38	3 24	60	3,577.871	4.9732	4.7586
2,200	2 6612	3.70	3.54	50	5,152.135	7.1613	6.8521
2,100	2.9207	4.06	3 88	1	12,880,337.930	17,903.6700	17,130.8500
2,000	3 2201	4.48	4.28				

The numbers given represent the oscillations in an hour of mean time of a *simple* pendulum, measuring from the point of suspension to the center of a heavy spherical bob attached to a fine thread, and oscillating through an exceedingly small arc in a vacuum.

The compound or material pendulum employed for regulating horological trains will give the number of oscillations indicated in the table when the length set opposite that number is equal to the distance between the centers of suspension and oscillation.

The assumption that the center of oscillation coincides approximately with the point at which the pendulum will rest horizontally on a knife-edge, is only legitimate when the rod is very light, and the weight of the pendulum acts nearly through the center of the bob.

The watchmaker will do well to employ a small platinum ball, suspended in front of a carefully graduated vertical rule, by a fine thread that can be lengthened or shortened at will. If the point of suspension is determined by a clamp that is opened or closed by a set screw, it will be easy to adjust this pendulum to the length indicated in the table, and, by making it oscillate side by side with the compound pendulum under consideration, to ascertain the approximate position of the center of suspension of this latter.

The length of the pendulum giving 1 oscillation in an hour (12,880,-337.93 meters, or 507,109,080 inches), affords a useful datum for certain calculations with reference to the lengths of pendulums. For an oscillation of 2° the lower end will travel through a space of 280 miles.

In the above table all dimensions are given in meters and millimeters. If it is desirable to express them in feet and inches, the necessary conversion can be at once effected in any given case by employing the following conversion table, which will prove of considerable value to the watchmaker for various purposes.

Inches expressed in Millimeters and French Lines.			Millimeters expressed in Inches and French Lines.			French Lines expressed in Inches and Millimeters.		
Inches.	Equal to		Millimeters.	Equal to		French Lines.	Equal to	
	Millimeters	French Lines.		Inches.	French Lines.		Inches.	Millimeters
1	25 39954	11.25951	1	0.0393708	0.44329	1	0.088414	2.25583
2	50.79908	22.51903	2	0.0787416	0.88659	2	0.177628	4.51166
3	76.19862	33.77854	3	0.1181124	1.32989	3	0 266441	6.76749
4	101.59816	45.03806	4	0.1574832	1.77318	4	0.355255	9.02332
5	126.99771	56.29757	5	0.1968539	2.21648	5	0 444069	11.27915
6	152.39725	67.55709	6	0.2362247	2 65978	6	0.532883	13 53497
7	177.79679	78 81660	7	0.2755955	3.10307	7	0.621697	15 79080
8	203 19633	90.07612	8	0.3149664	3.54637	8	0.710510	18.04663
9	228.59587	101.33563	9	0.3543371	3 98966	9	0.799324	20.30246
10	253.99541	112.59515	10	0.3937079	4.43296	10	0.888138	22.55829
						11	0.976952	24.81412
						12	1.065766	27.06995

A meter is the forty-millionth part of a meridian of the earth. A decimeter is the tenth part of a meter. A centimeter is the hundredth part of a meter. A millimeter is the thousanth part of a meter.

1 meter		39.37079 inches,
10 decimeter	is	3.28095 feet,
100 centimeters	equivalent to	1.09363 yards or
1000 millimeters		0.00035138 miles

1 square centimeter = 0.15501 square inch.
1 square inch   = 6 45127 square centimeter.
1 cubic centimeter = 0 06103 cubic inches.
1 cubic inch   = 16.38618 cubic centimeters.

To Calculate the Vibrations of a Pendulum. Multiply together the number of teeth of the wheels, starting with the one that carries the minute hand (which makes one revolution per hour), but omit the escape wheel. Multiply together the numbers of leaves of the pinions, commencing with the one that engages with the center wheel. If the first product be divided by the second, the number obtained gives the *number of revolutions* of the escape wheel in an hour. Multiply this figure by *twice the number* of teeth of the escape wheel, and the product is the number of single vibrations performed by the pendulum in one hour. The vibrations of a balance may be calculated in precisely the same manner.

Mercurial Compensation. In the mercurial pendulum with a glass jar, the mercury does not answer so quickly to a change of temperature as the steel rod, and preference is therefore now generally given to thin metal jars; still the elegant appearance of the glass jar in a stirrup renders it suitable for show regulators, for which it is still retained. The following are the dimensions of a good seconds pendulum of this class: Steel rod, .3 inch in diameter, 43 inches long from top of free part of suspension spring to bottom of sole of stirrup; side rods of stirrup, .3 inch wide and .125 inch thick; height of stirrup inside, 8 inches, bottom of stirrup, .5 inch thick with a recess turned out to receive the jar; glass jar 7.6 inches deep and 2 inches in diameter inside, outside 2.25 in diameter, and 7.8 inches high; height of mercury in the jar about 7.4 inches; the weight of mercury 11 lbs. 12 oz. The steel parts may with advantage be annealed to guard against the possibility of magnetism.

The mercury divided between two jars answers quicker to changes of temperature.

Precision clocks with mercurial pendulums have jars larger in diameter than two inches, made of cast iron enameled on the inside, or of steel.

Great care should be taken, when filling the mercury jar, to avoid air bubbles. The best plan is, push the center of a good silk handkerchief into the jar and pour in the mercury through a long boxwood or other funnel with but a mere pinhole for the outlet.   When the whole of the mercury is poured in, carefully draw up the handkerchief by its four corners.   The jar of mercury, with a piece of bladder tied over the top, may then be subjected to a temperature of about 120° for a week or two.

It is important to get the mercury as pure as possible for a pendulum. A good way of removing impurities is to add sulphuric acid to the mercury and shake the mixture well.   The metal is then washed, and afterwards dried on blotting paper.   Another method of purifying mercury is to put it in a bottle with a little finely-powdered loaf sugar.   The bottle is stoppered and shaken for a few minutes, then opened and fresh air blown in with a pair of bellows.   After this operation has been repeated three or four times, the mercury may be filtered by pouring it into a cone of smooth writing-paper, the apex of which has been pierced with a fine pin.   The sugar and impurities will be retained by the cone. Some filter mercury by squeezing it through a piece of fine chamois leather.   In dealing with mercury, care should be taken to avoid the injurious vapor which rises from it even at the ordinary temperature of the air, and of course more freely at higher temperatures.

Wood Rod and Lead Bob.   A cheap and good compensating pendulum may be made with a wood rod and lead bob.   For a seconds pendulum the rod should be .5 inch in diameter, of thoroughly well-seasoned straight-grained pine 45 inches long, measuring from the top of the free part of the suspension spring to the bottom of the bob.   A slit for the suspension spring is cut in a brass cap fitting over the top of the rod, to which it is secured by two pins.   A bit of thin brass tube is fitted to the rod where it is embraced by the crutch.   The rating screw, .25 inch in diameter, is soldered to a piece of brass tubing fitting over the rod and secured by a couple of pins. Wooden rods require to be coated with something to render them impervious to the atmosphere.   They are generally varnished or polished, but painting them answers the purpose well.   Mr. Latimer Clark recommends saturating them with melted paraffin, The bob, 2.25 inches in diameter and 12 inches high, with a hole just large enough to go freely over the wood rod, rests on a washer above the rating nut.   Shorter pendulums for chime and other clocks are made of cherry, mahogany, and ebony, simply because in such small sizes pine does not allow of sound attachment to the ends.   These pendulums have generally lenticular-shaped bobs.   Such rods cost scarcely any more than brass or iron, and are infinitely preferable.

It is essential that the grain of a wood pendulum rod should be perfectly straight, for if the grain is not straight, the rod is likely to bend, causing the clock to go very irregularly.

Importance of Fixing.   Whatever kind of pendulum is used, it will not keep time unless it is rigidly fixed.   Just as engineer clockmakers invariably make their escape wheels and other moving parts too heavy, so clockmakers always seem afraid to put enough metal in their pendulum cocks and brackets, which have rarely enough base either. The beneficial effect of the heavy pendulum bobs, which it has been the custom recently to use for regulator and turret clocks, is often quite lost for want of sufficient fixing for the pendulum. For a regulator, the pendulum should be supported on a cast-iron bracket with a base at least 10 inches square, bolted right through the back of the case, which should be not less than an inch and a quarter thick. For a turret clock a bracket of a proportional size should be used, bolted to one of the main walls of the building, or, if attached to the clock frame, the rigid connection of the latter with the walls by means of girders or cantilevers should not be lost sight of. A timber frame fixing for a turret clock pendulum will never be satisfactory.

Length of Pendulums. One-second pendulums are long enough for all but turret clocks, and longer than two-second pendulums should not be used. The very long pendulums used by the old clockmakers for turret clocks in order to get, as they expressed it, "dominion over the clock," were unwieldy and unsteady from the action of the wind and other causes. The requisite "dominion" is now obtained by making the bob heavier.

Pendulum Error. The long and short vibrations of a free pendulum will only be isochronous if the path described is a cycloid, which is a curve described by rolling a circle along a straight line. If the generating circle, instead of being rolled on another circle, were rolled along a straight edge, it would describe a cycloid. But a pendulum swung freely from a point travels through a circular path, and the long arcs are performed slower than the short ones. This divergence from the theoretical cycloid was of great importance when the arc described was large, as it was of necessity with the verge escapement, and many devices were tried to lead the pendulum through a cycloid. With an arc of about 3° only, such as regulator pendulums describe now, the divergence is very small.

Escapement Error. The kind of escapement used also affects the time of vibration; for instance, it is found that, while with the recoil escapement increased motive power and greater arc causes the clock to gain, the contrary effect is produced with the dead-beat escapement. The pendulum error may, therefore, be aggravated or neutralized by the escapement error.

Temperature Error. With increase of temperature, the pendulum, in common with most other substances, lengthens, and the clock loses; with decrease of temperature the contrary effect is produced. The object of the compensation pendulum is to meet the error arising from change of temperature by keeping the distance between the point of suspension and the center of oscillation constant.

Barometric Error. With a decrease in the pressure of the air, and consequent fall of the barometer, the pendulum increases its arc of vibration; with an increase in the pressure of the air, and consequent rise of the barometer, the pendulum diminishes its arc of vibration. In the Westminister clock the pendulnm vibrates 2.75° on each side of zero, and Sir Edmund Beckett pointed out that with this large arc the circular error just compensates for the barometric error. Where the escapement is suitable, this is doubtless the best way of neutralizing the barometric error; but it is not applicable to the dead-beat, for extra run on the dead faces of the pallets or larger angle of impulse than usual is found to be detrimental, as the oil thickens.

Rolling or Wobbling. The path of a pendulum in plan should be a straight line. Any deviation from this will affect the regularity of its timekeeping. A want of squareness in the chops, or a twist in the suspension spring, will often cause rolling or wobbling. Many clockmakers fix the lower end of the spring with but one screw, so that the pendulum may hang plumb without danger of binding. If the pallet staff is not perfectly at right angles to the path of the pendulum, rolling may be caused by the oblique action of the crutch. This shows the necessity of care in adjusting the movement on the seat board in cased clocks, and is an argument in favor of attaching the pendulum of a turret clock to the frame of the movement, instead of to a separate wall bracket.

PENDULUM SPRING. The ribbon or ribbons of steel used in suspending the pendulum.

PERRON, M. A celebrated French watchmaker and author. Born at Besancon, in 1779.

PILLAR. Posts of brass used to keep the plates of a watch in position.

PILLAR PLATE. The plate of a watch to which the pillars are attached.

PINION. The smaller of two toothed wheels which are geared into one another. The tooth of a pinion is called a pinion leaf.

Pinion Grinder and Polisher. The ends of the leaves of pinions, when ground flat and polished, add very much to the beauty of a job when completed. Proceed to turn down your pinion in the lathe and fit it in the usual manner, ready for finishing. Now select a suitable chuck to hold the pinion in the lathe, and take a few copper cartridge shells, used in 22 or 32 caliber revolvers, and drill four holes in the end to fit the staff of the pinion you wish to polish. Fit a piece of wood about three inches long in the open end of the cartridge shells to use as a handle; do not allow the handle to enter the shell over one-fourth of an inch, so that it will not strike against the pivot of the pinion while polishing. Now file flat the closed end of the cartridge, and your grinding and polishing tool is completed. Insert the pinion in one of the holes of the shell so that the flat surface of the shell will come up squarely against the face of the leaves of the pinion. Apply a paste made of emery flour and sweet oil, and run the lathe at a high speed, pressing slightly against the pinion leaves. Transfer from one hole to another, to insure flatness. Clean off the pinion with benzine and examine to see that the marks of the turning tool are all out. If not, proceed as before. Take another shell prepared in like manner, and use crocus and oil, instead of emery, and grind out the scratches of the emery. After removing these, wash thoroughly in benzine, and with another copper shell proceed to polish, using a paste of diamantine and oil or alcohol. A good polish will soon appear. Care must be exercised to see that the work is thoroughly cleaned after each process. The shells can then be laid away in separate boxes for future use. During leisure moments you can prepare a number of these shells to fit almost any job, and you will find them very handy for many purposes.

PIN PALLET ESCAPEMENT. An escapement used mostly in French clocks, in which it is often placed in front of the dial. The pallets are formed of semi-circular stones; generally carnelian.

This excellent escapement (invented by M. Brocot), rarely seen except in small French clocks, appears to be worthy of more extended use. The fronts of the teeth of the escape wheel are sometimes made radial, as shown in Fig. 225; sometimes cut back so as to bear on the point only, like the "Graham;" and sometimes set forward so as to give recoil to the wheel during the motion of the pendulum beyond the escaping arc. The pallets, generally of carnelian, are of semi-circular form. The diameter of each is a trifle less than the distance between the two teeth of the escape wheel. The angle of impulse in this escapement bears direct reference to the number of teeth embraced by the pallets. Ten is the usual number, as shown in the drawing. The distance between the escape wheel and the pallet staff centers should not be less than the radius of the wheel multiplied by 1.7. This gives about 4° of impulse measured from the pallet staff center.

English clockmakers rather object to this escapement on account of the difficulty of keeping oil to the pallets, which is aggravated if there is much space between the root of the pallet stone and the face of the wheel. The effect of the want of oil is much more marked if the pallets are made of steel instead of jewel. Any tendency of this escapement to set is generally met by flattening the curved impulse faces of the pallets.

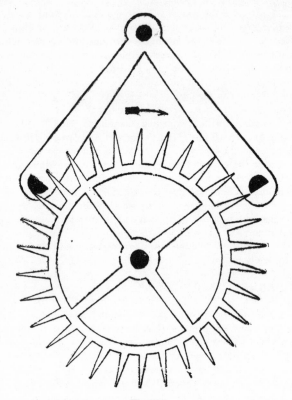

Fig. 225.

PIN VISE. An improved form of pin vise is that shown in Fig. 226, manufactured by A. J. Logan. It is hollow throughout its entire length

Fig. 226.

and closes together, the same as a chuck on the American lathe. It will hold a small drill or wire perfectly true and will be found very useful for many purposes.

PIN WHEEL ESCAPEMENT. The pin wheel escapement was invented by Lepaute about 1753. A clock escapement analogous in its action to the "Graham." The impulse is given by nearly half-round pins standing out from the face of the escape wheel. The one advantage over the Graham is that the pressure on the pallets is always downwards, so that excessive shake in the pallet staff hole, which may be

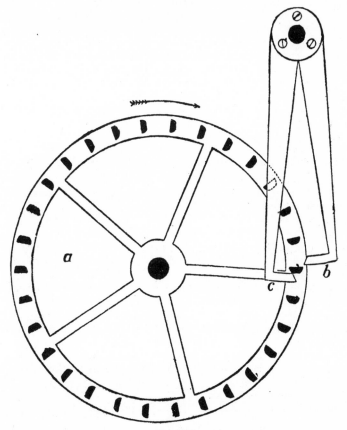

*Fig. 227.**

looked for in the course of time, especially in large clocks, would not affect the amount of impulse.

This escapement is used principally in turret clocks. The chief objection to it practically, is the difficulty of keeping the pins lubricated, the oil being drawn away to the face of the wheel. To prevent this a nick is

---

*a. Escape Wheel.   b and c. Pallets.

sometimes cut around the pins, close to the wheel, but this weakens the pins very much. The best plan is to keep the pallets as close as they can be to the face of the wheel without touching.

Lepaute made the pins semi-circular, and placed alternately on each side of the wheel so as to get the pallets of the same length. This requires double the number of pins, and there is no real disadvantage in having one pallet a little longer than the other, provided the short one is put outside, as shown in the drawing. Sir Edmund Beckett introduced the practice of cutting a piece off the bottoms of the pins, which is a distinct improvement, for if the pallet has to travel past the center of the pin with a given arc of vibration before the pin can rest, the pallets must be very long unless very small pins are used.

The escaping arc is generally 20, and the diameter of the pins is then 40 measured from the pallet staff hole.

Then with a given diameter of pin, to find the mean length of pallets, divide the given diameter by .069.

Or if the mean length of the pallets is given, the diameter of pins may be found by multiplying the given length by .069.

The opening between the extreme points of the pallets $= 2°$, that is, half the diameter of the pins.

With an escaping arc of $3°$ the mean length of the pallet arms is ten times the diameter of the pins.

The angle of impulse is divided between the pins and the pallets, and care must be taken that the pallets are not cut back too much. When a pin escapes from one pallet the bottom of the succeeding pin must fall safely on the rest of the other pallet. It is best before finishing the impulse planes to place the pallets in position and mark them off with reference to the pins. The thickness of the two pallets and one pin contained between them equals, less drop, which is very small, the space between two pins from center to center. The pallets are of steel, hardened at the acting parts, and screwed to a collar on the pallet staff. The rests are slightly rounded so as to present less surface to the pins, and the curves struck from a little below the pallet staff hole so as to be hardly "dead." The pins should be of gun-metal, or very hard brass, or aluminium bronze, round when screwed into the wheel, and cut to shape in an engine afterwards.

PITKIN, HENRY AND JAMES F. These two brothers, opened up a small factory in Hartford, Conn., in 1838, for the manufacture of watches. The movement, which was known as the "Pitkin Watch," and which is shown in Fig. 228, was the first machine-made watch manufactured in America. It was a three-quarter plate, slow train and about the diameter of the modern 16-size movement. The machinery used in its manufacture was very crude, and was all made by the Pitkin brothers. The cost of manufacture was so great, however,

that the Pitkin brothers could not compete with the cheap foreign
watches then imported, and shortly after moving the factory to New
York, which they did in 1841,
the project was abandoned. The
total product of the Pitkins was
about 800 movements.

PIVOT. The end of an arbor
or shaft that rests in a support or
bearing.

Length of Balance Pivots.
Saunier recommends the removal
of the endstone to see that the
pivot projects enough beyond the
pivot hole when the plate is
inverted. Remove the cock and
detach it from the balance.

Fig. 228.

Take off the balance spring with its collet from the latter and place
it on the cock inverted, so as to see whether the cock is central
when the outer coil is midway between the curb pins. Remove the cock
endstone and endstone cap, place the top balance pivot in its hole and see
that it projects a little beyond the pivot hole. Place the balance in the
calipers to test its truth, and at the same time to see that it is in poise. It
must be remembered, however, that the balance is sometimes put out
of poise intentionally. See *Poising the Balance.*

The Play of Pivots. Saunier gives the following rules for the play
of escapement pivots: In the cylinder escapement, about one-sixth the
diameter of the pivot; in the duplex escapement, about .1 the diameter
of the pivot; in the lever escapement, about one-eighth the
diameter of the pivot. A large hole causes the pitching of the depths to
vary with position, and a deficient play renders the escapement more
sensitive to thickening of the oil. There is less inconvenience when the
play is somewhat in excess than when it is deficient. In determining
the play of train wheel pivots, proceed as follows: Allow the train to
run down, and if it does so noisily, or by jerks, it may be assumed that
some of the depths are bad, in consequence either of the teeth being
badly formed, or the holes too large, etc. To test the latter point, cause
the wheels to revolve alternately in opposite directions by applying a
finger to the barrel or center wheel teeth, at the same time noting the
movement of each pivot in turn, in its hole. A little practice will soon
enable the workman to judge whether the play is correct. The running
down of the train will also indicate whether any pivots are bent. It is
important that the center pivots project beyond the holes in the plate and
bridge.

To Straighten Pivots. Saunier recommends that a number of straight holes be drilled in a plate at exactly right angles to its surface. Introduce the pivot into a hole that it fits with very little play, and redress it by causing the staff to rotate, at the same time holding the plate in the hand. Caution is necessary, since there is some risk of bending the pivot too far.

The Friction of Train Pivots. It is very important to reduce the friction of the wheel pivots to a minimum quantity, and to make it constant, so that the motive power be transmitted with the greatest possible uniformity to the balance or pendulum, which is necessary to enable the latter to maintain its arc of oscillation of the same magnitude. The friction of the pivots is due to the pressure of the motive power and the weight of the wheels. The wheel work nearest the motive power must have strong pivots, so that they possess sufficient resistance, neither wear the pivot holes to one side nor enlarge them, by which the friction would be increased, and at the same time alter the true point of engagement. In tenor with the distance of the wheels from the motive power, the thickness of their pivots must decrease because these latter sustain less pressure, and are subject to a greater velocity than the first parts.

Pivoting Cylinders. It often happens that cylinders are broken while turning down pivots. To avoid this proceed as follows: Select a piece of silver or German silver joint wire, the opening of which is slightly larger than the diameter of the cylinder (lower end); cut off a piece the length of the cylinder proper, leaving the pivot projecting through. Fill the cylinder with lathe wax and slip on the little piece of joint wire while the cement is quite warm. Proceed to true up by the pivot in the usual way and when the wax is quite cold, turn down and polish the pivot before removing from the lathe. If care is used in cutting the joint wire the proper length, it will answer as a gauge for the length of the cylinder. If a joint wire is properly cemented on the cylinder, it is almost impossible to break it. The lower part of the cylinder can be left in this condition and the upper part can be turned down to fit the balance, hair spring, collet and pivot. After this is done remove from the lathe and dissolve the cement in alcohol in a bottle.

Shape of Pivots. Pivots must be hard, round and well polished; their shoulders are to be flat, not too large, with ends well rounded off, so that they do not wear the cap jewel. The jewel holes must be round, smooth and not larger than is requisite for the free motion of the pivot which is surrounded with oil. Their sides must be parallel to those of the pivots, so that they sustain the pressure of the pivot equally at all points of their length. The holes, if of brass or gold, must have been hammered sufficiently hard, so that the pores of the metal are closed to prevent too rapid a wear. It is well if the oil sinks are of a size that will accommodate a sufficient quantity of oil, which, if too little, would soon dry out or become thickered with the worn off particles of the metal. The under-turnings of the pinion leaves are conical, but in such a way that the thicker part be nearest to the pivot, because by this disposition the oil is retained at the pivot by attraction, and does not seek to spread into the pinion leaves, as is often the case, especially with flat watches, in which this provision is frequently slighted.

PIVOT GAUGE. A steel plate with tapered slit for measuring the diameter of pivots.

PIVOT POLISHER. The pivot polisher is used for grinding and polishing conical and straight pivots and shoulders. It is also useful for drilling, polishing or snailing steel wheels, milling out odd places in plate or bridge where only a part of a circle is to be removed, etc. The circular base being graduated to degrees, it can be set at any angle. The spindle has a taper hole for drill chucks, which makes the fixture very useful for drilling either in the center or eccentric, and by using the graduations on the pulley of the headstock an accurately spaced circle of holes may be drilled. Fig. 229 is the American Watch Tool Company's polisher; Fig. 230, the Mosely, and Fig. 231, the Rivett pattern.

Fig. 229.

The polisher is used as follows: After the pivot is turned to proper shape, put on your polisher (spindle parallel with lathe bed), with lap back of pivot. Use cast iron lap first. (Square corners for square shoulders, and round corners for conical.) Lap for conical shoulder can be readily cornered with a fine file, and cross-grind with fine oil stone to remove any lines made by graver. Lines on end can be removed same way, or in fingers rubbed on piece of ground glass which has on it a paste of oil stone and oil well mixed.

Fig. 230.

This will rapidly bring them up to a sharp corner nicer than by the graver. On the iron laps use No. 1 crocus or very fine oil stone powder, well ground down in oil to a paste. When roughed out to your liking, wipe off the crocus, and with a little oil touch the pivot gently; repeat the second time. Then change lap for one of box-wood, and use crocus No. 4, very fine and ground down to paste. Proceed as with first lap, being careful at all times to keep the lap properly oiled and not pressed too hard against

Fig. 231.

the work, particularly in the last operation. Also be sparing of your grinding or polishing material. About three specks of polish with point of small knife is sufficient. Bring the lap up carefully against the work

Fig. 232.

until spread all the way around, then proceed, bearing in mind that grinding is not polishing, and that to polish nicely the work and lap must be very nearly the right shape. To thoroughly clean the laps, dip in benzine.

Fig. 233.

Fig. 232 illustrates the Johanson polisher, which is one of the latest on the market. Fig. 233 shows a front view of the same machine. It consists of a shaft mounted in nicely fitted boxes, adapted to give a lateral motion, which is controlled by set collars on the shaft as shown. The front end of the shaft is bored to receive the tapers of the

cutting tools, and also with an outside taper to hold the laps, the laps and
cutters being shown at Fig. 234, while the other end has a knob to enable
the fingers to control the lateral motion of the shaft as desired.   Pulleys
of hard rubber are fixed upon the shaft and two idlers are mounted on a

Fig. 234.

vertical stud at the rear.   The boxes which carry the shaft are swiveled
upon two screws in the base plate and are controlled by a lever, as shown
in Fig. 233, or they may be held rigidly in position by a set screw shown
under the lever.   This constitutes the tool proper.   When it is to be used

Fig. 235.

in the hand rest, a stud, shown in Fig. 233, is screwed into the base plate
and supports the tool in the hand rest, so as to be readily adjustable in any
direction.   When used in the slide rest, this stud is removed and the
plate clamped between two hollow cylindrical supports by a stud which

is slipped into the groove of the slide rest and fastened by a nut at the top, the whole forming a turret-like mount of great strength, as shown in Fig. 232, and upon which the machine can be readily swiveled in any direction.

Other cutters and laps may, of course, be used with the machine, so that it is capable of a wide range of work.

Fig. 235 illustrates the Hardinge pattern, which is a hand polisher. It is attached to the lathe bed the same as the T or hand rest. Grinding and polishing slips are furnished with this machine, which is very simple and inexpensive.

PIVOTED DETENT. A form of detent mostly seen in French chronometer escapements, which moves on pivots instead of through a weak spring, as in the English and American escapements.

PLATE. The plates of a watch are the discs of brass which form the foundation of the movement. The chief plate, called the pillar plate, lies underneath the dial; the side of it next the dial is recessed to contain the motion work; on the other side the pillars are fixed. Unless the watch has a " bar movement " there is another plate, kept a little distance from the pillar plate by the pillars, called the top plate. In full plate watches this plate, like the pillar plate, is circular. In three-quarter plate watches there is a piece cut out of the top plate sufficiently large to allow the balance to move in the same horizontal plane as the top plate. In half-plate watches the fourth wheel arbor is cut short, and its upper end carried by a cock, so as to permit of the use of a larger balance than would otherwise be the case. The plates of a clock are the two pieces of brass which receive the pivots of the train.

POISING TOOL. A tool used for poising or ascertaining if the metal in a balance is evenly disposed around the axis. See *Balance.*

POLISHING. See *Cleansing, Pickling and Polishing.* For polishing of steel, pivots, etc. See *Steel, Pivots, etc.*

POOLE, JOHN. An English chronometer maker of considerable fame and the inventor of the auxillary compensation which bears his name. He was born in 1818 and died in 1867.

POTENCE. A bracket used for supporting the lower end of the balance staff in full plate watches.

POTENTIAL ENERGY. Power to do work. A mainspring when wound possesses potential energy. The pressure exerted, multiplied by the distance traveled in winding, would be the measure of its potential energy. The potential energy of a raised clock weight is equal to its weight multiplied by the distance through which it can fall. The potential energy in foot-pounds of any raised weight $= \mathrm{w}\, h$, where w is the weight in pounds and h the vertical height in feet.

PUMP CENTER. The small, pointed steel shaft in the center of a universal head, which is used for centering the work.

PUSH PIECE. The movable part of a pendant used for opening the case. The small movable projection on the side of a case which is pushed in when setting the hands.

QUARE, DANIEL. Born in 1632 and died in 1724. He was the first to apply the concentric minute hand to watches and clocks and was the inventor of the repeating watch.

QUARTER RACK. The rack that regulates the striking of the quarters in a clock or repeater.

QUARTER SCREWS. The four timing screws in a compensation balance.

RACK LEVER. A watch escapement, said to have been invented by Abbe Hautefeuille in 1734. The lever terminated in a rack, which worked into a pinion on the balance staff.

RAMSAY, DAVID. Clockmaker to James I., and the first master of the Clockmakers' Company. He died in 1655.

RATCHET. A wheel having pointed teeth and fixed to an arbor to to prevent it turning backward. A click or pawl falls in between the teeth of the wheel and prevents it turning backward. See *Click*.

RATING NUT. A round nut, with a milled edge, screwed to the pendulum rod of a clock. It supports the pendulum bob, and by turning it to the right or left, the bob is raised or lowered, and the timekeeping of the clock altered. In the finest clocks a scale is engraved around the rating nut to serve as a guide to the amount it is turned.

RAYMOND, B. W. A Chicago capitalist and the first president of the Elgin National Watch Company. The first movement turned out from the factory, April 1, 1867, was named the B. W. Raymond in his honor. This movement was a success from the start and has done much toward establishing the reputation of the Elgin Company. Mr. Raymond died April 5, 1883.

RECOIL ESCAPEMENT. An escapement in which the teeth are pressed backward, or recoiled, by the pallets after coming to rest, as in the Anchor Escapement.

RED STUFF. Sesquioxide of iron, used for polishing brass and steel by mixing with oil. Crocus, rouge and clinker are various grades of red stuff.

REGNAULD. One of the first French clockmakers who attempted to compensate a clock against the effects of heat and cold.

REGULATOR. The small steel hand or lever to the shorter end of which the curb pins are attached, and which by moving from side to side practically shortens the hair spring. See *Curb Pins*.

2. A standard clock having a compensating pendulum and used for timing watches and clocks.

REID, THOMAS. Born in 1750 and died in 1834. He was a celebrated Scotch horologist and the author of a treatise on watch and clockmaking.

REMONTOIRE. A spring or other device which is wound by a clock and discharged at regular intervals. Its function is generally either to impart impulse to the pendulum or to cause the hands of the clock to jump over certain spaces. Although the word is derived from the French, it is not now used in that language, except to signify a stem-wind movement.

REPAIR CLAMPS. The magic repair clamps shown in Figs. 236

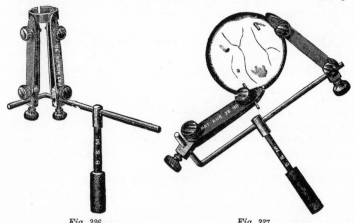

<table>
<tr><td>Fig. 236.</td><td>Fig. 237.</td></tr>
</table>

to 238, are used for holding various kinds of work in position, while repairing, soldering, etc. In addition to the uses shown in the illustrations, it is also applicable for dozens of operations that will suggest themselves to the possessor.

It is so arranged that the end screws can be used as feet and the handles as a support (as shown in the illustrations), so that the tool with

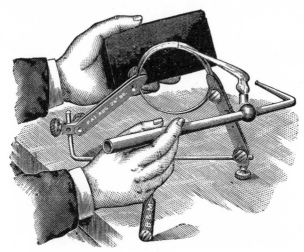

Fig. 238.

the work in it will stand up, leaving the operator free to use charcoal or asbestos block with one hand and the blow pipe with the other. It is especially valuable for holding dials, when soldering on feet.

REPEATER. A watch which indicates the time by repeating it by means of gongs or bells. There are hour, quarter, half-quarter, five minute, and minute repeaters. They were first made about 1676, and are said to be the invention of Edward Barlow, a clergyman. About the same time Daniel Quare, a watchmaker of London, was working on a model of a repeating watch. Barlow applied for a patent on his invention and Quare, hearing of it, determined to resist him, and succeeded in getting the backing of the Clockmakers' Company, who petitioned the king not to make the grant until the council could see and examine Quare's watch. The council investigated both watches and finally decided in favor of Quare, his watch having but one push piece, while in Barlow's there were two. Fig. 239 illustrates a half-quarter repeating watch by Nicole & Company. The principle of all repeating watches is the same, though some arrange the parts somewhat differently.

The small mainspring which supplies the power for repeating, is wound by pushing around a slide that projects from the band of the case. This slide is the extremity of a lever which presses against a pivoted

rack engaging with a segment on the barrel arbor.   There is underneath
a segment of greater radius containing twelvě ratchet teeth.   The number of hours to be struck is regulated by the position of the hour snail in
precisely the same way as the striking work of a clock.   At twelve
o'clock the lowest step of the snail is presented to the stop, so that the

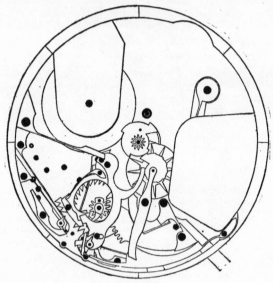

Fig. 239.

rack can be traversed its full extent.   In returning, each one of the
twelve ratchet teeth in turn lifts the hammer and strikes the hours.   The
quarter rack has two sets of three ratchet teeth each, and as the slide is
moved round the all-or-nothing piece, as it is called, releases the quarter
rack, against which a spring is constantly pressing.   The quarter rack is
stopped by the quarter snail.   After the hours are struck a curved finger,
or gathering pallet, on the barrel arbor presses the quarter rack to its
original position, and in passing each of the ratchet teeth, by pushing
aside a pallet fixed to the same arbor as the hammer, strikes a blow.
Whether one, two, or three quarters are struck depends, of course, on
the position of the quarter snail.

The half-quarter rack, with but one ratchet tooth, is placed on top,
and works with the quarter rack.   Between each quarter and seven
minutes past, it yields as it passes the lifting pallet.

The quarter snail, attached to the cannon pinion, is doubled with
steps just dividing each other, so that after the half-quarter the quarter
rack gets round a little nearer to the center of the snail than the half-
quarter rack.   This allows the spring catch which is mounted on the

quarter-rack, to lock the half-quarter rack, and then, after the quarters have struck, it lifts the hammer and strikes one more blow.

The hour snail is mounted on a star wheel, as shown, and the star wheel is moved by a pin in the quarter snail, or rather in the loose surprise piece beneath, which flies out to the position shown in the drawing directly the star wheel is moved. The surprise then prevents the quarter-rack reaching any step of the quarter snail, and consequently no quarters are struck. When the pin in the surprise piece comes round to the star wheel again, the pressure of the pin on a tooth of the star wheel causes the surprise piece to retire so that the third quarter and half quarter can be struck, but as the star wheel jumps forward the succeeding tooth flirts out the surprise.

The hammer arbors go through the plate, and the hammers are on the other side. The gongs of steel wire, fixed at one end to the plate, curl round it and lie between the plate and the end of the case.

There is also on the other side of the plate a train of runners for regulating the speed of striking. The centers of the wheels are indicated by dots on the left hand of the barrel. The last pinion is not furnished with a fly as in clocks, but there is a screw with an eccentric head, by means of which the depth of the last pinion can be increased or made shallower. This is found to be sufficient regulation, though latterly an escape wheel and pallets have been applied at the end of the train of runners to regulate the speed in some repeaters. This is perhaps more scientific than making a bad depth, but the pallet staff holes are found to wear very much, if not jeweled.

Five-minute repeaters seem likely to supersede all other kinds by reason of their simplicity, for they evidently involve but little more work in construction than quarter repeaters, and yet give the time more closely than half-quarters.

Rusty Gongs. They may be improved by polishing, first with a half-round polisher, and then finished with boxwood polisher on cork.

Causes of Failure. The flat shoulder of fly pinion in contact with a hollow sink. In a short time the shoulder will cut or wear a groove, fitting itself in the sink, and will stick in it, and when much worn no power of the spring will drive the train on. The pinion's shoulders should always act on a flat, not in a hollow surface; this is applicable to ordinary trains, as watches stop sometimes through end shakes being wrongly given by hollow-sinking the plate with a rounding face instead of a flat cutter.

Fly pinion the wrong size, or a little out of round. If the depth with such a pinion be altered to regulate the speed, it may stop the train.

The mainspring being bad and unadjustable, or binding in the barrel, sometimes through oil that has become too thick.

Too much oil applied, and very often in the wrong places. The studs and acting spring ends are essential places for the smallest portion of oil; but care should be taken that no oil flows between the racks, or between he surprise piece and snail, and none should be given to the case slide.

To Bend Gong Wires. The bending of a gong wire in a repeating watch, in order to free it from any point it touches, often results in diminishing the sound considerably. In such a case, Immisch advises as follows: If the spring touches on the outside and must consequently be bent inward, it should be laid upon a convex piece of brass corresponding in shape with the inner side of the spring at the place where it is to be bent; then, if the outside be slightly hammered with the sharp edge of a hammer, the small indentations produced will cause the outside to lengthen a little and the inside to contract in proportion. The change of form will be very gradual, and the granular disturbance, being spread over a large area, will not be great enough to affect the tone in the least. The more a spring is bent to and fro in any direction, the more it will lose its elastic force. In soft springs especial care should be taken to make any change very gradual, repeating the operation oftener rather than to bend too much at one time, and thereby necessitate the bending back of the spring. If a perfectly adjusted and very soft spring should be bent and brought back again to exactly its former position, the vibrations would be no longer isochronous, and by repeating the experiment the elastic force, or the spring curve, will become so small compared with that possessed by the body of the spring, that instead of exercising a control over the latter, its motion becomes subservient to it. A harder spring will bear a much greater amount of manipulation, and a Breguet spring, the form of which in itself necessitates a certain amount of bending, must always have a greater degree of hardness than that necessary for helical springs, in order that the advantage possessed by this form should be of the greatest possible use. It is also necessary that a certain time should elapse before ascertaining the result of the change affected. Metallic bodies possessing any degree of elasticity, if forced into a different shape, do not retain the newly acquired shape exactly, but have a tendency to return in some degree toward that shape from which they have been forced. The reactionary force becomes gradually less active, until after a time it ceases altogether. The time required for the shape to become permanent differs greatly with the degree of elasticity. It is sometimes desirable to bend a spring, but the repairer, being afraid of breaking it, abandons the idea. Suppose it is desirable to bend a side click spring of a Swiss bridge watch, which, by the way, is generally made of poor steel. Take hold of the end in which the screw goes with a pair of brass-nosed sliding tongs, holding it in the left hand; then press a piece of brass against the click, bending it in the direction desired, and at the same time holding it over the flame of a spirit lamp until the center, or spring part, becomes a straw, or dark red color. The fact that spring-tempered steel is brought to a dark red-blue twenty times over, will not reduce it below its former temper; on the contrary, it will tend to equalize and improve the temper, and render it less liable to break. Suppose a cylinder pivot, or any pivot of the escapement parts are bent, and you wish to straighten it by this process; take a small brass ring, fit it to the pivot and hold over the flame of the lamp, bending it at the same time in the desired direction.

Repeating Attachments. Fig. 240 illustrates the repeating attachment recently patented and put on the market by the American Repeating Watch Factory, of Elizabeth, N. J. The complete mechanism is arranged on a small plate which can be fastened to any of the American made movements by the aid of a few screws, and the construction is such that it can be wound either by the stem or by the repeating slide, the latter being similar to those used on all Swiss repeaters. The stem winding pattern can be applied to Elgin 16 size hunting, Illinois and Dueber-Hampden 16 sizes, Waltham 14 sizes and Lancaster 18 sizes, all hunting

movements. The repeating slide style can also be applied to these watches. The slide pattern is adapted particularly to Elgin 16 size open face and Elgin interchangeable 16 sizes and to Waltham and Columbus 16 size hunting and open face, Waltham 14 sizes, Illinois 16 sizes in open face, Howard 16 and 18 sizes and Paillard non-magnetic watches, both open and hunting. The attachment can also in various ways be applied to other American and Swiss watches. Fig. 240 represents the attachment

Fig. 240.

applied to an Elgin 16 size hunting movement. To attach this mechanism to a watch, first wind its mainspring completely and then let it down only one-quarter turn. Set stop wheel in position with its shoulder against the stop piece, to prevent further winding, place both racks above the stop wheel and let the mainspring drive the parts back to their normal position. The lever winding parts are arranged under the repeater plate and are similar in construction to those used in Swiss repeaters. The stem winding connection is composed of a ratchet wheel which is geared with the crown wheel of the stem-winding mechanism of the watch, and a ratchet stem, that passes through the wheel and both watch plates, carrying on its other end a pinion, that gears into the repeater barrel wheel, which winds its mainspring when the stem is turned to the left.

REPEATING RACK. A rack in a repeating watch which is shifted one tooth for each blow that is struck

REPEATING SLIDE. The slide on the band of a repeating watch case that is moved round to set the repeating work in motion.

RESILIENT ESCAPEMENT. A form of the lever escapement in which the lever yields, when pressed upon the outside by the impulse pin, and allows the pin to pass. See *Lever Escapement.*

REST. The *T*-shaped piece of metal attached to the lathe bed and on which the graver, peg wood, polisher, etc., is rested. It is also known as *T* rest and hand rest.

Back Rest. Among the many tools that watchmakers can make for themselves, one of the most useful is the tool illustrated in Fig. 241. It is a modification of what machinists call a "back rest." The only

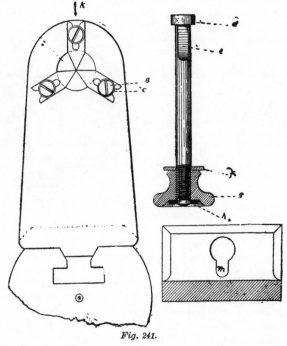

Fig. 241.

points in which it differs from that employed by the machinist is the shape of the jaws and the mode of fastening to the lathe bed. *a* shows the rest in position on the lathe bed, looking from right hand end of bed; *B* shows the base, looking from above, in direction of arrow *k*; *C* shows bolt for binding it to the lathe bed. It does not seem as though it needed much explanation, as it will readily be seen that the head *d* of bolt, passes up through the longitudinal slot in lathe bed, through the round hole in base of back rest, and slipped back into slot *m*, when about half a turn of the nut *g* binds it firmly to the bed. The washer *h*, on the end of binding screw, is riveted or soldered in place, and should be close enough to nut *g* to allow only about half a turn to loosen the bolt, as that is sufficient, and more would be time lost in running the nut back and forth to bind or loosen the rest. It will be seen that when the nut *g* is slackened it binds against the washer *h*, and it will stay there, and be just where you want it when you want to use it again. The jaws are of hard brass; about three sets, with points of different widths, will cover a good range of work. Those shown in Fig. 241 are suitable for such work as pivoting small French clock pinions, etc. It will be observed that the jaws are so made that they may be changed by slightly loosening the screws. The screw heads should have thin steel washers under them.

RING GAUGE. A gauge used by jewelers for measuring the internal dimensions of finger rings.

RIVETING STAKE. A steel block, pierced with a number of different sized holes. See *Staking Tool.*

ROBIN, ROBERT. A celebrated French watch and clock maker. He built many large turret clocks for the public buildings of France. Born in 1742 and died in 1799.

ROCKING BAR. The steel bar which carries the intermediate wheels in stem wind movements. Sometimes called the yoke.

ROLLER REMOVER. There are numerous designs in the way of roller removers upon the market, but lack of space prevents description and illustrations of them. Fig 242 illustrates the Hardinge remover, while Fig. 243 illustrates the Sheehan. They are both excellent tools and do the work in a satisfactory manner.

Fig. 242.

ROMILLY, M. A clever Swiss horologist. He was held in high esteem in Paris, where he passed the greater portion of his life. He was born at Geneva in 1714 and died in 1796.

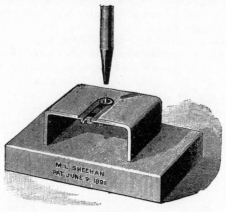

Fig. 243.

ROSE CUTTER. A hollow cutter, as shown in Fig. 244, used for reducing the size of wire, as in forming heads when making screws.

ROSE ENGINE. A form of lathe in which the rotary movement of the mandrel may be combined with a lateral, reciprocating movement

Fig. 244.

of the tool rest, the result being a movement of eccentric character. In this way many curves of an epicycloid or hypocycloid character and of great variety and beauty may be obtained by varying the rate of speed between the lathe mandrel and the lead screw, or splined rod which governs the motion of the tool post in the slide rest. The change gears are handled as in the ordinary engine lathe. Another form of this engine has a very heavy head, formed of a series of disks, circular in form, and placed concentrically on the shaft, so that they resemble a cone pulley having a large number of steps. These disks, instead of being true circles, are formed of a great number of facets, so that the discs constitute polygons of 64, 120, 180, etc., sides. The central mandrel bears an eccentric chuck and has lateral play, so that the facets, striking on a rigid roller, throw the mandrel alternately in and out of center, thus bringing the work regularly to and away from the cutting tool, making the tool cut a lozenge-shaped chip each time a facet on the disc is encountered by the roller. The work being held eccentrically in the chuck, these chips, or digs, are very fine and close at the center, and enlarged proportionately as they reach the outside of the watch case or other object being ornamented.

The work is done with tools which have been sharpened and polished so carefully as to make a " bright cut " on the metal, and the operator turns the lathe with one hand and watches the progress of the work with a glass.

ROUGE. See *Red Stuff*.

ROUNDING UP ATTACHMENT. The Webster rounding up attachment, shown in Fig. 245, is a very useful adjunct to the lathe. It is attached to the top of the slide-rest. To operate, a pointed taper chuck is put in the lathe spindle. The wheel to be rounded up is put into the fixture and the wheel adjusted vertically so that the point of the lathe center will be at the center of the thickness of the wheel, after which the lower spindle of the fixture should not be moved. Now remove the wheel, also the taper chuck, and put the saw arbor, with the rounding-up cutter, in the lathe spindle, and adjust the longitudinal slide of the slide-rest so that the rounding-up cutter will be back of and in

Fig. 245.

line with the center of the rounding-up fixture, after which the longitudinal slide of the slide-rest should not be moved. Now put the wheel and supporting collet in place, and proceed with the rounding-up.

ROY, PETER. Watchmaker to the King of France. Died 1785. Author of two works on horology.

ROZE, A. C. An eminent French watchmaker. Born in 1812, and died in 1862.

RUBY PIN. The impulse pin in the lever escapement.

RUBY ROLLER. The roller in the duplex escapement which locks the escape wheel teeth.

SAFETY PIN. In the lever escapement, a pin that when the hands are turned backward, prevents the pallets leaving the escape wheel.

SAFETY PINION. A center pinion which allows the barrel to recoil when the mainspring breaks.

SAPPHIRE FILE. A piece of flat brass to which a piece of sapphire, previously flattened, is attached by means of shellac. It is used for working upon garnet pallets and other soft stones. The sapphire is ground upon a diamond mill, and its surface rendered coarse, or fine, according to the mill used. A strip of copper and diamantine is sometimes used instead of sapphire files.

SCREWS. Odd sized screws, not to be had from the material dealers, may be readily made by means of the screw plate and rose cutter. The rose cutter is quite a valuable adjunct to the lathe, and is fixed to the spindle in the same manner as the chuck, and will be found exceedingly useful for quickly reducing pieces of wires for screws, etc., to a gauge. For screws, the wire should be of a proper size for the screw heads, and a cutter selected with the hole the size of the finished screw. The point of the wire is rounded to enter the hole of the cutter, against which it is forced by the back center of the lathe, the serrated face of the cutter rapidly cutting the superfluous metal, the part intended for the screw passing into the hole in the cutter. Some care is required in rounding the point of the wire, for if not done equally all around, the screw will not be true to the head.

To Remove Broken Screws. It sometimes happens that a screw gets broken off in a watch plate in such a manner that it is impossible to remove it with tools without marring the plate. In such an event proceed as follows: Put enough rain water into a glass tumbler to thoroughly cover the plate and add sulphuric acid until the water tastes a sharp sour. Place the plate in the solution and allow it to remain a few hours, when the screw will partially dissolve and drop out. Remove from the solution, wash thoroughly in clean water, then in alcohol and dry in saw dust. The solution will not injure the brass plate or gilding in the slightest, but care must be taken to remove all other screws or cement jewels, previous to immersion.

Any one having an American lathe can, with small expense of time and labor, make a small attachment which will easily and quickly remove a broken screw from the plate or pillar of any watch.

Take two common steel watch keys having hardened and tempered pipes—size, four or five—having care that the squares in each are of the same size and of good depth. Cut off the pipes about half an inch from the end; file up one of these for about one-half its length, on three equal sides, to fit one of the large split chucks of the lathe. Drill a hole in one of the brass centers of the lathe of sufficient size and depth, into which insert the other key-pipe, and fasten with a little solder. Soften a piece of Stubs' wire, to work easily in the lathe, and turn down for an eighth of an inch from the end to a size a little smaller than the broken screw in the plate; finish with a conical shoulder, for greater strength, and cross-file the end with a fine slot or knife-edge file, that the tool may not slip on the end of the broken screw; cut off the wire a half inch from the end and file down to a square that will fit closely in one of the key-pipes. Make a second point like the first one and fit it to the other key-pipe; harden in oil, polish, and temper to a dark straw color. Fit the brass center into the tail stock. To use, put the tools in place in the lathe, place the broken end of the screw against the end of the point in the lathe head; slide up the back center and fasten the point firmly against the other end of the screw, that it may not slip or turn; revolve the plate slowly, and the broken screw, being held fast between the two points will be quickly removed. To remove a broken pillar screw, place the broken screw against the point in the lathe-head, holding the plate firmly with the right hand, the pillar on a line with the lathe center; turn the lathe-head slowly backward with the left hand, and the screw will be removed. Should the tool slip on the broken screw, and fail to draw it out, drill a hole in the pillar in the lower or dial side, down to the screw point (if the size of the pillar from the plate will admit of so doing), and with the second point in the back center, remove the screw in the same manner as the plate screw in the first process. Five or six sizes of these points will be found sufficient for the majority of these breakages that may occur. See *Screw Extractor*.

To Blue Screws. See *Blueing Pan.*

Left-Handed Screws. A screw plate for left-handed screws can easily be made by screwing a good piece of steel of the desired size into a right-handed screw plate, removing, filing down on two sides, to leave only a knife edge, and hardening. Drill hole in steel plate and cut with the screw described by turning with reverse or left-handed motion. Left-handed screws can be made very successfully with this plate.

SCREW DRIVER. A well made and light screw driver is an important tool to the watchmaker. The point should be well polished and of a width nearly equal to the diameter of the screw head. One of

Fig. 246.

the best forms on the market is the Waltham, shown in Fig. 246. It has four different sizes of blades which are readily adjusted to position.

Screw drivers, are sometimes made in sets, the various width of blades being readily detected on the bench, as the color of the handle of each width is different.

SCREW EXTRACTOR. The Bullock Screw Extractor, shown in Fig. 247, is a simple yet very valuable accessory to the watchmaker, who finds he has a plate in which a screw has been broken off. To use this tool, first fasten it in your vice, then bring one end of broken or

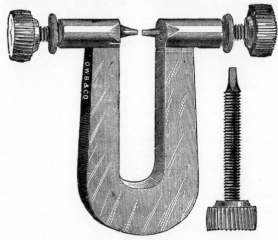

Fig. 247.

rusted-in screw against screw center and the broken screw head against screw driver; turn the washers so as to hold the broken screw firmly in place; turn the plate gently, and the broken screw will follow the screw driver point out of the plate. It may be necessary in some instances to turn the screw driver point against the broken head with a good deal of force in order to start the screw. A little benzine or kerosene applied to the screw will help to loosen it.

SCREW HEAD SINK CUTTER. This tool is not kept by material dealers, although a tool which somewhat resembles it, known as the countersinker, is. The countersinker does not have the central pivot for centering up by. We sometimes have American watches brought to us with the end-stone (cap jewel), broken, and a new one must be put in. The jewel, being set in brass, is held by two screws on opposite sides, the screw heads being let in, or sunk even with the surface, half of the screw head projecting over on the end-stone. The end-stones furnished by the watch companies are not sunk for these screw heads, but are round and of the proper diameter. These cutters will cut away from the jewel the space to be occupied by the screw head in a very few moments, and as perfectly as you like. All the American companies do not use the same diameter of screw head in the cock and potence, consequently you will be compelled to make a separate tool for the Waltham, Elgin, Hampden, Illinois, and other makes of watches, where the sizes are different. With a set of six of these cutters you can fit any American watch. They are easily made, and will repay you for the trouble.

Cut off a piece of wire of the required diameter, about one inch long, and place it in a chuck that fits it snugly, and turn one end to a center about forty degrees. Now reverse the wire in the chuck, and be sure it

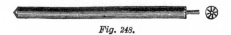

Fig. 248.

is true; select a drill that will pass through the screw hole in the cock or potence freely, and proceed to drill a hole in the center of the end of the wire, about one-sixteenth of an inch deep. Remove from the lathe, and with a sharp file and graver, proceed to cut a series of teeth as equal and even as possible. Use a good strong glass while working, and be sure you have every tooth sharp and perfect, as upon this depends the quick and nice work you expect from the tool. When this is well done, proceed to temper fairly hard, and polish up the outside to make it look workmanlike. Now select a piece of steel pivot wire, of a size that will almost fit in the hole drilled in the end of the tool, and polish down to the proper size to drive in the hole tightly. Allow this wire to project about one-sixteenth of an inch, taper the point and polish. The tool being completed, you are ready for work.

Select an end-stone of a diameter to fit tightly in the cock or potence, as may be required; place the hole jewel in place, and then the end-stone pressed down tightly against the hole jewel. Place your cutter in a split chuck that fits true; select a small or medium sized drill rest and place in the tail-stock spindle. Hold the cock or potence, with the jewels in place, against the drill rest, level, and proceeding to run the lathe at a fair speed, slowly feed the cock or potence to the cutter, the projecting pivot in the end of the cutter passing through the screw hole, and acting as a guide to keep the cutter in the center of the hole. Caution must be exercised, or you will cut the recess for the screw heads too deep, as these little cutters are very deceiving, and cut much faster than you would suppose. In fitting an end-stone, select one that is more than flush when the jewel hole and end-stone are in the proper position, and after sinking the screw head as described, turn off on the lathe almost flush or level. Make a small dot on one side of the end-stone, as a mark or guide in replacing it. Remove the end-stone and proceed to polish the top of the setting on a plate glass polisher.

SCREW PLATE.   A plate of hard steel in which are threaded holes of various sizes, for making screw threads.

SCREW TAP.   A tool for producing screw threads in holes.

SECONDS HAND REMOVER AND HOLDER.   The minuteness of the second hand makes it very difficult to manipulate. The little tool shown in Fig. 249 will be found very useful in handling these hands.   To use it, raise the spring with the thumb, and push the

Fig. 249.

tool along the dial astride the arbor; then let go the spring and raise the tool. The spring will hold the second hand firmly until replaced. For broaching, hold the tool, spring side down, firmly on bench or vice.

SECONDS HAND SETTING.   This improvement in watches is very useful, as it prevents a number of accidents or errors in the regulation.   The attempt to open the glass-bezel of the watch to turn the second hand with a pocket knife or other instrument to the right position, to make it correspond with the minute hand, should be avoided, as the second hand may be shifted or loosened on the pivot, or the ends of the hand may be bent so as to catch the other hands, which causes frequently the stopping of the watch; or instead of the front, the back of the watch is opened and with a penknife or pin, the balance is stopped, and it or hairspring may be easily bent, or even a pivot, jewel or end stone broken.   It is at any rate not good to touch a fine balance with any instrument whatever, to scratch the same, or even to stop the same, for the purpose of having the second hand in the proper position, because the most careful operator may accidently drop something into the watch, causing either stoppage or troubles of irregularities in the running or time keeping.

In the corresponding figures the invention is illustrated as applied to to pendant-set watches of well known construction. The second hand is attached to a small wheel *1*, placed upon a thin steel cannon, that fits firmly to the seconds-wheel pivot, as shown in Fig. 250. The stem-winding wheels are placed under the yoke, and the crown-wheel, intermediate winding-wheel, and the setting-wheel, as usual. The wheels *6*, *5*, *4* and *3* are flat, pivoted to the watch-plate, and are used to connect the small wheel *2* with the said stem-winding wheels. This wheel *2* is applied to a rocking-lever and held out of gear with the seconds-set wheel *1*, by the short arm of the lever resting against the circular edge of the yoke. The said lever is pivoted upon wheel *5*, to the watch-plate, and has a weighted arm *W*, which forms a weight to the lever, so that the same can change its position, by gravity, when the watch is held with its stem downward.   This is done when the seconds are required to be set.   The weighted part then holds the rocking-lever against the edge of the yoke, which is provided with a notch or stop *s*.   In the downward position, the stem is pulled outwardly, and the yoke is moved by the usual spring and mechanism, to the position shown in Fig. 251, to an *intermediate* position between the setting and winding positions, or plainly said, the winding-wheel *I* just passes freely the barrel-arbor wheel *B* and the setting-wheel is not yet engaged to the dial-wheel *D*.   The movement of the yoke being stopped by its notch or stop *s* coming in contact with the rocking-lever, which, by the gravity of its weighted part bearing against the edge of the yoke, *drops into* its notch *s*, thereby stopping the yoke on its way toward the setting position.   When the lever is caught by the notch *s* the same is turned on its pivot, so that its wheel *2*

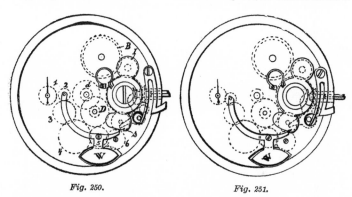

Fig. 250.   Fig. 251.

is brought in gear with the seconds setting-wheel *1*, and by turning the stem now, the second hand can be turned forward or backward to any second of the dial.   By doing this the watch can be held in any desired position, either horizontal or with its stem up, as it must be understood, that the lever is now held firmly into the notch of the yoke by the pressure or the yoke spring, which the weight of the lever cannot overcome, and therefore a sure connection is established between the second setting-wheel and the stem-arbor of the watch.   When the seconds hand has been adjusted, an *immediate* disconnection of the wheel *2* from the seconds wheel *1* is established by pressing the stem arbor inwardly, whereby the yoke is shifted or swung to the winding position, and the notch *s* away from the rocking lever, which is turned upon the edge of the yoke to its normal position as shown in Fig. 250. If the minute hand has to be set solely, the stem is pulled outwardly as usual, whereby the watch is held in any position except that with its stem downward, (which is only done in case the seconds hand has to be set, to produce the dropping of the rocking-lever into the notch *s*), and stops the yoke in its motion before reaching the setting position.   In holding the watch in the usual position, the weighted rocking-lever always passes *over* the notch and is held on the circular edge of the notch in this position, but the yoke can freely swing to its setting position, that is, its setting-wheel is brought fully in engagement with the dial-wheel for setting the minute hand. The second hand can either be operated before or after the setting of the minute hand, at will.

The Figs. 250 and 251 represent an Elgin 16 size open face pendant-set watch. Fig. 252 represents a Waltham 18 size pendent-set watch. The weight *W* is shown herein separated from the working-lever, that controls the wheel 2.   The stop *s* on the yoke is formed aside from the notch arranged into the circular edge of the yoke and the rocking-lever is always pressed against the same by a suitable spring.   The wheel *2* is

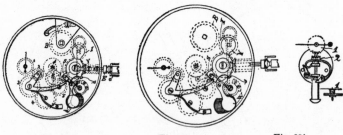

Fig. 252.   Fig. 253.   Fig. 254.

held out of gear with the seconds-setting wheel *1* as long as the said notch is not engaged by the rocking-lever, this being only the case, by first holding the watch with its stem *E* down, so that the weighted part *W* can engage the stop *s*, which is brought toward and against the same, when the stem is pulled outwardly. In this position the notch of the yoke is exactly moved in line with the end of the rocking lever and engaged thereby, which is turned with its wheel *2* out of connection with the seconds-set wheel *1*, as shown in Fig. 252. In pressing the stem inwardly, the yoke is again brought back to the winding position as usual and the notch away from said rocking-lever, which is thereby turned with its wheel *2* out of connection with the wheel *1*.   When the minutes are to be set, hold the watch in any position except with the stem downward, and pull the stem outwardly. The motion of the yoke is then produced by its spring to its fullest turn, that is, the setting-wheel *S* is brought in connection with the dial-wheel *D*, as usual.   It will thus be seen, that as long as the rocking-wheel is held against the circular edge of the yoke, the wheel *2* is held out of gear of wheel *1*, and can only connect with the same when the yoke is shipped around sufficiently and stopped by the weight, and this can be done only by pulling the stem out so that the notch can come in line with the end of the rocking-lever, which moves into the same and receives thereby the motion to set its wheel *2* into gear with wheel *1*.

Fig. 254 is a seconds-setting attachment which can be placed on key or stem winding watches of a peculiar construction. *1* is the seconds-hand wheel and the wheel *2*, which is placed on a small longitudinally movable stem, is shiftable in or out of connection with the said wheel *1* by the outward or inward motion of said stem. The invention was patented March 20, 1888, by Fred Terstegen, of Elizabeth, N. J.

SECTOR. A proportional gauge consisting of two limbs joined together at one end; used principally for sizing wheels and pinions.

SHELLAC. A resinous substance used extensivety by watchmakers and jewelers for holding work. Shellac is a corruption of Shell-lac. *Lac* is the original name of the resinous product which is exuded from an insect which feeds upon the banyan tree. In its natural state it incrusts small twigs and is known as *stick-lac*. It is then broken from the wood and boiled in alkaline water and the product, from its shape, is called *seed-lac*. It is then melted and reduced to thin flakes, known in commerce as *shell-lac* or *shellac*.

SHERWOOD, N. B. A clever mechanic, mathematician and inventor. He was born in New York state in 1823. In 1856 he entered the employ of Mr. Howard in the Waltham factory, and there his inven-

N. B. Sherwood.

tive genius was brought into full play in originating new tools and machines to do the work formerly done by hand. He not only conceived new ideas, but being an excellent draftsman, he placed them on paper and then entering the machine shop he put these machines together. Under his charge the jeweling department of the factory made a complete revolution over the old methods, and new methods and systems of doing work were introduced and the product doubled. Many of the machines and tools used to-day in watch factories were invented and first built by him. Among his many inventions were the counter-sinker or screw-head tool, for jewel screws; the end-shake tools, the opener, and the truing-up tools. In 1864 he interested capitalists and organized the Newark Watch Company. He died in October, 1872.

SIDEREAL CLOCK. A clock adjusted to measure sidereal time. It usually numbers the hours from o to 24. See *Time.*

SIDEREAL DAY. The interval of time between two successive transits over the same meridian of the vernal equinox, or first point of Aries. It is the true period of the earth's rotation. See *Time*.

SILVER. A soft, white, precious metal, very malleable and ductile and capable of taking a high polish. For Silver Plating, see *Electro-Plating*

Separating Silver. The silver-holding alloy or metal is dissolved in the least possible quantity of crude nictric acid. The solution is mixed with a srtong excess of ammonia and filtered into a high cylinder, provided with a stopper. A bright strip of copper, long enough to project beyond the liquid, is next introduced, which quickly causes separation of pure metallic silver. The reduction is completed in a short time, and the reduced silver washed first with some ammoniacal solution and then with distilled water. The more ammoniacal and concentrated the solulution, the more rapid the reduction. The strip of copper should not be too thin, as it is considerably attacked, and any little particles which might separate from a thin sheet would contaminate the silver. The operation is so simple that it seems preferable to all others for such operations as the preparation of nitrate of silver from old coins, etc. Any accompanying gold remains behind during the treatment of the metal or alloy with nitric acid. Chloride of silver, produced by the impurities in the nitric acid, is taken up by the ammoniacal solution, like the copper, and is also reduced to the metallic state; and whatever other metal is not left behind, oxidized by the nitric acid, is separated as hydrate, (lead, bismuth), on treating with ammonia. Any arseniate which may have passed into the ammoniacal solution, is not decomposed by the copper.

To Distingmish Genuine Silver. File or scrape the surface of the articles to be tested, rub the exposed portion on a touchstone and apply a test water consisting of 32 parts of distilled water and 16 parts of chromic acid. Rinse the stone in water and if the article is genuine silver a red spot will be left upon the stone, but if it is an imitation the mark will be unaffected. The finer the quality of the silver the more intense will be the red spot.

Silver Assay with Testing Tube. Place in the tube enough of the pulverized mineral to fill one inch of space, and on this pour nitric acid to occupy two inches more, and hold the mixture over the flame until the acid boils. The acid will dissolve whatever silver may be present, and must be passed through filtering paper to remove extraneous matter, and returned to the tube. Next add a few drops of water saturated with salt; any silver or lead that may be present will be precipitated in a cloudy form to the bottom. Drain off the acid, place the precipitate in the sunlight, and in a few minutes, if 'it contain silver, it will turn to a purple color, and may be again liquified by the addition of spirits of ammonia. The testing tube is formed of thin glass, about five inches long, and less than one inch diameter; bottom and sides of equal thickness. Where the tube is lacking, a cup may be used instead.

Silver Assay by Smelting. If no lead is present, mix 600 grs. of the pulverized ore with 300 grs. carbonate of soda, 600 grs. of litharge, and 12 grains charcoal in a crucible; add a slight coal of borax over all, put on the furnace, melt, take off, give it a few taps to settle the metal, let it cool, and remove the button.

To Clean Silver Plate. The tarnish can be removed by dipping the article from one to fifteen minutes in a pickle of the following composition: Rain water, 2 gallons, and cyanide of potash ½ pound; dissolve together, and fill into a stone jug or jar, and close tightly. The article after having been immersed, must be taken out and thoroughly rinsed in several waters, then dried with fine, clean sawdust. Tarnished jewelry can be speedily restored by this process; but be careful to thoroughly remove the alkali, otherwise it will corrode the goods.

Cleaning Silverware. Hyposulphate of soda is the simplest and most effective cleansing material for·silverware; it operates quickly and is cheap. A rag or brush moistened with the saturated solution of the salt cleanses, strongly oxidized silver surfaces within a few seconds, without the use of cleaning powder.

Cleaning Silver Tarnished in Soldering. Expose to a uniform heat, allow it to cool, and then boil in strong alum water; or, immerse for a considerable length of time in a liquid made of one-half ounce of cyanide of potash to one pint of rain water, and then brush off with prepared chalk.

Cleaning Silver Filigree. Anneal your work over a Bunsen flame or with a blowpipe, then let grow cold (and this is the secret of success), and then put in a pickle of sulphuric acid and water, not more than five drops to one ounce of water, and let your work remain in it for one hour. If not to satisfaction, repeat the process.

To Frost Silver. To produce a frosted surface upon polished silver use cyanide of potassium with a brush; the silver should not be handled during the process, but held between pieces of boxwood or lancewood. The proportion should be, 1 ounce of cyanide of potassium in 1 pint of water.

To Frost Silver. Silver goods may be frosted and whitened by preparing a pickle of sulphuric acid 1 dram, water 4 ounces; heat it and immerse the silver articles until frosted as desired; then wash off clean, and dry with a soft linen cloth, or in fine clean sawdust. For whitening only, a small quantity of acid may be employed.

To Frost Silver. The article has to be carefully annealed either in a charcoal fire, or with a blowpipe before a gas flame, which will oxidize the alloy on the surface, and also destroy all dirt and greasy substances adhering to it, and then boiled in a copper pan containing a solution of of dilute sulphuric acid—of 1 part of acid to about 30 parts of water. The article is then placed in a vessel of clean water, and scratch-brushed, or scoured with fine sand; after which the annealing or boiling-out is repeated which will in most cases be sufficient to produce the desired result. If a very delicate dead surface such as watch dials, etc., is required, the article is, before the second annealing, covered with a pasty solution of potash and water, and immediately after the annealing, plunged in clean water, and then boiled out in either sulphuric acid solution, or a solution of 1 part cream tartar and 2 parts common salt to about 30 parts of water. If the article is of a low quality of silver, it is well to add some silver solution, such as is used for silvering, to the second boiling out solution. If the article is very inferior silver, the finishing will have to be given by immersing it in contact with a strip of zinc in a silver solution.

SINGLE-BEAT ESCAPEMENT. An escapement in which the escape wheel moves only at every alternate vibration of the balance, or pendulum. The chronometer and duplex are the best known examples of single-beat escapements.

SKIVE. A circular saw used for slitting stones. It consists of a disc of iron fixed on a spindle between two collars or nuts. The free part is slightly dished to secure rigidity. Its edge is charged with diamond powder by pressing a hard stone against it, and gently pouring a little powder between the edge of the skive and the stone.

SLIDE REST. The slide rest is a tool holder to be used on a lathe; it is so universally used by all watchmakers that a full description is superfluous. Fig. 256 is a Moseley, and is a fair example of a modern slide rest for watchmakers' use. The tool holder varies with the different makers, but the rests proper are all made on the same general principle; that of two sliding beds working at right angles to one another and carrying a tool holder, capable of being raised, or lowered, or set at any desired angle.

Fig. 256.

SNAIL. A cam resembling a snail in form, used in the striking attachment to clocks.

SNAILING. The ornamentation of the surface of metals by means of circles or bars, sometimes erroneously called damaskeening

SNAP. A small catch, or fastening, as in a bracelet. The fastening of one piece of metal to another by springing of the edges, as in the bezel of a watch case.

SNARL. To emboss or raise figures upon metal work by driving the metal up from the back with a die or snarling iron, as in metal vases.

SNARLING IRON. An $\sim$ shaped steel tool which is used in snarling, or embossing metal vases, etc. One end of the snarling iron is placed in the vise, and the shank being struck with a hammer, the repercussion of the other end drives out the metal. The snarling iron is only used on vases, pitchers, and like hollow ware.

SOLDERING. The act of joining two metallic surfaces by means of a more fusible metal, or metallic cement. Solders are commonly divided into two groups, known as hard solders and soft solders; the former fuse only at a red heat, while the latter fuse at low degrees of heat. In hard soldering, it is frequently necessary to bind the parts to be soldered together with what is known as binding wire, which is made of soft iron, or the repair clamps shown in Fig. 238, or soldering forceps shown in Fig. 257. The blow pipe is used most extensively for soldering, although small soldering irons are used on the larger kinds of work. It is of the utmost importance that the meeting edges of all articles to be soldered be scraped, or chemically cleaned. While soldering, articles are usually placed upon a piece of charcoal, though asbestos, or pumice stone is better for the purpose. Charcoal emits gases from the coal while under the blowpipe, which enter into the alloy of gold or silver and render it brittle. To prove this, reduce a small piece of 10k gold to a liquid form on a piece of charcoal, and treat a piece similarly on a piece of asbestos or pumice stone, and after allowing each to cool, subject both to a heavy pressure, and note the difference in their malleability and ductility.

Hard Solders. Under this name very different alloys are used, depending upon the metals to be united. The following table shows the composition of various hard solders, which have stood a practical test for various purposes:

	Parts Brass	Parts Zinc.	Parts Tin.
Refractory - -	4.00	1.00	
Readily Fusible, - -	5.00	4 00	
Half White, - -	12 00	5.00	1.00
White, - - -	40.00	2 00	8.00
Very Ductile, - - -	78.25	17.25	

Gold Solders. Gold solders should approach the articles to be soldered in both color and fusibility as nearly as possible. The following gold solders are in general use:

	Parts Gold.	Parts Silver.	Parts Copper.	Parts Zinc.
Hard solder for 750 fine -	9.0	2.0	1.0	
Soft solder for 750 " -	12.0	7.0	3.0	
Solder for 583 " -	3.0	2.0	1.0	
Solder for less than 583 " -	2.0	2.0		
Readily Fusible Solder -	11.94	54.74	28.17	5.01
Solder for yellow Gold -	10.0	5.0		1.0

Silver Solders. The following hard silver solders have been thoroughly tested:

	Parts Fine Silver.	Parts Copper.	Parts Brass	Parts Zinc.
First - -	4		3	
Second -	2		1	
Third - -	19	1	10	5
Fourth -	57	28.6		14.3

Soft Solder. The soft solder most frequently used consists of 2 parts of tin and 1 of lead. The following table gives the composition of various soft solders with their respective melting points:

Number.	Parts Tin	Parts Lead.	Melts at Degrees F.	Number.	Parts Tin	Parts Lead.	Melts at Deg. F.
1 - - -	1	25	558	7 - -	1½	1	334
2 - - -	1	10	541	8 - -	2	1	340
3 - - -	1	5	511	9 - -	3	1	356
4 - - -	1	3	482	10 - -	4	1	365
5 - - -	1	2	441	11 - -	5	1	378
6 - - -	1	1	37	12 - -	6	1	380

Aluminium Solder. The following alloys are recommended for the purpose: 1. Melt twenty parts of aluminium in a suitable crucible, and when in fusion add 80 parts zinc. When the mixture is melted, cover the surface with tallow, and maintain in quiet fusion for some time, stirring occasionally with an iron rod; then pour into moulds. 2. Take 15 parts of aluminum and 85 parts zinc, or 12 parts of the former and 88 parts of the latter, or 8 parts of the former and 92 parts of the latter; prepare all of them as specified for No. 1. The flux recommended consists of three parts balsam copaiba, one of Venetian turpentine, and a few drops of lemon juice. The soldering iron is dipped into this mixture.

Soldering Fluxes. For hard solder use borax rubbed to a paste with water on a slate. For soft soldering dissolve a small piece of zinc in pure hydrochloric acid until effervescence ceases. Take out the undissolved zinc after 24 hours, filter the solution, add $\frac{1}{3}$ its volume of spirits of sal-ammoniac and dilute with rain water. This fluid is non-corrosive.

Soft Solder for Smooth Surfaces. Where two smooth surfaces are to be soldered one upon the other, you may make an excellent job by moistening them with the fluid, and then, having placed a sheet of tin foil between them, hold them pressed firmly together over your lamp until the foil melts. If the surface is fitted nicely, a joint may be made in this way so close as to be almost imperceptible. The bright looking lead, which comes as a lining for tea boxes, is better than tin foil,

To Dissolve Soft Solder. Nitric acid may be used safely for gold not lower than 12k, and is very effective. The following is suitable for all grades of gold and silver: Green copperas, 2 oz.; saltpeter, 1 oz., reduced to a powder and boiled in 10 oz. of water. It will become crystalized on cooling. Dissolve these crystals by the addition of 8 parts of spirits of salts to each part of crystals, using an earthenware vessel. Add 4 parts of boiling water, keep the mixture hot, and immerse the article to be operated upon, and the solder will be entirely removed without injuring the work.

Soldering Stone Set Rings. There are various ways for doing this, but the following will be found as good as any: Take tissue paper and tear it into strips about three inches wide, twist them into ropes, and then make them very wet and wrap the stone with them, passing around the stone and through the ring until the center of the ring is a little more than half full of paper, always winding very close, and then, fasten upon charcoal, allowing the stone to project over the edge of the charcoal, and solder very quickly. The paper will prevent oxidation upon the part of the ring it covers, as well as protecting the stone.

SOLDERING FORCEPS. By the use of this ingenious device, any article to be repaired can be adjusted in any desired position in a much shorter time, and with more accuracy, than by the ordinary process of binding with wire to a piece of charcoal. The Crane Patent Soldering Forceps are so constructed that any two pieces can be as readily brought together as can be done with the fingers, no matter at what angle or position you may desire them. Each part works independent of the

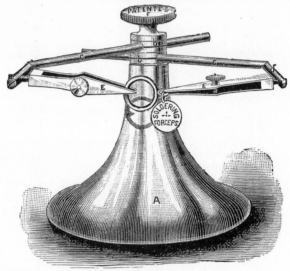

Fig. 257.

other, and the whole is held securely in place by means of a nut, as shown in Fig. 257, at *F*, and both hands being free, charcoal can be held behind the article, thereby concentrating the heat, the same as when held directly upon it. In soft soldering it can be used to great advantage.

The forceps *E E*, revolve in parts *d d*, which are fastened to arms *C C*, by means of a hinge joint. The arms *C C* run through the collars *b b*, so that they can be lengthened or shortened, and the forceps raised or lowered as desired. The collars *b b* turn independently of each other on base *A*, and being split, the whole is held firmly in position by nut *F*. See also *Tweezers*.

SOLDERING PADS. Figs. 258 to 260 illustrate Melotte's non-conducting soldering pads, which are reversible, and adapted to contain a small crucible and ingot mould on one side, a removable rim, shown in Fig. 258; a detachable handle, and various spring clamps as shown. Fig.

260 illustrates Melotte's new gas olow-pipe, which is used with these pads. This blow-pipe is simple and convenient, and, as will be seen by consulting the illustration, it consists of a blow-pipe of the ordinary form having a gas pipe inserted in the lower half, and a threaded hood or sleeve at the lower end, which changes the shape of the flame by screwing in or out, so as to vary the

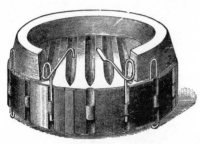

Fig. 258.

influence of the current of air upon the flame. A ring adapted to slip over the finger while working, is soldered to the middle joint of the pipe, and the quantity of gas is controlled by the stop-cock and

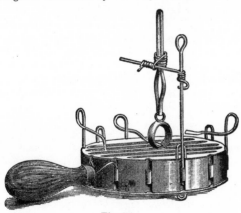

Fig. 259.

spring lever shown in the cut, the gas being supplied to the pipe by a rubber tube connecting it to the nearest gas jet in the usual way. Thus having the shape of the flame under control, and

Fig. 260.

the quantity variable at will, the workman is in position to accomplish the desired end speedily and effectually.

To use to the best advantage, set the jamb-nut so that with the valve lever in its normal position, the flame at the end of the pipe will just keep alight. The blow-pipe can then be laid down temporarily, and again used without the trouble of turning off the gas or relighting.

When used as a mouth blow-pipe, the most convenient way to hold it is with the third finger through the ring. For bellows work it is better to pass the ring over the index finger. The ring also serves, with the valve-lever, as a rest to hold the flame-nozzle away from the table when the blow-pipe is laid down temporarily.

To produce an oxy-hydrogen flame, connect the air-pipe with a cylinder of nitrous oxide, opening the cylinder-valve carefully, so as to permit the escape of only sufficient nitrous oxide to produce, with the illuminating gas, a very small flame. Regulate the illuminating gas flow with

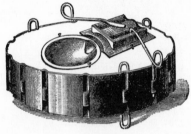

Fig. 261.

the thumb-screw, or with the finger on the lever of the blow-pipe valve.

For soldering, use the grooved face of the pad, with or without the removable rim (shown in Fig. 258), according to the work. The wire staples answer the double purpose of holding the removable rim in place and raising the pad from the table, with air-space underneath.

The spring-clamps are useful in holding the parts to be soldered, the loops in the metal band around the pad permitting them to be placed in any desired position.

For melting, use the reverse side of the pad, with the depression for melting-cup. Fig. 261 shows the melting-cup and ingot-mould in place. The shield is a flat piece of metal, with a lip at one end. The small melting-cups should always be used, as flux adheres to the pad, and pulls off particles of the fiber. The cup is held in place by two pins, inserted in the pad on either side, with the head bent over the edge of the cup. Place the shield upon the pad, with the lip in the depression underneath the edge of the cup; and fasten securely by placing pins through the notches in the edges. Then place the ingot-mold upon the shield, with the mouth of the proper matrix opposite the lip in the cup. To insure a smooth ingot, the ingot-mold should be slightly warmed, and oiled or waxed. After the metal is melted, tilt the pad gradually, carrying the metal toward the mold, and pour quickly. The handle of the pad can be attached at any point.

SPECIFIC GRAVITIES. The following table shows the specific gravities of numerous metals employed in the arts, together with their melting points, malleability, ductility, and tenacity.

Metals.	Specific Gravity.	Melting Points.		Order of Mallea-bility.	Order of Ductility.	Tena-city.*
		Fahrenheit	Centig'de			
Platinum___	21.40 to 21.50	Infusible except by the Oxyhydrogen blow-pipe.		6	3	274
Gold_____	19.25 to 19.50	2016°	1102°	1	1	150½
Mercury____	13.56 to 13.59					
Lead_____	11.40 to 11.45	612°	322°	7	9	27½
Silver_____	10.47 to 10.50	1873°	1023°	2	2	187
Bismuth____	9.82 to 9.90	497°	258°			
Copper_____	8.89 to 8.96	1994°	1090°	3	5	302
Nickel_____	8 40 to 8.60	2700°	1482°	10	10	
Iron_____	7.77 to 7.80	2786°	1530°	9	4	549
Tin_____	7.25 to 7.30	442°	228°	5	8	34½
Zinc_____	6.80 to 7.20	773°	412°	8	7	109½
Antimony_._	6.75 to 6.80	A little below red heat.				
Arsenic____ _	5.70 to 5.90	Volatilizes below fusing.				
Aluminium_	2.56 to 2.60	1300°	705°	4	6	300

SPECTACLE TOOL. Nearly every watchmaker knows what a troublesome thing it is to repair spectacle frames. When soldered, the solder will run through and fill the groove for the glass, and it is no easy matter to cut the solder out of the groove with a graver. The graver will slip, scratch and mar the frames in spite of the greatest care. This spectacle tool will cut out the groove in gold, silver, steel or any other spectacle frames in a moment's time, smoothly and perfectly. This tool is not for sale by material dealers, but can be made by any ingenious watchmaker. Take a piece of Stubs' polished steel wire, say number 40 by steel wire gauge, and one and a fourth inches long. Insert the wire in a chuck in your lathe, allowing the end to project about one-fourth inch; proceed to turn both ends to a center, as shown in Fig. 262. Select two female centers of the proper size; place one in the taper chuck of your lathe and the other in the tail stock spindle; fasten a dog on the piece of wire, and proceed to turn the wire even and straight throughout its entire length. Remove from the lathe, select a

*Number of lbs. sustained by 0.787 of a line in diameter in wires of the various metals.

split chuck that will fit snugly, place the wire in the chuck, allowing about three-eighths of an inch to project; remove the T rest of your lathe, and insert in its stead a filing fixture. By the aid of the index on the lathe pulley and the filing fixtures, proceed to square the end of the wire, (about one-fourth inch), of a size to fit in an American ratchet wheel. Now select two ratchets of the same thickness and size and place them on the square cut on the wire. Proceed to round up the balance of the square not occupied by the ratchets, and with the screw plate cut a nice full thread on the end up to the square. Now cut off a small piece of steel wire, the same in diameter as the body of the tool, true it in your lathe chuck and drill a hole in the center about one-eighth inch deep. With a screw tap, of the proper size to fit the screw on the end of

Fig. 262.

the shaft, which is now a small spindle, tap a good thread in the hole. This short piece is intended for a nut. With a graver cut it off to the desired length, replace the two ratchets and screw on the nut; replace the spindle in your lathe and turn up the nut round and true. While in the lathe, square half the length of the nut on two sides only. This is intended for a grab or hold for your pliers in removing the nut from the spindle. You can vary the width of the cut by using two or three ratchets as is desired. In order to make the groove rounding, the shape of the spectacle glass, hold an oil stone to the edge of the ratchets while revolving, which will round them very slightly. American ratchet wheels make good cutters and any width of groove can be cut. When the teeth get dull they can easily be sharpened or new wheels can be substituted. With this tool you can cut the solder out of spectacle frames in a few minutes. It will also prove useful in enlarging spectacle frames, in fitting new lenses.

SPLIT SECONDS. A variety of double chronograph in which there are two center-seconds hands.

SPRUNG OVER. A watch in which the hairspring is attached to the staff above the balance.

STAFF. An axis or arbor.

STAKE. An anvil. To fasten by means of a stake.

STAKING TOOL. A tool needed by every watchmaker, consisting of a shifting table or stake, around which holes of various sizes are arranged in a circle, so that any desired hole may be brought under a suitable punch moving in a vertical holder. Usually twenty-four tempered steel punches and four stumps are provided, which will be found sufficient to cover all the operations in the ordinary run of watch repairs,

Fig. 263.

and the ingenious workman can from time to time add to these by making punches in his spare moments, if he finds from experience that he is in need of punches of a different shape. Fig. 263 illustrates the Johanson combination staking tool on the front of which a hairspring stud indicator is arranged.

STAKING TOOL AND ANVIL. Smith's patent staking tool, anvil and screw holder, shown in Fig. 264, will be found a very handy

Fig. 264.

tool for removing and putting on rollers, for putting hairspring collet on balance staff, or for riveting in bushings. The plain staking block, or anvil, is usually made of a solid piece of polished steel, in the form of a cube, or circular as in Fig. 265. The example shown has a reversible center hub which makes it valuable for putting on hands, etc.

STAR WHEEL. The wheel of the stop work which is pivoted to the barrel and also known as the Maltese cross.

STEADY PINS. Pins used to secure two pieces of metal in relative positions, as a bridge and plate.

STEEL. Iron, when combined with a small portion of carbon. The varieties of steel are very great. Puddled steel is made from pig iron by a modification of the puddling process. Cast steel is made from wrought

iron or blister steel by mixing it with powdered charcoal, after which it is melted in a crucible, cast into ingots and rolled or hammered into plates or bars. Blister steel is made from wrought iron by interlaying it with charcoal and keeping it at a high temperature for a number of days.

Fig. 265.

Bessemer steel is made from the liquid cast iron as it comes from the smelting furnace by blowing air into it, thus burning out a portion of the carbon.

To Anneal Steel. There are nearly as many methods of annealing as there are workmen. The commonest methods are as follows: Heat to a dull red, bury in warm iron filings or ashes, and allowing the article to cool very gradually. Another method is to heat the piece as slowly as possible, and when at a low red heat put it between two pieces of dry board and screw them tightly in a vise. The steel burns its way into the wood, and on coming together around it they form a practically airtight charcoal bed. Brannt gives the following method, which he says will make steel so soft that it can be worked like copper: Pulverize beef bones, mix them with equal parts of loam and calves' hair and stir the mixture into a thick paste with water. Apply a coat of this to the steel and place it in a crucible, cover this with another, fasten the two together with wire and close the joint hermetically with clay. Then put the crucible in the fire and heat slowly. When taken from the fire let it cool by placing it in ashes. On opening the crucible the steel will be found so soft that it can be engraved like copper.

To Anneal Small Steel Pieces. Place the articles from which you desire to draw the temper into a common iron clock key. Fill around

it with brass or iron filings, and then plug up the open end with a steel
iron or brass plug, made to fit closely. Take the handle of the key with
your pliers and hold its pipe into the blaze of a lamp till red hot, then let
it cool gradually. When sufficiently cold to handle, remove the plug,
and you will find the article with its temper fully drawn, but in all other
respects just as it was before. The reason for having the article thus
plugged up while passing it through the heating and cooling process is,
that springing always results from the action of changeable currents of
atmosphere. The temper may be drawn from cylinders. staffs, pinions,
or any other delicate pieces by this mode with perfect safety.

Hardening and Tempering Steel. The process of heating steel to a
red heat and immediately chilling it is the same among all workmen, but
the agents employed for chilling are very numerous. The receipts here
given are from various sources, and the reader must adopt the one which
he finds on trial, is the best adapted to his wants.

In all cases the object should be heated to a red heat before plunging. If an object to be hardened is long and slender, it should
invariably be inserted in the hardening compound end-wise, otherwise it
will come out warped and distorted. The same rule applies to thin or
flat objects. A preparation is used in hardening, consisting of one tea-
spoonful of wheat flour, two of salt and four of water. The steel to be
hardened, is to be heated sufficiently, dipped into the mixture, to be
coated therewith, then raised to a red glow, and dropped into cold soft
water. Another method is to raise the object to the required heat and
then drop it into a mixture of ten parts of mutton suet, two parts of sal-
ammoniac, five parts resin and thirty-five parts olive oil. Oil, tallow,
beeswax and resin are also employed for hardening. If an intense brittle
hardness is desirable, drop the object into mercury or nitric acid. In heating very small or thin objects, they should be placed between two thin
pieces of charcoal and the whole brought to the required heat. In this
way you avoid uneven heating and hence it will be uniformly tempered.
When it is desirable to harden an article without discoloring its surface,
it should be placed in a metal tube or bowl of a clay pipe, and surrounded
with charcoal that has been previously heated to expel all moisture, and
when raised to the proper heat the whole should be immersed in the
hardening liquid.

Mat for Steel. The article to be treated must first be ground flat
and free from scratches in the usual manner. When this is accomplished take oil stone powder, mix it with oil and then add a little bluestone powder. Grinding is performed best upon a composition or iron
plate, or a file of the same material; glass is not as well suited for the
purpose. A large quantity of grinding powder and oil should be used.
Very hard articles take a good mat grinding with difficulty, and whenever possible it is advisable to anneal them blue.

Do not press too hard in grinding; the small grains of oilstone should assume a rolling motion, whereby they will to a certain extent, wear hollows with their sharp edges in the surface of the steel, all of which together will impart the handsome, mat appearance. If too much pressure is brought to bear, and the grinding material is too dry, it will cake on the steel and produce the disagreeable scratched surface so often seen.

The quantity of bluestone necessary for grinding can be scraped off from a large piece, after which the scrapings must be thoroughly crushed. The oilstone powder must not be too fine and should be of uniform grain. The proportions are 1 part of bluestone to 4 of oilstone powder.

Tempering. Before tempering, the surface of the object must be thoroughly cleaned and freed from grease by the application of oilstone dust, emery, or some like scouring agent. The object should not be handled with the fingers after cleaning, or it will be difficult to obtain the requisite tint. The following table by Stodart will be valuable to the student:

1	430° F	Very Pale Straw Yellow_____	220° C
2	450° F	A Shade Darker Yellow_____	235° C
3	470° F	Darker Straw Yellow_____	245° C
4	490° F	Still Darker Straw Yellow_____	255° C
5	500° F	Brown Yellow_____	260° C
6	520° F	Yellow tinged with Purple_____	270° C
7	530° F	Light Purple_____	275° C
8	550° F	Dark Purple_____	290° C
9	570° F	Dark Blue_____	300° C
10	590° F	Paler Blue_____	310° C
11	610° F	Still Paler Blue_____	320° C
12	630° F	Light Bluish Green_____	335° C

After letting an object down to the required color it should be allowed to cool gradually, and no artificial means used to hasten the cooling. A piece of steel may be let down to the same color several times without in any way injuring it or altering its properties. Tempering of small articles is performed satisfactorily by means of the bluing pan. (See Fig. 38). Small articles are also tempered by placing them in a vessel, say a large spoon, covering them with oil and heating them to the requisite degree. This is a favored method of tempering balance staffs and similar articles. The temper is usually judged by the color of the smoke; Saunier gives the following rule: When smoke is first seen to rise, the temper is dark yellow (or No. 2). Smoke more abundant and darker (No. 5). Black smoke still thicker (No. 7). Oil takes fire when lighted paper is presented to it at No. 9. After this the oil takes fire of itself and continues to burn. If the whole of the oil is allowed to burn away No. 12 is reached.

The Color of Steel at Various Degrees of Temperature. The following table gives the temperature corresponding to the various colors of steel when heated.

1	980° F	Incipient Red	525° C
2	1290° F	Dull Red	700° C
3	1470° F	Incipient Cherry Red	800° C
4	1650° F	Cherry Red	900° C
5	1830° F	Clear Cherry Red	1000° C
6	2010° F	Deep Orange	1100° C
7	2190° F	Clear Orange	1200° C
8	2370° F	White	1300° C
9	2550° F	Bright White	1400° C

Combined Hardening and Tempering. M. Caron, with a view to combining the two operations of hardening and tempering, suggested that the temperature of the water used for hardening, be heated to a predetermined degree. Thus the requisite temper may be given to gunlock springs by heating the water in which they are hardened to 55° C., or 130° F.

To Work Hard Steel. If steel is rather hard under the hammer, when heated to the proper cherry red, it may be covered with salt and hammered to about the shape desired. More softness can then be obtained, if required to give a further finish to the shape, by sprinkling it with a mixture of salt, blue vitriol, sal-ammoniac, saltpeter and alum; make cherry red again, sprinkle with this mixture, and hammer into shape. This process may be repeated until entirely finished. When ready, the steel is hardened in a solution of the same mixture. This method is recommended by prominent workers.

To Remove Rust. Kerosene oil (refined petroleum), or benzine are the best agents for the removal of rust, where the object is not pitted. When pitted, however, it can only be removed by mechanical means such as scouring with emery powder and oil.

To Prevent Rust. Rub the article with a mixture of lime and oil, or a mixture of equal parts of carbolic acid and olive oil, or with plumbago.

Anti-rust Varnish for Steel. The rusting of steel and iron tools and instruments is very perfectly prevented by coating them with a varnish made by dissolving 1 part white wax in 15 parts benzine, and applying with a brush. The very thin layer of wax forms a perfect covering for bright tools and when desired is very easily removed.

Browning or Bronzing for Steel. Aqua fortis and sweet spirits niter, each half an ounce, sulphate copper 2 ounces, water 30 ounces, tincture muriate of iron 1 ounce. Mix.

To Protect Steel from Rust. Immerse in a solution of carbonate of potash for a few minutes and it will not rust for years, not even when exposed to damp atmosphere.

To Temper Small Steel Articles. The tempering of small drills, for drilling holes in arbors, staffs, etc., which we find are very hard and difficult to perforate, may be effected in the following manner: After having filed the drill to its proper size (being careful not to flatten the cutting face), you then warm it moderately, not allowing it to become red, and run it into borax. The drill is thus coated over with a crust of borax and secluded from the air. Now it may be hardened by heating it only cherry red; after this it is inserted into a piece of borax, or what is better still, plunged into mercury; taking care not to breathe the mercury fumes. Drills prepared in this way, without being brittle, will become exceedingly hard and the watchmaker will be enabled to drill articles which could not otherwise be perforated with a drill. Do not use broken broaches to make your drills, as the steel in them is often burned, rendering the metal unfit for use in small tools. In order to make the quality of your drill a certainty, always take a new piece of round steel for the purpose.

To Harden Steel in Petroleum. According to B. Morgossy, the articles to be hardened are first heated in a charcoal fire, and, after thoroughly rubbing with ordinary washing soap, heated to a cherry red. In this condition they are plunged into petroleum; ignition of the petroleum need not be feared if no flame is near at hand. Articles hardened by this method show no crack, do not warp if plunged endwise, and after hardening remain nearly white, so they can be blued without further preparation.

Hardening Liquids. If water is used for hardening, 32° F. will be found about right for the sized articles hardened by watchmakers, and if the article is very small, ice may be added to the water. A solution composed of 1 quart of water, 1¼ lbs. of sal-ammoniac, 10 oz. of refined borax, 1¼ ozs. red wine, is used extensively for fine cutlery. A mixture of 1 lb. of resin, 3 ozs. of lard, ⅛ lb. train oil and ½ oz. of assafoetida is said to be excellent for fine steel work.

Directions for Plunging when Hardening. Thin articles, as steel plates, or articles of small diameter, such as drills, should always be plunged into the hardening compound, end or edge foremost to avoid warping. If an article is thicker on one side than the other, as a knife blade, the thick side should enter the compound first. Heat the article only as far as you wish to harden it and immerse it as far as it has been made red hot.

Tempering by Electricity. Watch springs have of late years been successfully tempered with the aid of electricity. The steel ribbon is passed through a bath of oil and an electric current of sufficient strength to keep it at the proper heat is passed through the ribbon.   The heating is thus effected without contact with the atmosphere and the spring is not liable to blister as in ordinary methods. The temper is drawn in the same manner and the heat can be controlled to a nicety and is uniform throughout. The spring is then finished by means of rolls.

Glass Polisher for Steel. French plate glass, ground on one side, makes a good polisher for flat work. A piece four inches square, nicely finished on the edge, is about the right size.

Tempering Magnets. M. Ducoetet uses the following process for tempering and magnetizing steel to be used as magnets. Two soft iron pole pieces are placed in the bottom of a water tight vessel and are connected with the poles of a powerful electro-magnet. The vessel is partially filled with water, and oil is poured into the vessel, which floats upon the surface of the water. The red hot bar is then passed through the liquids and comes in contact with the magnets. This softens the steel without depriving it of its power of being magnetized.

To Engrave Name on Steel Tools. Coat the tool or article, if made of iron or steel, with a thin layer of wax, draw the name, initials or design through the wax, exposing the metal, and place the tool in a mixture of 6 parts by weight of water and 1 part of sulphuric acid. In a few hours remove, and if etched sufficiently, wash in clean water and dissolve the wax by heat.

STOGDEN, MATTHEW. Inventor of the half-quarter repeating mechanism most used in English watches. He died in abject poverty, about 1770, at an advanced age.

STOP WORK. The mechanism which prevents the overwinding of a timepiece.

STRAIGHT LINE LEVER. That form of a lever escapement in which the escape wheel arbor, pallet and balance staff are all planted in a straight line, as in Fig. 266.

STUD. A small piece of metal which is slotted to receive the outer coil of the hair spring.

SULLY, HENRY. Born in 1680 and died in 1728. A celebrated watchmaker and the author of a work on horology. He was an an Englishman by birth, though he resided most of the time in France, where he died.

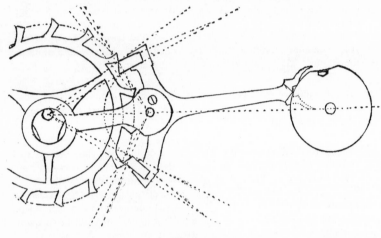

Fig. 266.

SUNK SECONDS. A watch in which the portion of the watch dial traversed by the seconds hand is sunk below the level of the rest of the dial. With sunk seconds, the hour hand may be closer to the dial than it otherwise could.

SURPRISE PIECE. A loose plate under the quarter snail of a repeating watch, which prevents the quarter rack reaching the snail if the mechanism is set going at the hour.

SWEEP SECONDS. A movement in which a long seconds hand moves from the center of the dial instead of at the bottom, as in chronographs and split seconds watches.

TABLE. The roller of a lever escapement that carries the impulse pin.

TAIL STOCK. The sliding block or support in a lathe that carries the tailscrew.

Half Open Tailstock. The half open tailstock shown in Fig. 267, is cut away so that the spindles can be laid in, instead of being passed

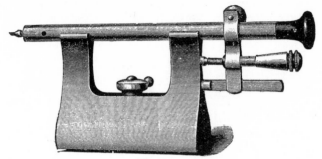

Fig. 267.

through the holes. This fixture will be found exceedingly convenient when several spindles are to be used for drilling, counterboring and chamfering.

Screw Tailstock. This attachment is very convenient for heavy drilling, the spindle being moved by a screw with hand wheel attached, as shown in Fig. 268.

Traverse Spindle Tailstock. This attachment, shown in Fig. 269, will be found very convenient for straight drilling. Where the watch-

Fig. 268

maker has a great deal of drilling to do, he will find this attachment invaluable.

TAVAN, ANTOINE. A celebrated French watchmaker who resided the better part of his life in Geneva. Born at Aost, France, in 1749 and died at Geneva in 1836.

TAVERNIER, LOUIS. A celebrated Parisian watchmaker who lived about 1800. He studied the cylinder escapement with great care and with considerable success.

TESTING NEEDLES. Small strips of steel with gold points, usually running from 4k. to 20k. inclusive, and used in conjunction with a touchstone for determining the quality of gold. The gold to be tested is first rubbed upon the touchstone, and the needle which most closely approximates to it in quality, in the judgment of the operator, is also rubbed upon the stone. The two marks are then treated with nitric acid and the difference in color indicates the difference in quality of the two marks. See *Touchstone*.

Fig. 269.

THIRD WHEEL. The wheel in the train of a watch which lies between the center and fourth wheels.

THIOUT, M. Watchmaker to the Duke of Orleans. In 1741 he published a work called "Traite d'Horlogerie," in two volumes.

THOMAS, SETH. One of the early American manufacturers of clocks. In 1810 Eli Terry sold out his clock factory to Seth Thomas and Silas Hoadley, two of his leading workmen, and this factory was the leading one for many years. The present corporation, known as the Seth Thomas Clock Company, is the direct successor of this humble beginning. March 31, 1853, the Seth Thomas Clock Company was organized with a capital of $75,000. Seth *Seth Thomas.* Thomas died January 20, 1859, being 73 years of age.

THREE-QUARTER PLATE. A watch in which enough of the upper plate is cut away to allow of the balance vibrating on a level with the plate.

TIME. The measure of duration. A particular period of duration. Time is measured by the interval between two successive transits of a celestial body over the same meridian; if measured by the sun, it is called solar time, or if by a star, sidereal time.

Absolute Time. Time irrespective of local standards or epochs; time reckoned for all places from some one common epoch; as all spectators see a lunar eclipse at the same instant of absolute time.

Apparent Time. Time as reckoned by the sun; the instant of the transit of the sun's center over the meridian constituting 12 o'clock.

Astronomical Time. Mean solar time, reckoned by counting the hours continuously up to twenty-four from one noon up to the next.

Civil Time, The reckoning of time for the common purposes of life The division of time into years, months, days, hours and seconds.

Sidereal Time. Time regulated by the transit, over the meridian of a place of the first point of Aries, or the vernal equinox, and chiefly used in astronomical observations.

The sidereal day is 3 m., 56 s. shorter than the mean solar day. The pendulum of a clock, to show sidereal time, must be a trifle shorter than that of one used to show mean time, both clocks having the same train. On or about the 15th of April the two clocks would agree, but from that time on there would be a divergence of 3 m., 56 s. per day. In the absence of a transit instrument and a table giving the right ascension of particular stars, Britten advises the selection of a window having a southern aspect, from which a chimney, or a steeple, or any other fixed

Days.	Stars Gain.			Days,	Stars Gain.		
	Hours.	Minutes.	Seconds.		Hours.	Minutes.	Seconds.
1	0	3	56	11	0	43	15
2	0	7	52	12	0	57	11
3	0	11	48	13	0	51	7
4	0	15	44	14	0	55	3
5	0	19	39	15	0	58	58
6	0	23	35	16	1	2	54
7	0	27	31	17	1	6	50
8	0	31	27	18	1	10	46
9	0	35	23	19	1	14	42
10	0	39	19	20	1	18	38

point, may be seen. To the side of the window attach a thin plate of brass having a small hole in it, in such a manner that by looking through the hole toward the edge of the elevated object, some of the fixed stars may be seen; the progress of one of these being watched, the instant it vanishes behind the fixed point a signal is made to a person observing the clock, who then notes the exact time at which the star disappears, and on the following night the same star will vanish behind the same object 3 m., 56 s. sooner. If a clock mark 10 h. when the observation is made, when the star vanishes the following night it should indicate 3 m., 56 s. less than 10 h. If several cloudy nights have rendered it impossible to compare the clock with the star, it will then be necessary to multiply 3 m., 56 s. by the number of days that have elapsed since the observation, and the product deducted from the hour the clock then indicates gives the time the clock should show. The same star can only be observed during a few weeks, for, as it gains nearly a half hour a week, it will, in a short time, come to the meridian in broad daylight and become invisible; to continue the observation, another star must be selected. In making the observation, care must be taken that a planet is not observed instead of a star; Mars, Jupiter, and Saturn are those most likely to occasion this error, more especially Saturn, which, from being the most distant of the three, resembles a star of the first magnitude. The planets may, however, be easily distinguished, for being comparatively near the earth, they appear larger than the stars; their light also is steady because reflected, while the fixed stars scintillate and have a twinkling light. A sure means of distinguishing between them, is to watch a star attentively for a few nights; if it change its place with regard to the other stars, it is a planet. See *Transit Instrument*.

Solar Time. Sun time. Time marked by the diurnal revolution of the earth with regard to the sun. A mean solar day is the average length of all the solar days in the year. The difference between true and mean time is called the equation of time. There are only four days in the year when the apparent and mean time are the same, and the equation of time nothing. These are December 24th, April 15th, June 15th, and August 31st. Between December 24th and April 15th, and between June 15th and August 31st, the apparent is always before the mean time, whilst in the remaining interval it is later.

TIMING. See *Adjustment*.

TIMING SCREWS. Quarter screws of a compensation balance.

TOMPION, THOMAS. Born in 1638 and died in 1713. He was buried in Westminister Abbey.

Thos. Tompion.

TOUCHSTONE. A piece of black basaltic rock, obtained chiefly from Silesia and used for testing the quality of gold. The piece of gold, or metal to be tested, is drawn upon the surface of the touchstone, and the streak left is treated with nitric acid. Nitric acid eats away the streak, if it is brass or any similar alloy, while if gold only the alloy in the gold is attacked. Testing needles of known alloy are then rubbed on the surface of the touchstone, and treated with the acid, and a comparison made. See *Testing Needles*.

TOURBILLION. A carriage in which the escapement of a watch is fitted, so that it revolves around the fourth wheel. The idea of the tourbillon, one of the almost numberless inventions of Breguet, is to get rid of position errors.

TRAIN. The toothed wheels in a watch or clock that connect the barrel or fusee with the escapement. In a going-barrel watch, the teeth around the barrel drive the center pinion, to which is attached the center wheel; the center wheel drives the third wheel pinion, which carries the third wheel; the third wheel drives the fourth wheel pinion, on which the fourth wheel is mounted; the fourth wheel drives the escape pinion, to which the escape wheel is fixed. The number of teeth in the various wheels and pinions is determined by the following considerations: The center arbor, to which the minute hand is fixed, always turns once in an hour, the fourth wheel, to the arbor of which the seconds hand is fixed, turns once in a minute, so that the product obtained by multiplying together the number of teeth in the center and third wheels must be 60 times the product obtained by multiplying together the numbers of third and fourth pinions. Two other points may be settled before deciding the rest of the train. 1st. The number of turns the barrel makes in 30 hours, which is the time allowed from winding to winding. Four turns would be a suitable number, and in that case the barrel would contain 7½ times the number of teeth in the center pinion. 2nd. The number of vibrations made by the balance in an hour. If 18,000 be decided on, then, assuming the escape wheel to have the usual number of 15 teeth, the escape pinion must make 10 rotations a minute, and the fourth wheel must have 10 times as many teeth as the escape pinion. The barrel teeth and center pinion, which have considerable pressure to bear, must be of adequate strength, but the pitch of the teeth and size of the wheels are gradually diminished as the train nears the escapement. In the last wheels of a train, small and light wheels are especially needed, so that they get quickly into motion directly the escapement is unlocked, and are stopped with but little shock when the escapement is locked again. The remarks on the train of a going-barrel watch apply equally to the going train of a clock. The considerations which guide in deciding the numbers for the striking train of a clock are the number of blows to be struck from winding to winding, the fall of the weight or turns of the barrel or fusee, as the case may be, and the number of pins in the pin wheel. English lever watches usually have either a 16,200 or an 18,000 train. American and Swiss watches, both lever and horizontal, have 18,000 trains as a rule.

TRANSIT INSTRUMENT. A telescope mounted at right angles to a horizontal axis. Used in connection with a clock or watch for obtaining the time of transit of a heavenly body over the meridian of a place. To watchmakers who make any pretense of a knowledge of their business, nothing can be more desirable or useful. A vague impression exists among them, that the transit instrument, used for this purpose, is so closely allied to the scientific, as to be serviceable only in the hands of the professional astronomer. This fact, taken in connection with the high cost of these instruments hitherto, fully accounts for the reason of their unfrequent employment.

These two causes, preventing the more general use of the transit, no longer remain, whatever may have been their force in the past. By an improvement in the mode of mounting, a ready means is furnished for setting up and placing the instrument in the meridian. Furnished with each transit are full printed instructions, describing each part in detail, the method of setting up, and taking observations, the whole of which is so plain and simple that every purchaser is surprised and gratified to find what was supposed to be difficult so easy to perform.

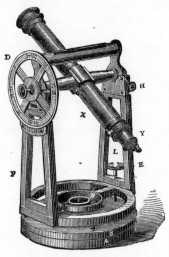

Fig. 272.

The principle involved in the use of the transit instrument is, that when in proper position, the center vertical line in the field of view of the telescope, shall be exactly on and represent the meridian, or true north and south line, of the place of observation. Hence, from the observed time of any heavenly body crossing the center or meridian line, may be determined the error of the timepiece used. The passage of any heavenly body across the meridian line is called its transit.

The stand on which the instrument rests, consists of two circular plates of metal, the lower of which, A, is to be screwed to a foundation of wood or stone; screw holes being provided for that purpose. The upper plate, B, turns upon the lower by means of a pivot, and the two are clamped together by a clamping screw. In the upper surface of the plate B, are sockets for receiving the three points on which the frame of the instrument rests.

When the clamping screw is loosened, ¡the entire instrument may be easily rotated horizontally upon the lower plate A, and when the clamping screw is tightened, the whole is rigidly held in position.

The telescope is ten inches long and fitted with an axis, the two pivots of which rest in the top of the frame F. At X is a sliding tube, which adjusts the focus of the object glass. The telescope is furnished with a diagonal eye-piece, E, which is made movable in a sliding tube at Y, to adjust the focus of the eye-piece. Small screens of colored glass are provided to protect the eye from the effects of the rays of the sun. On the axis of the telescope is attached a declination circle, D, used only for facilitating the finding of stars, when on or near the meridian, but not used in taking observations of the sun. Upon the pivots of the telescope is placed a riding level, for the purpose of leveling the axis of the telescope by means of the leveling screw L.

One of the pivots of the axis rests in a block made moveable by the horizontal adjusting screw.

The instrument must command an unobstructed view of the north star, and the sun at noon. Usually, the coping of a brick or stone building, easy of access, will be found the most convenient, but in the absence of this, a brick or stone pier, from sixteen to twenty-four inches square, built from four feet below to four feet above the ground, would be excellent, or a post six inches or more in thickness, firmly set in the ground would answer a very good purpose. A costly foundation offers no practical advantage and its greater expense need not be incurred. At the place chosen secure very firmly, a piece of plank two or three inches thick, of any suitable size, which should be well leveled, and thoroughly painted, top and bottom, to protect it against the action of the weather, and upon this plank screw the lower bed plate of the instrument. The instrument may be covered with a tight box, constructed to turn water and exclude dust, or, if removed after each observation, a tight cover should be made for the rotating stand, which must be left in its position.

The instrument is placed in position, or on the meridian line, by setting the center line in the field of view of the telescope, on the north star, at the time of night the said star is on the meridian, which time is calculated for any desired place and furnished in tabular form with each transit. Perfectly correct time for this operation, which is very simple, is not essential, but only as near as is in common use.

The instrument must now remain unmoved until a range mark has been obtained as follows:

On the day succeeding the setting of the center line on the north star, turn the telescope to the south, and notice some small object of a permanent character, which the center line bisects. This object is called the range, and may be at any distance from twenty feet to half a mile, but two or three hundred yards will be found best. If no convenient object can be selected, a range may be made by painting a small round spot on a permanent surface, at a point where the center line will bisect it. Before taking an observation the center line must always be set exactly on the range with the screw H, in order to secure an accurate adjustment in the meridian. The range may be either north or south, but the latter is the more convenient.

The purpose of the range mark is to furnish a means of keeping the instrument in the meridian without being obliged to re-set the center line on the north star.

METHOD OF TAKING AN OBSERVATION OF THE SUN.

Set the center line on the range, if off the same, and carefully level the axis, a few minutes before the sun comes in the field of view, which will be about four minutes before reaching the center line. As the telescope is an inverting one, the sun will appear to come in from the right hand side and pass across the field of view.

When the *first*, or advancing edge of the sun intersects the center line, the time must be noted by the watch, as in example. When the sun has passed entirely across the center line, which takes about two and a quarter minutes, note the time when the *last* edge intersects the center line, as in the same example.

Time of contact of *first* edge of sun with vertical line ___	11	43	14.5
" " " *last* " " " " " ___	11	45	30.
Divide by 2_____ 2)	23	28	44.5
	11	44	22.2
Add correction (from table supplied with instrument)___		16	12.5
	12	0	34.7
Subtract 12 hours_____	12		
Watch fast 34 seconds, 7 tenths_____		0	34.7

After adding the above correction, the difference between the result and 12 hours will be the amount the watch was fast or slow; fast, if more than 12 hours, and slow if less.

TRAVERSE SPINDLE GRINDER.   This tool will be found

Fig. 273.

very useful for grinding cutters, lathe centers, pump centers, reamers, counter sinks, squaring up barrel arbors after hardening, or any hardened steel tool. In the hand of an ingenious workman, it will be found exceedingly useful, as by its aid a great variety of work can be performed that cannot be accomplished without it. Fig. 273, is the Moseley pattern, and is designed to attach to the slide rest.

TURNS.   A small dead center lathe used but little in this country.

TWEEZERS.   The watchmaker will do well to purchase tweezers that are made of non-magnetic material, as they are no more expensive than ordinary ones of good make. Steel tweezers often become magnetized and by their use you convey the magnetism to the delicate parts of a movement. There are several makes of non-magnetic tweezers upon

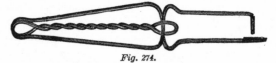

Fig. 274.

the market, all of which possess points of excellence. Soldering tweezers are made similar to Fig. 274, with hawk bill, for holding work while hard or soft soldering. See also *Soldering Forceps*.

TWO PIN ESCAPEMENT. A variety of the lever escapement having one small gold pin in the lever and two in the table, and the unlocking and impulse actions are divided between them.

UNIVERSAL HEAD. The universal head, shown in Fig. 275, has entirely superseded the clumsy universal mandrel in this country. It is more accurate, less clumsy and complicated and will perform the same work. The face plate is $3\frac{1}{2}$ inches in diameter, but by the use of two crescent-shaped slots, it will hold anything in size and shape of

Fig. 275.

watchwork. The pump center is operated from the back by the rubber knob and can be used either with or without a spring. The jaws, which will pass the center, are held in position on face plate by springs, and are fastened from the back. Peep holes are provided in these heads in order that the workman may examine the back of the work at all times. In the Moseley head, shown in Fig. 275, these holes are of taper form. Fig.

276 shows a universal face plate to be used on chuck in lathe.   It is smaller and less expensive than the universal head and answers very well for some work, but cannot be recommended very highly, as it is not as
accurate.   The pump center is used to
center from the back any object confined
in the jaws, but it sometimes becomes
necessary to mount the object by means of
wax upon a plate and hold the plate in the
jaws.   In such a case, the work must
necessarily be centered from the front.
This can be done accurately by means of
a piece of pegwood, as ordinarily done on
the lathe, by placing the point in the center

Fig. 276.

hole and the pegwood resting on the T rest, and observing if the free end of the pegwood remains stationary.   See also *Centering Tool.*

UNLOCKING RESISTANCE. The resistance opposed to unlock-ing by the adhesion between the locking faces of the pallets and the tips of the escape wheel teeth, and in the case of lever pallets by the draw of the locking faces.

VERGE ESCAPEMENT. A recoil escapement in which the pallet axis is set at right angles to the axis of the escape wheel.   The verge, the earliest probably of all the escapements, is shown in the engraving. It has no pretensions to accuracy, says Britten, in the presence of such escapements as the lever and chronometer.

The balance in this escapement has no free arc, and its vibration is limited to about 110° each way.   The escape wheel, or "crown wheel," as it is called, has either 11 or 13 teeth, and in the plan of the watch its arbor lies horizontally.   The balance staff, or verge, is made as small as proper strength will allow, and planted close to the wheel, so that the tips of the teeth just clear it.   The pallets, which form part of the verge, are placed at an angle of 95 or 100° with each other.   The latter angle is generally preferred.

The drawing is a plan of the escape wheel and verge, as they lie in the watch.   The width of the pallets apart, from center to center, is equal to the diameter of the wheel.   A tooth of the escape wheel is just leaving the upper pallet (*c*); as it drops off, the under tooth will reach the root of the lower pallet (*d*), but the motion of the verge will not be at once reversed.   The escape wheel will recoil until the impetus of the balance is exhausted.   The teeth of the wheel are undercut to free the face of the pallet during the recoil.

Generally in French, and occasionally in English watches, the pallets are even more open.   An increased vibration of the balance and less recoil can be obtained with a larger angle, but to get sufficient impulse the verge must be planted closer to the wheel. This necessitates cutting away a part of the body of the verge to free the wheel teeth. Then, as the wheel tooth impinges on the pallet almost close to the center of the verge, there is more friction on the pivots, and the wheel tooth gets

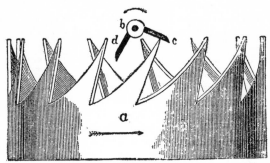

Fig. 277.

so small a leverage that the escapement often sets, unless the balance is very light. On the other hand, with the opening between the pallets only 90°, as it is in many English watches, the vibration of the balance is too small and the recoil too great. An opening of about 100° avoids the drawbacks incidental to the two extremes, and may therefore be adopted with advantage.

To ensure good performance the body or arbor of the verge should be upright, and when in the frames and viewed through the follower potence hole, should be seen crossing the balance wheel hole of the dovetail. The position of the eye should be in a line with the arbor of the balance wheel pinion when in the follower; the drops of the pallets equal, and the balance wheel teeth true.

VERNIER CALIPER. See *Gauge.*

VERTICAL ESCAPEMENT. An escapement in which the escape wheel is at right angles to the balance staff or pallet axis.

VIENNA LIME. A pure anhydrous lime, obtained from Vienna. It is extensively used for final polishing purposes, particularly in watch factories. The action of Vienna lime is different from most other polishing agents, for the effect is not produced, as in the case of rouge, by simple abrasion, for unless the lime be used while it is slacking, the result will not be satisfactory. The material should therefore be kept in air-tight bottles, and only enough for immediate use taken out at one time. Take a small lump from the bottle, slightly moisten with water and break down with any clean tool. Spread the lime paste on a box-wood slip and apply to the article to be polished, using quick strokes.

VULLIAMY, BENJAMIN LEWIS. He was born in London, in 1780, was grandson of Justin Vulliamy, a native of Switzerland, who emi-grated to London and became acquainted with Benj. Gray, of Pall Mall, married his daughter and succeeded to his business. Benj. Gray was clock-maker to the Crown in the reign of George II, and the position has been held by the Vulliamy family since his death. Benj. Lewis Vulliamy was an earnest student of horology, and was familiar with all the works of ancient and modern horologists. All of his productions were remark-able for their sterling excellence, but the branch to which he devoted the largest portion of his attention and time was the construction of turret clocks, and upon that subject he wrote several valuable pamphlets. He became a member of the Clockmaker's Company in 1809. He served every office in the Court of the Guild, and was five times elected master. He died January 8, 1854.

WATCH. A small time-piece to be carried in the pocket. The word watch is said to be derived from the Saxon *wæccan*, to awaken, which would seem to indicate that the earlier watches were of the alarm type. It is, however, much more probable that the term came originally from the watches of the night, and that portable timepieces were invented to mark them.

Cleaning and Repairing. As the movement is taken down, note should be taken of any needed repairs or alterations, either in the watch or case. See that the movement is tight in the case and that the stem turns easily. Examine movement carefully with eye glass and if a Swiss bridge movement, examine the depths of the wheels, see if minute wheel pinion touches the dial, and if balance pivots have too much side shake. Try the side shake of a Swiss bridge with a pair of fine and light tweezers. See if the guard and banking are correct. In a great many Swiss watches and also English watches, the jewel pin is too small for the fork, and often it does not enter properly. Memorize these little things as you go along, and repair them in this regular order. After examining the escapement, let the mainspring down; after taking the movement out of case, remove the hands first, with a modern tool made for that pur-pose, that does not interfere with the dial.

Now remove dial, and notice if it fits right; if the hand arbors come in the center of the holes. Oftimes this can be corrected by bending the feet with a pair of flat pliers, so the edge of the dial will correspond with the movement and the hand arbors. Sometimes, in American watches, the screws do not reach the dial feet; alter this by turning the shoulders off in lathe, so they will go further in. If the pins (when the dial is pinned on) are too high above the plate, fill them with a little pin and soft solder, and drill or punch new holes in the proper place. When you put a new dial on a Swiss watch, where the feet do not correspond with the holes, cut off the feet of new dial and file or grind the enamel flat around the feet and grind the enamel away with an emery wheel, where the new feet are to go. Now take a piece of copper wire, long enough for both feet, and the proper thickness, put it in lathe and hollow out the ends with a graver, so it will hard-solder flat on an old piece of dial copper about three-sixteenths of an inch round. If too large, put it in the lathe by the foot and turn it off. Now have feet prepared for new dial; take a little dissolved shellac and put it on the bottom of each of the dial feet and put the feet to their places in the movement plate.

Slightly moisten the places on the dial, where the new feet come, with dissolved shellac, and lay dial on these feet and see that second pivot comes properly through the dial, and that the edge of the dial corresponds with the edge of the movement plate. Now in this position let dial and movement lay over night, and in the morning the feet will be hard. Now lift your dial off carefully, turn it upside down, and bend up two brass clamps like a hair pin, but not so long, and clamp these feet on the flat part and lay this dial on a cork or piece of wood, feet up. Now put on your soft solder fluid, and blow a broad flame over it, and after the fluid has boiled you can put on your solder and blow again. Now dip it in a solution of cyanide of potassium, and wash off with soap and water, and brush dipped in clean water after the dirt is removed, Then dip it in alcohol, and dry in box-wood saw-dust.

The balance, of course, is removed during this process of fitting the dial. Now examine further and we find our center pivot worn and the hole in the bridge or upper plate too large. We now turn the pivot smooth with a graver, and grind with a pivot polisher, or a hand oil stone file, or pencil made of iron wire. Now clean off with pith, and polish with rouge or crocus. Now take the bridge or upper plate, and with a round face-punch in staking tool, close the hole. Now use a round broach and open the hole to its proper size, so it will fit the pivot correctly. Run this broach through, with the bridge screwed to its place, letting the broach go through the opposite hole at the same time. Now in an English watch, we may need a new bush, as the hole may have been bushed to one side and the center wheel be out of upright; but the question is, how to make the best job, so it will be strong, neat and workman like.

If you are compelled to put in a bush, or upright a hole in the center of a Swiss, English or American watch, first broach out the hole about twice its size and tap it with a fine thread. Now put in a threaded bush to fit snug; now rivet it in the staking tool, center the opposite hole in the universal head, center with a graver point and drill the bush in the lathe with a drill a shade smaller than the pivot. Now broach out in the lathe to suit the pivot and turn the bush off nicely with your slide rest.

After sharpening your cutter on an oilstone, run it over a fine emery stick to remove the burr on the cutting edge. Now, with moderate high speed, you can turn off this bush in good style. Should the endshake be too tight, lay your plate (English or full American), on a movement cup or ring, and with a wooden punch and hammer punch it outward. Treat a mainspring barrel in a similar manner when the end shake of the arbor is too tight, by laying it on a small silk spool, one end of the spool turned conically inward, so the outer edge only will touch the barrel. Strike the arbor with a horn, ivory or wooden mallet.

We oftentimes find American and English center pinions badly worn, so that when they are trued and polished up, there will be no shoulder left for the cannon pinion. When they are so badly worn as that, take a piece of steel, sometimes an old English cannon pinion (this will not have to be drilled), put it in lathe and turn a collar out of it, first preparing center pinion to receive this collar. Have this collar a little higher and a little thicker than the pivot is to be, and to go on loosely. Now soft solder it on to its place, wash clean and dry, and put the center wheel with its pinion back in the lathe and finish off with graver and oil stone, file and rouge, as before mentioned. The collar can be hardened and tempered in first-class style, by cutting a piece of binding wire through it and holding over the lamp and dipping in water or oil. Now you can clean it off by running a pointed peg-wood through it, then run over it with a fine emery stick, then lay on the bluing pan and turn to a dark chestnut color.

Take the mainspring out of the barrel, hold the arbor in the same way and revolve the barrel and you can see if it runs true. Now to true this barrel, either Swiss, English, or American, close the top or bottom hole with a round-faced punch, in a staking tool. In a Swiss, close the bottom, and in an English, the top hole. An American seldom needs this treatment. Now put barrel together and center it in universal head, and with a narrow and short cutter in slide rest open the hole that you closed to fit the arbor. When fitted, take it out and revolve it as before and our barrel will be dead true. Now in our key-winder Swiss, we find the ratchet worn, and it needs a new one. As the arbor and ratchet are one piece, we turn the ratchet about half off, edgewise. Now we turn it flatwise, and file or grind the square a little lower, so it will receive the new ratchet. This new ratchet must have a recess turned in it to fit over the part of the old ratchet. The square hole must fit the square snugly. Now, if this new ratchet is not too hard and the teeth not too fine, it will last better than the original. Now, in English watches, the square is oftentimes badly worn, or too small. In this case, draw the temper of the old square, turn it down by holding it in a step chuck by the fusee, taking off the great, or fusee wheel, and maintaining ratchet. After turning it down and squaring the pivot, cut a left-hand thread in a suitable piece of steel, and also on the old square (which, of course, is turned down in the step chuck), and fit this piece of steel on the old arbor, down to the pivot shoulder, against the stop cam. Now turn it down with a graver and square up the end in a lathe, and drill a very small hole through near the end of the square upper end. Now take and unscrew the new square and harden and temper it. Hold it over the lamp by a piece of binding wire, and dip in oil when cherry red. Now hold it in a chuck and clean it off with an emery stick. Now turn to a dark brown, screw back on, and grind and polish up. No graver is needed on this job after it is hardened and tempered. The thread need not go all the way down; half way will do, but the new square must go against the shoulder tight up to the lower round part of the square. When all done, put the little pin through, which keeps it from coming off when turned to the right.

On opening a barrel observe the condition of the mainspring, and the inside of the barrel head. Often, in good watches, the inside of the barrel head is not flat, and the mainspring scrapes it. Turn this flat with a step chuck and slide rest, at high speed, and sharpen the cutter as before mentioned. Now examine the mainspring, and see if it is the proper strength and width, and examine the hook, or brace, and stop work, the teeth of the barrel, etc. Now, sometimes in American watches, the barrel touches the balance; alter this by countersinking the lower hole of the arbor in the movement plate and bending the bridge down a little in the center, with a wooden spool and wooden punch, as in endshaking the center hole in American watches and the barrel arbor.

Oftentimes we find the winding pinion too shallow for the bevel wheel. Remedy this by either lowering the pinion deeper into the wheel, or the wheel into the pinion. Oftentimes, in Waltham watches of the old series, the intermediate winding wheel is too deep in the ratchet wheel. This can be corrected by the banking screw, by putting in one with a larger head. Now, very often the intermediate setting wheel is too shallow in the minute wheel. Correct this by stretching the lever where it touches the yoke, and taking off a little of the yoke where it banks for the hand setting. Remember that the yoke should be perfectly steady and firm, in turning the hands either way. The teeth of the minute wheel are often ruined when the cannon pinion is a little tight and the intermediate hand setting and minute wheels are too shallow. Never touch the arbor of the cannon pinion, but see that it is perfectly smooth and round. If the cannon pinion is too high from the plate, turn a little off from the under side. Take pinion off with a pair of brass-lined pliers. If the cannon pinion is too loose on the arbor (if a stem-wind), punch it in the same place, with a punch in the staking tool, having a V shaped stump to lay the cannon pinion on, and holding it with a peg-wood, or broach, while punching it. Use a punch a little rounding. A cannon pinion should work smoothly all around. Now, in a Swiss watch with a hollow center pinion, when its arbor is too loose, lay the arbor on a small flat anvil, or steel, or brass block, in front of you, not on vise, and hold a small square file across it, and tap it with a small hammer, rolling it while you tap it. This raises a nice burr all around it. If a little too tight, take it off with an oil stone slip. This can be done when the watch is clean and running.

Now examine the click, and see that it has a loose endshake and that the point goes freely in and out of the teeth of the wheel. Sometimes the point is too blunt, and in many cases, the click spring is too strong. Click springs should have a very low temper, and a nice slender shape, as the bending they perform is very little. They should not scrape on the plate, nor hold the click down too tight, if made like some Elgin clicks.

Now the end shake of the ratchet or ratchet wheel, should have some attention. You can easily manipulate this, if the ratchet is between the plates. End shake it with the winding arbor. Now we have the stem winding wheels, etc., in proper shape. The minute wheel pinion may rub on the dial. Remedy this by grinding the dial away with an emery wheel, and oftentimes free the hour wheel the same way. If there is too much end shake, put on a spring washer, cut it square and turn the corners up. We can examine the train from the third wheel to the scape wheel; see if the holes are large, and end shake correct. In some cases in Swiss watches, where the third and center wheels are under the same bridge, you can sometimes turn the shoulder of the lower pivot back.

Sometimes we find pivots too loose in their holes, and in some cases a new jewel can be put in to fit the pivot to a better advantage. In this case we must be guided by our practical experience, as in many other instances. True pinion or staff in a split chuck, flatten the old place, that you are to center with, on an oilstone slip, and center with a graver. Nine out of ten Swiss or English, and a few American pinions, can be drilled without annealing. Use oil and a properly made drill. For a bow drill use a rounding point, and in an American lathe an obtuse angle point, to cut only one way. Drill pinion or staff, and if you are compelled to draw the temper, do it in the following way: Use a cap made of copper wire, holding the opposite end of staff or pinion in a pair of brass-lined flat plyers; set copper cap on and blow a sharp blaze on the cap to blue article to be drilled. Remove the color with a peg-wood and rouge; first with rouge and oil, and then with dry rouge. Never leave a pinion or staff discolored. Now, if article cannot be trued in split chuck, cement it in, but you can true five out of every ten in a No. 1 Moseley lathe, without cement. For drilling it is not necessary that the article should run dead true; but it should be dead true, in turning the pivot on and finishing. Now, in pivoting after the hole is drilled and the plug is hammered in, turn your pivot to its proper shape with a graver and almost with the point. Turn pivot down to about three degrees thicker than pivot is to be. Now we have our

pivot finished with a graver. Now use an iron wire, about two millimeters thick and about five inches long, flattened about one inch on one
end with a file, filing crosswise, and now and then retouching with a fine
file. This is done so the file lines or marks will retain the grinding
powder to be used with oil. For a staff pivot, always file the corner off
a little, so it will conform to the conical shoulder, and file or grind, holding the oil-stone charged file so the latter and the pivot will traverse at
an acute angle. This is done to prevent the pivot from lining. Now, if
down to the desired size and shape, use another such tool, made of brass
or zinc and charged with rouge and oil, and polish pivot in the same
manner that you grind it. At last touch it up with dry rouge and a peg-
wood. Diamantine and oil or alcohol can also be used to good advantage before using the rouge.

After all repairs, clean your work in the following manner: Use good
benzine or gasoline and cyanide of potassium; a lump as large as a walnut to a pint of water. Keep in a glass or china cup with a cover on it.
Clean the lever in benzine only and dry in the sawdust. Have an alcohol cup, with cover, plenty of clean soft water (in cold weather use warm
water), and a medium soft brush, like a paint brush, about a half inch
thick for the benzine. A long, three or four row brush, to use with good
castile soap and water, and three, four or more pieces of brass wire made
into loops or strings, by bending an eye on each wire like a fishing hook.
The wire can be almost any length, from three to six inches, and from
three-tenths to five-tenths mm. thick. This, with about three pints of
boxwood sawdust, put through a sieve to get out the coarse particles, and
a soft camel's hair brush to use dry on the work after it has been cleaned,
completes the outfit for cleaning. Put a wire through the top plate,
hang in the benzine, and brush it carefully with the benzine brush, principally the pivot holes. After this has been done, pick up the stem
wheels, wheels and small parts, unscrew the safety pinions, and wash
and clean with the wheels. Oil the thread sparingly when you put it
back. String all of these small parts on a wire. Put the lower plate on
with the barrel. Use a very thick wire for the balance (dip it separately),
and move it about in the benzine; dry it in sawdust, dip in cyanide solution, in clear water, then in alcohol. Then move it about in the sawdust; this will clean the balance and hair spring and roller. After the
plates and wheels have gone through the benzine or gasoline, dip them
in the cyanide and wash with brush and water and castile soap. Dip in
clean water, then in alcohol and then in sawdust. By this process, every
speck of oil will be removed, and the gilding or nickle finish will not be
injured, as with old fogy chalk, and a variety of powder. Sometimes
the dirt in the pinion is thick and hard, and it must be removed with
peg-wood; sometimes it has been oiled with linseed oil and left to dry;
this can be boiled off in oil and cleaned as mentioned. To get dirt or
hard gum out of the wheel teeth, make a kind of pad with stiff writing

paper, draw the edge of these papers through the teeth; this will clean them nicely. When taking the cleaned parts from the sawdust, hold them with Dennison's watch papers, and brush off with a three or four row soft camel or fine goat hair brush. In setting the watch up, set the stem work up first and oil it properly. Right here, in oiling, is where it requires judgment. For the stem work use a heavier oil than for the train. Use refined clock oil for the stem wheels, as they necessarily require a heavier oil, and it also has less tendency to spread. Use watch oil in oiling the center pivots, and they, being large, should have more oil than the third, fourth and scape wheels, etc. Put the proper amount of oil on the end-stone, or cap jewel, before putting the latter to its place; also the barrel arbor. Oil the pallet faces sparingly before putting the lever to its place. Now if your balance and hair spring are true and in poise, and the pivots have their proper freedom and end shake, and the roller its proper freedom, and everything is all right throughout, your watch will move off all right. To ascertain if exactly in beat, hold a peg-wood against the teeth of the fourth wheel, and move it slightly forward, and observe the motion of the balance. If one pallet throws the balance further than the other, turn the hair spring by the collet slot, so that the lift will be equal on both pallets. When in beat, examine the escapement again; see if the balance clears the stud, cock, center wheel, etc. See if all the screws are tight, and by all means have the hair spring so the second coil will not get into the curb pins. After this the train can be oiled. The barrel pivot next to the ratchet, or ratchet wheel, should be oiled before the ratchet wheel is put on. It is well to oil the balance jewel holes after it has been put in beat, on account of dragging in dust with the pivots if they should be oiled before. After this put on the dial wheels; do not oil the minute wheel posts; see that the hour wheel has its proper end shake. In cheap watches put on a thin washer to steady the hour hand and wheel; put the dial on, and see that the second and hour wheel sockets are in the center of the holes after the dial is properly fastened. If you have any steel hands to bend, it will pay you to bend them with a pair of hot tweezers, as this will prevent breaking them. Now set your second hand with your second pendulum regulator, and regulate pendant up. Meantime you can clean the case with water, ammonia and a soft cotton rag. An old tooth brush can be used in the corners. Stiff joints in front case can be loosened up with benzine. This will take the dirt out, and the joints will work free. Cases should be cleaned, like all other repaired work. Often we find balance hole jewels entirely too thick, so they will take an unreasonably long pivot to reach through them. To remedy this, use an iron point charged with diamond powder, that fits the concave of the jewel, and then polish in the same manner with a finer grade of diamond powder, diamantine and rotten stone. Keep the jewel wet with water in grinding and polishing, and use the highest speed you can produce. Care must be taken in this operation, as it requires a little experience. Like everything else, you will find a great deal of difference in grinding a garnet or a ruby or sapphire, also in polishing them. Zinc and lead points are used in polishing with diamantine and rotten stone and water. If the above process is understood it can be quickly done. The hole can also be polished, but in some cases it will pay better to put in a new and perfect jewel.

Sizes of Watch Movements. Swiss and French watches are measured by the French ligne (line) which is one-twelfth of an inch of a Paris foot. One line equals .088814 of an English inch, or 2.25583 mm. The movements are spoken of as 14-line, 18-line, 19-line, etc. Mr. Aaron L. Dennison is said to be the inventor of the system employed for the sizing of American watches and he first applied it to the watches made by the American Horologe Company, about 1851. He took one inch as a basis of measurement and called it o; he then took a second inch and divided it into 30ths and numbered the movements according to the number of 30ths that they exceeded an inch. For example, a watch that measured 1 16-30 inch, was called a 16-size, and one that measured 1 18-30 inch was called a 18-size, etc.

WATCH BOW PLIERS. Pliers of a peculiar shape, as shown in Fig. 278, and used for manipulating watch bows.

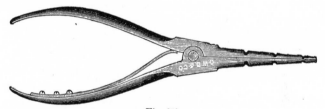

Fig. 278.

WATCH CASE TOOL. The Hopkins' patent watch case tool is designed for the two-fold purpose of easing a case when it opens too hard, and for making one stay shut when it opens too easy. It is illustrated in Fig. 279. The part D is intended only for use when the spring catch of a hunting case has worn the case so that it will not stay shut.

For making a back case stay shut when it opens too easily, use the cutting tooth B, in the following manner: Rest the beveled edge of the tool from A to C, down level on the ledge against which the dome or back case closes, as represented in the illustration, taking care to keep the end A as well as the tooth B down level on the ledge, and inward against the part to be re-undercut, in which position, with the end D resting in the hollow of your right hand, back of the little finger, and with your thumb resting on the inner cap to steady your hand, hold the tool thus quite still, and with your left hand give a circular movement to the watch, crowding the part to be under cut against the tooth *B*, that is, instead of shoving the tool forward to produce the cutting, hold the tool still, and crowd the part of the case to be cut against it as described. By thus renewing the under cut of the catch edge, even a badly worn case may be made to shut and stay shut nicely.

Fig. 279.

For easing the cap or the back case of a watch when it opens too hard, rest the end *A*, of the tool, down on the inside of the dome, with the handle inclining backward at an angle of about 45°, and with one of the sharp edges extending from *A* to *C*, brought to bear against the snap edge that requires to be eased, in such a way that it will give a shaving (not a scraping) cut; carefully shave off the edge, thus, to the extent required. In this way even the most delicate case may be eased without the slightest marring or injury to it. In case of roughness of the snap edge, burnish it carefully with the back of the tool; or rubbing a bit of beeswax around the edge will often be found of service in cases of this kind.

WATCH HAND PLIERS. Fig. 280 shows Horton's combination watch hand pliers for removing watch hands, second, hour and minute. It also takes the place of the 9-hole hand sliding tongs.

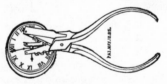

Fig. 280.

WATCH PAPERS. These were circular pieces of paper, silk, velvet, or muslin, placed in the outer cases of the old watches, and were decorated with verses or devices; some of them were very elaborate specimens of scroll work, and had a miniature painted in the center, others merely bore verses. Later this same device was used by repairers as a means of placing a business card in the watch. Many old watches in various collections contain over a dozen of these cards, of repairers in whose hands the watch has been.

WATCHMAKERS. Sometimes the watchmaker and jeweler is desirous of telling how old a certain movement may be and the following alphabetical list of watch and clock makers may aid him in fixing the age approximately. The date after the name gives approximately the year in which the watchmaker was in business. The date is only approximate and is based on the year in which he became a member of the Clockmakers' Company, if an Englishman, and in the case of watch makers of other countries is based upon reliable data, so that as a whole the dates are very nearly correct.

A

Abbott, John, L. C. 1703.

Abbott, Peter, L. C. 1719.

Abbott, John, L. C. 1740. Son of Peter.

Adams, Francis, L. C. 1840.

Adams, J., L. C. 1843.

Addis, William, L. C. 1756.

Addis, Geo. Curson, L. C. 1785.

Alcock, Thomas, L. C. 1630.

Allen, Elias, L. C. 1630.

Almond, Ralph, L. C. 1670.

Ambrose, Edward, L. C. 1637

Ames, Richard, L. C. 1653. Died 1679

Ames, Richard, L. C. 1677.

Andrews, John, L. C. 1688.

Appleby, Joshua, L. C. 1735.

Archer, Henry,* L. C. 1630.

Arnold, John. 1760. Born 1744. Died Aug. 25, 1799.

Arnold, John Roger, L. C. 1740.

Askel, Elizabeth, L. C. 1740.

Aspinwall, Sam'l, L. C. 1590.

Atkins, Francis, L. C. Born 1730. Died 1809.

Atkins, Geo, L. C. Born March 25, 1767. Died 1855. Son of Francis.

Atkins, Sam'l Elliott, L. C. 1831.

Aveline, Daniel, L. C. 1763. Died Aug., 1772.

B

Backquett, David,† L. C. 1632.

Bailey, Jeffery, L. C. 1665.

Barrand, Paul P., L. C. 1802.

Barrow, Nathaniel, L. C. 1680.

Barrow, Sam'l, L. C. 1696.

Barrow, John, L. C. 1705.

Basire, John, L. C. 1760.

Bartram, Simon,† L. C. 1630.

Bange, Edward,‡ L. C. 1700.

Bayes, John, L. C. 1658.

Bayley, Thomas, L, C. 1785.

Baylie, Jeffry, L. C. 1650.

Beauvais, Simon, L. C. 1690.

Beck, Christopher, L. C. 1785.

Beckner, Abraham, L. C. 1640. Died 1665.

Bell, Benj. L. C. 1660. Died 1694.

Benn, Anthony, L. C. 1755. Died 1763.

Bennett, John, L. C. 1850·

Berry, John, L. C. 1715.

Berthoud, Ferdinand. Born 1729. Died 1807.

Berthoud, Louis. 1775.

Bertram, William, L. C. 1720. Died Aug., 1733.

Bidlake, Francis, L. C. 1800.

Billinghurst, Hen., L. C. 1760.

Blackborow, Jas., L. C. 1730. Died July, 1746.

Blackburn, William, L. C. 1785.

Blisse, Ambrose, L. C. 1656.

Bosley, Chas., L. C. 1760.

Bouchet, J., L. C. 1728.

Bouquet, David, L. C. 1640. Died 1665.

Bouquett, Solomon, L. C. 1650.

Bowen, Francis, L. C. 1650.

Bowley, Devereux, L. C. 1718. Born 1697. Died 1773.

Boyear, William, L. C. 1633.

Bradley, Langley, L. C. 1719.

Breguet, Abraham Louis, Paris. Born 1747. Died 1823,

L.—Carried on business in London.

C.—Member of the Clockmakers' Company.

*One of the first wardens of the Clockmakers' Company and a charter member.

---

†Charter member of the Clockmakers' Company.

‡An apprentice of Thos. Thompion.

Brooke, John, L. C. 1632.
Brown, Henton, L. C. 1726.
Brown, James. L. C. 1761.
Browne, John, L. C. 1680.
Bucklee, David, L. C. 1785.
Bull, John,† L. C. 1632.
Bullby, John,† L. C. 1632.
Burgis, John,† L. C. 1622.
Bushman, John Baptist, L. C. 1785.

C

Cabrier, Charles, L. C. 1697.
Callet, F., Paris. Born 1744. Died 1798.
Cam, William, L. C. 1686.
Carlton, John, L. C. 1630.
Carrington. Robt., L. C. 1760.
Carrington, Thomas, L. C. 1762.
Carrington, George, L. C. 1785.
Carpenter, Thos., L. C. 1785.
Carter, William, L. C. 1800.
Carter, John, L. C. 1825. Died May 5, 1878.
Cavendish, Richard, L. C. 1800.
Cext, Cathrine, L. C. 1735.
Chamberlain, Nath., L. C. 1700.
Charlstrom, William, L. C. 1800.
Charrington, Saml., L. C. 1756. Died 1768.
Chater, Eliezer, L. C. 1760.
Chater, James, L. C. 1780.
Chater & Son, L. C. 1790.
Cheney, Wither, L. C. 1768.
Child, Richard,† L. C. 1632.
Child, Henry, L. C. 1640. Died 1665.
Chisman, Timothy, L. C. 1785.
Clarke, George,† L. C. 1632.
Clarke, Henry, L. C. 1817.
Claxton, Thomas, L. C. 1656.
Clay, William, L. C. 1656.
Clement, William, L. C. 1685.
Clerk, George, L. C, 1785.
Clewes, James, L. C. 1670. A great clockmaker.
Closon, Peter, L. C. 1625.
Clows, John, L. C. 1707.
Collingridge, Edmund, L. C. 1800.
Comfort, William, L. C. 1656.
Cooke, Lewes,† L. C. 1630.
Cooke, John, L. C. 1656.
Copeland, Alex., L. C. 1800.
Copley, Thomas, L. C. 1632.
Coulson, Robert, L. C. 1800.

Coxeter, John, L. C. 1650.
Coxeter, Nicholas, L. C. 1650.
Crayle, Richard, L. C. 1630.
Crouch, Edward, L. C. 1711.
Cumming, Alexander, L. C. 1760. Died 1813.
Cuper, Josias,† L. C. 1632.

D

Daniell, William,† L. C. 1632.
Daniell, Isaac, L. C. 1656.
Dawson, Thomas,† L. C. 1630.
Day, Edmund, L. C. 1692.
Debaufre, James, L. C. 1712.
Debaufre, Peter, E. C. 1689.
Decka, John, L. C. 1757.
De Charmes, Simon, L. C. 1691.
Delander, Daniel, L. C. 1699.
Delander, James, L. C. 1668.
Delander, John, L. C, 1670.
Delander, Nath., L. C. 1668.
Delander, Nath., L. C. 1740.
DeLaundre, Peter, L. C. 1640.
Dent, William, L. C. 1674.
Desbois, Daniel. L. C. 1825.
Deuchesne, Pierre, Paris. 1740.
DeWellke, Christianus, L. C. 1630.
Dolley, Thomas, L. C. 1800.
Dorrell, William, L. C. 1785.
Drake, John, L. C. 1656.
Droeshout, John,† L. C. 1632.
Drury, James, L. C. 1720.
DuChesne, Claudius, L. C. 1693.
Duncombe, R. Jr., L. C. 1790.
Dunlop, Conyers, L. C. 1750.
Durand, Oswald,† L. C. 1630.
Dutton, Mathew, L. C. 1792.

E

East, Edward,† L. C. 1630.
East, Jeremie, L. C. 1656.
Ebsworth, John, L. C. 1665.
Edlin, Geo., L. C. 1810.
Ellet, William, L. C. 1771.
Ellicott, John,§ L. C. 1726.
Ellicott, Edward, L, C. 1823 Died July, 1836.
Erbery, Henry, L. C. 1656.
Etherington, George, L. C. 1684
Everell, John, L. C. 1730.
Exelby, James, L. C. 1718.

---

† Charter member of the Clockmaker's Company.

§ Clockmaker to King George III.

F

Faulkner, Edward, L. C. 1727.
Feilder, Thomas, L. C. 1707.
Fenn, Daniel, L. C. 1759.
Fenn, Samuel, L. C. 1785.
Fenn, Joseph, L. C. 1831.
Finch, John, L. C. 1697.
Fisher, Rebeckah, L. C. 1720.
Foreman, Francis,† L. C. 1630.
Foreman, Michael, L. C. 1800.
Francis, William, L. C. 1800.
Frodsham, William James, L. C. 1802.
  Died June 28, 1850.
Frodsham, Charles, L. C. 1845.
Fromanteel, A., L. C. 1632.

G

Ganthony, Richard, L. C. 1820.
Ganthony. Richard Pinfold, L. C. 1833.
Gibbs, Thomas, L. C. 1700.
Gibson, Edward, L. C. 1785.
Gibson, James, L. C. 1660.
Gillpine, Edward, L. C. 1630.
Gilpin, Edmund,† L. C. 1632.
Glenny, Joseph, L. C. 1800.
Glover, Boyer, L. C. 1760.
Godbud, William, L. C. 1656.
Goode, Charles, L. C. 1686.
Goodwin, Thomas, L. C. 1657.
Goujon, Stephen, L. C. 1752.
Grant, John, L. C. 1781.
Grant, John,¶ L. C. 1828.
Gravell, William, L. C. 1829.
Graves, Benjamin, L. C. 1697.
Gray, Timothy, L. C. 1633.
Graham, George, L. C. 1715. Born
  July 7, 1673. Died Nov. 20, 1751.
Green, James, L, C. 1664.
Green, James, L. C., 1776.
Green, John, L. C. 1711.
Green, Joseph, L. C. 1723.
Greene, James, L. C. 1685.
Gregory, Jeremie, L. C. 1652. Died
  1685.
Gregory, Jeremeah, L. C. 1694.
Gregory, Robert, L. C. 1678.
Gregory Thomas, L. C. 1671.
Grennel, Richard, L. C. 1735.

---

†Charter member of the Clockmakers'
  Company.
¶Five times master of the Clockmakers'
  Company.

Gretton, Charles, L. C. 1672.
Griffiths, Edward, L. C. 1800.
Grimes, Thomas, L. C. 1670.
Grinkin Robert,† L. C. 1632.
Grinkin, Edmund, L. C. 1656.
Grove, Richard, L. C. 1785.
Guy, Henry, L. C. 1702.
Guy, Charles, L. C.

H

Hacket, Symon,† L. C. 1632.
Halsted, Robt., L. C. 1690.
Hamilton, Dr. Robt., L. C. 1784.
Hancorne, Thomas, L. C. 1680.
Harker, G., L. C. 1842.
Harper, Henry, L C. 1664.
Harris, John,† L. C. 1630.
Harris, Anthony, L. C. 1683.
Harris, Henry, L. C. 1711.
Harris, William, L. C. 1821.
Harrison, John, L. C. 1720. Born 1693.
  Died March 24, 1776.
Hatton, Jos. York, L. C. 1800.
Hatton, James. 1810.
Hayes, Walter, L. C. 1670.
Heerman, John, L. C. 1691.
Hemmen, ——— L. C. 1646.
Henshaw, Walter, L. C, 1685.
Herbert, Cornelius, L. C. 1720.
Herring, Jos., L. C. 1770.
Higgs, Peter, L. C. 1759.
Hill, Benj., L. C. 1650.
Hill, John, L. C. 1630.
Hiorne, John, L. C. 1736.
Hobson, John, L. C. 1630.
Hodges, Nathaniel, L. C. 1681.
Hohwii, Andreas,‖ Amsterdam. Born
  1803. Died 1886.
Holden, Onesiphorus, L. C. 1630.
Holland, George, L. C, 1630.
Holland, Thomas, L. C. 1642.
Hollidaie, Edward, L. C. 1656.
Holloway, Robert, L. C. 1682.
Horne, Samuel, L. C. 1660.
Horne, Henry, L. C. 1760.
Horsman, Stephen, L. C. 1709.
House, Thomas, L. C. 1632.
Howse, William, L. C. 1769.
Howse, Charles, L. C. 1779.
Howse, John, L. C. 1672.
Hubert, James, L. C. 1700.
Hubert, Charlotte, L. C. 1730.

‖Chronometer maker to the Dutch Marine.

Hubert, Davıd, L. C. 1735.
Hue, Pierry, L. C. 1632.
Hughes, Thomas, L. C. 1734.
Huggeford, Ignatius, L. C. 1670.
Hunt, John, L. C. 1670.
Hunter, Thos. Sr., L. C, 1780.
Hunter, Thos. Jr., L. C., 1798.

I

Ireland, Henry, L. C. 1668.
Irving, Alexander, L. C. 1795.

J

Jackson, John, L. C. 1788.
Jackson, John, Jr., L. C. 1813.
Jackson, Martin, L. C. 1713.
Jackson, Richard, L. C. 1632.
Jaques, William, L. C. 1708.
Jarratt, John William, L. C. 1785.
Janatt, Richard, L. C. 1680.
Johnson, Thomas, L. C. 1720.
Johnson, John, L. C. 1760.
Johnson, Roger. L. C. 1630.
Jones, Evan, L. C. 1656.
Jones, Henry, L. C. 1663.
Jones, Henry, L. C. 1697.
Jones, Henry, L. C. 1680.
Jones, John, L. C. 1754.
Jones, Owen, L. C. 1785.
Jones, William, L. C. 1785.

K

Knibb, Jos., L. C. 1670.
Kotsford, William, L. C. 1685.

L

Lambe, Thomas, L. C. 1632.
Lea, Thomas, L. C. 1763.
Le Conte, Daniel, L. C. 1676.
Lecount, Peter, L. C. 1800.
Lecount, Peter, L. C. 1787.
LeCompte, James, L. C. 1687.
Lee, Cuthbert, L. C. 1676.
LeFebuce, Charles, L. C. 1687.
Lello, Jas., L. C. 1655.
Levy, Jonas. L. C. 1825.
Linnaker, Samuel, L. C. 1630.
Litherland, Peter, Liverpool, 1790.
Locker, John, D. C. 1733.
Loddington, Isaac, L C. 1725.
Long, Henry, L. C. 1780.
Long, John, L. C. 1677.

Long, John, L. C. 1698.
Loomes, Thomas, L. C. 1650.
Lord, Richard, L. C. 1632.
Lowndes, Jonathan, L. C. 1633.
Lyons, Richard, L. C. 1675.

M

Maberly, John, L. C. 1730
Marchant, Samuel, L. C. 1698.
Markwick, James, L. C. 1666.
Marriott, John, L. C. 1791.
Maisden, John, L. C. 1723
Masters, James, L C. 1800
Masterson, Richard, L. C. 1630.
Mather, Francis, L. C. 1656.
Matthews, William, L. C. 1761.
Mattchet, John, L. C. 1656.
Mattocks, John, L. C. 1785.
McCabe, James, L. C. 1803.
Meredith, Launcellott, L. C. 1656
Merigeot, John, L. C. 1761.
Merrill, Chas., L. C. 1800.
Merry, Chas., L. C. 1762.
Metcalf, Geo. M., L. C. 1785.
Merttius, Sir George, L. C. 1706.
Midnall, John,† L. C. 1630.
Miles, Sep., L. C. 1800.
Million, William, L. C. 1671.
Mitchell, Robert. L. C. 1760.
Moodie, David, L. C. 1656.
Morgan, Richard,† L. C. 1630.
Morgan, Thomas, L. C. 1645.
Moss, Thomas, L. C. 1785.
Moseley, Elinor, L. C. 1730.
Mulford, John, L. C. 1742.
Mudge, Thomas, L. C. 1738.
Mottram, John, L. C. 1790.

N

Nathan, Henry, L. C. 1673.
Newell, William, L. C. 1800.
Newman, Robert, L. C. 1800.
Newman, John, L. C. 1800.
Newcomb, Joseph, L. C. 1800.
Nicacius, John, L. C. 1642.
Norris, Edward, L. C. 1680.
Nourse, Thomas, L. C. 1761.

O

Okeham, Edward,† L. C. 1632.
Overzee, Gerard, L. C. 1678.

---

†Charter member of the Clockmakers
Company.

P

Parkwick, James, L. C. 1690.
Patmore, Peter, L. C. 1813.
Pace, Thomas, L. C. 1634.
Pattee, Thomas, L. C. 1800.
Payne, Southern, L. C. 1762.
Pearce, William, L. C. 1785.
Peachy, Newman, L. C. 1760.
Pennock, John, L. C. 1650.
Pepys, John, L. C. 1700.
Perigal, Francis, L. C. 1748.
Perigal, F. S., Jr., L. C. 1785.
Perry, J. A., L. C. 1841.
Pettit, William, L. C. 1632.
Pitt, William, L. C. 1780.
Pitt, Thyar, L. C. 1790.
Pistor, Edward, L. C. 1790.
Pistor, John, L. C. 1790.
Planner, Thomas, L. C. 1701.
Plumley, William, L. C. 1771.
Plumley, William, Jr., L. C. 1793.
Poole, Robert, L. C. 1773.
Potter, Harry, L. C. 1787.
Potter, James, L. C. 1800.
Prigg, John, L. C. 1761.
Proctor, William, L. C. 1800.

Q

Quare, Daniel, L. C. 1670. Born 1632. Died 1724.

R

Ramsey, David, L. C. 1630.
Ranier, John, L. C. 1785.
Rawlins, James, L. C. 1785.
Reead, Thomas,† L. C. 1632.
Reeve, Thomas, L. C. 1638.
Reid, Thomas, L. C. 1775. Born 1748. Died 1824.
Richards, Hugh, B. C. 1728.
Richardson, John, L. C. 1800.
Richardson, James, L. C. 1780.
Rimbault, Paul, L. C. 1770.
Rimbault, Stephen, L. C. 1800.
Ringmader, Dublin, Ireland, 1792
Rivers, David, L. C. 1773.
Rivers, William, L. C. 1786.
Robins, William, L. C. 1797.
Robinson, Francis, L. C. 1717.
Robinson, Robert, L. C. 1756.
Robson, William, L. C. 1801.
Rogers, Isaac, L. C. 1776.
Rogers, Thomas, L. C. 1810.
Rogerson, William, L. C. 1760.
Rooker, Richard, L. C. 1728.

Roothwood, Robert,† L. C. 1632
Russell, Nicasius, L. C 1680.

S

Sadleir, Samuel, L. C. 1718.
Sargeant, Nath. L. C 1775.
Saunders, Daniel. L. C. 1632.
Scafe, William, L. C. 1741.
Sellars, John, L. C. 1686.
Shaw, John, L. C. 1704.
Shaw, Anna, Maria, L. C. 1738.
Sharp, John, L. C. 1832.
Shelton, John, L. C. 1760.
Shelton, Thomas, L. C. 1830.
Shelton, Sampson,† L. C. 1630.
Shepheard, Thomas, L. C.† 1632.
Sherwood, William, L. C. 1732.
Sidey, Benj., L. C. 1753.
Silver, Fredk., L. C. 1800.
Sinderby, Francis, H., L. C. 1800.
Skinner, Mathew, L. C. 1740.
Smith, John,† L. C. 1630.
Smith, Robert, L. C. 1645.
Smith, Susana, L. C. 1752.
Snelling, James, L. C. 1728.
Somersall, Richard, L. C. 1785.
Sowery, Andrew, L. C. 1676.
Speakman, William, L. C. 1691.
Speidell, Francis, L. C. 1669.
Spencer & Perkins, L. C. 1790.
Stafford, John, L. C. 1733.
Stanton, Edward, L. C. 1686.
Stamper, Francis, L. C. 1682.
Stephens, Joseph, L. C. 1744.
Stephenson, Thos. S., L. C. 1800.
Stevenson, Adam, L. C. 1785.
Stones, Thomas, L. C. 1722.
Storer, Robert, L. C. 1760.
Street, Richard, L. C. 1710.
Ssmidt, Gersen, L. C. 1630.
Stubbs, Gabriell, L. C. 1675.
Style, Nath., L. C. 1748.
Styte, Richard, L. C. 1782.
Swell, George, L. C. 1688.

T

Tayler, Edward, L. C. 1800.
Taylor, Geo., L. C. 1700.
Taylor, Jasper, L. C. 1694.
Taylor, Jasper, L. C. 1746.
Taylor, John, L. C. 1702.
Taylor, Samuel, L. C. 1799.
Taylor, Thomas, L. C. 1703.

† Charter member of the Clockmakers Company.

Thomton, Henry, L. C. 1699.
Thwaites, John, L. C. 1785.
Tompion, Thomas, L. C. 1671.
Tomlinson, William, L. C. 1725.
Townsend, Joseph, L. C. 1670.
Trubshaw, John, L. C. 1709.
Tutet, Edward, L. C. 1762.

U

Underwood, William, L. C. 1790.
Upjohn, Francis, L. C. 1785.

V

Valentine, Chas. D. F., L. C. 1800.
Vernon, Samuel, L. C. 1756.
Vick, Richard, L. L. 1720.
Viet, Chaude, L. C. 1700.
Viet, Mariane, L. C. 1720.
Volant, Ely,† L. C. 1630.
Voutrollier, James, †L. C. 1632.
Vulliamy, Benj. Gray Justin, L. C. 1790.
Vulliamy, Benj. Lewis, L. C. 1809.
Vulliamy, Justin Theo., L. C. 1810.

W

Walker, John,† L. C. 1632.
Ward, John, L. C. 1789.
Ward, Thomas,† L. C. 1632.
Webster, Henry, L. C. 1709.
Webster, Richard, L. C. 1800.
Webster, Robert, L. C. 1695.
Webster, Samuel, L. C. 1761.

Webster, William, L. C. 1729.
Weeks, Thomas, L. C. 1657.
Wheeler, Thomas, L. C. 1655.
Wheeler, Thomas, L. C. 1681.
Whichcote, Samuel, L. C. 1741.
Wickes, John, L. C. 1785.
Williamson, Joseph, L. C. 1716.
Willin, William, L. C. 1800.
Willow, John, L. C. 1620.
Wilson, James, L. C, 1740.
Windmills, Jos. Jr., L. C. 1670.
Windmills, Thos., L. C. 1711.
Wontner, John, L. C. 1800.
Wray, Hilton, L. C. 1777.
Wrightson, Thomas, L. C. 1730.
Wynn, Henry, L. C. 1680.
Wyse, John, L. C. 1669.
Wyse, John, L. C, 1710.
Wyse, Joseph, L. C. 1687.
Wyse, Luke, L. C. 1694.
Wyse, Mark, L. C. 1719.
Wyse, Peter, L. C. 1693.
Wase, Richard, L. C. 1679.
Wyse, Robert, L. C. 1695.
Wyse, Thomas, L. C. 1686.

Y

York, Thomas, L. C. 1716.
Young, James, L. C. 1785.

† Charter member of the Clockmakers Company.

WEBSTER, AMBROSE. Mr. Webster was born in Southbridge, Mass., July 16th, 1832, and attended the common schools in that town until 1847, when he went to Springfield, Mass., attending the school there until 1849.

He then commenced a four years' apprenticeship in the Springfield Armory, being the first apprentice taken after the Armory was under military rule, i. e , under superintendency of the ordinance department. After serving his apprenticeship, he worked on locomotives with Blanchard & Kimball, locomotive builders. In 1853 and 1854 was on the Richmond & Danville Railroad as machinist and engineer. In 1855 he worked on the gun stocking machinery, built by Ames Manufacturing Company, Chicopee, that went to Enfield, England, arsenal. In 1857 he went to work for Appleton Tracy & Company, who were succeeded by the American Watch Company. Was appointed foreman of the machine shop of the American Watch Company in December, 1859, and master mechanic in 1862. In 1875 was appointed assistant superintendent, retaining also the duties of master mechanic, which position he held until the spring of 1876, when he left the employment of the company and spent six months in a much needed rest, and in visiting the various watch and clock companies of the country, making a thorough study of their methods. In the spring of 1857, Mr. Webster was the only machinist regularly employed ten hours per day as a machinist and tool maker, in the watch and watch case industries of this country, and probably the only one in the world. Dnring Mr. Webster's connection with the watch industry the business has increased until there are now 500 machinists connected with the various watch factories, from 200 to 250 connected with various watch case factories, and over 200 in the various watch tool factories.

Under Mr. Webster's management, the machine shop of the American Watch Company developed into a force of 70 men, and the daily product of the company was increased from five watches per day to 350. When making five watches per day, if the "Boston east winds" were strong, they were unable to turn out any, as the gilding operations could not be performed. In the fall of 1876 Mr. Webster entered the partnership of the American Watch Tool Company, taking its general management.

At that time they were making about 50 lathes per year. They immediately commenced the erection of a factory building, and when completed, increased their force from six men to eighty, taking a large contract to equip an English watch factory, and in 1878 commenced the work of equipping the Waterbury Watch Company. This establishment was planned, erected and equipped to make 1,000 watches per day, by Mr. Webster and the American Watch

Ambrose Webster.

Tool Company. While at Waterbury he formed the acquaintance of Mr. Woodruff, of the Seth Thomas Clock Company, and used his influence in inducing that company to commence the manufacture of watches, and subsequently built a large amount of machinery for them.

When Mr. Doolittle organized the New Haven Watch Company, he used Mr. Webster's experience in the building of machinery, and subsequently in the plan of their factory at Trenton, and equipping the same. The Cheshire Watch Company also called upon Mr. Webster for assistance in the same line, as did the Hampden Watch Company, in the erection of their last building in Springfield. When Mr Wendell organized the Aurora Watch Company, having been acquainted with Mr. Webster for some time, he consulted him in relation to the erection of a factory, and gave him large orders for its equipment.

The American Watch Tool Company has, under his management, built machinery for all the American watch companies, and many foreign, until they have on their books, as customers, 25 watch companies, for whom they have turned out $300,000 worth of machinery, and seven clock companies, for whom they have furnished machinery to the amount of $55,000. Probably no person in the world has had so intimate connection with the watch industry as Mr. Webster. He has among his correspondents nearly all the foreign watch companies, and probably no man is better known in connection with the watch industry than he. He has been frequently called upon to appraise watch factories, plants, etc., and advise with the general managers regarding the development of their business.

WHEELS AND PINIONS. In the construction of watches and clocks, it is necessary to transmit motion from one arbor to another, so that the arbor which is driven rotates more quickly than the one which drives it. If it were practicable to use rollers with smooth edges for transmitting such motion, the diameter of the rollers would be inversely proportionate to the number of rotations made by their arbors in a given time. For instance, the distance apart of two arbors from center to center measures 3.7 inches, and it is desired that for every time the arbor from which the power is taken rotates the other shall rotate eight

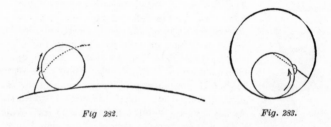

Fig 282.   Fig. 283.

times. The distance between the arbors is divided into nine equal parts, of which eight are taken for the radius of the driver, which rotates only once, and one part for the radius of the follower, as it is called, which rotates eight times. Although it is not practicable to drive with smooth rollers, which would slip unless pressed so tightly together as to cause excessive friction, the circles representing the rollers are the basis on which the wheel and pinion are constructed. They are called the pitch circles. The acting parts of the teeth of the driver is beyond its pitch circle, and the acting parts of the teeth of the follower within its pitch circle. In most of the toothed wheels with which watchmakers are concerned, the driver is the wheel and the follower the pinion. The shape for the acting part of the wheel is an epicycloid, a curve generated by rolling one circle on another.

In Fig. 282 is shown a portion of a circle representing the pitch diameter of the wheel, and on it a smaller circle rolling in the direction of the arrow. If these two are made of brass, or any thin material, and laid on a sheet of paper, a pencil fixed to the circumference of the small roller will trace a curve as shown. This curve is the acting part of the wheel tooth.

The acting part of the pinion leaves must be produced by the same sized roller as was used for the points of the wheel teeth, but in a different manner. The pinion flanks should be hypocycloidal in form. A hypocycloid is obtained by rolling one circle within another, instead of upon it. The most convenient size for the generating roller for both wheel and pinion is half the pitch diameter of the pinion. In Fig. 283 is a circle representing the pitch circle of the pinion, with another circle half its size rolling within it, and in this case the point described by the pencil would be a straight radial line, which is a suitable form for the pinion.

Teeth formed in this way will transmit the motion uniformly at the same speed as though the pitch circles rolled on each other without teeth, and will also meet another important requirement. The action between the teeth will take place almost wholly after the line of centers, that is if the pinion has not less than ten leaves. The difference between

Fig. 284.   Fig. 285.

the engaging and disengaging friction is great, especially if the surfaces in contact are not quite smooth. Wheels which have any considerable portion of their action between the teeth as they are engaging, or before the line of centers, not only absorb considerable power thereby, but wear out rapidly. With a larger generating circle, more of the action between the teeth of the wheel and the leaves of the pinion would take place after the line of centers, which is a consideration with low numbered pinions, but then a larger generating circle traces a pinion leaf too weak at the root.

The pitch circle of the wheel is spaced out so that the teeth and spaces are equal. To allow of necessary freedom, the teeth or leaves of the pinion are less in width than the spaces. The distance between the center of one leaf and the center of the next may be divided into .6 for space and .4 for leaf *

---

*The "pitch" of wheels and pinions is the portion of the circumference of the pitch circle between the center of one tooth and the center of the next.

The pinion leaves are finished with a semi-circular piece projecting beyond the pitch circle, as seen in Fig. 284. They would work without if properly pitched, but would not be safe as the depth became shallow from the wearing of the holes. Some prefer a Gothic shaped projection like Fig. 285, which is of the epicycloidal form, the same as the wheel teeth. This is a very suitable form if the pinions are low numbered, for, although with it the action takes place more before the line of centers, a safer depth is insured.

The teeth of the wheel are extended within the pitch line to allow of clearance for the addendum of the pinion. The root or part of wheel tooth within the pitch line is generally radial.

The corners at the bottom of the tooth may be rounded for strength, but these round corners must not be so full as to engage the points of the pinion leaves. The action should be confined as nearly as possibly to the epicycloid on the wheel, and the hypocycloid on the pinion. In watches, the roots of all the wheels and pinions are left square, except the roots of the barrel, or great wheel teeth, and the roots of the center pinion leaves, which should always be rounded for strength. There is then less danger of the teeth stripping if the mainspring breaks.

If the pinion is to be used as the driver and the wheel as the follower, as is the case in the motion work of watches and clocks, the points of the pinion teeth must be epicycloidal, and the roots of the wheel teeth hypocycloidal, struck with the same generating circle. For the convenience of using wheels and pinions indiscriminately as drivers and followers, engineers generally use a generating circle whose diameter = the pitch × 2.22 for the points and roots of all wheels and pinions of the same pitch. The tip of the addendum is removed in both wheels and pinions.

If more than two wheels gear together, the acting parts of all should be struck from the same sized generating circle. The number of teeth in a wheel bears exactly the same proportion to the number of teeth in a pinion with which it gears, as the diameter of the pitch circles of the wheel and pinion bear to each other. If the pinion whose pitch circle is .8 of an inch in diameter has 10 teeth, then the wheel with a pitch circle 6.4 inches in diameter will have 80 teeth, because .8 is contained 8 times in 6.4, and 10 × 8 = 80. But the outside or full diameter of a wheel or pinion is not proportional to the pitch diameter. The addendum, or portion of the tooth beyond the acting part bears reference rather to the size of the generating circle and to the width of the teeth, than to the diameter of the wheel or pinion.

Lantern pinions work very smoothly as followers, though they are unsuitable as drivers. The space occupied by the shrouds precludes their use in watches, but in the going parts of clocks they answer well.

For the convenience of ready calculation, it may be assumed that the addendum of the wheel teeth increases the size of the wheel by three teeth. For instance, the pitch diameter of a wheel of 80 teeth is 2 inches. Then its pitch diameter would bear the same proportion to its full diameter as 80 does to 83; or 80 : 2 :: 83 : 2.07, which is the full diameter.

In the same way it may be taken that the circular addendum increases the size of the pinion by 1.25 teeth, and the epicycloidal addendum by 1.98, or nearly 2 teeth.

If the pinion is to be used as the driver, it must have the epicycloidal addenda to insure proper action. I believe an opinion prevails among some watchmakers that the circularly rounded pinions may be used as

Fig. 286.

drivers if they are sectored large, and they are so used for motion work, but such a practice is altogether wrong.

In the motion work of keyless watches, the followers are used as drivers when the hands are being set, and a good form of tooth for motion work generally may be obtained by using for roots and points of both wheels and pinions a generating circle of a diameter equal to twice the pitch. This gives a short tooth which will run smoothly when at full width. The form of gearing suitable for the train permits of too much shake for motion work.

WHEEL CUTTER. The wheel cutter is a valuable addition to the lathe. Several different styles of these tools are made, each possessing points of merit. They are designed for cutting all kinds of wheels and pinions used in key and stem-wind watches. When the cutter spindle is vertical the belt runs directly to it from the countershaft, but when horizontal the belt passes over idler pulleys held above the lathe. These idler pulleys are also used to run the pivot polisher. Fig. 286 illustrates the American Watch Tool Company's wheel cutter, while Fig 287 is Moseley's pattern.

Fig. 287.   Fig. 288.

WHEEL VISE. Rose's patent wheel vise, shown in Fig. 288 is used for holding all kinds of watch wheels while undergoing repairs, such as putting in new teeth, removing rust from pinions, etc., and for holding balance wheels while putting in or removing the screws, taking the hair spring or collet from staff, or for any work where the safety of the wheel is involved.

WIGWAG. The wigwag is used for polishing the shoulders of pinions, pinion leaves, staffs and pivots, and for numerous other operations. The formation of these tools differs according to the ideas of the various makers, but in principle they are alike. These tools are used extensively in all the American watch factories.

INDEX.

351

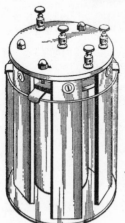

Go to Headquarters Every Time.

It is Best for Yourself and Prevents Delays.

H. H. KAYTON,

84 NASSAU ST, NEW YORK,

IS HEADQUARTERS FOR

WATCH MATERIALS, TOOLS,

OPTICAL GOODS, ETC.

I am the sole importer of the celebrated Union Brand of Main-springs, every spring being warranted. Price $1.25 per dozen or $12.00 per gross. I also control the sale of the well-known "Union" Brand of gold and silver solders. Best in the market and warranted.

Sole agent for Fuller's Stone Setting Cutter. Price, $1.00 each.

Manufacturer of Kayton's Marble Polish Restorer for French clock cases. Price, 25 cents per bottle.

I Carry the Largest and only Complete Stock of Materials for the Lancaster Movements.

Special Agent for the Hopkins Lathe and all other makes of Watch-makers' Lathes.

Orders promptly filled. No unnecessary delay. Experienced and practical men in charge of the various departments.

Mail Orders Solicited and Filled from any Catalogue.

OUR MOTTO:—BEST GOODS AT LOWEST PRICES.

Anything and Everything in the shape of
Dials Made to Order from your own
Designs or from ours.

Dials with Portraits, Monograms, Landscapes,
Yachting Hunting, Fishing, Base Ball, Tennis, or
in fact any design. Society designs a specialty.
Complete Stock of Plain and Fancy Dials always
on hand.

THE RIVETT LATHE LEADS THE WORLD.

HIGHEST
AWARD
at the . . .
World's
Columbian
Exposition.

The **RIVETT LATHE** and
STAKING TOOL. The "Rivett"
is the embodiment of modern mechanical
perfection, and is recognized as such by fine mechanics. The attachments are
covered by several valuable patents, and practical watchmakers who need a tool of
this kind should not fail to investigate. Send for catalogue, new price list and
list of jobbers who keep our lathe.

MADE BY THE

FANEUIL WATCH TOOL CO.

BOSTON, MASS.

Electro Plating Outfits

—FOR—

GOLD. SILVER. NICKEL. COPPER. ETC.

WE FURNISH COMPLETE OUTFITS FOR

Electro Plating, Polishing, Buffing, Burnishing and Lacquering.

SEND FOR ILLUSTRATED CATALOGUE

Showing Dynamos, Batteries, Polishing Lathes, Felt Wheels, Cotton Buffs, Vienna Lime, Burnishers, Walrus, Lacquer, Cyanide Potassium, Gold Rouge, Gold Solution, Silver Solution, Nickel Solution, Copper Solution, Anodes, Tripoli, Crocus.

THE HANSON & VAN WINKLE CO.

MANUFACTORY AND OFFICES:

219-221 MARKET STREET, NEWARK, N. J., U. S. A.

WESTERN BRANCH:
35-37 S. Canal St., Chicago.

NEW YORK OFFICE:
81 Liberty Street.

The Largest Manufacturers of Electro Plating and Polishing Material and Apparatus.

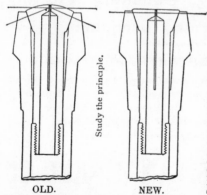

American Watch Tool Co.,

STONEY BATTER WORKS,

CHYMISTRY DISTRICT,

WALTHAM, MASS,

MAKE THE

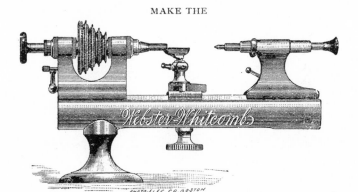

WEBSTER-WHITCOMB LATHE

Our Mr. Webster began designing lathes in 1860; This is his Latest and Best.

By the introduction of special and costly tools we have brought the price of lathes down from $80.00 in 1876, to $36.00 in 1894.

WHO HAS DONE MORE FOR THE CRAFT THAN WE?

Remember our full address when you send for price lists

Oskamp, Nolting & Co.

Mammoth Wholesale Jewelers of America,

COR. 5TH AND VINE STS.   CINCINNATI, O.

Distribute a monthly bargain sheet, which is of great interest to all legitimate jewelers throughout the world. This house probably introduces more new novelties than all the other houses put together. Graduates of Horological Schools will find the house of Oskamp, Nolting & Co. best suited for the purpose of selecting a new outfit. Some of the reasons are their large and varied stock, everything that is new, and last but not least, the house that will sell to you on very favorable terms.

◎ ◎ ◎

Correspondence Solicited.

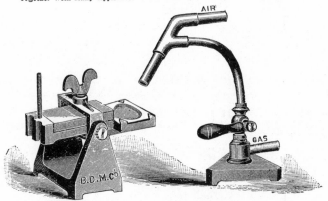

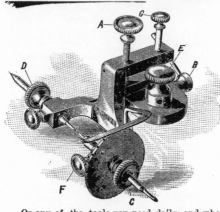

Canadian Horological Institute

133 KING STREET EAST,

H. R. Playtner, Principal. **TORONTO. ONT.**

ARE YOU interested in technical education? You are? We would like to claim your attention for a moment. The watchmaker requires a thorough, practical and theoretical education; we teach both branches, and all students must attend the lectures and drafting lessons, as they explain why and wherefores, and are alone worth more than the cost of tuition. In the practical department, students make all kinds of difficult repairs, and construct watches and chronometers from their own designs.

We aim to have the best school, and so far as America is concerned, we have it. Our shortcomings are, we cannot teach horology in one year. To tell the truth, this institution is run independently of what other schools may do. Why? Because our aims are high and it is only by having a thoroughly reliable school in every respect that our objects can be accomplished. We refer especially to our "System of Instruction," length and beginning of terms, examinations and awarding of diplomas, etc. No other school on the continent is our equal or even rival in these respects.

New term begins on first of September of each year, when intending students should be on hand.

OUR CATALOGUE, the finest one issued, will be sent to any address upon application.

PRACTICAL BOOKS

.... FOR ....

Watchmakers AND Jewelers.

FOR SALE BY

GEO. K. HAZLITT & CO.,

91 PLYMOUTH PLACE,   **CHICAGO.**

Staff Making and Pivoting. Practical directions for making new staffs from raw material. By Eugene E. Hall. Chapter I. The raw material; the gravers; the roughing out; the hardening and tempering. Chapter II. Kinds of pivots; their shape; capillarity; the requirements of a good pivot. Chapter III. The proper measurements and how obtained. Chapter IV. The gauging of holes; the side shake; the position of the graver. Chapter V. The grinding and polishing; the reversal of the work; the wax chuck. Chapter VI. Another wax chuck; the centering of the work. Chapter VII. The finishing of the staff; pivoting; making pivot drills; hardening drills; the drilling and fitting of new pivots. Illustrated with 24 engravings. 48 pages. Paper covers--$ 25

Watch Repairing. By N. B. Sherwood. Contents: The Bench and its Accessories; The Vise and Oilstone; Lathe Appliances; The Jacot Lathe; Depthing Tool; Expanding the Web of a Wheel; The Spreading Tool and its Use; The Rounding-Up Tool; Stud Remover; Opening the Regulator; Roller Remover; Replacing Broken Teeth; Graining Polishing Blocks; Polishing Steel Work; Polishing Pivots; Superiority of Conical Pivots; The Cutting Engine; To Cut 'Scape Wheels; Replacing Broken Arbors; Hardening and Tempering. Illustrated. Price-- 35

The Watchmakers' and Jewelers' Practical Hand Book. A guide to the student and a workshop companion for the practical watchmaker. Hundreds of valuable suggestions from private formulas and the best authorities, together with hints on making certain repairs. An invaluable book for the workman. The most valuable book for the money ever offered to the trade. Fifth Edition, Revised and Enlarged. Edited and compiled by Henry G. Abbott. Illustrated with 154 zinc etchings. 118 Pages. Flexible muslin, 50 cents. Paper covers------- 35

Prize Essay on the Detached Lever Escapement for watches and timepieces. A practical and theoretical treatise, by Moritz Grossman, to which the first prize was awarded by adjudicators appointed by the British Horological Institute, London. 118 pages, bound in paper covers, with 20 full page plates, bound in a separate volume. Two volumes, price, 1 50

Acme Record of Watches Bought and Sold. A complete record for dealers in watches, by which they can at all times tell what watches have been sold, by whom bought, price paid, profit made, etc., and in case of the watch being imperfect, the dealer can readily ascertain from whom he purchased it, or if stolen he has a full description of them which should materially aid in their recovery. Books of 3,000 Entries, substantially bound---$1 00

The Acme Record of Watch Repairs. A simple and economical method of recording watch repairs. Book of 1,000 entries, substantially bound 1 00

The Acme Record of Jewelry Repairs. A simple and economical method of recording jewelry and miscellaneous repairs. Book of 1,000 entries, substantially bound--- 1 00

The Acme Watch Guarantee Book. If you desire to increase your watch repair business, purchase an Acme Guarantee Book, and advertise the fact that you "give a written guarantee with all work turned out." These books are printed with a stub so that you may keep a record of all guarantees made, with date, name of owner, description of movement and case, repairs, etc. They are bound in heavy, substantial covers. printed on good paper and perforated all around so they can be easily torn out.

Books of 200 Guarantees -- 1 00
Books of 300 Guarantees ------ ------------------------------------ 1 25
Books of 500 Guarantees --- 2 00

The Escapements. Their Action, Construction and Proportion. All watch and clock escapements thoroughly illustrated and described. Illustrated with twenty diagrams. Paper Covers Price............ ...**$ 50**
Same in cloth binding.. 75

Prize Essay on Watch Cleaning and Repairing. By F. C. Ries. This work took the first prize, (offered by The American Jeweler) in competition with thirty-six other writers. Contents: Examination of the Movement; Taking Down; Fitting the Dial; Fitting Center Pivot and Bridge; Bushing; Endshake; Worn Center Pinions; Truing the Barrel; Repairing the Ratchet; Putting on Square on a Fuzee; Examination of Main-spring; Stemwind Mechanism; Examination of Train; Imitation Gilding; Pivots; Making Balance Staff; The Hairspring; Jeweling; Cleaning in General. Price... 25

Watch and Chronometer Jeweling. By N. B. Sherwood. A complete treatise on this subject and the only one in print. Contents: Peculiarities of Gems used in Making Jewels; Requisite Tools and How to Use Them; Shaping and Polishing the Jewel; Opening the Jewel; Setting the Jewel; The Endshake Tool; General Hints to the Repairer. Illustrated. Price... 35

General Letter Engraving. By G. F. Whelpley, the acknowledged authority on engraving. His latest and best work. Contents: General Hints to Beginners; Lines and Curves; Originality; Practice Material; Position of Graver; Treatment of Gravers; Correct Spacing; Coffin Plate Engraving; Necessary Tools; Laying out the Work Preparation of Plate; Use of Gravers; Methods of Cutting; Slope and Height of Letters; Inclination of Graver; Transfering; Letters Appropriate for Long and Short Names; Harmony in Laying Out; Touching Up; Difficult Materials and their Treatment; Tools and Materials; Sharpening Gravers; Choice of Tools; Engraving in Rings; Gravers for Same; Engraving Blocks and Stands; Ciphers, their Formation and Ornamentation; Inscriptions; Best Manner of Cutting; Ciphers as Compared with Monograms; Monograms and their Treatment; Figure Monograms or Cipheroids; Intertwining, Complex Monograms; General Treatment. Copiously Illustrated. 112 pp. Paper $1.00. Cloth..1 25

The Watchmakers' and Jewelers' Practical Receipt Book. A workshop companion, comprising full and practical formula and directions for solders and soldering, cleaning, pickling, polishing, bronzing, coloring, staining, cementing, etching, lacquering, varnishing, general directions for finishing all metals, hundreds of miscellaneous receipts and processes of great value to all practical watchmakers and jewelers. This is the only book on the market to-day that gives full and complete directions for etching names, portraits, etc., in the bowls of souvenir spoons and silver articles in general. This so-called trade secret is sold by certain persons at $5.00. Dozens of other "trade secrets" that are advertised for sale in trade papers at from $1.00 to $5.00 can be found in this book. Worth its weight in gold to any practical watchmaker and jeweler. 132 pages, illustrated. Paper covers, $1.00. Fine English muslin binding.. 1 25

Poising the Balance. An Essay of unusual merit. By J. L. Finn.... 25

Hairspringing. A complete treatise on the art of hairspringing. By A. Z. Price... 25

Adjustments to Positions, Isochronism and Compensation. The only work on the subject in print. 50 pp. Illustrated. Price.......................... 25

Repairing Watch Cases. A practical treatise on the subject. By W. Schwanatus. Contents: Repairing the Pendant; Lining Pendant Holes; Work at the Joints; Soldering the Bezel; The Closing of the Case; Taking Out the Dents. 40 pp. Price............................... 25

Jewelers' Practical Receipt Book. Contains a mass of most valuable receipts, formulas and information, gathered from the best and most reliable sources. Fifth edition, revised and enlarged. 48 pp. Price... 15

Prize Essay on the Balance Staff and Cylinder. By P. W. Eigner. This essay took the first prize offered by the American Horological Society. Gives methods for turning, grinding and polishing, from staff to pivots. Illustrated with numerous engravings. Paper covers......... 25

Compensating Pendulums and How to Make Them. A practical treatise on the construction of mechanically perfect Pendulums, for the use of watchmakers. By J. L. Finn and S. Riefler. Illustrated. Paper covers, Price... 35

Abbott's American Watchmaker and Jeweler. By Henry G. Abbott. An Encyclopedia for the Horologist, Jeweler, Gold and Silversmith. Containing Hundreds of Private Receipts and Formulas, Compiled from the Most Reliable Sources. Complete Directions for Using all the Latest Tools, Attachments and Devices for Watchmakers and Jewelers.

Among other things contained in this volume may be mentioned a thorough explanation of adjustments, both to positions and isochronism; directions for making all the alloys used by a watchmaker, jeweler and metalworker; a review of all the escapements, their action, construction and proportion, together with diagrams of each escapement; an exhaustive treatise on balances, their expansion and contraction, auxiliaries, sizes and weights and direction for poising; the balance staff, and full and complete directions for making and replacing new staffs, together with the use of the graver in turning and the manipulation of measuring instruments; directions for making twenty different cements of great value to the watchmaker and jeweler, including lathe wax; directions for cleansing, pickling and polishing all kinds of metals; magnetism and the use of the various demagnetizers; electro-plating, bronzing and staining all metals; gauges of all kinds, and directions for using; soldering and directions for making all kinds of hard and soft solder and fluxes; steel, its treatment in annealing, hardening, tempering, etc.; watch cleaning, repairing, etc.; a treatise on wheels and pinions; directions for using all modern tools and appliances; and hundreds of miscellaneous receipts, formulas and hints on all kinds of work, of great value to every workman. This edition contains forty-four pages more than former editions, and each page contains one-third more matter than the pages of former editions. An alphabetical list of over five hundred European watchmakers who manufactured watches prior to 1800, with years in which they carried on business, from which the watchmaker can easily establish the age of any movement that a customer may desire to know about; an alphabetical list of all books on horology published in the English or French language, prior to 1850; portraits and sketches of all the celebrated watchmakers of the world from 1600 to 1894. 354 pages. Illustrated with 288 engravings. Paper covers, $125. Fine muslin--**$1 50**

A Simple and Mechanically Perfect Watch. By Moritz Grossmann. A Prize Essay on the Construction of a Simple yet Perfect Watch. Written in a masterly manner by one of the greatest of Horological Authors. Illustrated with many engravings. From the standpoint of the practical man at the bench this is one of the most exhaustive essays ever written on the subject and no practical workman can fail to appreciate it. 96 pages. 38 diagrams. Paper, 75c. Fine muslin --------- 1 00

The Watchmakers' Library. This book consists of a collection of the best articles from the various trade journals of this country and Europe, among the authors being Moritz Grossmann, M. Kessels, Chas. Spiro, Chas. Reiss, Herman Horrman, P. M. Youlen, M. Sandoz, Herman Grosch, James U. Poole, E. Sordet and Vincent Lauer. The papers are all of a practical nature and of great value to the practical watchmaker, the whole forming a volume of 290 pages and index. In Paper Covers------------------ 1 00

Prize Essay on the Balance Spring and its Technical Adjustments (Baroness Burdett Coutt's Prize). By M. Immisch. A description of the invention of the balance spring, its effect upon the art of watchmaking; the effects of inertia of the balance; resistance of the air; balance adjustment by means of turning screws and washers; proportions of spring and balance; nature of spirals; lengths of balance vibrations and their effect upon the timing; pinning in equal and unequal coils; the Breguet spring; making its curves; pinning; regulating isochronal springs, etc. Fully illustrated with numerous engravings and diagrams. Cloth. Price-- 1 00

Repairing Repeating Watches. By C. T. Etchells. A practical treatise on the subject and the only one in print. Fully illustrated. The most vexatious repairs that come to the watchmaker are those on repeating watches—and yet they are the most profitable if you know just how to make them. Not every watchmaker can make them, and that is just why they are profitable. Do you how? If not, why not? You are never too old to learn. Paper covers----------------------------------- 35